ETHNIC PERSPECTIVES

IN

AMERICAN LITERATURE

Selected Essays
on the European Contribution

A Source Book Edited by

Robert J. Di Pietro and Edward Ifkovic

The Modern Language Association of America
New York   1983

Copyright © 1983 by
The Modern Language Association of America

Library of Congress Cataloging in Publication Data
Main entry under title:

Ethnic perspectives in American literature.

   Includes index.
   1. United States—Literatures—History and
criticism—Addresses, essays, lectures.
I. Di Pietro, Robert J. II. Ifkovic, Edward, 1943-
PN843.E8   1983   810'.9   82-14265
ISBN 0–87352–126–9
ISBN 0–87352–127–7 (pbk.)

Published by The Modern Language Association of America
62 Fifth Avenue, New York, New York 10011

Contents

Introduction

Walt Whitman called America a "nation of nations." Every new group that participated in the building of our country has expanded and enriched America's cultural base. Until recently, however, these groups were not substantially represented in the literary anthologies prepared for use in our schools. In spite of the cultural pluralism of the American public, textbook writers have been wont to favor an ethnically neutral mainstream in their choice of authors to represent the United States. Not too long ago, many critics considered American literature an offshoot of British literature. For many decades, those writers who responded to the ethnic experience in America remained largely unknown, and the special strengths they contributed to our literary patrimony went unrecognized.

During the past few years, however, a new awareness of ethnic diversity has arisen among educated Americans. Ethnic pluralism, once anathema to those who espoused the melting-pot theory, has become a positive, stimulating force for many in our country. This change in attitude has begun to affect educators. University courses in ethnicity have proliferated. MELUS, the Society for the Study of Multi-Ethnic Literature in the United States, has firmly established itself and continues to grow. Its journal has become a comprehensive keynote publication concerned with expanding the definition of American literature to include long-neglected ethnic materials. A rich repository of documents in Italian, Hungarian, Slovenian, and other languages has been gathered in the archives of the Immigration History Research Center at the University of Minnesota, Saint Paul. The Center for Migration Studies on Staten Island, New York, has become active as a publisher of studies on ethnic groups in America. The passage of the Ethnic Heritage Act by the U.S. Congress has led to the creation of innovative school curricula in many parts of the United States. Undoubtedly inspired by the raising of black, brown, and red consciousness over the past two decades, members of various European ethnic groups have shown a new interest in their heritage.

With this new interest has come the realization that we need a variety of resources with which to meet the challenge of the new courses in ethnic literature already appearing in various high schools and universities. We now have extensive bibliographies, such as Wayne Miller's *Comprehensive Bibliography for the Study of the American Minorities*, with its accompanying handbook. Also, collections of scholarly articles (for example, the two-volume *Ethnic Literature since 1776: The Many Voices of America*, ed. Wolodymr T. Zyla and Wendell N. Aycock) cover a wide range of ethnic diversity. Undigested source materials can be found in the *Encyclopaedia Britannica's* Makers of America series; for textbook anthologies, one can consult Edward Ifkovic's *American Letter: Immigrant and Ethnic Writing* or Lillian Faderman and Barbara Bradshaw's *Speaking for Ourselves.* The *Harvard Encyclopaedia of American Ethnic Groups* (1980) is another important resource. As editors of this collection of essays, we are conscious of yet another vital need: to make available to the teacher-researcher a handy volume focusing on the major writers and themes associated with European ethnic groups in the United States.

The volume consists of twelve essays, each the product of a scholar or scholars of a specific ethnic area. Given the purpose of the volume and the limitations of space, we unfortunately could not include all European ethnicities. Furthermore, to make subjects manageable within the space allotted, a broader topic has in some essays been narrowed to a more limited topic. For example, Franco-American literature is represented in this volume only by writers living in New England. With such limitations in mind, however, we have made every effort to provide a cross section of groups from eastern, western, southern, and northern countries of Europe.

The essays appear in alphabetical order, according to the name of the ethnic group they represent. Without exception, the individual essays reflect the larger, multiethnic fabric of America and reveal the interrelations among ethnic groups as depicted by the writers themselves. As editors, we were motivated by the idea that our perspective should recognize the contributions of both sexes, of different ages, and from all periods of our history. We gave our contributors complete freedom to organize their essays in the way they thought best. Most have followed a chronological order. Some, however, have chosen a thematic organization. Whatever the order, they have given careful consideration to major writers, themes, and periods.

America's Ethnic Heritage

What do we Americans know about our origins? Collectively, not as much as we would like to know. Some ethnic groups—such as the Hispanics, Asiatics, American Indians, and blacks—have come to the public consciousness by being declared minorities. Others—like the Irish, Italians, Germans, and Poles— are numerous but rarely the object of legislation. Still others—the Latvians, Slovenes, and Icelandic people—are almost unknown among the general population. In all, more than fifty groups compose our ethnic heritage. Throughout the nineteenth century, beginning around 1815, over fifty million people left their native lands and headed across the oceans for America. Of these, some thirty-five to forty million came to the United States. The onset of World War I dramatically curbed emigration, but by that time millions of people from Europe had restocked the American population. Cities like New York, Boston, and San Francisco were filled with variously dressed, multilingual men, women, and children—all definitely (and sometimes defiantly) outside the mainstream of conventional "American" life. The open-door policy for immigrants began to close in 1914, when drastic discriminatory legislation was enacted. Yet many writers heralded the new "Americanization" process: "in the story of liberty a new constellation will appear, and its name will be America—many peoples, but one nation."[1] Many immigrants were infused by the same spirit, and one of them, Israel Zangwill, coined the famous description of America as a huge melting pot.

Actually, the peopling of our shores had gone on steadily since the earliest British, Dutch, Spanish, and French colonizers arrived. Although various groups came to America for religious or political freedom—in Puritan New England, for example, and later, during the post–World War II period—most were motivated by the wish to improve their earthly lot. The New World held out the promise of material comfort, freedom of choice, and security for one's children. Here the peasants of the Old World would be free to advance on the basis of their own determination. In the seventeenth century, the Western Europeans came.

Joint-stock companies like the Virginia Company of London (1607), the Dutch West Indies Company (1624), the Massachusetts Bay Company (1630), and the New Sweden Company on the Delaware River (1638) were commercial enterprises that encouraged settlement by people from western Europe.

As the nation grew, the call for people increased. Population meant wealth; many children signified prosperity on the land. Indentured servitude, by which one's passage to America was paid in return for four or five years of service to the sponsor, became a common practice. According to some estimates, as many as two thirds of those living south of New England during early Colonial times were indentured servants. The East Coast remained largely English until 1680 when shifting policy in England discouraged emigration. The breach was filled by people from other lands. Other nationalities began to arrive in large numbers, many of whom were responsive to the religious tolerance offered by William Penn in his settlement. He welcomed into his fold not only Quakers but Germans, Scotch-Irish, and Mennonites. Sephardic Jews first entered America around 1654, and a colony of Huguenots (French Protestants) began forming in 1685. In an effort to turn the Old Dominion into a new Tuscany, Thomas Jefferson encouraged Italians to come to Virginia. One of these settlers, Philip Mazzei, worked closely with Jefferson in formulating his views on government and politics.

The New World was fast becoming a diversified, multiethnic continent. At one point, eighteen languages were spoken in the Dutch colony of New Amsterdam. By the time of the Revolution, the thirteen colonies may well have been English in language and social instituions, but other ethnic populations were clearly in evidence. The census of 1790 revealed the pattern: 60% English, 14% Scottish or Scotch-Irish, 9% German, 4% Catholic Irish, and 13% other groups. Blacks, who were considered property, and Indians, who were totally ignored, did not appear in census tabulations, but their presence certainly contributed greatly to the multilingualism of early America. The Slovene-American writer Louis Adamic draws our attention to several interesting points of history: the black tradition of fighting for liberty, which dates from 1526; the staging in 1619 at Jamestown, Virginia, of one of the first rebellions by a handful of Polish, German, and Armenian workers; the fathering of the ideal of freedom of the press in the 1730s by the German printer John Peter Zenger; the writings on equality and freedom of Jefferson's

Italian friend Mazzei; and the Irish contribution to the political-military movement that finally won American independence.[2] Indeed, the first stitch in the multiethnic fabric that is America was made the moment Columbus touched shore with his motley crew of Spaniards, Portuguese, Dalmatians, Italians, Jews, and who knows what other ethnic strains.

In 1815, the approximate beginning of the great migration, the United States had a population of 8.4 million. By 1914 over thirty-five million aliens had entered the country. This great migration began in Ireland and the German Rhine Valley, then moved to England, Scandinavia, northern Germany, Poland, Russia, down through the Austro-Hungarian Empire, Greece, and Italy. Historians traditionally divide the migration into three distinct periods. Until 1860 the Celtic immigrants entered America from Ireland, Scotland, and Germany. The attraction for America grew as drastic changes took place in Europe. For centuries, the European population had remained relatively constant. Then improved medical care and new technology brought about a higher infant survival rate, and the resultant boom in population severely taxed the available land resources. Between 1750 and 1850 the population doubled, and the economic level of the people began to decline. In Ireland, peasants had come to depend on the potato, the one staple in abundance. When that crop failed in 1845 and again the following year, starvation decimated the Irish population. The situation worsened throughout the decade, and some 1 million Irish flocked to America between 1850 and 1860. Eventually a total of 4.5 million would come. Over 1 million Germans, suffering similar miseries in their native land, particularly in the southern Rhineland, also emigrated during this first stage, bringing the total to nearly five million people entering America before the Civil War.

But if Americans were occasionally hesitant about the vast hordes entering their ports before 1860, the situation changed after the Civil War. The rise of industry and commerce precipitated by the war called for a steady source of cheap labor. Then, as always in our history, immigrants built our industries, roads, bridges, and homes. The importation of people became a profitable business venture, as steamships assumed control of the Atlantic lines, and cheap steerage passage, which meant either salvation or death to millions, came into its own. Shipboard conditions were so bad that one out of every ten immigrants died on route. From 1860 to 1890, in the second stage, popularly termed the Teutonic, the immigrants were mainly English, northern German, Scandinavian, and Bohemian. In England the enclosure movement strangled the landless peasants and contributed to the exodus. Counting both the first stage and the second, four million left England, together with some six million from Germany and two million from Scandinavia. These people left simply because they could not stay where they were. The decline of fisheries in Scandinavia, the crop failure in Norway in 1847, and the cruel practices of absentee landlords throughout all Europe had the same result. The Atlantic Ocean became a pathway, delivering poor and frightened masses to Castle Garden, the immigrant station in New York City.

The largest and most recent stage, the Mediterranean-Slavic, began in 1890 and lasted until 1914, when World War I curtailed the European flow. A total of twenty million people entered during this last stage, one million a year in 1905, 1906, 1907, 1910, 1913, and 1914. The peak year was 1907, when 1,285,349 aliens landed on American soil, most entering through Ellis Island, which had replaced Castle Garden as the port of entry. Lacking land and suffering from overtaxation by oppressive and decadent governments like that of the Austro-Hungarian Empire, they looked to America for a new life. Two million East European Jews, largely from Russia, fled economic limitation and brutal czarist pogroms. Some were literally forced from their homes. Many were merchants, artisans, shopkeepers, religious leaders, and scholars. Five million Italians came, along with eleven million others from eastern Europe, the Balkans, and Asia Minor. Among them were Ukrainians, Slovaks, Bohemians, Hungarians, Poles, Greeks, Croats, Serbs, Slovenes, Lithuanians, Estonians, Albanians, Syrians, and Armenians. Clashes were inevitable between these newcomers from southern and eastern Europe and the already English-speaking Germans and Irish who had preceded them. A million people a year, few speaking the dominant language, clustered in the industrial ghettos of the urban centers. How, indeed, could these people become Americans? In the minds of many who were already here, America had aged enough to worry about the preservation of traditions. By 1914, nativist sentiment had grown and become blatantly discriminatory. When World War I ended and immigrants again streamed in, politicians actively sought ways to cut off the influx of southern and eastern Europeans. Nativist legislation in 1924 and 1929 ended the great migration. The year 1924 marked a great dividing line in American history—the end of American open-door policy on immigration.

Edward Corsi, commissioner of immigration in the 1920s, labeled the last stage the "new immigration" as opposed to the "old"—that is, pre-1890—immigration, and the terms eventually came to be used to isolate and discriminate. The new immigrant inspired the restrictive legislation, and nativists applauded the old immigrant as the repository of invincible and steadfast American values. Nativists viewed the new immigrants as impervious to assimilation. The Colonial period attracted the attention of most American historians. Only a few, such as Marcus L. Hansen, exhorted us not to forget the role of the immigrant in the industrial revolution. Most worried that we had become a chaotic society. In 1930 seventy-three percent of the residents of New York City were foreign-born or of immigrant parentage. One could walk only a few blocks in that city and hear people speaking a dozen different languages, just as one can today.

While the United States has always been a multiethnic nation, each new immigrant group has had to struggle to take its place among the established groups. Oddly enough, the main-stream way of life that has evolved in America reflects the contributions made by succeeding waves of new people but does not afford easier entry to any outsider. Those in the mainstream consider themselves immersed in democracy and knowledge. Those outside view the insiders as intolerant, bigoted, aloof, and insensitive. Some nineteenth-century main-stream Americans could espouse democracy and yet engage in anti-Irish demonstrations such as those of the 1840s and 1850s, when signs appeared announcing "No Irish Need Apply." As industrialization introduced new problems and tensions into American life, established citizens were likely to blame them on the new immigrants. The widely publicized strike of 1877, followed by a seven-year depression, frightened mainstream Americans. The new immigrants became the scapegoats for all social ills. They were blamed for the ghettos in which they were forced to live. They were accused of causing the economy to flag. Anti-Catholicism (a throwback to the strident Know-Nothing party of the 1850s) increased. Henry F. Bowers began his influential American Protective Association (APA) in Clinton,

Iowa, in 1887, and the largely midwestern organization rallied against Catholicism. In 1915, the Ku Klux Klan was revived in Georgia in support of one hundred percent Americanism. The objects of its hatred were Catholics, Jews, and blacks.

The presence of aliens in large numbers contributed to another growing fear: radicalism. Since 1848, when the United States received groups of "forty-niners"—Germans fleeing the collapse of the liberal revolution of 1848 in their homeland—mainstream Americans had feared radical ideologies. Johan Most, a German anarchist, brought his philosophy to America in the 1840s, and scattered groups of radicals came throughout the rest of the nineteenth century. The Socialist party appeared at the turn of the century, and its immigrant membership led to the stereotyping of all immigrants as pervasive radicals and danger-ous anarchists. In reality, a small number of the immigrant population were radicals. Most had no definite politics. One fundamental characteristic of immigrants has been their conser-vatism and their abiding faith in a fair and just America. Most came here to find financial security and to establish families. Long inured to tradition, they cast no favorable eye on radical change. But nativist Americans could not separate the conspicu-ous few anarchists from the majority, who were law-abiding and hard working. Frequently, cartoons appeared in periodicals depicting swarthy, shabby Russians or Jews running through the streets with round, lighted bombs—the hallmark of the anarch-ist. Stereotyping spread to other groups: Italians always carried stilettos, and Slavs sabotaged factories. In 1891, a mass lynching of eleven Italians (including a young boy) in New Orleans was led by the town's most respected citizens.

Much of this blatant antipathy toward the new immigrants jelled into a cult of Nordic superiority. Some Americans of northwestern European extraction came to think of themselves as innately superior to the lesser "breeds" of Europeans, Africans, and Asiatics. They praised themselves for their contributions to law, sophisticated social patterns, belles lettres, and all the other trappings of civilization. They set themselves up as the sole custodians of fair play, honesty, the protection of womanhood, and the integrity of the white race. Some self-styled historians even traced the origins of the New England town meeting back to the law and order of the primeval, dark Germanic forest. The old guard, led by people like Henry Cabot Lodge, distinguished Boston Brahmin that he was, irrationally and with scarcely concealed bias, attacked the new immigrant. Madison Grant, a "scientist" and founder of the New York Zoological Society, wrote *The Passing of the Great Race* (1916), a book that was to have devastating effects. The Jews received the full force of his hatred. Adolf Hitler later read and appreciated Grant's writings. "O Liberty, White Goddess! Is it well to leave the gates unguarded?" cried Thomas Bailey Aldrich in his popular poem "Unguarded Gates."[3]

Thus the years of legislative exclusion began. The restrictionists claimed that there was no longer room for immigrants in America. The new Jim Crow (separate but equal) laws managed to curtail the little remaining freedom of blacks. Asiatics had become personae non gratae, especially on the West Coast, where their back-breaking labor was no longer so much in demand. Congress excluded the Chinese from immigration in 1882. Other laws enacted in 1882, 1891, 1903, and 1907 forbade entry to those who suffered from disease, had criminal records, or held radical views. In 1908 a gentleman's agreement with Japan cut off Japanese immigration. Despite the veto of Presidents Grover Cleveland, William Howard Taft, and Woodrow Wilson, a literacy test for citizenship was made law in 1917. A yearly quota of 150,000 immigrants was imposed. Each country was given a quota proportionate to the number of its people already here, according to the census of 1890. By selecting that year, the legislators excluded most Italians, Slavs, and Jews. In addition, they excluded Asiatics. This unjust law remained on the books for half a century, even though various allowances were made for political refugees from Nazi terrorism and for post–World War II displaced persons, some 600,000 of whom eventually entered America. In 1952 the McCarran-Walter Immigration Act continued these discriminatory practices, despite the opposition of men like Dwight Eisenhower, Harry Truman, Hubert Humphrey, and John Kennedy. Not until 1965 did Congress change the law, drop the national-origins clause, and enact a more equitable quota system.

Against the backdrop of our social history, ethnicity has been remarkably resilient. The old urban ghettos of the Irish in Boston and of the Jews and Italians in New York are slowly disappearing. Now, one speaks of neighborhoods and the values inherent in a healthy community. New ethnic groups continue to come: the Puerto Ricans in New York, the Cubans in Miami, and the Indo-Chinese in many American cities. Perhaps we are beginning to accept our multiethnicity. The black movement of the 1960s made practically invisible people suddenly very visible. "Black is beautiful," the buttons proclaimed. We are now discovering Afro-Americans of the past, from Phillis Wheatley, slave poet, to Nat Turner, slave revolutionist. This racial consciousness eventually spread to the American Indians. Vine Deloria's *Custer Died for Your Sins* is but one of many recent contributions of this group to our American literary patrimony.

The new black and red consciousness has been a major force in the recent recognition of ethnicity by all Americans. Even white Anglo-Saxon Protestants are beginning to view themselves as one among many groups. While exclusionary practices and prejudices have not totally disappeared, awareness of the full spectrum of American multiethnicity has fostered a desire by many third-, fourth-, and fifth-generation Americans to rediscover the old ways. No longer victimized so overtly by discrimination, these white ethnics want to remember the traditions from which they grew: the music, the foods, the old beliefs, and the stories passed down through the generations. What the second generation wishes to forget, according to Marcus Lee Hansen, the third strives to remember.⁴ Perhaps we are about to realize Louis Adamic's dream of a diversified America that seeks to share and profit from its diversity. "I'm Polish," a young student may declare. Questioned further, he will probably admit that his great-grandparents came to the U.S. in the 1890s, that he knows no Polish, and that he has never been to Poland. And yet the hold of ethnicity is such that he feels confident in labeling himself by a nationality that is really not his own. Pushed even further, he can be made to define himself by no other term than "American." What does America mean to him? How has his Polish heritage contributed to his nature in the 1980s? Almost daily the strands of our national multiethnic fabric become brighter and more distinctive. An Irish Catholic is elected President, and a few years later, a Polish American aspires to the White House. An American Indian wins the Pulitzer Prize for fiction, and a black civil rights leader wins the Nobel Peace Prize. An Italian-American congressman and an Italian-American judge become guardians of American democracy in the infamous Watergate affair.

Yet, the Kerner Report in 1968 maintained that we remain essentially a racist country. Any facile, optimistic views of a completely integrated America would be difficult to support at this time. Transforming the national metaphors from "melting pot" to "mosaic" is not easy. Indeed, the pieces of that national mosaic have been cemented in place with much congealed blood and sweat. We must all continue to work at making the beauty of our multiethnicity shine through the dullness of racism that threatens to cloud it.

In one way or another the immigrant experience has touched all Americans. In the editors' opinion, we need to study our ethnicity, not simply in a naive, filiopietistic manner, but in order to understand more fully what we are. With an understanding of ourselves and our fellow Americans, we can appraise more meaningfully the state of our society and the directions in which our leaders would take us. As Mary Antin stated, "America is the youngest of nations, and inherits all that went before in history. And I am the youngest of America's children, and into my hands is given all her priceless heritage, to the last white star espied through the telescope, to the last great thought of the philosopher. Mine is the whole majestic past, and mine is the shining future."[5]

Ethnic Literature

Is there a definition of ethnic literature with which we can be comfortable? For that matter, can we be certain that ethnicity, by itself, has been adequately defined in all that has been written about it? Based on an old Greek root meaning "nation," ethnicity in our modern sense is often more emotion than reason. It describes a feeling of belonging to a group. Furthermore, the group is not necessarily coterminous with a national boundary or equal to a specific race. It soon becomes obvious to anyone working in the field that the ways of being ethnic vary considerably. Not everyone is Irish in the same way, or Italian, or Jewish. To insist on uniformity of behavior and beliefs in order to define the dimensions of an ethnic identity would be to slip into stereotype. While some groups conform neatly to an ethnicity based on historical and cultural tradition, other groups define their ethnicity according to less concrete criteria—isolation, alienation, and so forth.

Labeling a literature ethnic can be just as precarious as the articles in this book reflect. First of all, the writing in question must meet whatever standards of evaluation the analyst may wish to apply. One might decide, as Edward Ifkovic and Carol Bachman do in their essay on Russian-American literature, that good ethnic literature uses the ethnic setting to convey universally human concerns and themes. To that definition, Rose Basile Green ("Italian-American Literature") would add that the literature must project consistent and continuing values that are unique to the group in question. Enikö Molnár Basa ("Hungarian-American Literature") puts forth four determining characteristics of ethnic literature: (1) it must be about the experiences of an ethnic group in America, (2) it must be written by a member of the group, (3) it can be in English or in the native language of the group, (4) its audience must be ethnic.

The effort to agree on a definition of ethnic literature will continue. Meanwhile, we can point to features that recur in the literature of different groups. First of all, most ethnic literatures in America are shaped in some way by the writers' contact with the dominant society. Some exceptions might be found, such as the Franco-Americans of New England, who, according to Armand Chartier ("Franco-American Literature"), write against a background of standard French culture and language. Yet they share with Italian Americans the theme of struggle against the deethnicizing policies of a Roman Catholic church dominated by Irish Americans.

Ethnic literatures often display generational differences. Whereas writers of the first generation are wont to respond to conditions in the old country and loss of an old way of life (see Jerzy Maciuszko, "Polish-American Literature"), second-generation writers concern themselves with identity problems and the contrasts between the ethnic group and the mainstream. The third generation often draws closer to the first and seeks to rediscover its roots or recover older life-styles. As Rose Basile Green observes, even the genre may change over time. In an early phase, the writings of an ethnic group are often expository (history, descriptions, and political reports, for example), but they may become creative later on.

Italian-American authors often write about the family and about alienation. They cover the broad range of social conditions in America, and many of them are well known to the general American reading public: Paul Gallico, Bernard De Voto, Mario Puzo, and Lawrence Ferlinghetti. Russian emigrants have written out of deep-seated political or religious concerns. The reader is reminded that the Russians were not only immigrants in the early years of the 20th century but also colonists at an earlier time in Alaska and in Northern California.

Americans who maintain an ethnic identity, according to Richard Tuerk ("Jewish-American Literature"), often retain some feeling for what is happening in the land of their origin, as with Jewish Americans whose self-image improved as a result of Israel's victories in wars with the Arab states.

Dorothy Skårdal ("Scandinavian-American Literature") questions whether there is a unified Scandinavian literature at all. In fiction as in real life, Norwegians are often taken for Swedes, Swedes for Danes, and so on. She concludes that they respond to their American experience in practically identical ways and therefore have produced a unified literature. A prevalent theme in Scandinavian-American literature is doubt about and fear of the New World. This view is not surprising since many of these people settled in the vast northern plains where they were cut off from the mountains and seacoasts that they once knew.

Some ethnic literary traditions are difficult to treat as separate entities; Robert Bishoff, for example, tells us that writers in the German-American tradition have merged over the years with writers of mainstream American literature. The same difficulty applies in part to Jewish-American writers, many of whom—Norman Mailer, Saul Bellow, and Philip Roth, for example—have become prominent in recent times.

Smaller ethnic groups, such as the Romanians and the Portuguese, are more likely to be represented by authors writing in the native language than by those writing in English. Greek-American writers, however, are often as fluent in Greek as they are in English. Some Greek-American poets and novelists have anglicized names—Ariadne Thompson, Charles E. Jarvis, and Nicholas Gage. Others, like Elia Kazan, are better known to the general public for achievements not connected directly with their writing talents (see Alexander Karanikas, "Greek-American Literature").

The editors are certain that readers will find much that is new and much that is provocative in the pages of this volume. American literature is still very young. The full ripening of its many diverse fruits awaits us.

Robert J. Di Pietro
Edward Ifkovic

Notes

[1] Royal Dixon, *Americanization* (New York: Macmillan, 1916), p. 196.

[2] *A Nation of Nations* (New York: Harper, 1945), pp. 1–2.

[3] Quoted in Howard B. Grose, Pref., *Aliens or Americans?* (New York: Missionary Education Movement, 1906).

[4] "The Problem of the Third Generation Immigrant," in Oscar Handlin, *Children of the Uprooted* (New York: Grosset, 1966), pp. 255–73.

[5] *The Promised Land* (Boston: Houghton, 1912), p. 364.

Franco-American Literature: The New England Experience

Armand Chartier

For my father, Monsieur Joseph Emile Chartier

Introduction

Many Americans of French descent came to this country by way of Canada, especially Quebec and Acadia, as did the Franco-Americans of New England, whose literature is discussed here. Major events in the United States and Canada precipitated three phases of immigration, beginning in 1776, when French Canadians fought with American colonists in our struggle for freedom. Some of these volunteers chose to remain here after the Revolution, and they were given tracts of land on the shores of Lake Champlain. Later, after the insurrection of 1837–38, a number of *patriotes* sought political refuge in northern New England and remained even after amnesty had been granted them.

But by far the largest number came during the period from 1840 to 1930. Accurate figures on the immigration will probably never be established,[1] but the founding of Saint Joseph's parish in Burlington, Vermont, attests to the existence of organized Franco-American life by 1850. The indifference of the Canadian government toward the economic well-being of a growing population, illustrated by inadequate policies for land development, explains the restiveness of the French Canadians in mid-nineteenth century. Given, too, the post–Civil War industrial boom in New England, we may then understand why several hundred thousand immigrants were drawn to such mill towns as Lewiston, Manchester, Lowell, and Woonsocket.

Adjusting to the general scorn they encountered from Anglo-Americans and the Irish, the French set about establishing ethnic parishes—more than one hundred fifty would eventually be created—and obtaining French-Canadian and Franco-American priests to minister to them. This proved difficult because of the Irish conviction that Catholicism in the United States had enough prejudice to overcome without becoming multilingual and multicultural. Amid mutual distrust and misunderstanding, the French and the Irish remained in a state of open ideological warfare for nearly a century, the French-Canadian immigrants remaining loyal to their traditional cultural framework, which linked the French language and the Catholic faith.

Thus the boundaries of ethnic life were delimited during the early years of the immigration. The goals were to resist assimilation and to preserve the cultural heritage, to adapt to the milieu, and to seek fulfillment as Americans of French descent. Roman Catholicism and the French language were the foundations of this construct, a fact difficult to overemphasize or overestimate. By 1900, an astonishing multiplicity of organizations existed to further those goals. French-language newspapers with identical objectives proliferated; so did the fraternal insurance societies whose resources served the cause to varying degrees. Other organizations were formed, some ephemeral, others durable, centered on virtually every human activity from athletics to theater. Of special interest are the literary and drama groups (whose history has yet to be written) and the press, which did so much to encourage the development of Franco-American literature. Obviously, proximity to Quebec and Acadia facilitated the preservation of the French cultural heritage. Formal and informal contacts, at either the personal or the institutional level, were enormously helpful in keeping the culture alive. As a consequence, assimilation was indeed forestalled until the recent past. Its impact since World War II, however, has been devastating, but there are still signs of ethnic vitality, particularly on the local level.

Franco-American literature has yet to achieve national visibility; in fact, several writers have fared better in Quebec than in the United States.[2] Franco-American writers have always been isolated from one another. Hence, there have never been any schools, movements, or coteries to encourage the exchange of ideas and foster a sense of solidarity. Isolated from their contemporaries, with a few exceptions, the writers have been isolated across the generations as well; novelists of the 1960s, for example, seem unacquainted with the work of their predecessors. For these reasons, one cannot speak of a tradition of Franco-American literature.

Limiting our discussion to the literature produced by the Franco-Americans of New England, we encounter a relatively small body of work. To flourish, a literature needs more time and a much larger population. Moreover, when socio-economic conditions conducive to the literary life finally began to prevail, large number of French Americans had become assimilated, so that the existence of *any* Franco-American literary works at all is surprising. One must remember, too, that for over a century, the dominant ideology was that of survivance, a doctrine advocating the preservation of ethnic heritage, with the Catholic faith, the French language, and French-Canadian traditions as bases. This doctrine favored self-expression of a utilitarian rather than of a primarily aesthetic nature. Within this context, many writings were responses to assimilation, which was seen as a threat of total extinction. Franco-American thinkers therefore saw the need to defend, to justify, to shed luster on the group by relating in essays and newspaper articles without number the exploits of their forefathers and the achievements of members of the group.

No complete history of Franco-American literature has been attempted since the 1940s, and few general studies exist.[3] Nothing definitive has ever appeared, probably because of the lack of resources for an exhaustive survey of the three hundred French-language newspapers published in the United States since the Revolution. Many of those newspapers have contained poetry, fiction, and essays of interest to the literary historian and, even more, the cultural historian. There are gaps, too, in our knowledge of Franco-American folklore and popular literature; indeed, the sociology of Franco-American literature (for example, studies telling us what was read and by whom) has remained a matter of fascinating conjecture.

If scholars ever undertake a definitive Franco-American literary history, they should give a generous place to such nontraditional genres as historical works, polemical writings, sermons, and speeches. Restricting literary history to poetry, fiction, and drama would distort the reality of Franco-American literature beyond recognition. A thorough evaluation of all extant writing might well reveal that the major contribution has, after all, been made in that area vaguely called the literature of ideas.

Oral Tradition

Like other literatures, Franco-American literature began with an oral tradition, brought from France to Canada by the early settlers in the seventeenth century. Many of its elements date back to medieval France. In the forests and villages of New France this wealth of folk songs, legends, and folktales was transmitted down through the generations, reaching New England's mill towns by the middle of the nineteenth century. Expressing joy or melancholy, songs—folk ballads; paddling songs; drinking songs; songs of sailors, fisherman, shepherds; religious, military, satirical, and comical songs; the traditional laments, berceuses, and carols—increased in number along with the population, and the repertoire was vast. Patriotic selections such as "La Marseillaise" or "O Canada" are still sung by Franco-Americans today, as are many other spirited chansons, including some that praise the French-Canadian woman—for example, "Vive la canadienne!" This, then, is the earliest poetry, the poetry of the people.[4]

The advent of the modern age has virtually eliminated the telling of folktales and legends from the daily lives of Franco-Americans. But until the 1950s and 1960s many immigrants were still alive and ready to repeat the legends and tales about the werewolf, the will-o'-the-wisp, or the *Chasse-galerie,* the last being a variation on the Faust theme.[5] Until now, there has not been a concerted effort to collect and preserve the diverse elements that constitute Franco-American folklore.[6] One can safely assert, however, that most of it is French-Canadian folklore that the immigrants brought with them as part of their cultural heritage. One must hope for a serious study of this field before all traces of it vanish.

Poetry

Confronting a century of poetry and at least twenty worthy names, I have structured this discussion around dominant modes. Hence, I am proposing a three-part division according to the predominance of the lyric, the didactic, or the ethnic element in any given body of work. Of course these elements are not reciprocally exclusive, and I wish to emphasize that the chosen rubrics reflect predominant elements only.

We owe the first collection of Franco-American lyric poems to the novelist Anna-Marie Duval-Thibault (1862–1958), whose *Fleurs du printemps* was published in Fall River, Massachusetts, in 1892. The emphasis on love and suffering, love and death, and nostalgia for a lost love situates the work well within the Romantic tradition, more specifically in the melancholy mode of French Romantics such as Alphonse de Lamartine. The presence of twelve English-language poems (in a total of forty-nine) points up the author's bilingualism, to be sure, but it also bears witness to the existence of a linguistic dilemma as significant today as it was a century ago.

A note of desolation dominates the meditations on life found in the *Voix étranges* (1902) of Joseph-Hormidas Roy (1865–1931). Life here is seen as a desert where an oasis is a mirage, a vanishing dream. Roy wrote many lines, in fact, on the haunting power of the dream, the dream one must resist as a perilous lure. In pieces both philosophical and elegiac, he keeps restating his fear of being a victim of the dream yet keeps contrasting the sublimity of the dream with the banality around him, constantly reminding himself that dreams are destined to oblivion. A related, recurring notion is the ideal, a mere glimpse of which brings despair into the poet's soul, though more than once he has glimpsed "enchanted castles far up in the clouds" (*Anthol.,* p. 41).

There appears to be less languor in the poetry of Joseph-Amédée Girouard (1865–1938), but his *Au fil de la vie* (1909), like Duval-Thibault's *Fleurs du printemps,* is in the same Romantic-melancholic vein. A more definite sense of place emerges from certain poems—"Aux montagnes blanches" ("An Old Orchard")—in which the natural setting is described for its own beauty but is also used as a backdrop for the poet's musings on the transience of youth, the sadness of the human condition, or the mystery of our existence. Fortunately, such ponderousness is offset by striking poetic imagery.

Supremely serious about literature, almost totally devoted to poetry, Louis Dantin (1865–1945), the pseudonym of Eugene Seers, was one of the foremost French-Canadian and Franco-American literary critics of the 1920s and 1930s. His own poetry barely exceeds the five thousand lines published in two principal collections, *Le Coffret de Crusoé* (1932) and *Poèmes d'outre-tombe* (1962). Much of it is confessional, even the reference to Robinson Crusoe alluding to Dantin's sense of exasperated solitude, a recurring theme in his poetry. "Optimisme" expresses his confidence in the power of art to transform all into beauty, an essential tenet in an aesthetic creed that provided him with reasons for living.

Henri d'Arles (1870–1930) wrote history, art criticism, essays on social questions, and more poetic prose.[7] He is assuredly one of the few immigrants from Quebec who succeeded in being a priest, an author, a dandy, and an aesthete. Aloof, preeminently disdainful of the prosaic, he was active in life at his own level, writing tracts on the importance of the French language, which he seemed to value only slightly less than he valued God, who was above all the Supreme Artist. Every line Henri d'Arles wrote bespeaks his lifelong quest for elegance and refinement. He has left us a number of nature descriptions, verbal landscape paintings remarkable for their sumptuous imagery, their concern for nuances of color and accuracy of detail.

Nostalgia dominates the poetry of Georges Boucher (1865–1956) to the point that he expressed in "Ultimate volonté" (*Anthol.,* p. 171) the wish to be buried in Quebec, the native province he loved and missed. His *Chants du Nouveau Monde* appeared in 1946 and contained revised versions of two earlier collections, one of them titled *Je me souviens* ("I Remember"), which more than coincidentally happens to be the motto of Quebec. His poetry is his life relived and includes much reminiscing about youthful friendships and about all that reminds him of his native land, down to the solitary tree by the village church ("L'Arbre," *Anthol.,* pp. 164–65). Melancholy becomes obsessive, so much does his memory dwell on his beloved dead; these are heroes of his youth, vanished friends, or, more tragically, children lost in infancy. It might be argued, however, that he surpassed his other efforts in his "Ode à Québec," an ode in the classic mold, a vibrant homage to the capital city of the native country.

Encouraged and guided by Louis Dantin, Rosaire Dion-Lévesque (1900–74) became *le poète national franco-américain*, obtaining prizes and decorations from the governments of France, Canada, and Quebec. In his first major work, *Les Oasis* (1931), he demonstrated his mastery of both the sonnet and the mood poem. Religion is a major source of inspiration in this poetry of stained-glass windows, solitary churches, and poetic homages to the Blessed Virgin. Quite different is *Vita* (1939), which contains an exuberant tribute to Walt Whitman, Dion Lévesque's "new Christ," the liberator and spiritual forebear from whom he has learned the full acceptance of physical love.[8] A lengthy sequence on sensual love, "Inamorata," concludes on a bitter note, as the poet records the victory of the great void, when love ends. Within the broad context of the poet's religious thought, sensual love appears not to have been a conflicting theme and reveals total self-acceptance, as "Magnificat" bespeaks: "I am what You have willed that I should be, and such as You have shaped me...for Your glory and Your agony" (p. 25). *Vita* also evinces the poet's ongoing love affair with nature, especially in "Petite Suite marine," a short series of seascapes, with rhythms often imitative of the ocean.

Dion-Lévesque's *Solitudes* (1949) deals in large part with the dialects of humanity's quintessential aloneness and the individual's repeated attempts to reach other human beings by developing bonds of kinship, friendship, affection, or love. Of these, love is by far the most significant in this poetry, and for its birth or growth, nature serves as a setting, not for decorative purposes, but as an integral part of the process.[9] This suggests a double harmony: between the lovers themselves and, on the metaphysical level, between the lovers and the world about them. Significantly, when the beloved leaves, nature becomes ugly ("L'Absente,", pp. 58–60). In *Quête* (1964), the last published volume of Dion-Lévesque's works, ennui asserts itself again; his Catholic faith remains intact, while the poet himself remains true to his origins by proclaiming, in the language of his fathers, his deep attachment to *his* city, *his* woods, and *his* river, the "indolent Merrimack."

Several intriguing writers have not yet published their verse in volume form, and one can only reiterate the hope that this gap will soon be filled.[10] From what little we have seen, we know that the poetry of Gabriel Crevier (b. 1908) is suffused with quiet mysticism; the poet views nature as a book to be deciphered in religious terms. He has evoked the tranquil beauty of dusk, for example, as a solemn offertory ("Crépuscule"), whereas "Les Feuilles d'automne," "La Neige," and "Parfum de mai" are nature poems with philosophical or religious overtones. These selections also bespeak a sharpness of vision, a delicateness of touch, a gentleness of tone, and a scrupulous attempt to choose the most poetic *mot juste*.[11]

Rodolphe-Louis Hébert (b. 1913) has also neglected to

publish his "Collected Works," poems scattered in various journals from New Hampshire (*Le Canado-Américain*) to Texas (*Le Bayou*). Some of these pieces have a density, a hermetic quality, and a solemn tone reminiscent of Mallarmé.[12] This quality appears in "Soir d'automne à Salem" and "Vitrail IX," a sumptuous evocation of a stained-glass window that itself evokes the tragic story of John the Baptist and Salome. In both, Hébert has raised allusion to the level of art. In a different vein, he has given us impressionistic renderings of Arizona ("Les Trois Palmiers"), his native Rhode Island ("Reverdie pawtuxetoise"), and, in his memorable "Rue des Remparts," a Monet-like representation of Quebec City, its cliffs, walls, and port, with the Isle d'Orléans just beyond its own golden bridge.

Paul-P. Chassé (b. 1926), critic, essayist, and historian, has published two collections of dithyrambic poetry marked by sustained intensity and variegated imagery. *Et la mer efface. . .* (1964) underscores the impossibility, despite repeated efforts, of achieveing human love. Underlying this theme is the belief that human beings cannot communicate totally, perhaps not even meaningfully, although communicating with others would appear to be one of humanity's elemental needs. A different nexus of themes is developed in the lengthy lament on the assassination of President Kennedy, "Saisie d'une vie," which movingly combines mourning, anguish, and unanswered questions. The author's second collection, *La Carafe enchantée* (1968), reveals an evolution toward diversification of form. The most impressive sections are the series of "Suites." "Suite abbatiale," for example, voices an overpowering sense of total futility, and the "Suite latine" records the quest for love, ponders the disappearance of the beloved, and moves through phases of bitterness to ultimate resignation.

The work of Normand Dubé (b. 1932) is characterized by spontaneity and abundance. In many ways, his two published collections are the poetry of the Saint John River Valley in northern Maine: *Un Mot de chez nous* and *Au coeur du vent*.[13] Here, nature is of the essence, primarily as a source of images but also as the medium for the poet's interaction with the cosmos. In the manifold moods of its seasonal variations, nature seems omnipresent in Dubé's tales, fables, and meditations. The child recurs frequently, as does the couple, both being endowed with great significance. Other figures are seen or heard: an immigrant widow in 1854; Théophile, the old Acadian raconteur, sage, and clown; a nurse watching a patient slowly die; an eskimo speaking of himself with simplicity and eloquent succinctness. But to date, the great summing up of this poet's beliefs is in the lenghthy "La Graine pousse," an expression of hope, an affirmation of life, particularly of the life that extends from the poet's ancestors through him to his children and beyond (in *Au coeur du vent,* pp. 61–71).

One should not infer that the writings of those designated here as didactic poets thoroughly lack the lyric qualities associated with the three generations of poets just discussed. To avoid misunderstanding or misrepresentation, one must insist that the question is merely one of degree, of dominant modes, and, obviously, of a need for rudimentary classification that is subject to revision and refinement. Rather diversified, for example, is the inspiration of Rémi Tremblay (1847–1926)[14], whose "Emigré Canadien" (*Anthol.,* p. 24) is a lyric tribute to the industrious, God-loving immigrant. His "Le Drapeau du 14ᵉ" (*Anthol.,* pp. 24–29) is an epic description of the Civil War battle at Cold Harbor, Virginia, in which the poet and other French-Canadian and Franco-American volunteers took part. On balance, the work is more successful as narrative than as poetry, and it contains less moralizing than most of his other poems display. Indeed, Tremblay was above all a satirist, and in this sense he belongs to the Franco-American didactic tradition. Since he spent only part of his life in the United States, however, most of his production is of interest to students of Quebecois rather than of American literature. We should still mention his "Le Chant de l'ouvrier" (*Anthol.,* p. 31), in which he inveighs against capital's exploitation of labor, and his "Lettre d'un abonné" (*Anthol.,* p. 30), a denunciation of the boor who makes preposterous demands of the beleaguered Franco-American newspaper editor.

Louis-Alphonse Nolin (1849–1936) wrote several selections characterized by straightforward moralizing rather than by satire. He left two unpublished manuscripts, "Poèmes détachés" and "Vers les cimes," the latter apparently suggesting that the purpose of his entire poetic effort was to urge his readers upward, toward moral and spiritual summits.[15] His poems in Chassé's *Anthologie* (pp. 65–72) were written in just such a spirit, and his well-integrated world view is apparent in his themes: the elusiveness of human fulfillment is universal ("Le désenchantement"); pleasure, ambition, disgust, regret—all is vanity, except life after death ("Sous les cyprès"); life's only purpose is to lead us to eternity ("Fugitives Années"); one must see beyond the illusory appeals of life to the essentials. Nolin was also a staunch defender of the Franco-American cultural heritage.

Aristide-D.-M. Magnan (1863–1929) was one of those patriot-priests who never completely left his native country, and, in fact, he returned there to continue his service as a priest and died in Quebec while still in the active ministry. The Catholic faith, which he saw as an integral part of the cultural heritage to be zealously defended, is omnipresent in his work, including the poetry collection he published in 1923, *Rime et raison*. Through the written as well as the spoken word, he urged Franco-Americans to resist assimilation, but his poems indicate broader interests. In "La Ligue des Nations" (*Anthol.*, pp. 75–77), he ridicules what he perceives to be the arrogance and utopianism of Woodrow Wilson. Elsewhere, in the tradition of Boileau and Voltaire, he rather ruthlessly satirizes those who believe in Darwin's theory of evolution ("Une Conversion," *Anthol.*, pp. 77–78). And at least once he shared with us his apocalyptic vision of the world's end, when, he believed, the dead will rise for the final judgment (*Anthol.*, pp. 78–79).

Equally concerned about the preservation of the French cultural heritage was Philippe Sainte-Marie (1875–1931), whose *En passant* appeared in 1924. In "Soleil de demain" (*Anthol.*, pp. 82–84), he urges us to look toward the future not only with confidence but in enthusiastic anticipation of the wonders it will bring. Such buoyancy compensates perhaps for the pessimism of a piece such as "Le Franco-Américain d'origine, son nom, sa langue" (*Anthol.*, pp. 87–88), in which he fulminates against Franco-Americans who showed their disloyalty by breaking with their ethnic past. Sainte-Marie calls them "dupes," "apostates," and "renegades" because they yielded to assimilation by altering their names. Like La Bruyère, he is adept at satirizing well-defined types. He portrays the actress, for example, as vain, fatuous, and brainless ("Eglantine," *Anthol.*, pp. 85–86) and the physician as lofty, pretentious, and exploitative ("Nos Médecins," p. 86).

Obviously, poets such as Magnan and Sainte-Marie are not one-dimensional; though primarily didactic, they share with other ethnic poets a deep concern for the preservation of their cultural heritage. Among ethnic poets, we include those whose primary focus is on ethnic themes (Franco-American history, traditions, manners, for example), whose poetry contains clear reflections of the Franco-American experience, or whose works are self-consciously Franco-American in other ways. In *Au seuil du crépuscule* (1924), by Charles-Roger Daoust (1865–1924), one finds several elegiac evocations of ethnic life, like "Premier Anniversaire" (*Anthol.*, pp. 58–59), which recalls a heroic deed carried out by Georges Charrette of Lowell, Massachusetts, during the Spanish-American War. There are other reasons for believing that the strikers in "La Chanson de la grève" (*Anthol.*, p. 60) are Franco-Americans: what other strikers would combine, in such proportions, submissiveness, a thought of revolt, hope for justice in the afterlife, and a note of gaiety and prayerfulness? The sonnet titled "A L'occasion de la mort de Louis Fréchette" represents a justice that is more than poetic, for it is a posthumous tribute to the French-Canadian poet who took a continuing interest in Franco-American life. "La Sentinelle" is a short piece, full of fervor and hope for the future of a Franco-American newspaper bearing that name.

Joseph Thériault (1860–1938) in *Loisirs et vacances* (1929) depicted the northern New England region, its history as well as its geography, perhaps more clearly than any other Franco-American poet. "Une Excursion à Montréal, P.Q." (*Anthol.*, pp. 153–54) describes the towns and lakes in New Hampshire's White Mountains. "La Rivière Connecticut" is appropriately subtitled "Une Page d'histoire" (*Anthol.*, pp. 154–55), while another poem recounts "Le Massacre Bradley" (pp. 155–57). "L'Etat du Vermont" (pp. 157–58) evokes the pioneering spirit of a people with a proud history. "Québec" (p. 159) expresses hope for the future of the native country.

Joseph Lussier (1867–1957) has left us amusing sketches of fellow Franco-American journalists in his *Silhouettes par Nemo* (1946), a light, unpretentious collection, full of bonhomie, private jokes, and expressions of solidarity with colleagues throughout New England.

Radically different from the work of Daoust, Thériault, and Lussier is that of George McFadden (b. 1951). Whereas his predecessors wrote in traditional French verse forms, McFadden uses English free verse, with bits of French interspersed throughout. Surprisingly (because it comes so late), this is the poetry of revolt and protest, undergirded by angry questioning and doubts about the wisdom of the emigration from Quebec. "Rocky Garden Where the Weeds Grow" (*Anthol.*, p. 275), "Through Mill River Junction" (pp. 277–78), "Promenade in a Circle"

(p. 278), and other poems tell of the seamy life in a New England mill city; they tell, too, of the bitterness and disenchantment wrought by a "symphony of sterility" (p. 279).

The Novel

The first Franco-American novel, *Jeanne la fileuse* (1878) by Honoré Beaugrand (1848–1906), raises problems of classification. Beaugrand himself stated that his effort was "less a novel than a polemical work,"[16] an assertion that needs to be qualified, since *Jeanne la fileuse* contains a love story developed at considerable length, elements of the historical novel, and, especially important, certain attributes of the novel of manners. Since, moreover, the author's intent was to refute arguments concerning the alleged misery and wretched living conditions of the immigrants, arguments advanced by several political figures in Canada, the work is understandably tendentious.

Among the many noteworthy aspects of this novel is its firm grounding in French-Canadian history and folklore. Part One takes place in Quebec and tells us much about life in the native country during the first seventy-five years of the nineteenth century. One custom of the time was storytelling, and Beaugrand gives us two outstanding examples of well-constructed tales. One is the popular legend, "Le Fantôme de l'avare ("The Miser's Ghost"); the other takes the reader out to the hinterland, the celebrated *pays d'en haut,* around 1825. The author also transcribes the lyrics of the folk song "Canot d'écorce qui va voler," offers a memorable vignette of the hay harvest, and describes a family conflict based on the Insurrection of 1837–38, thereby indicating that the feelings aroused by that controversial revolt could still be stirred several decades later.

The second half of *Jeanne la fileuse* deals with the immigration itself, and Beaugrand takes great pains to situate it within its historical context. The result is substantive as social history but aesthetically dubious, especially when the novelist-just-turned-historian turns pamphleteer, denouncing the idleness of the Canadian government when inhabitants by the tens of thousands sought economic relief by immigrating southward. Beaugrand also points with pride to the upward mobility of some immigrants after their arrival in the United States. He then returns to the main story line, chronicling the immigration of the

Dupuis family, who settle in Fall River, Massachusetts. There are digressions, however, on the excellence of American railroads, the history of Fall River, statistics on the growth of that textile city, and notes on the development of ethnic life. After these "excursions," the focus shifts from descriptions of the customs and mores of the French-Canadian immigrants in general to the specific life of one particular immigrant family; hence one gets the impression of moving repeatedly from essay to novel. Though seriously flawed, the work is indeed a novel and contains many facts about and insights into the early phase of the French-Canadian immigration. That it is one of few such works makes it all the more valuable.

Les Deux Testaments (1888), by Anna-Marie Duval-Thibault (1862–1958), another early effort, has little in common with Beaugrand's work, except that both are novels of manners dealing with the immigration. Because Duval-Thibault wrote *Les Deux Testaments* as a serial for a Franco-American newspaper, the book has many characteristics of the French *feuilleton,* above all a complex love story. Still, it does provide glimpses of the French Canadians who settled in the Yorkville section of New York City and who founded Saint Jean-Baptiste parish. It also points up the existence of a problem still relevant a full century later, namely, the conflict of "two cultures, a private French culture and a daily, external Anglo-Saxon culture."[17]

Canuck (1936), by Camille Lessard (1883–1972), is the French-language novel that most successfully evokes the transplanting of a French-Canadian family to the United States. The difficulties of leaving a beloved country for an unknown land, the complexities of moving from a rural life to an urban industrial setting, and cultural conflicts for which the immigrants were unprepared constitute the work's substance. The author succeeds in the attempt to embody these abstractions in adequately individualized characters. The father of the Labranche family, for example, has yielded to the greed encouraged by the prosperity of the United States. The influence of materialism could be all the stronger on French-Canadian immigrants if we remember that in Quebec people were urged to de-emphasize material goods and to concentrate on spiritual values. The open revolt of Labranche's daughter against his greed makes him adopt a moderate stance between two diametrically opposite value systems. For such episodes and for its generally realistic portrayal of immigration, *Canuck* deserves to rank high on a list of Franco-American novels.

More limited in scope is *Sanatorium* (1938), by Paul Dufault (1894–1969), whose purpose is to describe life in a sanatorium, a setting favorable to solitude, whether it be the solitude of a group isolated from society for medical reasons or the solitude of the individual within this group. One of the characters, a doctor, ably transforms his situation into one of creative solitude with a strong emphasis on study and reflection. As a result, he cultivates his nostalgia for his native Quebec and delights in the prospect of a patient, cured, returning to the rural life in his native land. The doctor also reflects a good deal on the question of social progress, both in Quebec and in the United States, and soon begins to advocate a form of progress based on the kind of disinterest and total giving of self characteristic of the heroic founders of Canada in the seventeenth century. This preoccupation with the social problems of both countries is rare in Franco-American literature.

The Delusson Family (1939), by Jacques Ducharme (b. 1910), has a fascinating, cleverly conceived spiral structure. It begins with the arrival in Holyoke, Massachusetts, of Jean-Baptiste Delusson in 1874 and records the life of an immigrant family in a textile town. The Delussons are typical of the thousands of French Canadians who became Franco-Americans over the course of one or two generations. They are a family for whom a French church and school are of paramount importance. A great dream is to see one of their children enter religious life, and the dream is fulfilled when their son Léopold becomes a priest. Other dreams come true for the Delusson family when their economic condition allows them to move away from "the Flats" and up to "the Hill" and again when two of their children are able to enter the field of retail merchandising, instead of stagnating in the mills. Another remarkable achievement occurs when they make one final move from "the Hill" to a farm. Thus the family returns to the land, thereby fulfilling a dream cherished by many immigrants but realized by few. In this manner, the cycle (actually a spiral) is complete, since the family has moved from the country to the city and back to the country, but at a higher economic level.

With his tragically divided cultural identity, Jack Kerouac (1922–69) was the permanent transient visitor, never completely at home, never at home to stay. His most explicitly ethnic works are *The Town and the City* (1950), *Doctor Sax* (1959), *Visions of Gerard* (1963), and *Satori in Paris* (1966). Moreover, specific references to his ethnic origin occur in virtually all of his twenty published works, and his French-Catholic upbringing certainly formed his vision of life to an astonishing degree. Even his transcontinental journeys betray the coureur de bois, the French-Canadian version of the eternally restless nomad.

The Town and the City relates the coming of age of the eight children of the Martin family, first in a New England mill town, then in New York City. It is a story of second- and third-generation Americans still trying to adapt to their environment, hence the questioning, the self-doubt, the sense of not belonging. The more sensitive children must deal with feelings of inferiority, as might be expected in descendants of a conquered people. *Doctor Sax* is a phantasmagoric evocation of a Franco-American childhood in the "Little Canada" of Lowell, Massachusetts. *Visions of Gerard* is a tribute to Kerouac's older brother, who died at age nine, who embodied the idea of sanctity, who taught Kerouac to revere life, and who impressed Kerouac with his Franciscan love for animals. The novel conjures up the agony of Gerard's fatal disease, bedside visits by the local French-Canadian nuns and the ironically named pastor, Father Lalumière, and, unforgettably, scenes of the wake and funeral.

Satori in Paris recounts Jack Kerouac's journey to France on a genealogical mission that turns into a romp when Kerouac discovers that he can indeed communicate with the natives in their own language. A generally light work, *Satori in Paris* does contain serious passages on the significance of family names and the relation between the Franco-American dialect and standard French. All this suggests that his good friend Allen Ginsberg was justified in calling him "The Great Rememberer." Either intentionally or atavistically, Jack Kerouac was faithful to the motto of Quebec, *Je me souviens* ("I remember").

Grace Metalious (1924–1964), the author of *Peyton Place,* the succès de scandale of the 1950s, wrote one novel on the Franco-American experience, *No Adam in Eden* (1967). She may well have drawn on her own childhood and youth, since her maiden name was de Repentigny. The work is unusual in that it shows us a distortion of traditional French-Canadian values carried out in a spirit of revolt amounting to a negation of life. One of the main characters, Monique Bergeron, condemns herself to being forever alone in a desert of her own creation, refusing to learn the English language or to become an American citizen. Thus, she resists assimilation but simultaneously keeps trying to bury her French-Canadian past. The result is total isolation followed by insanity. The novel can be read as an implicit denunciation of evil illustrated by an inverted spirituality, for we see here much more than an anatomy of sin; we see something that might be termed satanism.

Gérard Robichaud's *Papa Martel* (1961) reaches beyond the sometimes melancholy fate of the Franco-Americans and studies the harmony a family can achieve by fully accepting its ethnic heritage and, at the same time, adapting to a different cultural environment. This is the story of a family held together by love—love understood as giving and sharing. Louis and Cécile Martel, the loving parents, create a home in which the keynote is joie de vivre. They bring up their children to emulate the parents as the children develop their own personalities.

The Martels, as typical Franco-American parents, pass on to their children the teachings of the Catholic church, but they manage to avoid the rigorous morality that has plagued French Canadians and Franco-Americans for centuries. They avoid that excess by their intelligent use of the French *esprit critique,* an ethnic resource too seldom tapped by Franco-Americans in their religious lives. Cécile Martel evinces the same spirit of discernment again when she brings about curricular reform in the parish school.

The Martel family also lives a fully bilingual and bicultural life. They read and discuss both French- and English-language newspapers, they are familiar with the great historical figures of France, French Canada, and the United States as a result of frequent sessions of reading aloud. There is an obvious nostalgic note in *Papa Martel,* but the nostalgia transcends the wistfulness Gérard Robichaud may have felt when he wrote his novel. What we witness in this work is something poignant: a precious, irrecoverable moment in time, when an immigrant family carried out its own manifest destiny, moving from one culture to another, yet understandably clinging to the old while grasping the new. It is a moment of transition, a major turning point like that experienced by millions of ethnic American families.[18]

Quite different in mood is David Plante's *The Family* (1978), the only Franco-American novel set in Notre-Dame-de-Lourdes parish in Providence, Rhode Island. The reader is struck above all by the bleakness of this fictional world. Plante's primary interest here may not be ethnicity, but the work contains numerous reminders of the characters' ethnic origins. French expressions and phrases, for example, are scattered throughout the novel, as are reflections on linguistic problems and observations indicating that French is the private language used for prayer and for speaking with immigrant grandparents, whereas English is the public language used to communicate with society at large. At a deeper level, the novel makes it clear that even in the 1950s Jansenistic thinking—an integral part of French-Canadian Catholicism—was still a reality, at least in the lives of the parents' generation. But apart from its participation in parish life, this family lives in frightful isolation, the novel conveying no sense whatever of ethnic solidarity.

Franco-American historical novels range in subject matter from the international to the local, from the seventeenth century to the nineteenth, but this diversity must not suggest a systematic effort or an abundance of works in this category. On the contrary, I have found only four novels worth mentioning. The first is the work of the poet, wandering journalist, and volunteer in the Union Army, Rémi Tremblay. *Un Revenant: Episode de la Guerre de Sécession aux Etats-Unis* (1884) has a complicated double plot, part of which relates a melodramatic series of events in Quebec, while the rest deals with the Civil War. The latter aspect is by far the more successful of the two, perhaps because the teenage soldier who observes and takes part in the horrors of war is the author himself. His descriptions of life in army prisons and of the battles at Petersburg and Cold Harbor are especially noteworthy. *Un Revenant* remains, then, a flawed work, but it can be viewed more positively as a tribute to and a reminder of the several thousand French Canadians and Franco-Americans who served with honor in the Civil War.

Georges Crépeau (1868–1913) wrote other works besides *Bélanger ou l'histoire d'un crime* (1892), but they are lost. The story of *Bélanger*, taken from local history, tells of a *crime passionnel* that took place among the Franco-Americans of Lowell, Massachusetts. Apparently, Crépeau never anticipated that his novel would be read outside Lowell, since in several instances he refers directly to actual places and persons so well known to his local readers that he deems description unnecessary. *Bélanger* is therefore a unique novel written solely for a local readership, but clearly its author was too modest. The work is still of interest to us today, even to non-Lowellites, because of the author's thorough knowledge of his fellow Franco-Americans and his ability to convey something of their thinking, their spontaneous responses, their speech rhythms. In addition, the author attempts to offer a plausible explanation for a crime never resolved, to shed a ray of light on the mystery of human violence.

Mirbah (1910–12), by Emma Port-Joli (pseudonym of Emma Dumas, 1857–1926), was also inspired by local history, more specifically by the early Franco-American history of Holyoke, Massachusetts. The work contains useful information on the arrival of the first French-Canadian settlers in the Holyoke area and a detailed account of the fire that destroyed Précieux Sang Church in 1875. The author provides an extremely vivid description of the fire and its aftermath, along with valuable documentation on the role of religion in the lives of the survivors.

The sources of *La Fille du roy* (1954), by Gabriel Nadeau (1900–79), date back to the seventeenth century, when French colonists were settling in Canada—or la Nouvelle-France, as it was then called. *La Fille du roy* is an unjustly neglected minor masterpiece whose only serious defect is its underdevelopment. It is the only fictional piece completely inspired by the early history of the native country, and it works so well that one is sorry other writers have not turned to this same source. The simple story involves the consequences of François Barnabé's refusal to marry Louise Colpron, the *fille du roy,* a protégée of the king and one of the many girls sent to the colony for the express purpose of marrying and contributing to New France's demographic growth. Barnabé has refused to marry his assigned partner because Louise Colpron is unspeakably ugly. What follows justifies the subtitle, *conte drôlatique,* as we meet every manner of colorful character in a remarkable succession of comical scenes. Nadeau uses a diversity of narrative techniques and tells the entire tale in delightfully archaic French.

The propaganda novel, or *roman à thèse,* is a problematic subgenre in which literature is subordinate to the propagation or demonstration of an idea. There are probably no more than two such novels in the entire corpus. The first, *La Jeune Franco-Américaine* (1933) by Alberte Gastonguay (b. 1906), appeared during the golden age of Franco-American life. By then, the fusion of various cultural elements had taken place, and one could properly speak of a Franco-American soul. In mill towns throughout New England, the French were interacting with the

Americans around them, yet the group was asserting itself without arrogance; it had achieved an enviable cohesiveness; it appeared to be succeeding in warding off assimilation while at the same time it was adjusting to the Anglo-American ambience. While *La Jeune Franco-Américaine* exemplifies the dominant Franco-American ideology of the 1930s, *L'Innocente Victime* (1936) by Adélard Lambert (1867–1946) defends the same ideology but proposes a radical solution to the dangers of assimilation: stop immigration. In the novel Lambert makes his attitude toward Quebec especially clear. It lies somewhere close to cult and worship. Because of its glorious past and its simple, peaceful present, Quebec embodied for him an ideal beside which the appeal of American materialism vanished. Indeed, it is perhaps not fortuitous that one of the main characters in his novel was lured to the United States by the promise of fast money and then was deceived, on his arrival here, in such a way that he found himself an unwitting member of the U.S. Army. While one might regret Lambert's excessive idealization of Quebec, to the detriment of this country, one should examine his thought in the larger context of the debate between defenders of urban life and advocates of a return to the land. Lambert was so imbued with love of country that he himself returned to Quebec.[19]

The poet Louis Dantin has given us an autobiogrphical novel that contains elements of the novel of manners. Living in self-imposed exile in Boston after leaving the priesthood, Dantin developed a special empathy for the blacks of Roxbury, befriended several, and had a passionate affair with a black woman. *Les Enfances de Fanny* (1951; Eng. version, *Fanny,* 1974) recounts that affair in considerable detail, after relating Fanny's life in the South and in Roxbury before her love affair with Dantin.

Although this work is autobiographical, some aspects of it are not convincing, largely because the cultural gap between the two lovers is so wide that one wonders how they can possbily communicate meaningfully. Dantin is more successful in his depiction of ghetto life, as he conjures up black customs and mores in extremely vivid scenes. In like manner, he conveys something of the blacks' moral fiber—the courage and patience with which they approach their daily lives, for example. Implicit is a protest against racial injustice, along with a vague portent of eventual racial strife.

As the foregoing discussion suggests, few Franco-American novels have appeared in the recent past. We may well be witnessing a phenomenon similar to what Rose Basile Green calls "the revulsion into non-Italian-American themes, a reflection of the Italian-American's rejection of his immediate national heritage in an attempt to identify himself with the broader American culture."[20] This phenomenon may well explain the choice of subject matter by authors like Paul Théroux, Robert Cormier, and Richard Belair. All of them willingly admit that they are of French-Canadian ancestry, yet all of them write on nonethnic themes. Still, they are certainly young enough to continue writing novels for many years; one of them *might* begin writing on something as close to him as his own origins. In this connection, it is worth noting that *The Family* was David Plante's sixth novel.

Theater

By the 1950s, Franco-American authors had written approximately fifty plays, most of which were never printed, but this hardly begins to suggest the vitality of the theater in Franco-American centers. The first *club dramatique* was founded in Marlboro, Massachusetts, in 1868, and by 1930 one hundred fifty such clubs existed and had produced some nine hundred plays. These groups consisted of theater lovers who, responding to popular demand, produced mostly melodrama, although clubs did perform some plays by Molière as early as 1877 in Southbridge, Massachusetts.[21]

One of the few extant plays by Franco-American authors is a short comedy in verse, *Reflets de vie conjugale,* by Louis-Alphonse Nolin.[22] This *saynète* offers a light treatment of a serious subject, the marital difficulties of a couple seemingly entrenched in selfishness. After an altercation during which husband and wife review their grievances, they separate, briefly, in distress; after recognizing the true love that underlies their surface differences, they reconcile. Their daughter, pretending to be unaware of their difficulties, congratulates them for being a model couple, in the hope that they will mend their ways. In a final flourish, they sincerely resolve to do so.

First produced in 1976, *Un Jacques Cartier errant,* by Grégoire Chabot, is a rather acidulous satire on the contemporary Franco-American situation as seen by one of the group's angry young men. At the anecdotal level, Jacques Cartier (who, in 1534, was the first European to reach Canada) comes down from heaven to observe the present state of the North American French. He visits a bar in a New England mill town and learns, to his horror, that the North American continent is not French, as he, in the sixteenth century, had presumed that it would be. While briefing Jacques Cartier, the other characters reveal a number of ethnic traits that, according to the author, are responsible for the grim plight of today's Franco-Americans. Yet despite all, the French side of the Franco-American persists and wants to endure. The play itself can readily be seen in this light. Written in the Franco-American dialect, it is an obvious plea for the development of an indigenous Franco-American culture, a culture better attuned to the realities of a younger generation. It might itself be viewed as an act, a step toward the evolution of this desired culture.

Different in tone and spirit is the historical drama *With Justice for All* by Guy Dubay (1976). The play recreates events that took place in Maine's Saint John Valley in the 1860s and 1870s. It concerns the attempted eviction of French-American farmers in the valley by a group of business people striving in an unscrupulous manner to compensate for certain losses. The scene shifts from business offices to the Maine State House to the home of one of the farmers, finally to the Superior Court of Aroostook County. This shifting point of view has the obvious advantage of acquainting us with the varying contentions of the principals and, of particular interest, with the mentality of Franco-American farmers.

The Essay

The Franco-American essay has been a means of advocating the ideology of survivance, the attempt to instill in the people the will to survive as an identifiable, distinct group, through the preservation of their entire cultural heritage. This ideology led to many utopian or idealistic writings dealing with "desirable" manners and morals. The writings were often characterized by a tone of righteousness, indignation, or even outrage, a tone inspired by the gap between what actually existed and what was willed by the clergy and other ethnic thinkers.

Such writing is well illustrated by *Les Franco-Américains peints par eux-mêmes,* a collection, published in 1936, of short essays by different writers summarizing Franco-American thought in the 1930s. The work is divided into four sections dealing with ethnic organizations, the French language and its preservation, stumbling blocks, and the current situation in each New England state. The essays, originally given as radio talks in Montreal, combine the objectivity of the exposé with the explicit purpose of propagating the ethnic "faith"—that is, stressing the group's achievements while urging readers to draw inspiration from those achievements. Certain essays in this collection are especially noteworthy because of the ideas they convey, their stylistic merit, or both.

Considering that the French love ideas and tend to defend them passionately, it is not surprising that polemics have played a role in Franco-American history. During the past 125 years, countless minor ideological skirmishes have occurred, along with others of greater import, but the most significant controversy originated in Woonsocket, Rhode Island, in the 1920s. Characterized by high emotional responses, the struggle is commonly referred to as *l'agitation sentinelliste,* and it pitted an indeterminate number of Franco-American militants, the Sentinellistes, against their Irish-American bishop and a considerable number of moderates. The Sentinellistes opposed the bishop's decidedly assimilationist policies, including in particular his highly centralized administration of all individual parishes in the diocese. That a centralized method of administration was the norm in every American diocese, as opposed to the relative autonomy enjoyed by the parish in Quebec, did not impress the militants.

The essential questions, then, dealt with priorities: Did one's Catholic faith require uncritical submission to the bishop? Or was the preservation of ethnic heritage, including the Catholic faith, possible despite the hostility of the church hierarchy? Members of the warring factions vehemently debated these and related questions in their newspaper. Edited by J. Albert Foisy, *La Tribune* was the forum of the moderates, and its goal was to annihilate the opposition. *La Sentinelle,* edited by Elphège-J. Daignault, the leader of the movement, strove to bring about reform in the church and was not above using derision, abuse, and vitriol in its repeated denunciations of the assimilationist enemy. The use of such tactics explains why the Vatican eventually condemned the paper.

Of equal interest to the literary historian are the books that resulted from the controversy. J. Albert Foisy's *Histoire de l'agitation sentinelliste en Nouvelle-Angleterre, 1925–1928* (1928; Eng. trans., 1930) is a virulent denunciation of the opposition; it reeks rancor and profound hatred of the Sentinellistes. Elphège-J. Daignault's *Le Vrai Mouvement sentinelliste en Nouvelle-Angleterre, 1923–1929, et l'affaire du Rhode Island* (1936), the leader's account of the movement, refutes Foisy's book and unequivocally lays the blame for the entire matter at the bishop's doorstep. Shrill tone and intemperate language mar both works.

Yet another intriguing aspect of this ideological warfare is the role played by France and French Canada in providing models, structures, arguments, ideas, and so forth. It is known, for example, that theologians and public figures in Quebec became involved in the dispute, expressed opinions, and made suggestions. It is also known that *L'Action Catholique* (Québec) and *Le Droit* (Ottawa), newspapers that defended the cultural rights of French Canadians against English-Canadian recalcitrance, were models for Daignault's *Sentinelle*. But our knowledge of these matters has not evolved beyond generalities.[23]

Including history in a discussion of Franco-American literature is far less paradoxical than it may appear if our definition of literature includes what French literary historians have long referred to as *la prose d'idées*. We should also consider that most Franco-American historical writings have a distinctly subjective character that we expect from "literature." This subjectivity derives largely from the stringent Catholic orientation evident in virtually all the historical works published since the beginning of the immigration. It also derives from the tradition of making history an instrument in the defense of *la cause*. This use of history as propaganda partly explains its abundance, for the writing of history was encouraged by a Church-dominated elite determined to keep vivid the memory of not only the heroic French past in North America but also the more recent immigrant past. Here again, Quebec played a role in shaping Franco-American thought, a vital role, with a cult of the past so fervent that the literary masterpiece of nineteenth-century Quebec is François-Xavier Garneau's *Histoire du Canada depuis sa découverte jusqu'à nos jours*.

As early as 1891 French-Canadian Jesuit Edouard Hamon published *Les Canadiens-français de la Nouvelle-Angleterre,* a lengthy (484 pp.) work that emphasizes the "divine mission" of the Franco-Americans: the conversion of New England Protestants to Roman Catholicism. Despite the bias, this first general history contains much reliable data on the immigrants, as do Alexandre Bélisle's *Histoire de la presse franco-américaine et des Canadiens-français aux Etats-Unis* (1911) and Aristide Magnan's *Histoire de la race française aux Etats-Unis* (1912).

A strict chronological approach to Franco-American historiography reveals that these early general histories were followed by several local histories, such as Félix Gatineau's *Histoire des Franco-Américains de Southbridge, Mass.* (1919), Alexandre Bélisle's *Livre d'or des Franco-Américains de Worcester, Massachusetts* (1920), Marie-Louise Bonier's *Débuts de la colonie franco-américaine de Woonsocket, Rhode Island* (1920), and Thomas Albert's *Histoire du Madawaska* [Maine] (1921). There has also been a plethora of parish histories, many of them written to commemorate the founding of the parish. These are far too numerous to list here, but their importance should at least be signaled, since they frequently contain sermons, speeches, or other primary source material of interest to the literary or cultural historian.[24]

What the French call *la petite histoire* extends beyond the local histories just mentioned. The expression also refers to institutional histories and to histories of a given tradition; these too are abundant, diverse, and significant to anyone interested in Franco-American intellectual history. They include works such as Adolphe Robert's *Mémorial des actes de l'Association Canado-Américaine* (1946)[25] which relates the activities of a mutual benefit society involved, since its foundation, in Franco-American group life, and Adrien Verrette's *La Saint-Jean-Baptiste, Manchester, New Hampshire: Historique 1868–1938,* which recounts the annual commemorations of the French-Canadian national holiday, as observed in a Franco-American urban center. A recent addition to *la petite histoire* is Marguerite Cyr's *Mémoires d'une famille acadienne de Van Buren, Maine* (1977), a fascinating combination of regional, local, and family history and Acadian folklore.

The most important contribution to Franco-American historiography has been made by Adrien Verrette (b. 1897), a priest and patriot who has devoted his life to promoting "the cause." In addition to several histories of La Saint-Jean-Baptiste, he has written several parish histories, the most impressive being *Paroisse Sainte-Marie, Manchester, New Hampshire: Cinquantenaire 1880–1930* (1931), a massive (400 pp.) survey containing biographical sketches of the pastors, chapters on the development of the city of Manchester, the local evolution of the Catholic church, the Franco-American colony, the parish itself, parochial institutions, parish life, Franco-American social action, and the fiftieth anniversary of the parish. The work deserved to become a model, and it may indeed have inspired other historians, but, very much to our loss, no one else has written on so grand a scale. In addition, Verrette has been a loyal chronicler of Franco-American life since 1938, when he wrote the first in a series of some fifteen volumes entitled *La Vie franco-américaine* (1937–52), an annual compilation of the year's achievements in all major fields of endeavor. The series was succeeded in the 1950s by the annual *Bulletin de la Société Historique Franco-Américaine*, also edited and, in large part, written by Verrette.

Autobiography

In the realm of autobiography, one should cite the "Journal intime" of Henri d'Arles, which expresses in highly stylized language the effusions of an aesthete who was profoundly moved by nature's varying moods.[26]

Souvenirs et portraits (1965), by Adolphe Robert (1886–1966), is a collection of sketches and vignettes drawn from the author's childhood and youth in Quebec, his immigration to New England, and his role as a leader in Franco-American activities for several decades. His description of his nineteenth-century French-Canadian background conveys a sense of solidarity, a deep sense of belonging, the exact opposite of alienation. He belonged to a society with a well-defined body of manners, customs, rituals, and traditions, many of which he evoked in his book. He was to have a determining influence on the Franco-American world into which he arrived as a young college graduate in 1907. Similar, in this respect, to men such as Adrien Verrette and Thomas-M. Landry, Adolphe Robert was both a thinker and a doer. He helped define and propagate the ideology of survivance, one fortunate aspect of which involved frequent contacts with the rest of the French-speaking world. He makes clear in his book that he himself maintained these contacts, both on a personal level and as an "official" representative of various Franco-American organizations.

Quite different is *Inside, Looking Out* (1971), by Harding Lemay, who has spent most of his life in New York City, far from the Franco-American centers of New England but who nevertheless refers to his French-Canadian origins several times in his personal memoir. From the standpoint of literary history, however, the work raises questions that only close cooperation between the historian of ethnic literature and the social scientist can answer. On the surface, the work's overtly ethnic content is slight. But considering the author's repeated references to his origins and considering, too, Michael Novak's contention that it takes four or five generations to immigrate (that is, four or five generations must pass before full assimilation occurs), it would probably be erroneous to dismiss works such as Lemay's as mainstream. Hence one must give a close psychological, sociological, and anthropological reading to *Inside, Looking Out* before one can determine what is universal here and what is truly, uniquely Franco-American.[27]

Conclusion

Close cooperation between ethnic literary historians and social scientists should rank high on the list of scholarly desiderata. We are all familiar with the results of such cooperation in Europe, particularly in France, where the losses sustained by literary history have been greatly offset by the massive gains produced by radical new approaches to literature. It is my contention that only an interdisciplinary approach could begin to resolve riddles such as possible "hidden ethnicity" in a given body of work. Resolving such riddles may well add to the existing corpus of ethnic literatures in the United States. In this respect, we could do worse than ponder the words of Irving Howe:

> Tradition broken and crippled still displays enormous power over those most ready to shake it off. And tradition seemingly discarded can survive underground for a generation and then, through channels hard to locate, surface in the work of writers who may not even be aware of what is affecting their consciousness.[28]

Notes

[1] It is generally agreed that the Franco-American population of New England does not exceed two million. For statistical data, see Yolande Lavoie, *L'Émigration des Québécois aux Etats-Unis de 1840 à 1930* (Quebec: Editeur Officiel du Québec, 1979).

[2] Increasingly, scholars in Quebec are treating Franco-American writers as Quebecois who happen to live in New England, even though they might have been born there or lived there for most of their lives. See, for example, the articles on the works of Rémi Tremblay and Anna-Marie Duval-Thibault in Maurice Lemire, ed., *Dictionnaire des oeuvres littéraires du Québec*, Vol. I (Montréal: Fides, 1978). Additional articles on Franco-American writers will appear in subsequent volumes of the *Dictionnaire*.

[3] The most important works to date are Mary-Carmel Therriault, *La Littérature française de Nouvelle-Angleterre* (Montréal: Fides, 1946); Paul-P. Chassé, *Les Poètes franco-américains de la Nouvelle-Angleterre 1875–1925* (Somersworth, N.H.: Abbaye de Thélème, 1968); also available as Diss. Université Laval 1968; Paul-P. Chassé, *Anthologie de la poésie franco-américaine de la Nouvelle-Angleterre* (Providence: Rhode Island Bicentennial Commission, 1976), hereafter cited in the text as *Anthol.*; Richard Santerre, "Le Roman franco-américain en Nouvelle-Angleterre, 1878–1943," Diss. Boston Coll. 1974; and Armand B. Chartier, "The Franco-American Literature of New England: A Brief Overview" in W. T. Zyla and W. M. Aycock, eds., *Ethnic Literatures since 1776: The Many Voices of America* (Lubbock: Texas Tech Press, 1978), I, 193–215, a short survey of recent writing. Armand B. Chartier, "Pour une problématique de l'histoire littéraire franco-américaine" in Claire Quintal and André Vachon, ed., *Situation de la recherche sur la Franco-Américanie* (Québec: Conseil de la Vie française en Amérique, 1980), 81–100. Richard Santerre, ed., *Anthologie de la littérature franco-américaine de la Nouvelle-Angleterre* (Manchester, N.H.: National Materials Development Center, 1981). 9 vols.

[4] Resource materials dealing with the French-Canadian folk song include Eusèbe Viau and J.-Ernest Philie, *Chants populaires des Franco-Américains* (Woonsocket, R.I.: Union Saint-Jean-Baptiste d'Amérique, 1931); Frédéric-Ernest-Amédée Gagnon, *Chansons populaires du Canada* (Montréal; Beauchemin, 1952), 8th ed.; Marius Barbeau, *Répetoire de la chanson folklorique française au Canada* (Ottawa: Musée National du Canada, 1962); Edith Fulton Fowke and Richard Johnston, *Chansons de Québec* (1958; Waterloo, Ont.: Waterloo Music Co., 1973).

[5] Some useful sources are Honoré Beaugrand, *La Chasse-galerie: Légendes canadiennes* (Montréal: Fides, 1973) and Aurélien Boivin, *Le Conte littéraire québécois au XIXe siècle: Essai de bibliographie critique et analytique* (Montréal: Fides, 1975).

[6] The most extensive and reliable source materials to date are the publications of the Archives de Folklore, Université Laval, Québec. The newly established Institut d'Etudes Françaises et Franco-Américaines at Assumption College, Worcester, Mass., directed by Claire Quintal, has recently begun a collection of folklore materials.

[7] Representative works of Henri d'Arles (pseud. Henri Beaudé) include *Laudes* (1925), *Estampes* (1926), and *Miscellanées* (1927).

[8] Rosaire Dion-Lévesque (pseud. Léo Lévesque), *Vita* (Montréal: Valiquette, 1939). Dion-Lévesque also published an excellent translation of excerpts from *Leaves of Grass: Walt Whitman, ses meilleures pages* (Québec: Presses de l'Univ. Laval, 1965).

[9] Rosaire Dion-Lévesque, *Solitudes* (Montréal: Chanteclerc, 1949).

[10] Efforts made by the National Assessment and Dissemination Center for Bilingual Education (Cambridge, Mass.) and by the National Materials Development Center (Bedford, N.H.) should be supported and supplemented by any means possible.

[11] For the basic data on Gabriel Crevier, I am indebted to Ernest B. Guillet, "French Ethnic Literature and Culture in an American City: Holyoke, Massachusetts," Diss. Massachusetts 1978.

[12] The most readily available illustrations of Hébert's work and of the work of several other poets discussed here are to be found in Chassé, *Anthologie* (see n. 3).

[13] Normand Dubé, *Un Mot de chez nous* (Fall River,Mass.: National Assessment and Dissemination Center, n.d.) and *Au coeur du vent* (Cambridge, Mass.: National Assessment and Dissemination Center, 1978).

[14] Representative works include *Caprices poétiques et chansons satiriques* (1883), *Coups d'ail et coups de bec* (1888), and *Boutades et rêveries* (1893).

[15] Louis-Alphonse Nolin's manuscripts have been preserved at the Library of the Oblate Fathers, Natick, Mass.

[16] Honoré Beaugrand, *Jeanne la fileuse,* 2nd ed. (Montréal: Presses de la Patrie, 1888), p. 5; my translation.

[17] Santerre, "Le Roman franco-américain...," p. 86; my translation.

[18] Gérard Robichaud's second novel *The Apple of His Eye* (1965) also takes place in a New England mill town with a large Franco-American population.

[19] The novel *L'Innocente Victime* was serialized in *Le Droit* and is therefore difficult to find, but like Duval-Thibault's *Les Deux Testaments* and Crépeau's *Bélanger ou l'histoire d'un crime* before it, Lambert's novel will be reissued by the National Materials Development Center, Bedford, N.H.

[20] Rose Basile Green, *The Italian-American Novel* (Rutherford, N.J.: Fairleigh Dickinson Univ. Press, 1974), p. 23.

[21] See Gabriel Nadeau, "Le Théâtre chez les Franco-Américains," *Bulletin de la Société Historique Franco-Américaine,* 1 (1955), 69–74.

[22] In Antoine Clément, ed., *L'Alliance française de Lowell* (Manchester, N.H.: L'Avenir National, 1936), pp. 58–64.

[23] A full half-century after the "agitation" a realistic assessment of the movement remains impossible.

[24] A complete listing of either parish histories or local histories does not seem to exist. For a partial listing, see the sources indicated in note 3 and in Armand Chartier, "Selective and Thematic Checklist of Publications Relating to Franco-Americans," *Contemporary French Civilization*, 2 (1978), 469–512.

[25] See also Gérald Robert, *Memorial II des actes de l'Association Canado-Americaine, 1946–1971* (1975).

[26] Censored excerpts from the "Journal intime" of Henri d'Arles have appeared in *Bulletin de la Société Historique Franco-Américaine,* NS 2 (1956), 132–42; 4 (1958), 133–44; and 5 (1959), 129–57.

[27] Oral history has broadened the range of autobiographical statement. Tamara K. Hareven and Randolph Langenbach have used this technique in *Amoskeag: Life and Work in an American Factory City* (New York: Pantheon, 1978). The work deals mainly with the Franco-Americans of Manchester, New Hampshire, and sparked controversy from the day of its publication.

[28] Irving Howe, *Jewish-American Stories* (New York: New American Library, 1977), p. 13.

German-American Literature

Robert Bishoff

German-American ethnicity is elusive. On the one hand, it seems to possess all the characteristics inherent in standard definitions of ethnic identification in the United States. On the other hand, so many aspects of the German character have become an organic part of the standard definition of "American" that it is often impossible to distinguish one from the other. In short, the hyphenated adjective "German-American" is often redundant, and on many levels and in many respects "German-American" ethnicity is, in fact, "American" ethnicity. The German influence on what has come to be known as the "American character" is second only to that of the English Puritan pilgrims. The reason for this influence is simple enough. Germans have been an active force in the formation of this country since Colonial times, and they have been here in large numbers. Since the early decades of the eighteenth century, Germans and Americans of German extraction have constituted almost a quarter of the population of the United States.

Because of the complex interrelations between the standard "American" character and German-American ethnicity, any attempt to present a concise overview of German-American literary activity and its relation to the traditionally accepted examples of the national literature is extremely difficult. Yet this complex relation indicates the importance of developing an awareness of and appreciation for a significant body of writings that sometimes run parallel to the literary mainstream, sometimes diverge from it, and sometimes become a part of it.

Any effort to present an introduction to and an overview of German ethnic contributions to American literature must, in the beginning, recognize three significant facts. First, the presence of German thought and writing in the United States is a long and varied one. Second, the number of German works produced in this country indicates the large size of this group. And, finally, the geographical diversity and divergent interests of the German immigrants have resulted in a great variety of literary genres. Although a brief outline of its history might make German immigration seem to parallel the experience of several other non-English groups, a significant and fundamental difference is that German migration to America had more continuity, involved more people, and touched more places than the migration of any other European ethnic group.

In his classic exploration of the immigraion experience, *A Nation of Nations*, Louis Adamic points out that

> In 1900 the United States had nearly 2,700,000 immigrants born in Germany, and another three-quarters of a million Germans from other European countries. They were the newest part of the estimated nineteen million people of German stock then forming twenty-seven percent of the American population.[1]

At the beginning of the twentieth century, these nineteen million German Americans were scattered throughout every part of the nation. They established communities in such diverse geographical regions as Pennsylvania, central Texas, and the midwestern states of Missouri, Illinois, and Wisconsin. Their interests, activities, professions, and religious beliefs reflected the great diversity that characterized American society as a whole at the beginning of the twentieth century. There were German artisans, scientists, professors, farmers. Some were members of various Protestant religious sects; some were Catholics; some were Jews. They were settling—or were already settled—in densely populated cities, in small towns and villages, in isolated rural areas. There were those who had eagerly and hastily become assimilated into the mainstream of American culture, and there were those who held staunchly to the culture and traditions of the land of their origin. Some German Americans could trace their family roots back to the early colonists of New York and Pennsylvania, and others had only recently arrived on American shores. And by 1900 a body of literature already reflected the diverse regional and ethnic experiences of this sizable percentage of the American population.

The historical beginnings of German-American literature read much like a scenario for the origins of mainstream American literature. Late in the seventeenth century, a group of religious pilgrims seeking a place in which to practice their beliefs freely struggled to form a viable community in the unfamiliar wilderness of what is now the northeastern United States. These pilgrims, Mennonites led by Franz Daniel Pastorius, had arrived in Philadelphia in 1683 on the ship *Concord*, sometimes called the *Mayflower* of German immigration. By 1690 Pastorius and his followers had formally founded the German colony of Germantown, Pennsylvania. The experiences of this band of settlers were not unlike those of their English contemporaries to the north in New England, and the written records of those experiences were parallel as well.

Pastorius, one of the most learned men in the America of his day, an intellectual, and an educated equal of Cotton Mather, became the first major representative author of German-American poetry and imaginative prose. The literature that he and his compatriots produced was largely of a religious-didactic or practical-informational type that paralleled in content and form the mainstream literature then being produced by the English-speaking colonists. Mainly consisting of political and theological writings, travel diaries, and settlement records, the earliest examples of German-American literature were generally "literature" only in the broadest sense of the word, and as such, the only real and significant way in which they differed from most traditional mainstream writing of the period was that they were in German rather than in English. Since the writings of Pastorius and the other early German colonists were not written in the dominant language of the time, they had practically no effect on American thought outside their own immediate area. Nonetheless, they were important to the ever-increasing numbers of German immigrants who continued to arrive in America at the end of the seventeenth century and the beginning of the eighteenth century.

Franz Daniel Pastorius, who might be called the father of German-American literature, was both an able, practical leader and a man of ideas and ideals. He composed works in Germantown as early as 1690 and often expressed his philosophy of life and his experience in short rhymes and epigrams. Among his longer poetic works "Gegen die Negusklaverei" particularly stands out because it is one of the earliest literary expressions of opposition to slavery recorded in the colonies. Earlier, in 1688, the people of Germantown had composed, under his leadership, the first public protest in America against slavery. Pastorius' principal work was a geographical description of the Germantown area, published in 1700. Less distinguished for its literary merit but a pleasant curiosity nonetheless is his *Hive, Beestock Mellitrophium Alvear or Rusca Aprium*, a scrapbook of about a thousand pages in eight languages which Pastorius began in 1796. Pastorius found more practical outlets for his linguistic abilities, however, in teaching English to his fellow immigrants and in becoming the first known teacher of German in America. He also compiled a primer that became the first schoolbook printed in Pennsylvania. Consequently, although the literary aspects of Pastorius' writing failed to make him a significant force in the development of mainstream American literature, the practical aspects of its content did play an influential role in the emerging consciousness of a newly developing national identity.

Among the significant examples of early German-American literature, works by Pastorius' contemporaries Johannes Kelpius, Konrad Beissel, and other leaders of German religious sects are worthy of note. Kelpius and Beissel were both mystics and prolific hymnists whose religious lyrics formed the roots of lyric poetry in the German-speaking colonies of seventeenth-century America. The Ephrata community in Pennsylvania, under the leadership of Konrad Beissel, became the center for original hymns and choral music in the colonies. Beissel's best lyrics often transcended the narrow dogmatic limitations of pietism and revealed the "mystic imagination" and artistry of a serious lyric poet. His descriptions, in certain poems, of America as a new Eden, an earthly paradise, are of special interest, particularly because that attitude resembles the feelings expressed in English-language works of the period. In 1730 Beissel published one of the first German-language books in America, *Goettliche Liebes—und Lobesgethoene*, which was printed by no less an influential member of the Pennsylvania colony than Benjamin Franklin. Other notable poets among the late seventeenth- and pre-Revolutionary eighteenth-century German-American colonists include Ludwig von Zinzendorf, who wrote, in German, hundreds of verses on American themes; Johan-Christopher Friedrich Cammerhof; Abraham Wagner; and Justus H. C. Helmuth. In general, religious lyrics, specifically for hymns, were the major literary contribution of the early German-American colonists.

Writing of a more practical, utilitarian, and factual type was fairly abundant among the German-speaking colonists of pre-Revolutionary America. Valuable records of the formation of various religious settlements constitute a large part of the literature of the period and offer important, enlightening descriptions of the country as it then was. The Moravians, in particular, kept carefully detailed records that provide insights into the experience of colonization. Travel books and sketches extolling the beauties and possibilities of the American landscape reflect a typical pioneer zeal for the new land, a zeal that culminated in abundant patriotic works celebrating the struggle for independence and the virtues of the newly emerging nation. And, while little of the factual writing done in German was translated into English, many patriotic and political writings of the English-speaking colonists were translated into German. One such work was the Declaration of Independence, which was in fact published in a German-language Philadelphia newspaper before the original had been published in the English press. The practical, utilitarian German-American writing up to and during the Revolutionary War is, therefore, most significant because it reflects a growing awareness of a new political, social, and national identity that paralleled and often interrelated with the more predominant and visible developing awareness of the English-speaking colonists.

The effects that the Revolutionary War and its aftermath had on German-American literature in general and especially on the works emerged from the large, established Pennsylvania German communities are succinctly summarized by Robert Ward in "The Case for German-American Literature":

> The period following the War for Independence through the first three decades of the nineteenth century is marked by religious didacticism and concern for the effects of the war and the question of statehood. The major works are hymnals, lyric poetry, and nonfictive prose. Some of the themes treated by writers of this period are the plight of the Redemptionists, slaves and Indians, public hangings, epidemics and disease, the emergence of new industries, the hard winters suffered by the settlers, the exploitation of children, and the New England bias against the foreign element.[2]

The large-scale German immigration that began early in the eighteenth century centered primarily in Pennsylvania, and there the literature that Ward describes was most fruitful and abundant. It was also in the Pennsylvania of the late eighteenth and early nineteenth centuries that the best-known, most distinctive, and longest-lived German-American society and literature began to develop.

As I have already pointed out, the Pennsylvania German culture actively began to develop late in the seventeenth century, but this culture was directed and determined by a handful of scholars who had been educated in German universities. The language and customs were principally German. The average German colonist held as much as possible to the Old World ways, relying on educated leaders to serve as a bridge to the predominantly English-speaking world. Pre-Revolutionary German American was essentially a nonhyphenated experience in which two different cultures existed side by side. The deaths of the European scholar-leaders, however, along with the large influx of new German immigrants following the Revolutionary War, effected a change that resulted in what has come to be known as the Pennsylvania Dutch culture.

The characteristics and customs of the Pennsylvania Dutch culture are too complex to dismiss with a superficial discussion. They offer interesting insights into the German-American ethnic experience. For purposes of discussing German-American ethnic literature, however, let it suffice to say the the Pennsylvania Dutch culture provided a unique way of viewing experience and a unique dialect for expressing that view. Pennsylvania Dutch culture was essentially the result of the homogenization of two other cultures—the German and the English—and the Pennsylvania Dutch dialect and literature were a direct result of the hyphenization of the German-American ethnic experience.

At the outset, the Pennsylvania Dutch culture was not a literary one, and not until almost midway through the nineteenth century were any conscious attempts made to create a literature in the Pennsylvania German dialect. In the seventeenth- and eighteenth-century German-American settlements, High German was considered the accepted language for serious writing, and the emerging regional dialect was regarded as lacking in dignity. Although the workaday language of the Pennsylvania Germans was principally that of the Palatinate region of Germany, an ever-increasing number of commonly used words were either English or a compound of English and German. This emerging vernacular reflected the cultural evolution that occurred in German-American settlements throughout the eighteenth and early nineteenth centuries, and it is not, therefore, surprising that the written literature of the new Pennsylvania Dutch culture should follow only after the language and social customs of that culture were firmly established.

Also, as several social historians have indicated, the early Pennsylvania German settlers were primarily concerned with practical matters of physical well-being and financial success rather than with the conscious creation of art. Nonetheless, by the midnineteenth century, a literature had emerged that was American in spirit and a real part of the literature of the United States, even though it was written in a unique non-English dialect.

In its earliest written form, Pennsylvania German literature began primarily as dialect letters printed in Pennsylvania Dutch newspapers during the years between the Revolutionary and the Civil War. These letters, which flourished in the decade preceding the Civil War, were often earthy attempts at satire and humor resembling the folk art typical of a developing culture rather than the sophisticated artistic works of an established tradition. For this reason the writing in pre-Civil War Pennsylvania German letters bore little or no resemblance to the works of Emerson and Thoreau or Hawthorne and Melville. While English-American literature in the post-Revolutionary era reflected the continuance of a traditional cultural heritage, the German-American writing of the period illustrated the emergence of a wholly new culture.

Around 1849, Louis Miller wrote one of the earliest examples of dialect literature from the Pennsylvania Germans, a lively and popular driver's song, but not until the Civil War did the Pennsylvania Dutch make a conscious effort to build a body of literature in their own language. Composed chiefly of educated professionals—teachers, ministers, doctors—the first group of conscious Pennsylvania Dutch writers attempted to add morality and gentility to their works as a means of transcending the overt earthiness of the earlier letter writers. As a result, much of the literature produced in this period epitomizes the excessive sentimentality common to English writing during Victorian times. A large part of the dialect verse written by such early Pennsylvania Dutch poets as Henry Harbaugh, Eli Keller, Ludwig Wollenweber, and Edward Rauch, to name only a few, was concerned chiefly with the enjoyment of home and infused with a strong sense of nostalgia for the "good old days." Another early poet, Lee Grumbine, urged his fellow Pennsylvania writers to embrace this theme when he wrote, "The common range of everyday human experiences, human activities, human feelings, these are the materials and opportunities for the Pennsylvania

German poet."[3] Some scholars have suggested that the nature of the dialect is as much responsible for this attitude as is any temperamental tendency toward sentimentality. Certainly the few attempts of Pennsylvania Dutch writers to go beyond the range of everyday experiences have not been as artistically successful as the works dealing with more common, everyday subject matter.

A work such as "Heemweh" by Henry Harbaugh, the earliest and best known of the poets, achieves a considerably more successful artistic effect than does Edward Rauch's Pennsylvania German translation of passages from Shakespeare. Even Rauch seems to have been aware of this fact, since he ultimately chose to make his translation of the ghost scene in *Hamlet* a burlesque, thereby pointing up through exaggeration certain limitations of the dialect. To recognize that the Pennsylvania Dutch dialect is not necessarily suited to loftiness or grave dignity, however, does not mean that this body of literature should be dismissed as insignificant and inconsequential. At best these works celebrate the commonplace: the washerwoman, the fisherman, the thrush, the crow, the country store, the cider mill. This is a folk literature from a unique American culture, expressed in a unique American voice.

Though Pennsylvania Dutch writers continued to develop throughout the last half of the nineteenth century, a real body of literature and a community of writers actually emerged only after the establishment of the Pennsylvania German Society in 1891. Such writers as Edward Hermany, Henry Lee Fisher, Rachel Bahn, and Abraham Howe worked throughout the last half of the nineteenth century, keeping the dialect literature alive by occasionally writing for the popular Pennsylvania Dutch magazine, *The Guardian*, for the regional newspapers, or sometimes simply for sheets to be distributed to friends. With the formation of the Pennsylvania German Society and the annual publication of its *Proceedings*, however, an established central outlet for the dialect literature became a reality and ensured writers not only a publication source but also a forum for serious discussion of their work. By the beginning of the twentieth century, then, Pennsylvania Dutch literature had come of age.

Throughout the nineteenth century and well into the twentieth, poetry remained the favorite literary form of the dialect writers. Among the few authors of prose fiction, Thomas Hess Harter and Charles More are worthy of note. Harter developed his fictional character, Gottlieb Boonastiel, as a means of responding to injustice and political corruption through a series of letters published in Herter's own newspaper. As the character evolved and became bolder in his attacks on influential persons, he grew increasingly popular. Ultimately the Boonastiel letters were collected and published in book form. These works were probably the best-sellers among the dialect books. In style they most resemble the earlier *Spectator* of Addison and Steele. Unlike the Boonastiel letters, the works of Charles More are true examples of the short story form. While his stories, such as "Der Wiescht Mann van der Flett" and "Die Kutztown Mael," tend to be heavily melodramatic and sentimental, they are nonetheless carefully crafted, suspenseful, sustained renderings in pure Pennsylvania Dutch. More's ability to weave Romanticism and realism, pathos and humor, into genuinely artistic literary products establishes him as a significant voice in Pennsylvania German and German-American literature.

Although literature in the dialect continues to be written—the works of the poet John Birmelin being only one notable example—the most significant body of twentieth-century literature from the Pennsylvania Dutch country has been in English. When, around the turn of the century, local color writing heavily influenced mainstream American literature, a parallel movement was once again occurring in Pennsylvania German writing. Three of the most popular authors of Pennsylvania German local color stories were Helen Martin, Elsie Singmaster, and Katherine Loose, who used the pen name Georg Schock. Helen Martin was the most prolific and popular of these writers, but the works of Singmaster and Schock are artistically superior and display the authors' sympathy, insight, and thorough knowledge of the people and the region. In more recent years, several novels about the Pennsylvania Dutch people and their culture have become a part of popular American literature. These include such works as Conrad Richter's *The Free Man*, Pearl Buck's *Portrait of a Marriage*, and John O'Hara's *A Rage to Live*. As these works indicate, by the middle of the twentieth century, the Pennsylvania German experience had become an essential element of the general American experience, and writers of Pennsylvania German descent such as Conrad Richter have become a part of the American literary tradition.

While the Pennsylvania German literary tradition is the oldest, the most familiar, and perhaps the most sustained element of the German-American literary tradition, it is not the only significant body of German-American ethnic writing. Writing of some type appeared, of course, wherever Germans settled throughout the eighteenth and nineteenth centuries. There are in fact examples of deliberate attempts to create German-American literature in such diverse places as South Carolina, New York, and Tennessee. Nonetheless, Pennsylvania was the center for a type of German ethnic literature that for the most part runs parallel in both style and content to the developing literature of the nation as a whole. One could suggest, although this is a gross oversimplification, that one reason for the parallel nature of this German-American literary movement rests in its specific origins as a literature of immigrants whose purposes and experiences were similar to those of their English counterparts.

In the nineteenth century, however, at least two other significant bodies of German-American literature developed. Each had its origins in circumstances distinctly different from those of the early northeastern immigrant experience, and each produced a literature that at times diverged considerably from that of nineteenth-century English-American literature. For the sake of simplicity, we can label these two literary countertraditions Texas German-American literature and Midwestern German-American literature.

Like Pennsylvania, Texas became a particularly significant center for German-American ethnic literature primarily because of its large German population. In 1900 a third of the population of Texas was of German descent, and many of this number had been in the state for well over half a century. The immigrants who came to Texas in the nineteenth century differed, however, from the seventeenth- and eighteenth-century Pennsylvania settlers in certain basic and significant ways. As a result, the literature produced in the German communities of Texas did not follow the same patterns as that produced by the colonists in the northeast. Essentially the German population in Texas during the nineteenth century was made up of or descended from migrants, immigrants, and emigrants. Each played a distinct role in establishing the Texas German-American cultural experience and in the literature that resulted from that experience.

In general the earliest Germans to arrive in Texas were nonintellectual migrants who traveled to that region at the time of the Anglo-American colonization during the opening decades of the nineteenth century. Frederick Law Olmsted in *A Journey through Texas* (1857), describes these earliest German Texans as being "of a somewhat humble and promiscuous description." Some were farmers and craftsmen, but "there was a certain number, as among the early settlers of Virginia, who were suffered to escape justice at home on condition of becoming colonists; who were, in short, sentenced to Texas."[4] This brief description is sufficient at least to suggest a basic contrast between the earliest German element in Texas and the band of religious pilgrims that Daniel Pastorius had led into Pennsylvania more than a century before. Interestingly, though, not all the Germans who migrated to Texas in this early period were nonintellectual.

Among the various people who traveled to or through the area at this time were at least two important figures in the history of German-American literature. The first, Valentin Hecke, was a traveler-explorer who published the earliest German book that dealt with Texas. This work, *Reise durch die Vereinigten Staates* (*A Journey through the United States*), was published in Berlin in 1820. Two chapters in the two-volume work are devoted exclusively to Texas. Although they contain an extensive description of the area and its inhabitants, the chapters serve primarily to suggest a plan by which the Prussian colonization of the Texas area could build up the Prussian navy and increase trade with North and South America. In time the work did spark at least two attempts at German colonization. The first was made by the Germanic Society of New York in 1839, and the second and more significant was undertaken by a group of Hessian noblemen in 1842. Although both attempts were ultimately doomed to failure, they did attract large numbers of German immigrants to Texas between 1836, when it won its independence from Mexico, and 1845, when it joined the Union. The Mainzer Adelsverein, as the association of Hessian noblemen was called, was especially concerned with attracting colonists to support its political purpose, and it produced a great deal of literature designed not only to attract Germans to Texas but also to prepare them for life in the New World.

The second important intellectual and literary figure among the German migrants in early eighteenth-century Texas was Karl Postl, an Austrian political dissident who ultimately became Charles Sealsfield, the first important German-American writer to devote himself to fiction. Postl, or Sealsfield as he became known after his migration to Texas, began his literary and political career as an Austrian clergyman and the author of a work published anonymously and entitled *Austria as It Is, or Sketches of Continental Courts, by an Eyewitness*. As a result of this work, Sealsfield became a political criminal, fleeing Austria and arriving in New Orleans in 1823. He traveled extensively in the United States and Mexico, but Texas particularly impressed him. His first English-language publication, *The United States as They Are, in Their Political, Religious, and Social Bearings*, printed in England in 1828, was followed by a historical novel, *Tokeah, or the White Rose*, which is set primarily in the Neches River area of Texas.

Tokeah has been compared in both style and content to Cooper's *Leatherstocking Tales* and Helen Hunt Jackson's *Ramona*, though some critics have suggested that the Sealsfield novel is technically superior. The Comanche and Creek Indians play an important part in *Tokeah*, and the title character is a chief of the Creeks. El Sol, the lover of Tokeah's daughter Canondak, is the chief of the Comanches. Other more or less historical characters in the novel include the pirate Jean Lafitte and General Andrew Jackson. Published in Pennsylvania, where Sealsfield was then residing, the well-received novel established an audience for the author on both sides of the Atlantic.

Along with *Tokeah*, two other fictional works by Sealsfield had an important influence on German immigration to Texas. The first—"Nathan, the Squatter Regulator; or, The First American in Texas," included in a collection of works entitled *Life Sketches from the Western Hemisphere*—presents a Daniel Boone–type character who preferred to brave the dangers of the wilderness rather than remain under the confines of a restrictive society. The character of Nathan is one of Sealsfield's most original creations and one of the more interesting characters in early American fiction. The second work, *Das Kajutenbuch oder National Charakteristiken*, is probably the best of Sealsfield's historical romances. It deals with the Texas war for independence and contains some of the finest descriptive passages in Sealsfield's writing. The story is essentially an extended, romantic exploration of why the central character chose to come to the unsettled lands of Texas. "Nathan" and *Kajutenbach* created a great deal of German interest in Texas and helped to promote the Adelsverein's enterprise.

Sealsfield's significance as a writer goes beyond his importance as a recruiter of immigrants to the new land, however. He made his primary contribution by preserving for posterity certain typical American characters of the first half of the nineteenth century. As a result of Sealsfield's knowledgeable, fair, and sympathetic presentation of characters, customs, and institutions, the *Southern Review* wrote, "the Germans are the only peoples who have a comparatively just appreciation of America."⁵

The literary output during what might be termed the immigrant period of the Texas German-American experience, from 1836 through 1845, was chiefly limited to official reports, descriptive literature, and guidebooks for prospective newcomers. Because of the political nature of this immigration, particularly that promoted by the Adelsverein, and the sponsorship of this colonization by German royalty, the literature differed markedly in tone and style from that produced in other parts of the United States and by other ethnic groups. Victor Bracht, Prince Carl von Solms-Braunfels, Ferdinand Roemer, and A.H. Soergel, among many others, wrote specifically for a German rather than German-American audience. Prince Solm-Braunfels, for example, wrote his chief work with one purpose in mind: to inform prospective German immigrants of what they might expect in Texas. His description of the non-German people of the region is negative in many respects, although he does praise their courage and determination.

A. H. Soergel's *Neueste Nachricten aus Texas* is unique in that it is mainly a critical commentary on earlier German-American authors of Texas. Soergel attempts to correct the misinformation of some, while praising others as informed advisers to immigrants. A significant and prolific novelist of the period was H. E. Belani (Carl L. Haeberlin). Belani's *The Texas Emigrants* has special interest historically because it relates incidents in the lives of several prominent figures of the time.

Around the middle of the nineteenth century, after Texas statehood was firmly established, the Mainzer Adelsverein ceased to exist and the numbers of new German settlers declined considerably. Emigration replaced immigration, and many later arrivals came as members of small groups of political dissidents and revolutionaries who had been forced to flee from their native land. Sketches of pioneer life and histories of the settlements replaced the immigrant guidebooks of the earlier decades. In 1857 Peter August Moelling wrote what was apparently the first German book published in Texas, *Travel*

Sketches In Poetry and Prose. This work fairly represents the general type of writing being produced by Texas Germans at that time.

The most important writer of this period, however, was August Siemering. Because of his support of revolutionary political activities in 1848–1849, Siemering had been forced to emigrate from Germany to the New Braunfels, Texas, area. Siemering found many kindred spirits in the area and continued his rebellion against tyranny by attacking the political structure and purposes of the already weakening Adelsverein. Selma Raunick in her concise but thorough study, "A Survey of German-American Literature in Texas," on which much of this discussion of Texas German writing is based, offers the following description of Siemering's political activities in Texas:

> During the activities of Adelsverein and after its dissolution, criticism pro and con was heard everywhere. Much of the criticism was published in Germany; a number of critics also used their pens in Texas. Among these Siemering took an active part, accusing the German princes and other aristocrats of having been in league with England in order to reduce the number of slave-holding states. The majority of the liberty-loving Germans were opposed not only to social or political dominance of one group over another, but to the dominance of one race over another. Siemering was radically opposed to the aristocratic party and therefore had little sympathy with the "Adelsverein" which was composed of noblemen. Others, as for instance L. Constant and F. E. Walther, also criticized the Adelsverein severely, though but few implied selfish political and personal motives to the Association. (p. 38)

In addition to his political activities, Siemering, although opposed to both war and slavery, served as an officer in the Confederate army. He also founded one of the most prominent German newspapers of the day, organized an English paper, and edited a German daily in Saint Louis. In addition, he published several historical sketches, factual accounts of life in Texas, and novels. His most interesting novel, *Ein Verfehites Leben* (*A Failure*), published in 1876, is based on actual experiences of Texas Germans during the Civil War period.

While most German writing in Texas during the last half of the nineteenth century was primarily factual or historical, some interesting fiction did appear. George Willrich's novel *Erin-nerungen*, for example, is set in both Germany and Texas but is most interesting for its treatment of the "woman question" and slavery. The story of a German immigrant family, *Joy Follows Sorrow; or, The Settlers of Texas* by Gustav Duvernoy, is a well-written adventure story with a clearly defined plot. Fiction, however, was not the most popular form of written expression among the political activists who emigrated to Texas at this time. Many found journalism to be a more natural outlet for their literary talents and, consequently, several influential German-American newspapers were established during this perod. For the most part these newspapers and their editors were avid spokesmen for democratic ideals and principles.

Since the beginning of the twentieth century, most Texas German-American literature has been of a historical nature. As Selma Raunick says, "There are about half a dozen scattered novels and a few biographies of predominantly cultural and historical value. One author of note, Clara Palacios, who has a number of novels and a volume of poetry to her credit, appears at this time" (p. 39). The best writing during this period, of which the works of Clara Palacios are an outstanding example, tends to be realistic rather than romantic, presenting the harsh realities of the pioneer existence and the customs and folklore of the variety of cultures that have continued to coexist in Texas and the Southwest.

It is interesting to note that the German-American experience in Texas did not result in a culture similar to that of the Germans in Pennsylvania and that, unlike the Pennsylvania Dutch, the Texas German community, despite its size and activity, has not carved a place for itself in the national literature. Texas German-American customs or locales have not figured significantly in any popular mainstream literature thus far produced in the United States. Curiously, the two novels on the western frontier experience that have probably enjoyed the most success — Owen Wister's highly popular work, *The Virginian*, and Conrad Richter's critical success, *The Sea of Grass* — though both written by authors of German-American descent, are set in locales other than Texas. When Richter did treat the German-American experience, in *The Free Man*, he returned to his own roots in Pennsylvania instead of combining it with his interest in the Southwest by dealing with Germans in Texas.

While it is understandable, perhaps, why Richter would choose to return to Pennsylvania for his German-American materials, one can only speculate on why the Texas German-

American culture and literature have failed to become a part of the American literary mainstream. Whatever the causes might be, the written record of the German-American ethnic experience in Texas remains very much a regional literature.

The third major German-American literary tradition in the United States, the midwestern movement, follows roughly the same chronological pattern as the Texas movement. Again, however, because of certain unique circumstances in its origins, the midwestern German-American culture and literature developed individual characteristics. If one can argue that the development of the German-American literature of Pennsylvania paralleled that of mainstream American literature and that Texas German-American literature diverged from the mainstream and moved into a type of isolated regionalism, then one can suggest that midwestern German-American writers were in part responsible for the creation of a countermainstream American literature. In short, German-American communities in the Midwest, through their customs, beliefs, and writing, had a direct impact on the shaping of the contemporary American character and the resultant body of literature. Two basic reasons for the impact of the midwestern Germans on the general American cultural and literary experience are the specific characteristics of the immigration that produced the German society and the specific locations in which the people settled.

Between 1820 and 1920 well over five million Germans arrived in the United States. A large percentage of these newcomers settled in the midwestern states of Missouri, Indiana, Illinois, Iowa, Ohio, Michigan, Minnesota, and Wisconsin. Unlike the German settlers in Texas, who found themselves in small scattered frontier towns like New Braunfels and Austin, many midwestern settlers ended their journey in such developing urban centers as Chicago, Saint Louis, and Milwaukee. The experience of busy, expanding city life left a marked impression on both the culture and the literature of the German communities that were in these areas.

Additionally, many of these urban midwestern German settlers were well-educated intellectuals of high social rank who brought with them an intense belief in certain social and political ideas, which they continued to articulate effectively after arriving in the new country. The Forty-eighters who emigrated to this region around the midnineteenth century are especially notable in this respect, because they counted among their numbers an extremely high percentage of journalists, college professors, university students, and literary figures who had been exiled from Germany as a result of their revolutionary political activities.

> They were young; they were fired with enthusiasm, with energy; they possessed skill of pen and of speech. In all the leading cities of the United States east of the Mississippi they exerted a potential influence in the educational movements of the time, and naturally their activity soon extended to the significant political movements that foreshadowed the great struggle of the Sixties.[6]

Wisconsin in particular was receptive to these emigrants, and as a result the state became a major center for midwestern German-American political, cultural, and literary activity in the nineteenth century.

Although a strong argument could be advanced, perhaps, for looking at either Missouri or Illinois as a representative model for the examination of midwestern German-American literary activity, Wisconsin with its large German-American population (thirty-four percent of the state in 1900) and its early established cultural center in Milwaukee can effectively serve that purpose. Wisconsin, regarded by many as the most Germanic state in the Union, developed largely as a result of a Germany-in-America movement similar to the ones that had occurred in Texas and Missouri. While the Wisconsin movement, like those in the other two states, was doomed to failure, it nonetheless had a strong impact on the politics and culture of the entire midwestern region and ultimately on the nation.

In 1830 Wisconsin was an undefined wilderness populated largely by Black Hawk Indians, and twenty years later it was an officially recognized part of the United States with a population of over 300,000 non-Indian settlers. German migration alone accounted for most of this growth and development. During the 1840s a campaign began to recruit German settlers to the developing territory, and the result was impressive.

Franz Loher's romantic travel essays containing lush descriptions of Wisconsin's natural beauty along with a plan for the development of a politically powerful Germanic enclave in the area were especially influential in attracting Germans to this part of the Midwest, as were the pamphlets that Moritz Schoeffler published in his Milwaukee printing office. The Wisconsin

Territory, on receiving statehood in 1848, immediately provided
official support for these efforts to draw Germans to Wisconsin,
and this move resulted in the great influx of German political
emigrants called Forty-eighters.

Hundreds of German emigrants began arriving weekly in the
new state, and Milwaukee served as the distribution center for
settlers. As a result, the city became a rich, vital German cultural
center. German-language newspapers, journals, theaters, and
literature flourished in the 1850s, earning for Milwaukee the title
"the German Athens." So entrenched was the German community in Milwaukee, and in certain other midwestern cities as
well, that European social customs could hold their own against
active protest by the Anglo-American-Puritan segment of the
society. Milwaukee Germans could, for example, rebel against
rather than capitulate to such anti-European customs as the
puritanical blue laws. In general, European definitions of the joys
of life could be cultivated rather than repressed by the demands
of life in an essentially non-German nation. As a result, a spirit of
confrontation developed, providing an impetus for sustaining
Old World customs and practices, fostering introspection among
the intellectuals of the community, and creating an attitude
toward life in America that manifests itself in politics, business,
religion, art, and literature.

Literature benefited greatly from this spirit of cultural
confrontation. The most intellectual and gifted German Americans in the state were inspired to new heights of creative activity
and, with the help of the many good German-language newspapers, journals, and periodicals then being printed, were able to
find a forum for their expressions.

The literary scene in Milwaukee during this midnineteenth-
century period was so intense that conflicting ideologies sur-
faced even within the German ethnic community. Known as the
War of the Grays and the Greens, the literary battle that ensued
as a result of these conflicting ideologies was between the old,
conservative German-American element and the radical, idealistic Forty-eighters. The writing of the Grays, on the one hand, was
rooted firmly in religious ideas and closely aligned with Anglo-
Puritan social and political conservatism. The Greens, on the
other hand, were free-thinking, cynical, and passionate writers of
a literature that was socially and politically liberal and artistically
accomplished. In the end, the Greens won the day, both in
Wisconsin and throughout the midwestern German-American

literary community. As a result, the spirit of cynical, iconoclastic radicalism that the Forty-eighters brought to America established a firm foothold and had a permanent effect on the politics, culture, and literature of the United States.

Perhaps the most obvious indication of the Forty-eighters' impact not only on German Americans but on the larger national culture is that, largely as a protest against their activities, some members of the Anglo-American majority established the Native American and Know-Nothing movements.

> But the struggle, ending as it did with defeat of Know-Nothingism, was all to the good — it strengthened enlightened Americanism. Historians now are agreed that the intellectual German immigrant of the middle nineteenth century was one of the most valuable elements in the New Immigration. From the 1850's on the group produced a huge number of unusually effective Americans in industry, and business, politics, education, medicine, journalism, the labor movement, the Army, and the arts. (Adamic, p. 178)

Among those effective contributors to the arts were several significant Wisconsin poets, including Mathilde Anneke, Konrad Krez, Augustus Steinlein, Edmund Maerklin, and Rudolph Puchner. Probably the best-known work produced by a member of this group is "To My Fatherland," by Konrad Krez. This poem, which has been reprinted in virtually every German-American anthology since it was first published, illustrates not only the artistic mastery of lyric verse form that these poets exhibited but also the strong personal attachment that they felt for the German homeland, culture, and customs. Puchner's "Farewell to Germany" and Maerklin's "At Parting" are other notable examples of both the lyric talent and the chauvinistic sentiments evidenced in "To My Fatherland."

Mathilde Anneke, an accomplished poet and novelist, was the spiritual center of this group of Wisconsin writers, influencing the others by her exhibitions of courage, determination, and endurance. An advocate of equal legal rights for women in both Germany and America, Anneke had been an active force in the failed German revolution. She had edited a revolutionary newspaper and served as a member of her husband's staff on the German battlefields. In America she lectured in major cities of the Midwest and the East, published the *Frauenzeitung*, wrote poetry and fiction, and inspired others to do the same. Her actions and her writings exemplify the zeal that infused the intellectual German-American community in the last half of the nineteenth century.

This mention of Wisconsin German-American poets is not intended to suggest that the literary output of the Forty-eighters was limited either to Wisconsin or to lyric poetry. Mathilde Anneke is only one of several prolific women writers among German-Americans in the last half of the nineteenth century. Therese Robinson, Edna Fern, and Lotte Leser were, along with Anneke, influential authors of prose fiction that was frequently infused with social activism. Edmund Maerklin, in addition to writing lyric poetry, composed one of several popular memoirs on the Civil War. Other popular memoir novels were written by Fredrich Harter and Fredrich Hassaurek. Urban mystery novels and sketches of German-American city life were made popular by authors such as F. G. Ahrens, Philipp Berger, Johann Rittig, and Adolf Schaffmeyer. The German-American theaters, which flourished in Milwaukee and in most other major cities throughout the Midwest, produced plays by Viktor Precht, Friedrich Ernst, Friedrich Schnake, and others who dealt specifically with American themes.

In general, Wisconsin was simply a representative part of an active literary and political community that flourished among the midwestern German Americans throughout the last half of the nineteenth and the early part of the twentieth century. Nowhere, perhaps, is this representativeness more apparent than in the person of Carl Schurz. Schurz, who became one of the most influential figures in nineteenth-century America, began his life in this country as an exiled Forty-eighter in Wisconsin. He became in time an important leader in the Republican party — United States senator from Missouri, ambassador to Spain, and secretary of the interior; an influential editor of the *Westliche Post* in Saint Louis, the *New York Evening Post*, and the *Nation*; and a biographer — *Life of Henry Clay*. Distinguishing himself in all these endeavors, Carl Schurz reflected not only the abilities inherent among the midwestern German Americans but something of their common zeal and passion for social and political reform as well.

The German-American literature of the latter part of the nineteenth century is often marred by implausible plots or poor characterization (in the works of such popular authors as Owen Wister, Joaquin Miller, Bayard Taylor, and Henry Timrod), but it does frequently reveal authors with an extraordinary gift for capturing minute realistic detail. More important, it embodies an aesthetic that values the investigation of social behavior and commitment to social criticism and reform. Considering the active proliferation of this literature throughout midwestern America, it is perhaps more than a coincidence that a socially critical, naturalistic mainstream literary movement countering in significant ways the eastern traditional mainstream should emerge here in the opening years of the twentieth century. Certainly it is no surprise that Theodore Dreiser should become one of the major figures in this movement. Dreiser is surely the most significant figure in German-American ethnic literature and a social critic whose attitudes and approach descended directly from his midwestern German forebearers. In many respects the Dreiser canon can be seen as a compendium of the greatest strengths and the greatest weaknesses in midwestern German-American literature. Although a detailed examination of Dreiser's work is not within the scope of this study, an important point is that he is the most significant link between German-American ethnic literature and the countermainstream naturalistic movement that has become such an important part of the twentieth-century American literary experience. Dreiser's *Jennie Gerhardt* is one of the chief American literary works dealing with the German experience in this country, and it is a major representative work of naturalistic fiction. The impact of the German-American ethnic literary tradition on Dreiser and on the entire naturalistic movement of which he is a part is an area rich with possibilities for scholarly exploration.

Although Theodore Dreiser may loom largest among prominent literary figures of German descent in twentieth-century America, he is by no means alone. Among his contemporaries, both chronologically and philosophically, H. L. Mencken stands out as an effective leader in the attack on the New England Puritan thought that has always dominated the American character. Works by other, less aggressively anti-Puritan authors of German descent have also played influential roles in the shaping of the twentieth-century American character. Pearl Buck, John Steinbeck, Louis Untermeyer, Joyce Kilmer, Frederick Prokosch, and Conrad Richter are all of German ancestry. Richter's *The Free Man* (1943) deals with a German immigrant boy's life. Two other novels dealing with Germans in America are George Freitag's *Lost Land* (1947) and George Hummel's *Heritage* (1935). These names by no means exhaust the list of major twentieth-century American literary figures that German immigration produced, but they do represent some of the most significant figures in our national literature.

Finally, not even a superficial overview of German-American ethnic literature would be complete without some mention of the emigrants who came to this country between the two world wars. One need only cite such names as Thomas Mann, Heinrich Mann, Erich Maria Remarque, Fritz Unruh, Ernst Toller, and Bertolt Brecht to suggest the literary significance of this period of emigration. While these and other figures of world prominence did not all remain in this country, their work influenced and profited from the American experience. They have become a part of an ethnic literary tradition that began in the earliest years of the American experience and continues as a vital part of this experience to the present day.

Today, German-American ethnic literature still flourishes, in the writings of popular mainstream authors descended from German immigrant stock and in the small regional publications in communities that still hold staunchly to their German ethnicity. Dora Grunewald, Lisa Kahn, Bernhard Mack, and Lisel Muller are a few of the emerging authors. Whether running parallel to the mainstream, diverging from it, or blending with it, German-American ethnic literature has had and continues to have a strong part in the creation of an ever-evolving American literature and American character.

Notes

[1] Louis Adamic, *A Nation of Nations* (New York: Harper, 1944), p. 183.

[2] Robert E. Ward, "The Case for German-American Literature," *The German Contribution to the Building of America*, ed. Gerhard K. Friesen and Walter Schatzberg (Worcester, Mass.: Clark Univ. Press, 1977), p. 378.

[3] Quoted in Frederic Klees, *The Pennsylvania Dutch* (New York: Macmillan, 1950), p. 409.

[4] Quoted in Richard O'Connor, *The German-American: An Informal History* (Boston: Little, 1968), p. 87.

[5] Selma Metzenthin Raunick, "A Survey of German-American Literature in Texas," *German-American Literature,* ed. Don Heinrich Tolzman (Metuchen, N.J.: Scarecrow, 1975), p. 30. Tolzmann has done the most important and extensive bibliographical studies on German Americans.

[6] Henry E. Legler, "A Wisconsin Group of German Poets," *German-American Literature*, p. 18.

Greek-American Literature

Alexander Karanikas

Introduction

Courses in modern Greek literature, language, and history are offered for credit in many colleges and universities. Some were initially promoted by members of the Modern Greek Studies Association, founded at Princeton in 1969. Most relate to Greece, of course, but the scholarly study of Greek America has also expanded in recent years. Such systematic study goes back at least to 1911, when Henry Pratt Fairchild published *Greek Immigration to the United States.* Thomas Burgess followed with *Greeks in America* (1913). Since then many books and monographs, including master's theses and doctoral dissertations, have helped to make the Greek minority one of the more thoroughly researched in the nation. The most authoritative account to date remains *The Greeks in the United States* (1964) by Theodore Saloutos. Of late an interesting adjunct to these endeavors by social scientists has been an inquiry into the modern Greek presence in our literature, with respect to both fictional characters and creative writers.

Until now the bibliographies either sparely reported or completely ignored the Greek ethnic component. The two-volume collection of essays *Ethnic Literature since 1776: The Many Voices of America,* by W. T. Zyla and Wendell Aycock (1978), for example, has no section on this subject. A fairly sizable segment on Greek Americans does appear in Wayne C. Miller's *Comprehensive Bibliography for the Study of American Minorities* (1976), although its listing of Greek writers and Greek characters in American fiction is incomplete. The standard literary indexes that mention immigrant and ethnic works are also unsatisfactory. The current popularity of the ethnic dimension in American literature promises to hasten the needed bibliographical work. The establishment of MELUS, for the study of the multiethnic literature of the United States, indicates the growing value that scholars are placing on the new literary emphasis. Greek immigrants did not begin to arrive in large numbers until the 1890s. Coming mostly from peasant and pastoral backgrounds, unlearned and poor, they did not immediately express in writing the wonder, anguish, and triumph of their odyssey. Their initial publications were both utilitarian and ephemeral — Greek-language newspapers such as *Atlantis, National Herald*, and Chicago's *Greek Star.* Some earlier accounts consisted of fugitive narratives and personal history deriving from the Greek Revolution, captivity and atrocity tales, and reminiscences. During the nineteenth century many non-Greeks visited Greece, however, and wrote interesting though usually impressionistic travel essays. Most of them wanted to learn at first hand if four hundred years of Turkish enslavement had left in the Greeks any traces of their classical greatness. Stephen A. Larrabee's excellent *Hellas Observed* (1957) documents these reports as well as many other works, including those that reflect the "Greek fever" of support for the Greek revolutionary cause. A valuable extension of Larrabee's pioneering research is the more recent *American Poets and the Greek Revolution (1821–1828)* by Alexander Papas and Marios Byron Raizis. Subtitled *A Study in Byronic Philhellenism*, the book records how American poets celebrated in verse the rebirth of modern Greece.

The writings cited by Larrabee, Papas, and Raizis help to illustrate the impact of Hellenism on the early years of our republic. They form a useful intellectual background for the contribution made by Greek ethnics to American literature. By "ethnics" I mean any Greek writers, regardless of place of birth, who have lived and worked in the United States, and by "Greek" I mean any person who has at least one Greek parent and does not deliberately flee from his or her heritage by change of name (unless through marriage) or by other means. I assume, of course, that writers of Greek descent can contribute to American literature even if they choose never to write about their fellow Greeks.

No scholar can know for sure, at this stage of research, how many Greek Americans can qualify as writers by virtue of having published worthy poems, stories, or essays. In the 126 issues of *Athene* magazine, the leading American journal of Hellenic thought, a couple hundred more or less minor authors were represented during the twenty-seven years of publication from 1940 until 1967. Many others have published in Greek newspapers, written privately printed booklets, and so on. The Greek press has often published poetry and short fiction. These scattered and rather slight works may have some value for term and seminar papers — that is, if one can locate them to begin with; they have not as yet been gathered and cataloged at any central location. Even many books by the forty or so relatively important Greek-American authors are so long out of print that they cannot be readily assigned as texts. In time, no doubt, the archives of Greek Americana will be as complete as money and effort can make them. Then, on microfilm and through inter-library loans they will be available to students throughout the country.

Lafcadio Hearn, the first major writer usually regarded as Greek, at least in part, presents the problem of not having shown any interest in modern Greece. Born on the Greek island of Lefkas, Hearn had an Irish father and a Greek mother, Rosa Tessima. She was "Grecian" or "predominately Greek," as he writes, although she may have been Maltese or Maltese with a Greek heritage. Hearn alludes frequently to classical Hellenism in his many essays, yet he never uses a modern Greek in his fiction. He does portray rather exotic ethnic types such as Creoles, Polynesians, and Japanese. As a writer and teacher he spent much of his adult life in Japan; he left Lefkas at an early age and never went back. After the age of seven, in fact, Hearn never again saw his parents. Thus, even though he enjoys permanent stature in American literature and despite the accident of having a Greek mother, Hearn cannot be considered a Greek ethnic.

Poetry

No college course in Greek-American literature can ignore the dozen or more poets for whom the muse has sung in the promised land. The works of more recently published authors like Olga Broumas and Evans Chigounis are readily available, but those of poets such as George Koutoumanos, who wrote early and exclusively in Greek, are not. Some of the poems deal with Greek ethnic subjects; yet, on the whole, the Greek-American poets concentrate on topics that are more personal than narrowly chauvinistic. That is not to say that a consciously

"Greek" act, idea, or emotion cannot at the same time have universal meaning. Nevertheless most of the works written by the poets mentioned here do not reveal a specific ethnic origin. I am presenting these poets in roughly chronological order with some comment on the intrinsic worth of their work.

Demetrios A. Michalaros

Until his death in 1967 Michalaros was known nationally primarily as the editor of *Athene* magazine and locally in Chicago for his weekly television program, *Greek Panorama*. A poet turned journalist, Michalaros also edited *American Hellenic World* in the 1920s. As a young poet he published two volumes, *The Legend of America* (1927) and *Sonnets of an Immigrant* (1930). In her Foreword to the *Sonnets*, the famed social worker Jane Addams compares Michalaros with Jacob Riis and other immigrants who left a record of their arrival and adjustment. "In Old Ionia" eulogizes his village of Alachata on the western coast of Asia Minor. "Wanderlust" cites an episode that contributed to his leaving — a ship anchored in the bay where he heard stories about America. The poem "I Am the Immigrant" praises the newcomer as the builder of America who lifts mountains, digs canals, masses the bricks, and runs the machines. Of the several plays that Michalaros wrote the best is perhaps *Theodora* (1931), about the empress for Justinian. The play premiered at the Studebaker Theater in Chicago and received such headlines as "Greek Immigrant Proves His Mettle" and "Ditch Digger Sees His Play Produced." Among other books by Michalaros are *Protagoras* (1937) and *The Minoan* (1958), the first a long poem about the noted Sophist and the second about the adventures of Antalos, a mythical Cretan hero. For his long editorship of *Athene*, Michalaros was honored by the Friends of Literature, who gave him their Ferguson Award, and by the king of Greece, who gave him a plaque.

George Koutoumanos

Much admired as a "people's poet," Koutoumanos composed in Greek enough poems to fill several volumes. Were poets in America as widely read as they are honored, the best of his work would have long since been rendered into English. From 1907 to 1964 his poetry appeared in slim, privately printed books and in

Greek-language newspapers. Rae Dalven and John Prevedore translated some of his verse for various issues of *Athene*. In "A Saugatuck Landscape," Koutoumanos praises the region in Michigan where he retired to write and live out his days. In "Dance of the Grecian Maidens" the poet, as master of ceremonies, welcomes the girls to participate in a festival of youth. In 1968 the writer Theano Papazoglou-Margaris delivered a lecture on Koutoumanos, in Greek, which is available as a pamphlet. She calls him the finest of the earlier Greek-American poets, one who captures well the dreams, the agonies, the nostalgias, and the hopes of the immigrant. In his verse he also supports many social causes dedicated to improving the lot of humanity.

Paul Nord

Several poets write equally well in both Greek and English. One uses his real name, Nikos Laides, in Greece, and the name Paul Nord in America. His poems tend to be epigrammatic, satiric, and witty. Like a fellow poet, the columnist Paul Denis, he belongs to the cultural scene of New York City. Greece knows him for his poems, essays, songs, and translations of Shakespeare, Tennyson, and others. Nord's mock epic in English, *Salamander* (1946), elicited from Albert Einstein a warm letter of praise. The more than eighty poems in *Chaos Revisited* (1964) appeared first in the Jamestown, New York, *Sun*. Acerbic humor such as one finds in Nord's pithy verse seeks to reduce humanity's folly and greed. A number of his poems and short stories appeared in *Athene* magazine.

Andonis Decavalles

A versatile author, Decavalles is also a teacher, scholar, critic, editor, and translator from the Greek into English. He has for many years edited *Charioteer*, an ambitious and high-quality review sponsored by the New York cultural society, Parnassos. *Charioteer* brings to American readers, in English translation, the best poetry and fiction of modern Greece. Decavalles has written several books of poetry as well as critical studies of Eliot, Pound, Elytis, and Prevelakis. His collection in Greek, *Armoi karabia lytra* (1976), won the Academy of Athens Poetry Prize of 1977. With the demise of *Athene* in 1967, *Charioteer* remains the

longest surviving Greek-American journal, and as such becomes
an increasingly valuable repository of modern Greek literature.

Rae Dalven

Translators of the works of Greek poets and novelists have been
busy since the 1940s, when Dalven issued *Poems* (1944),
written by the Greek-Jewish poet Joseph Eliyia. She worked in
the tradition of Aristides E. Phoutrides, a brilliant Harvard
scholar who introduced the great Kostis Palamas to America.
Harvard published *Life Immovable* (1919) and *A Hundred
Voices* (1921), and Yale offered a play by Palamas, *Royal
Blossoms* (1923). Phoutrides also collaborated with Demetra
Vaka in translating a fine volume entitled *Modern Greek Stories*
(1920). Dalven followed up her book on Eliyia with *Modern
Greek Poetry* (1949), another pioneer translation, and later with
The Complete Poems of Cavafy (1961). Dalven's play, *A Season
in Hell*, was produced off Broadway at the Cherry Lane Theater
in 1950. Among her other writings are a critical study, *Anna
Comnena* (1972), and *The Fourth Dimension* (1977), selected
poems of Yannis Ritsos.

Kimon Friar

Long before Friar undertook the Herculean task of translating
The Odyssey: A Modern Sequel (1958), by Nikos Kazantzakis, he
was established in American letters as poet, critic, editor,
lecturer, and teacher. Friar has taught at Adelphi, Amherst, Iowa,
and Minnesota, among other places. His critical articles and
translations of Greek poets from Cavafy to Ritsos have appeared
in many magazines. He prepared the poetry section for *Introduction to Modern Greek Literature* (1969), edited by Mary P.
Gianos. During its relatively brief life, Friar edited *Greek
Heritage*, an impressive quarterly founded by Christopher G.
Janus. Friar has compiled several anthologies and texts including,
with John Malcolm Brinnin, *Modern Poetry: American and
British*. He did a great service for world literature by gathering,
translating, and publishing *Modern Greek Poetry* (1973). In
another book, *The Sovereign Sun* (1974), Friar presents the best
poems of another major Greek poet, Odysseus Elytis. His
crowning achievement, however, remains *The Odyssey: A Mod-*

ern Sequel. Friar lives in Greece but visits the United States periodically to lecture and teach.

Byron Vazakas

One of the best and most prolific Greek-American poets, Vazakas was born in Reading, Pennsylvania, in 1907. His work has appeared in *Accent, Yale Review,* and other prestigious journals. Vazakas' first book, *Transfigured Night* (1946), marked him as a major precursor of the Greek-American literary awakening that was in the offing. William Carlos Williams in his introduction greeted Vazakas as a genuine inventor who had "completely done away with poetic line as we know it, a clean sweep, not a vestige of it left." To replace the line, he had "found a measure" based on music, with its primal appeal to the "pure ear." Vazakas dedicated his title poem to Arnold Schoenberg. Of the fifty poems included, none deals with Greek ethnic subjects. The same is true of the fifty poems in his second volume, *The Equal Tribunals* (1961). Vazakas' interest in music continues with poems such as the "Ballet of the Noble Stairs, " "Martial Music," "Masks of Chopin," "Night Fugue," "Music in America," "The Mozart Pavilion," and "Late Music." Other poems allude to art and literature; in form and diction they appeal to the aesthete rather than to the casual reader.

Vazakas was named the Amy Lowell Poetry Traveling Scholar, 1962–64, an experience that resulted in his third volume, *The Marble Manifesto* (1966). By this time he had won national recognition. *Library Journal* called him "Unquestionably one of the best contemporary poets." Most of the poems in *Manifesto* were inspired by the sights and sounds of England, from the band playing at Brighton to the poet's rubber soles squeaking on the floor of the British Museum. The title refers to the Elgin marbles, whose classical nudity shocked the Victorian sensibility. Vazakas dedicated his next book, *Nostalgias for a House of Cards* (1970), to the memory of his "old friend," William Carlos Williams. Among the fifty poems are some that advance a chronology of personal experiences, from his early childhood until, as an adult, he evokes Emerson and Whitman in present-day Boston. Although Vazakas frequently alludes to ancient Greece, calling one section of *Nostalgias* "The Trials of Oedipus," he makes no aesthetic use of the Byzantine or the modern Greeks. His own father is the only Greek immigrant he mentions.

Evans Chigounis

Chigounis also dedicated a volume of poetry to Williams, saying in *Secret Lives* (1972), "To the American master William Carlos Williams who would tell me that writing is a very human thing to do and to my father Charles who was a Greek." His volume appeared in the long-standing poetry series of Wesleyan University Press. The first section, "South," contains fourteen poems about places in South and Latin America written in free verse and containing varying degrees of experimentation. The poet, through his verse, visits Peru, Argentina, Mexico, Chile, Brazil, commenting about past and present as he goes. The second part, "Other Directions," includes forty-six poems on a wide variety of subjects. Chigounis writes some prose poems, as does Vazakas. He deals with modern Greek material in two poems, "Hasapiko," a folk dance, and "Peoples Heroes," inspired by the funeral of Nikos Kazantzakis.

Olga Broumas

A new poet of great promise, Broumas writes sharply and sensitively from an activist position asserting the power of the feminine. *Beginning with O* (1977) appeared as Volume 72 of the Yale Series of Younger Poets. She uses English, her adopted language, with surprising control and finesse. Stanley Kunitz in his foreword notes her "explicit sexuality and sapphic orientation" and adds, "Among the most impressive features of Broumas' supple art is her command of syntax, rhythm, and tone." Many poems and parts of poems unabashedly describe the physical aspects of lesbian love. In another comment Kunitz says, "It does not seem at all presumptuous for Broumas to link herself with the goddesses of the Hellenic age, for she has honest ties of kinship to that age in blood and spirit." He refers to a cycle of poems entitled "Twelve Aspects of God" wherein Broumas casts a mythic and classical aura about lesbian lovemaking; in effect, it becomes a special way to celebrate the human body. With understandable fondness she honors the women who pointed the way for her: Anne Sexton, Sylvia Plath, Virginia Woolf, and Adrienne Rich. That her poems also express a social conscience, fired by her feminist views, is shown in "the knife & the bread," written "for the women of Cyprus, '74." One may well wait to see where Broumas' fine talents will go from "O."

Other Greek-American Poets

Additional poets include Theodore Giannakoulis, who wrote poems for *Athene* and helped edit it for a time. *Athene* also printed many stories from *Fairy Tales of Modern Greece* (1930), which Giannakoulis prepared with Georgia H. Macpherson. Another Greek-American poet, Constance Elinore Hatson, published a creditable first volume entitled *Who Know Not Leaf* (1947). She also wrote articles for a New York language newspaper. More recent poets include Konstantinos Lardas whose *And in Him, Too; In Us* (1964) was nominated for a Pulitzer Prize. Lardas has published in many journals here and abroad. His story "The Broken Wings" appeared in *The Best American Short Stories of 1973*. The poems of Alexander Karanikas have been printed in newspapers and journals since the 1930s; in two books, *When a Youth Gets Poetic* (1933) and *In Praise of Heroes* (1945); and in such anthologies as *Port Chicago Poets* (1966), edited by Don A. Torgersen, and *Hold Fast to Dreams* (1969), edited by Arna Bontemps. Another poet, Eleni Floratou-Paidoussi, was born in the United States, spent her youth in Greece, then returned to this country after World War II. Her poems include both personal lyrics and political statements. *Cycles of Silence and Screams* (1975) laments the fascism of the junta years and expresses hope for a democratic future. A second volume, *Twenty Strophes and Other Poems* (1976), continues her lyrical appraisal of life's sadness and joys.

Prose Fiction

Greek-American novelists are more numerous than the poets and they use more ethnic material. They have also reached a much larger audience, and their works are more readily available. A student can discover some of the same themes in both the poetry and the fiction: the diaspora, the odyssey, nostalgia for the lost homeland. The novel as a genre, however, has much more scope for ethnic-based plot, for characterization, for the description of ethnic customs, ideology, and illusive soul. The novel has sufficient magnitude to allow the author to deal with the alienation inherent in the immigrant experience and to extend the action to whatever triumph or loss is consistent with the organic aesthetic purpose of the work.

In a number of novels and short stories the conflict between the generations serves as a basis for the plot. A frequent source of tension is the son's or daughter's decision to marry a non-Greek. The fiction of other ethnic writers makes similar use of this basic problem. Perhaps no other decision so profoundly tests the degree of assimilation achieved by the parents. In fighting against nature, so to speak, the parents are invariably, and often sadly, defeated. Their ethnic dreams appear to founder, break, and die. Nor does wealth or social class make any difference in the outcome. The rich daughter in Ariadne Thompson's *The Octagonal Heart* and the poor son in Harry Mark Petrakis' *Lion at My Heart* face equally fierce opposition when they "betray" their *ethnos*. The clash over marriage (or over "learning Greek," for that matter) raises the broader question of identity: to be or not to be a Greek, though born in America. Or, more exactly, what does it mean to be *both* Greek and American?

The coming of World War II made the Greek war hero a viable protagonist in American literature. Non-Greek authors such as Leon Uris and Glenway Wescott were inspired to dramatize the heroic Greek resistance to Nazi occupation. In Tom T. Chamales' *Never So Few* the Greek hero fights and dies in distant Burma, whereas in Petrakis' *In the Land of Morning* he returns home to Chicago, where, echoing the myth of Orestes, he helps to wreak a violent revenge on his mother's lover. In the war fiction the Greek is far removed from the earlier diaspora and process of assimilation. Nobody now questions his right to be an American. He has other, usually more personal, problems to face and resolve.

Some novels set in the postwar period — *The Arrangement*, by Elia Kazan, for example — have protagonists who are only incidentally Greek. The fact of their ethnicity plays a very subordinate role; in that aspect they tend to resemble Greek characters created by non-Greek authors. They are Greek in name only. They are no longer called bad names; they do not confront a hostile, bigoted environment; they do not have to choose from a limited number of jobs. Greeks are now free, like any other Americans, to make their mistakes on their own, to be great lovers, adventurers, business and social successes or failures, and sometimes comic or mad figures. The price that they pay for almost full assimilation is the almost total loss of their ethnicity.

Theano Papazoglou-Margaris

A fairly complete and varied treatment of the Greek immigrant informs the five collections of short stories published by Papazoglou-Margaris. One of them, *The Chronicle of Halsted Street* (1962), won the second government prize in Athens — a high honor, since the award had never before gone to a Greek living outside Greece. Unfortunately for the general reader, Papazoglou-Margaris writes only in her native Greek, and only a few of her stories have been translated. Like Kimon Friar, Demetra Vaka, and Elia Kazan, Papazolglou-Margaris has an Anatolian (Turkish) background, which is often seen in her characters. What she admires in the poetry of Koutoumanos emerges in her fiction as well: the longing and the bitterness, the dreams and nostalgia of the early Greek immigrants. Moreover, she delights in the whimsical, the ironic, and sometimes the starkly tragic when fate intervenes to demolish hope and ambition. Ethnicity permeates her work; she is always aware that her characters are Greeks. Her books include fully developed short stories as well as relatively brief narrative sketches. They are *Eftihia and Other Stories* (1939); *A Tear for Uncle Jimmy* (1958); *The Chronicle of Halsted Street* (1962); *Notes from Chicago* (1967); *George Koutoumanos* (1968); and *The Adventures of Uncle Plato* (1972). For many years Papazoglou-Margaris has also written weekly columns of commentary for Greek-language newspapers. *Athene* printed two of her stories, "The Nymphs of Lake Michigan" and "Theia Giannitsa" in English translation. A volume of selected and translated stories by her would be useful since she is the last and the best of those still writing in Greek.

Demetra Vaka (Brown)

This vital and prolific author used both her maiden name and her married name; on several occasions she collaborated with her husband, Kenneth Brown. A polyglot from Turkey, she used English with great skill. She arrived in America at eighteen, learned English, married, and spent a busy lifetime writing, traveling, and supporting causes such as the Greek War Relief during World War II. Through her more than fifteen books she sought to interpret Turkey and the Near East to the West, in the hope that more understanding among peoples might lead to peace and security. Her novel *Bribed to Be Born* (1951) was issued after her death in 1946. The autobiography she left behind, *A Heart for Any Faith,* came out as a serial in *Athene* but has not yet appeared in book form. Her career as a writer began in 1907 with a romance entitled *The First Secretary.* Her first prose work, *Haremlik* (1909), unveils the suppressed status of Turkish women under the old dispensation, before Kemal Atatürk's revolution began to move the nation forward.

In her last work, *Delarah* (1943), Vaka makes an eloquent appeal for love between the Greeks and the Turks. Many delightfully comic touches emerge from the basically grim situation — the agitation and violence of the Young Turks (1909) demanding that Sultan Abdul Hamid adopt a new constitution. Delarah, the young pampered daughter of Ali Pasha, becomes friends with Alcmene Floras, the bright daughter of a Greek banker. As their friendship grows, Delarah experiences a mental and emotional awakening. When turmoil convulses the country, Ali Pasha "gives" Delarah to the Floras family, who manage to escape to Vienna. Of all Vaka's works, *Delarah* most deserves to be reissued for today's readers.

A. I. Bezzerides

Best known as a Hollywood screen writer, Bezzerides also wrote three novels: *The Long Haul* (1938), *There Is a Happy Land* (1942), and *Thieves' Market* (1949). The first and last are novels about the tough San Francisco produce market. The hero of *Thieves' Market* is a volatile young Greek, Nick Garcos. He blames his mother for driving Yanko, his father, to death with her constant complaining. To haul and sell produce Nick teams up with Ed Kennedy, a rough man who knows all the dirty tricks. Most of the story deals with the buying and selling of two truckloads of apples, during which time Nick proves strong but naive. In the end he learns how to recoup his losses and get revenge on the master thief, Figlia. *The Long Haul* also describes trucking in California, but it has no Greek characters. Bezzerides, of Greek and Armenian descent, dramatized the life of the Tarpon Springs spongers in the film *Beneath the Twelve Mile Reef.* The most valuable of his works from an ethnic point of view, *Thieves' Market,* is also a regional novel that qualifies as proletarian fiction.

Mary Vardoulakis

The first novel depicting the Greek as immigrant is *Gold in the Streets* (1945) by Mary Vardoulakis. She was attending Wellesley College when this work won the Intercollegiate Literary Fellowship sponsored by Dodd, Mead. Set in 1906, *Gold in the Streets* takes a group of immigrants from pastoral Crete to the mill town of Chicopee, Massachusetts. Vardoulakis' characters show real ethnicity, an element usually missing from fictional Greeks in earlier novels by non-Greeks. George Vardas, a young Cretan, leaves for America because of trouble over a girl and a conflict with his cousin Nicholas over land rights. In Chicopee he and other Greeks cope with the hostile Polish workers. The Greek community grows, and more immigrants arrive, including Greek girls. They all expect to find "gold in the streets" — the dream that lured millions of Europeans to our shores. The novel lacks much of the real day-to-day suffering, but it does express the loneliness of the newcomers and their nostalgia for Crete. *Gold in the Streets* ends happily with the arrival of Nina. Better prospects lie ahead for George Vardas; the mills in nearby Hartford pay as much as fifteen dollars a week. Maybe George and Nina will still find the gold; after all, they have seen only half the streets. Despite her brilliant and precocious beginning, Vardoulakis did not write any other fiction.

George Demetrios

An artist as well as author, Demetrios wrote his first book, *When I Was a Boy in Greece,* in 1913, and thirty-four years later he wrote another, the small classic *When Greek Meets Greek* (1947). The twenty-five "episodes" — stories and sketches — in this fine collection often embody a moral or lesson and a style as spare and laconic as that of Aesop's Fables. The Greeks of Demetrios are wise, foolish, kind, pigheaded, conceited, lazy, shrewd, funny, conniving, compassionate, thieving, mad — in short, very alive and human, and quite Greek. Their good qualities are sometimes undermined by faults and follies as they seek, by hook or by crook, by labor or by cunning, to survive in their strange adopted land. Demetrios characterizes them with a few telling strokes of his pen: the wrestler Leonidas, who poses for sculptors until he meets Mary, and then he poses only for her; Pericles of Boston, who loses all his money in the stock market; the adventurer Anastasios, who is discovered cheating an intellectual friend out of fifty dollars; the clever Prokopios, who manages to trade a horse and cart for a theater; Gus Pappas, who returns to his village in Greece and explains to an octogenarian why he misses America; and so on. The lasting literary value of *When Greek Meets Greek* is evidenced by its having been reissued in 1970 in the Short Story Index Reprint Series. Demetrios effectively seeks humor, not social or historical significance, in his delightful limning of modern Greeks.

Roxanne Cotsakis

A resident of Atlanta, Cotsakis represents with distinction the women writers of Greek descent, even though her only publication has been the novel *The Wing and the Thorn* (1952). No other single piece of fiction contains so complete a record of Greek customs. Among much else in her ample novel, Cotsakis describes and explains the relevant symbolism of Greek Easter, name days, baptism, weddings, and funerals. A scholar can abstract from her story an authentic account of the ethnic rituals that assimilation threatens to erode or change. Cotsakis also details the issues that resulted in the founding (as it happened in Atlanta) and the growth of the American Hellenic Educational Progressive Association (AHEPA). She follows the fortunes of an immigrant, John Pantellis, who stubbornly retains and defends his "Greekness" against all American influences. He creates all kinds of difficulty and anguish for those nearest and dearest to him. Only when he visits Greece after World War II, a much older man, does he realize that he has been too boorish and parochial in his nationalism — and especially when he meets an "American" woman who speaks better Greek and knows much more about Greece than he does.

Ariadne Thompson

Whereas Vardoulakis writes about Cretan peasants turned mill workers and Demetrios deals with former Macedonians now living in New England, Ariadne Thompson in *The Octagonal*

Heart (1956) records the life of a wealthy Greek family during and after World War I. In a vivid and evocative manner the author recreates her childhood spent at Parnassus, the family's baronial estate in a suburb of Saint Louis. The patriarch of the house was the first Greek Orthodox bishop to be ordained in America; Thompson's father was a successful businessman who was also the Greek consul. Her book chronicles a segment of Greek-American life far removed from that of the immigrant who arrived poor, illiterate, and alone. The main conflict concerns whether or not Aphrodite, a cousin, should be allowed to marry a nice non-Greek boy. The headstrong Aphrodite also wants to become a doctor, another unheard-of ambition for a Greek girl of the aristocracy. In the end Aphrodite wins on both counts, gaining a husband as well as a career. Unfortunately, the octagonal house burns down; a new house rises on the old ashes, but it can never take the place of the fondly remembered one that went up in flames.

Tom T. Chamales

The first novel by Chamales, *Never So Few* (1957), not only struck a strong popular chord but also introduced the Greek-American war hero to the reading public. Con Reynold leads a band of about six hundred loyal Kachins behind Japanese lines. He is a foxy leader who, though greatly outnumbered, outwits the enemy. He has great understanding, patience, and courage. Con Reynolds is a thoroughly American Greek, a kind of Hemingway hero of Greek descent, fighting the Japanese in the Burmese jungle. He fulfills the requirements of the Hemingway code, which includes drinking, loving, and facing danger with stoicism. The Kachins under his command get the perilous assignment of providing intelligence for General Stilwell's offensive. After many battles and after two wounds in combat, Con Reynolds is killed by a booby trap in Rangoon.

The Greek hero of Chamales' *Go Naked in the World* (1959) belongs to the rich and decadent North Shore above Chicago. Nick Stratton returns as a lost and bitter young war veteran to contest the wishes of his domineering father. Old Pete Stratton, the owner of a theater chain, pressures Nick to marry a girl named Pat Rakis so that the Stratton empire can acquire many theaters in the South. Instead, Nick falls in love with Nora, who is eventually revealed to him as Chicago's highest-priced call girl. She also turns into a drug addict. Disheartened, Nick leaves home for a small island in the Florida Keys. There, completely alone, he begins to write a novel, which succeeds and opens up a new life for him. The accidental death of Tom T. Chamales, at thirty-six, deprived America of a writer who had only begun to realize his promise.

Thomas Doulis

Doulis has written several books: *Path for Our Valor* (1963), a novel about paratroopers in peacetime; *The Quarries of Sicily* (1969), another novel; *George Theotokas* (1975); *Disaster and Fiction* (1977); and *A Surge to the Sea* (1977), a study of Greek immigrants in Oregon. The setting for *Path for Our Valor* is Fort Mosby, Tennessee, home of the 43rd Airborne Division. What happens to Sergeant Gus Damianos is one of the three story lines that converge in this tale of a massive and dangerous maneuver called Operation Razor Blade. Damianos leads a jump to look over the Crossroads Drop Zone. The men respect him as a hardened veteran who knows and loves his work. Doulis rounds out Damianos' character by describing his private problems, which centered on Sophie, who is pregnant with his child. Damianos feels bitter toward life, yet he survives and finds an identity and a freedom that he can live with — or at least he can continue to skydive after tragedy strikes others in the ill-fated Operation Razor Blade.

The Quarries of Sicily concerns a young American author, Gordon Warrington, who has discovered and translated the works of Stamos Patrinos, a neglected Greek genius. As Patrinos condemns the disastrous Athenian invasion of Sicily, so Doulis by implication condemns the American involvement in Vietnam. A serious problem for Warrington arises over the motion picture to be based on Patrinos' novel. Will it be a superficial and commercial film made by Gainsborough or a more honest effort directed by the Italian, Carlo Patriarchi? Complications lead to revelations about Patrinos' past, and Warrington finds out why some powerful Greeks are content to let him remain unknown on the island of Chios. In the end, artistic integrity wins out over easy profit.

Daphne Athas

Athas' several books include a vivid prose work, *Greece by Prejudice* (1962), and four novels, *The Weather of the Heart* (1947), *The Fourth World* (1956), *Entering Ephesus* (1971), and *Cora* (1978). Although it has no Greek characters, *The Fourth World* is a powerful story of life in a school for the blind. In *Entering Ephesus* a family with a Greek father goes from wealth in New England to relative poverty in the South. For more than a year, Pavlos Episcopoulos (changed to Bishop), has been in Ephesus, a university town in North Carolina. He raises tomatoes but without much success. When his wife Clara, a Mayflower descendant, arrives with his three daughters, they find P.Q., as he is nicknamed, renting a former funeral home in the heart of the black district. Perhaps the emotional high point in this book about maturation comes when the youngest girl, Sylvia, is run down and killed by a truck. The Bishops receive a check for $1,500, barely enough for the funeral. The final blow befalls them at the end when, unable to pay the rent for the decrepit mortuary, they must leave to start anew once more, this time in a tent on land they hope to own. The character of P.Q. is memorable. A Greek with a brilliant mind, he can readily allude to the classical philosophers, but he is compelled by a sardonic fate to deliver laundered linen on a bike.

H. L. Mountzoures

The literary career of Mountaoures began when he sold a story to the *Atlantic Monthly.* "The Buoy" from the *Atlantic* and twelve other stories appear in his collection, *The Empire of Things* (1968). Greek characters have significant roles in several stories. Philip Neros, the protagonist of Mountzoures' first novel, *The Bridge* (1972), is five at the beginning of the novel and twenty-six at the end. Philip belongs to a large family, the depression lingers on, and times are hard. Their neighborhood is filled with other ethnic types: Syrians, Italians, Irish. The Greek customs that the Neros family observes are carefully described. During Philip's long journey to manhood he learns to adjust to being both a Greek and an American. He goes to school, enters military service, and returns to a home tense with acrimony. The mother is apparently insane. The bridge symbolizes a conflict between the generations as well as the problems of growing up as a Greek in a non-Greek society. At twenty-six Philip must seriously examine himself to learn in what direction he wants to go.

Elia Kazan

After winning much acclaim as a film and stage director, Kazan wrote a novel, *America America* (1962). The story begins in 1896 with war impending between Greece and Turkey. An Anatolian Greek boy, Stavros Topouzoglou, suffers many reverses and works hard to reach America, the land of his dreams. After a massacre of Armenians, his father sends Stavros to Constantinople, with all their valuables, to secure a partnership with a supposedly rich cousin and then bring the rest of the family there for comparative safety. On the long pilgrimage Stavros is robbed by Abdul, the friendly thief, whom Stavros stabs to death. Only by becoming the lover of Madame Kebabian, the wife of a rich rug merchant, does he finally make it to Ellis Island. There he anglicizes his name to Joe Arness; he is soon happily at work shining shoes.

Kazan's very successful second novel, *The Arrangement* (1967), dramatizes a crisis in the life of Eddie Anderson, an advertising executive whose real name is Evangelos Topouzoglou and who is a descendant of Joe Arness of *America America*. Eddie's many extramarital affairs are meaningless because he loves none of his mistresses. He loves his wife, Florence, even though she has become sexually inadequate. Then Eddie meets Gwen, and his problems begin when he falls in love with her. His previous and precarious arrangement falls apart. Florence divorces him. Eddie finally ends up with a new arrangement, this time with Gwen, and not as an advertising executive but as a writer.

The author's next two novels depart from Greek ethnicity and seek a wider relevance: *The Assassins* (1972), about the sickness and violence of our society; and *The Understudy* (1974), about the modern world of theater and film. Elia Kazan's next work, *Acts of Love* (1978), is the only novel by a Greek American about the sponge colony of Tarpon Springs. One of its major characters, Costa Avaliotis, was once a famed sponge-boat captain, and the legendary sponge center serves as the setting for much of the plot. The main interest, however, concerns the wealthy and confused American girl Ethel Laffey. Although only twenty-two, she has already had many affairs in many places, and now, in search of stability, she marries Teddy Avaliotis, a young Greek navy man whose father, Costa, furiously objects. Ethel's marital vows apprently mean nothing; she continues her affairs, claiming that she wavers between wanting discipline and craving freedom. Being terribly "wicked," she even allows Costa to seduce her; then, to punish her treachery to his son, Costa chokes her to death. A plea of temporary insanity saves Costa. Teddy soon finds a new and more pliable girl to wed. All these events, even the murder of Ethel, are "acts of love."

Charles E. Jarvis

The process of growing up as a Greek American dominates Jarvis' *Zeus Has Two Heads* (1976). His hero is twelve-year-old Socrates Genos, and the setting is Lowell, Massachusetts — called Cabot City in the novel. A good deal of Greek ethnicity permeates the story. The boy's mother fears that he suffers from the evil eye, and Jarvis describes Mrs. Magisa's method of exorcism. A Greek dunce in school is named Vlakas (fool). During the summer and fall of 1932 the presidential campaign stirs the people of Cabot City. That the Greeks believed Roosevelt would save them from further poverty indicates how strongly the ethnic enclaves supported him. Jarvis writes about the local Greek politicians and gamblers. The focus of the novel, however, is the Genos family and its many woes. The eldest son Leander dies from pneumonia. The poverty worsens. The Epilogue has Socrates wandering about the rainy city, wondering what will happen next.

In a second novel, *The Tyrants* (1977), Jarvis continues to write about the Greeks of Cabot City. Now the protagonist is the leading Greek-American politican, Peisistratus Zacharias. With his coffeehouse as a base, he builds an ethnic political machine that eventually shares some power with the Irish organization led by Jim Bailey. By handing out jobs and other favors Peisistratus survives for a quarter of a century. Through him and his Diogenes Democratic Club, the Greek immigrants and their offspring enter public life. The two novels by Jarvis constitute an interesting report on the ethnic and political life of an industrial New England city during the depression.

Nicholas Gage

A relative newcomer among Greek-American authors is Nicholas Gage, whose latest novel, *The Bourlotas Fortune* (1975), explores the jet-set world of Greek shipowners. Gage was born in Greece in 1939, migrated to the United States, and eventually won recognition as a reporter for the *New York Times*. Attachment to his homeland resulted in *Portrait of Greece* (1971). Gage's special knowledge of the underworld is reflected in three books: *The Mafia Is Not an Equal Opportunity Employer* (1971), *Mafia, U.S.A.* (1972), and a novel, *Bones of Contention* (1974). The two books about the mob are factual accounts based on Gage's years of research and reportage. In *Bones of Contention* two young criminals seek to dispose of some stolen paintings while FBI agents concoct an ambitious plan to capture both the paintings and the thieves.

The Bourlotas Fortune deals with the shipping industry and its significant Greek component. Ethnic details add flavor and authenticity. *Bourlotas* ("fireship") refers to an episode during the Greek Revolution. The Bourlotas saga begins on the island of Chios in the early nineteenth century and ends in the present, after Kosmas Bourlotas has built a rich empire. Gage shows how World War II and the Korean War elevated the Greek shipowners to positions of great wealth and power. The real rivalry between Onassis and Niarchos has a fictional parallel in the bitter contest between Bourlotas and Malitas. Gage looks closely into the private lives of his Greek tycoons, and what he reveals about greed and decadence does not always create a positive picture.

Harry Mark Petrakis

Of Greek-American novelists writing today, Petrakis is the most openly ethnic. His first novel, *Lion at My Heart* (1959), is set near the South Chicago steel mills. Like several other Greek stories, it exploits the generation gap between immigrants and their offspring. The lion of the title is Varinakis, a strong father whose son Mike works in the same steel mill. Mike wants to marry an Irish-American girl named Sheila Cleary. Such a wish constitutes a betrayal of country and of all traditions cherished by the parents. Objection to the marriage, however, means unwarranted interference in the son's personal affairs. Here, in a free country, can we not be free to marry whom we please? A virulent hatred develops between the father, who loves his Greek heritage, and the son, who loves a girl who happens to be Irish. At the end there is no reconciliation.

The many Greek characters in Petrakis' works run the gamut from good to evil; some are saints or heroes, other are devils, while not a few are fools and clowns. His second novel, *The Odyssey of Kostas Volakis* (1963), describes the coming to America of a Greek family and its troubles here. Kostas Volakis and his wife, Katerina, have three sons. One of them, Alex, feels that his father hates him, and this feeling of rejection leads to tragedy: he kills his younger brother Manuel, as Cain killed Abel. The novel concludes with the despairing father making a visit to the prison to see his lost son, a pilgrimage of sorrow he had once vowed never to make.

While composing his first two novels Petrakis kept selling short stories to magazines as different from one another as the *Saturday Evening Post* and *Playboy.* They are available in two highly praised collections: *Pericles on 31st Street* (1965) and *The Waves of Night* (1969). In the meantime he was also writing *A Dream of Kings* (1966), the story of a rather quixotic hero, Leonidas Matsoukas. Somewhat of a Zorba, Matsoukas is a fun-loving rogue with good intentions, great gusto, and a real love of life. He resorts to cunning when more laudable means fail. Often a loser, Matsoukas has an invalid son whom he wishes to take to Greece for treatment. Before he can leave, he makes love to a hot-blooded widow. He cheats at cards; he fights a Turk and must beg for his life. Petrakis enlarges Matsoukas into a quasi-epic or mock-epic figure. At the end, we pity him for his flaws.

Petrakis continued to enlarge characters and create modern myths when he wrote *In the Land of Morning* (1973). Alex Rifakis, the protagonist, bears a strong resemblance to Orestes of the *Agamemnon.* He returns from Vietnam, tired of death, only to find a trying situation at home. During his absence his father has died, broken-hearted after losing his grocery to Antonio Gallos in a game of chance. Gallos heads an underworld empire, the glittering heart of which is a nightclub called the Temple of Apollo. Asmene Rifakis, Alex's mother, becomes the mistress of the rich gangster. Her daughter Eunice, like Electra, wants her wayward mother to be punished. Before the novel ends, Gallos lies dead at the hands of Zervas, an old friend of the Rifakis family. Alex leaves Chicago for the Southwest, where he hopes to build a new life.

In *The Hour of the Bell* (1976) Petrakis departs from Chicago's Greek community and goes back to the Greek Revolution. He provides a panoramic view of the major events on both land and sea, from the autumn of 1820 through the following summer. The climax occurs at the Battle of Tripolitsa. Petrakis lists fifty-one principal characters, most of whom are Greek, although some are Turkish. Among the Greeks are some important clerics, from the levelheaded Bishop Germanos to the fanatic monk, Papalikos, who wants to kill all the Turks. Other Greeks are important sea captains, mountain chieftains, and assorted revolutionaries both historical and fictional. The real include the legendary Kolokotronis; the imaginary, the grizzled leader Vorogrivas and the heroic Captain Boukouvalas, who lives long enough to lead a crucial charge against the enemy. *The Hour of the Bell* begins a projected trilogy that will see the success of the revolution and the birth of modern Greece.

Other Greek-American Writers

At least eight additional authors should figure in any course on Greek-American literature, and Jim Dilles is such a writer. In *The Good Thief* (1959) he tells of a Greek family in California. Costa Desmas finds himself unemployed after a strike in his packing-house. A crisis erupts when his twelve-year-old son Stavro, aided by two friends, steals a steer and hides it in their cellar. Costa is arrested and he takes the blame on himself; eventually, however, he emerges as the hero. Another author, Thalia Selz, in "The Education of a Queen," published in the *Partisan Review,* describes the coming to maturity of a sensitive girl with a Greek father and an American mother. The short novel was reprinted in *The Best American Short Stories* (1962), and in the following year it won an O. Henry award. Another writer whose works have a strong ethnic content is Dean Brelis, whose *My New Found Land* (1963), set in Newport, Rhode Island, has a Greek boy as protagonist. Dimitri suffers a crisis in loyalty toward his alcoholic father, John, but eventually he has a rebirth of faith in himself, his father, and people in general. George Christy in *All I Could See from Where I Stood* (1963) dramatizes both the humorous and the sad problems of a boy growing up as a Greek American in western Pennsylvania. Stephanos hates everything Greek. A Greek girl, Lekky, commits suicide because she cannot marry a non-Greek. In time Stephanos becomes somewhat less hostile toward his ethnic heritage.

Theodore Vrettos describes the Nazi occupation of Greece in *Hammer on the Sea* (1965). A nonfiction work by Vrettos, *A Shadow of Magnitude* (1974), recounts the acquisition of the Elgin marbles by England, at the expense of Greece. In his second novel, *Origen* (1978), the author re-creates the life and times of the early Christian period. The most ambitious piece of fiction by Konstantinos Lardas is *Tree of Man* (1968), a tribute to the author's grandfather. With the planting of a victory garden as his central event, Lardas pens a lyrical memorial to his Greek family. George N. Rumanes sets *The Man with the Black Worrybeads* (1973) in the port city of Piraeus during the Nazi occupation. Two acts of sabotage organized by the hero, Petros, dominate the plot. In the first, three oil tankers are destroyed; in the second, an entire convoy. The climax occurs when, because of a misunderstanding, Petros is killed by his friend Nico. Athena G. Dallas-Damis in *Island of the Winds* (1976) describes the Chios of 1822 and the Turkish massacre of its inhabitants. The action also involves the tribulations of a Greek woman, Helena, and the fate of her twin sons. Dallas-Damis has written a second historical novel, *Windswept* (1979). She has translated *The Fratricides* and three plays by Nikos Kazantzakis.

Conclusion

The major immigrant and ethnic themes either stated or implied in the foregoing accounts may be summarized as the social conditions in the donor country (Greece); a definition of the American dream and its effect on the immigrant; the archetypal odyssey, the journey to the promised land; the attitudes of the receiving community; alienation, the "suspended souls," the pull from two cultures; the ethnic enclave, Greek Town; the novel as study in class mobility, the transition from peasant to industrial worker to entrepreneur; the establishment of roots in a strange environment; the process of Americanization; the ethnic backward glance, nostalgia for the lost homeland; the aesthetic use of the Greek heritage, from myth to Zorba to *gyros*; the fear of defeat and failure, the failed immigrant; the clash between first and second generation over degree of ethnic compromise, choice of occupation, education, and marriage; ethnic humor; inherited superstitions; the role of religion and the church; psychological problems that result from alienation and related causes; the changing role of Greek women, their new opportunities; the results of financial success on morality; the formal and aesthetic use of Greek ethnicity in plot, characterization, tone, thematic unity, and emotional effect.

Enough works by Greek Americans are available in both paperback and hardcover to serve as texts for either a quarter or a semester course. Much material that is not in print may be found in any sizable library. The rare volumes may usually be secured through inter-library loan. Students who know modern Greek can study authors such as Koutoumanos, Papazoglou-Margaris, and Decavalles, who write primarily in Greek. Because most of the works cited are written in English, however, the instructor should have no problem acquiring relevant material.

The works of three of the best poets of Greek descent are avilable in paperback editions: Byron Vazakas' *Equal Tribunals, The Marble Manifesto,* and *Nostalgias for a House of Cards* (reissued as *Poems of Byron Vazakas*); Evans Chigounis' *Secret Lives;* and Olga Broumas' *Beginning with O.* Most of the poems are not particularly ethnic but they represent a literary contribution by an ethnic minority.

The fiction still in print in paperback allows for a wider range of study in terms of both form and content. The five novels by Elia Kazan lead the list: *America America, The Arrangement, The Assassins, The Understudy,* and *Acts of Love.* A paperback edition of Harry Mark Petrakis' *A Dream of Kings* was published, but is no longer in print. The recent *A Petrakis Reader* issued by Doubleday is very useful, however, especially since the author uses Greek characters almost exclusively. Other novelists in paperback are Tom T. Chamales, *Never So Few;* George N. Rumanes, *The Man with the Black Worrybeads;* Athena G. Dallas-Damis, *Island of the Winds;* and Charles E. Jarvis, *Zeus Has Two Heads* and *The Tyrants.*

Should they be needed as texts, the following hardcover works by Greek Americans may also be assigned: A. I. Bezzerides, *Thieves' Market,* recently reprinted; George Demetrios, *When Greek Meets Greek;* Nicholas Gage, *The Bourlotas Fortune;* Harry Mark Petrakis, *The Hour of the Bell;* Theodore Vrettos, *Origen;* and Daphne Athas, *Cora,* a new novel about a Greek American searching for his ideal girl. No doubt as interest in ethnic studies grows, more of the older and rarer works cited here will be reprinted to meet the demand.

Bibliographical Note

Among useful secondary sources are the following: Thomas Burgess, *Greeks in America* (Boston: Sherman, French, 1913); Henry Pratt Fairchild, *Greek Immigration to the United States* (New Haven: Yale Univ. Press, 1911); Alexander Karanikas, *Hellenes and Hellions: Modern Greek Characters in American Literature, 1825–1975* (Urbana: Univ. of Illinois Press, 1981); Stephen A. Larrabee, *Hellas Observed* (New York: New York Univ. Press, 1957); Wayne Charles Miller, ed., *A Comprehensive Bibliography for the Study of American Minorities* (New York: New York Univ. Press, 1976); Charles C. Moskos, Jr., *Greek Americans: Struggle and Success* (Englewood Cliffs, N.J.: Prentice-Hall, 1980); Alexander Papas and M. Byron Raizis, *American Poets and the Greek Revolution (1821–1828)* (Thessaloniki: Inst. for Balkan Studies, 1971); and Theodore Saloutos, *The Greeks in the United States* (Cambridge: Harvard Univ. Press, 1964).

Hungarian-American Literature

Enikö Molnár Basa

What is Hungarian-American literature? Who are its representatives? How many Americans have heard of George Kemény? Of George Szécskay? Of Teréz Stibrán, or Imre Sári Gál, or József Bakucz? Yet who has not heard of Joseph Pulitzer, Ferenc Molnár, or György Faludy? The answers to those questions might indicate some of the distinctions and definitions that we need to make when we consider ethnic literature, particularly Hungarian-American literature. The definition will need to be partly historical and partly sociological and linguistic. What will emerge from this examination, however, is a realization that here is another part of American literature that is unknown to many students or that is known only sketchily and from generalizations. And, while we cannot always trace direct influences and continuity, we will see that a new, dynamic force is making its contribution to American literature now in the works of several fine poets who write about the American experience from a special perspective.

Ethnic literature, as defined elsewhere in this work, is literature written about the experiences of an ethnic group in the United States by members of that group. It may be in the native language or in English; it may be written by immigrants or by their native-born descendants. I will make certain adjustments in this essential definition to suit the nature of the literature that has been produced by Hungarians in the United States over the past 160 years.

I will, for example, not discuss the works of the well-known newspaperman Joseph Pulitzer or of the popular dramatist Ferenc Molnár, or even of the journalist-essayist György Faludy. They and many others who write for Hollywood, Broadway, television, newspapers, and other media are outside the scope of this survey. Although Hungarian by birth, Pulitzer was an American newspaperman whose writings did not reflect the ethnic experience. Molnár, although he did live in New York at the end of his life, remained a Hungarian dramatist of international reputation. Faludy and many others like him followed this cosmopolitan-international pattern: he lived in the United States briefly, but his writings remain personal expressions that reflect little of either American or Hungarian life.

This is the first category of omissions. The second includes those writers who, while living and writing in the United States, do not really deal with the American experience. In most cases, their subject matter remains Hungary and Hungarians. Many were respected and successful writers in Hungary before 1945, and they continue to write in the same style and often from the same perspective. They are known and recognized here (and more and more in Hungary) as representatives of Hungarian literature, but they are not ethnic writers. For this reason I have omitted such a noted author such as Albert Wass.

Between these two groups is a third, whose most prolific representative is probably Lajos Fűry. Authors in his group write about the American experience but do so from a distance, as we shall see later.

Similar adjustments in the definition of ethnic literature will be necessary in discussing works written by Americans who have used ethnic settings in popular works but who remained apart from the real experience. Their books, however, are well known and should be mentioned because they give a picture of the Hungarian American.

A historical overview will help introduce individual writers and works. For, while the authors wrote in different genres, a chronological progression often explains the literary developments and helps to establish the individual authors within the larger picture of Hungarian-American literature.

Such literary activity can be said to have begun in the 1850s, when participants in the Hungarian Revolution of 1848 came to the New World. They published the first newspaper, *Magyar Száműzöttek Lapja (Hungarian Exiles' Journal)*, but it failed, as did another early publication, *Magyar Amerika (Hungarian America*, 1879). Accounts of life in America during the 1850s can be found in letters and journals. Two published sources are Tivadar Ács's *New Buda* (Budapest, 1941), which chronicles the settlement founded by László Ujhazy, a follower of Kossuth, in the Missouri valley, and *A Száműzöttek (The Exiles)* (Budapest: Hungaria, 194?). The settlement did not survive, partly because most of the men enlisted in the Union army during the Civil War. While there is a wealth of other material in letters, diaries, travel essays, and descriptions of American life, until recently little has been done to make these materials available.Edmund Vasváry spent a lifetime collecting such materials, and the results of his work are on microfilm in the collection of the American Hungarian Foundation in New Brunswick, New Jersey. (The originals have been sent to the Somogyi Library in his native Szeged, in compliance with the provisions of his will.) Only recently have scholars started to catalog the voluminous collections or to publish monographs or excerpts; because the task is great, it proceeds slowly.

An even earlier account should be mentioned in this context, although the work was not published in the United States. *Journey in North America,* by Sándor Bölöni Farkas, first appeared in Transylvania in 1834, a year before Alexis de Tocqueville's much more famous *Démocratie en Amèrique.* Two translations have been published recently: a scholarly one by Árpád Kádárkay (Santa Barbara: ABC-Clio, 1978), containing only those parts that chronicle Bölöni Farkas' experiences in and observations on the United States and a complete account by Theodore and Helen Benedek Schoerman (Philadelphia: American Philosophical Soc., 1977), which includes Farkas' description of the Atlantic passage and his digressions on such Hungarian-related matters as Captain John Smith's adventures in Transylvania before his journey to Virginia.

But these accounts are outside the scope of Hungarian-American literature, particularly when it is viewed from an ethnic perspective. With the large-scale immigration of the last years of the 19th century and the early years of this century, a viable literary life and a new literary tradition evolved. This first period began with imitative literature and produced a great many works of nostalgia about Hungary, but gradually the writing became more original and turned to American life for its subject matter. Written for the thousands of agricultural workers and peasants who left Hungary to seek better opportunities in the mines and factories of the United States, the literature consisted mainly of poems and stories about immigrant life; sometimes the journalist-author indulged in rather strong editorializing. Some of the significant works will be discussed later.

The second period does not really begin until after World War II. Immigration patterns changed between the wars, as the rate of immigration declined; there was a parallel decline in the quantity and sometimes even the quality of original Hungarian-American literature. The refugees from World War II began to arrive around 1950, and while these immigrants were perhaps the most intellectual, they did not bring about a literary revival. The political orientation that most newspapers and journals had adopted intensified, as did the Hungarians' alienation from American life. The consequent duality kept the cultural and intellectual organs of the Hungarian community remote from the America of the 1950s and the 1960s and close to the topics, themes, and settings of prewar Central Europe or to the war itself and its attendant upheaval. Such a duality was undoubtedly possible because this new wave of immigrants no longer looked to the newspapers, churches, and local organizations to help it bridge the cultural gaps and adjust to life in the United States.

The last phase of this evolution is a result of the Hungarians who came to the United States after the failure of the Revolution of 1956. This wave continues to be augmented by new arrivals, many of them writers. They do not share the conservative views of the older group, nor do they view their presence in the United States as temporary: they have assimilated with vigor and are producing a surprisingly large body of literature that is Hungarian in language and in certain elements of style and imagery but that is otherwise contemporary American.

During the first period of Hungarian literary activity — that is, the early decades of this century — we find only Hungarian-language material. The few English-language books about the Hungarian immigrant experience were either produced by American authors or written years after the experience occurred. The work of Kemény, Szécskay, Klara Hollos, Agota Illés, the anonymous contributors to the newspapers or the composers of folksongs truly reflect the experiences of these early immigrants who came to work in the mines and factories of the Northeast. The men often came alone, intending to return when they had saved enough money to buy some land. Sometimes the wives and sweethearts followed, or the men met women here and married to settle in the States after all. Most settled in Hungarian communities that had been built around the mines and factories; because labor agents in Hungary did much of the recruiting and because the men wrote letters home about the good life or at least about the opportunities available here, such settlements often reflected one or another region of Hungary.

Yet, in spite of a certain sense of community, there was a need for more formal associations. Newspapers were soon established, churches were founded, and fraternal organizations sprang up. All served to perpetuate the language and culture of the old country and to aid in the acculturation process. The Cleveland *Szabadság* (*Liberty*), founded in 1891, was one of the more successful papers. It later moved to Pittsburgh and gradually incorporated other newspapers, which is one reason it has survived. Another early paper with remarkable staying power is the *Amerikai Magyar Népszava* (*American Hungarian People's Voice*), which began as a daily in 1899 and is still published. A range of political ideologies was represented even when the papers devoted a considerable portion of their space to literary selections. *Előre* (*Forward*) was a socialist paper, unlike the two mentioned above, which were and are conservative and nationalistic. Religious groups also had their organs. The *Katolikus Magyarok Vasárnapja* (*Catholic Hungarians' Sunday*), for example, provided an opportunity for many Hungarian-American writers to publish their works, particularly in its earlier years and to some extent while it was still under the editorship of István Eszterhás. In its almanac, *Históriás Kalendárium*, also, such writings were occasionally represented, though as with many other publications, many of the literary pieces were Hungarian classics. Also, Calvinist and Jewish papers served both the religious and the cultural needs of their readers.

Two Hungarian-American writers mentioned earlier, Kemény and Szécskay, also earned their living as newspapermen. Their work reflects the needs and interest of this first large wave of Hungarian immigrants. George (György) Szécskay (1880–1958)and George (György) Kemény (1875–1952) share the themes of isolation, loneliness, homesickness, and at times, strident nationalism. While neither was a good poet, both wrote much poetry, for the genre seemed to be in demand. (Hungarian literature has always been dominated by poetry, and even now poets are read and are more influential than in most other countries.) Their poetry is imitative, modeled on that of Petőfi and his followers and on folksongs. The readers sought the familiar, and these songs reflected part of their cultural heritage and could express new problems, desires, and aspirations. Yet, while the forms were conservative, the content often showed a wide range. The concerns of the working class dominate, but occasional verse for holidays and festivals and patriotic and lyrical poems can be found. Neither Kemény nor Szécskay approached the socialistic tone of some other writers, although the political and social conditions that had forced the emigration of what the Hungarian poet Atilla József called the "million and a half reeling" Hungarians (his own father among them) are always present in these writings. In his *András Vas,* Kemény comments:

> Although he worships the motherland devoutly
> The oppressed peasant still has no home there.
> Wide-mouthed they teach the concept of homeland—
> Those who selfishly claim all the fruits of the earth;
> And while at noisy parades the proud flags fly:
> The working millions do not even merit bread.[1]

The poem in which these line appear typifies the blend of conservative Hungarian values and satiric, nonviolent criticism of the Hungarian regime. This narrative poem in twelve cantos is closely imitative of János Arany's *Toldi;* it chronicles the efforts of a group of peasants to escape the hopeless cycle of poverty by emigrating to the United States. Hardship, loneliness, and disappointment plague them, yet, in spite of the drudgery and the setbacks, one hope remains: if not they, at least their children will have a better life and will learn skills, trades, and professions.

Similar ideas are expressed in "Az amerikai magyarokhoz." Kemény laments the hard fate of the Magyars in the homeland, citing historical — namely, Tartar, Turkish, and German (i.e., Austrian) rulers — as well as social pressures that prevented the country from developing its full potential. In the new land

> . . . he has earned
> His just deserts. Hungarian spirits flaming
> Strew their light over far-flung regions,
> And the orphan driven from his home
> Finally becomes a man.

But this respect was not won easily, and much had to be endured before acceptance came:

> Here: he was not yet known; there: he was falsely known;
> The dew rarely fell here on Hungarian flowers,
> But even without dew the spiritual garden
> By virtue of ancient strength, will blossom.
> And the homeless orphans even dared to hope.

Yet, in spite of all the hardships and the snubs, the hostility gradually faded and the sense of not belonging to either world diminished:

> We came to be at home here, we were no longer accused there
> And the disturbed soul was able to regain its peace.[2]

Kemény's contemporary, George Szécskay, chronicles some of these hardships in his tales of the miners of the Alleghenies. He began his career as a writer in Hungary in 1897 and emigrated to America in 1904. After working as an assistant to the editor of *Tárogató* (1904), he moved to McKeesport, Pennsylvania, and became associated with the *Hungarian Star* shortly thereafter. When that paper merged with the *Szabadság,* Szécskay moved to Cleveland and in 1906 returned to New York to work on the *Magyar Hírlap* (*Hungarian Courier*). In 1912 he took over the editorship of the *Amerikai Magyar Népszava* (*American-Hungarian People's Voice*), where he continued his literary activities until his death. Thus, he followed the same pattern as many other Hungarian-American writers. He was a keen observer of life, but his poetry only occasionally rises above the mundane. His prose pieces, however, are well-written vignettes of life in the mining towns of Pennsylvania and West Virginia with only an occasional venture into heavy-handed symbolism in the more nationalistic of the satirical prose pieces.

It is not surprising that his first book, *Idegen világban* (*In a Strange Land,* 1909), is chiefly a collection of nostalgic pieces. Yet the description of an evening in a New York café (*A new yorki Gulyás evenyun*) gives a good account of the lives of displaced workers. "A levél" ("The Letter") is a poignant comment on the death of a miner whose wife learns of his death only months later when the letter reaches her in Hungary. While Hungarian events and holdiays are the subject of most of his occasional poetry, a sensitive philosophical comment on the San Francisco earthquake shows Szécskay's increasing involvement in American life:

> Behold, in the evening a yet mighty, gilded city stood
> On the foam-washed shores of the ocean,
> The setting sun's thousands of playful rays
> Broke shimmering on its proud towers —
> By morning — all things were over, were finished.[3]

So he begins. Then he sketches the devastation that no one could foresee, no one could prevent, and that touched all San Francisco equally.

Vándordalok (*Wanderer's Songs*) is a collection of poems that Szécskay wrote under the emotional impact of World War I.[4] The subject matter is Hungary, and the concerns are Hungarian. Poems from the era of World War II in his *Őszi tarlózás ötven éves mezőn* (*Autumn Gleanings on a Fifty-Year-Old Meadow*) also contain comments on the war, but these reflect the emotional struggle of an American Hungarian.[5] His "Apám... Anyám" ("My Father... My Mother") is an allegory of the father-mother relation the two countries hold for him; it concludes with the compromise he must find. His third book, *Baltimorei rapszódia* (*Baltimore Rhapsody*), shows a further development.[6] As the title suggests, American cities and places serve as the leitmotif. The symphony of Baltimore, the title poem, is characteristic: it begins with a description of the busy port city and its industries but moves on to comment on the hard lives of the workers, primarily through an interesting imaginary dialogue with Edgar Allan Poe and the author. In "A Minnehahanál" ("By the Minnehaha") and "Mississippi... Mississippi" Szécskay uses the rivers chiefly as departure points for sentimental thoughts, but "Mississippi," written in Dubuque, Iowa, is a tribute that matches Mark Twain's in its expression of admiration for the "father of waters." The mighty American river made an impression on Szécskay; in fact, several works of these years exhibit admiration for the natural wonders as well as the industrial achievements of the United States. Other pieces, however, look on the other side of life: he chronicles the decline of Hungarian communities in "Két templom" ("Two Churches"); while the mining town could once support both a Catholic and a Calvinist church, the whole settlement is now falling into ruin as a result of strikes and fires.

Szécskay's prose pieces, his best works, are found in his fourth book, *Őszi tarlózás ötven éves mezőn*. This is a collection of fifty years' work, and the sketches he wrote between 1920 and 1925 represent the peak of his literary output. These stories chronicle the life of the early immigrants, and they deserve a place in the mainstream of American literature.

"Sánszky Béla halála" ("The Death of Bela Sanszky") is the tale of a man who, though he had above average opportunities, failed both in Hungary and in this country. While working as an agent for a Hungarian newspaper, he dies one day while crossing a West Virginia mountain ridge to reach yet another mining community. Szécskay makes it clear that Béla's salary, though not good, was sufficient to provide for a home and a family. Béla, however, is an alcoholic, and his need for liquor is more than adequately met on the road, while the communities he visits will generally provide shelter and food as well. Szécskay blends his description of the late autumn West Virginia woods with some other information on the region, then still wild and relatively unexplored and peopled by suspicious moonshiners. Szécskay's comments on the mountain people are sympathetic: he opposes Prohibition because he believes that it makes criminals out of the law-abiding men and women of the hills. He also defends the Hungarian settlers who continued to distill brandy as they always had. But he sees Prohibition as an even greater threat to the native mountaineer for whom alcohol represents the only cash crop from small plantings of corn in the tiny mountain clearings. "Húsz mérföldes gyalogás" ("A Twenty-Mile Hike") is an account of a walk along a mine spur line to the main rail line in West Virginia. Szécskay's sensitive portrayal of nature is as important a part of this literature as is his compassionate attitude toward the men along the line, isolated as they are from civilization and fully dependent on the mine.

Several stories such as "Szeredás Pista szerelme" ("The Love of Pista Szereda"), "Jókus Barnabás házassaga" ("Barnabas Jokus' Marriage") and "A rossz előjel" ("The Bad Omen") present the lonely life of the miners, who worked long hours and lived in boardinghouses while they saved money for a wife, a family, or a return to Hungary. The boardinghouses were generally run by the wife of a miner. She did all the work and acted as banker and sometimes adviser to the men; often she became the lover of one or another of them, and these affairs live on in story and song. Yet such behavior was not generally condemned, perhaps because most people recognized the hard work the miners did.

The second and third stories revolve around just such a situation. Barnabás Jókus waits a long time to marry, but when he notices gray hairs mingling with his dark locks, he seeks a wife in the mill towns of New Jersey. Soon after the wedding, however, he notices signs that his wife is flirting with the boarders while he is in the mines: the knife marks on the lintel of the kitchen door are replicas of the marks he himself once left in his own former landlady's kitchen while he sought words to express his feelings for her. "The Bad Omen" recounts an unsuspecting husband's superstitious fear that he will die in a mine explosion. Trying to avoid what he believes is destined to happen, he goes home during the noon break, only to find his wife in bed with one of the boarders who is on a different shift. In his rage he kills both, and the omen is fulfilled, though in an unexpected manner.

"The Love of Pista Szeredás" is a more positive tale. The youngest son of agricultural laborers in Hungary, Pista makes good by rising to the position of coachman to the local judge. But he falls in love with the judge's wife, though she knows nothing of his adulation. One day, after returning from a party, the couple quarrel, and the judge strikes his wife. Pista, in a rash move, defends her. After that, he has no choice but to leave, something he does readily, as his brothers and sisters are already in America. A strong and determined worker, he rises to become a foreman and represents the workers in the union; in short, he is an eligible bachelor. But he continues to carry a torch for the woman he once loved. Then, while in town to attend a union convention, he meets her again. She has left her husband and come to America, where she earns her living as a singer and a call girl in cheap bars. After the encounter, Pista is finally released from her spell, and he marries a local woman.

The stories of Szécskay chronicle the hard life of the miners, particularly of the single men, who had but one goal: to save enough money to bring their wives or sweethearts out of Hungary or to marry someone here and with her help be able to earn enough to escape the grinding cycle of work and debt. Few of them reached their goal, but their sons and daughters were able to succeed as skilled workers and even to enter professions. The exploitative nature of labor–management relations is taken for granted, as are both the psychological and the phsycial dangers of the workers' lives. All in all, these stories offer a more depressing picture of life in the United State than do the works of other ethnic writers, such as Stibran, Anthony, or Bell.

A poignant story that Szécskay wrote in 1942 illustrates this point: an old immigrant is just as destitute at eighty after a lifetime of work as he had been earlier, but his children at least have escaped and moved into American society. "Barna János hadiszolgálatra jelentkezik," ("János Barna Reports for the Draft") recounts the old man's attempt to enlist in the United States Army. He had emigrated in 1906, and now, after many years of work in the mills of Homestead, Pennsylvania, he has been laid off without a pension. Although he could survive on his small plot of land and the charity of his friends, he determines to enlist; he has a grandson in the army. Arriving at the recruiting station in Pittsburgh, he announces, "I wish to be a soldier, to go to war for America." When asked his age, he proudly replies that he is eighty, that he was once an officer with the Hungarian hussars, and that he can still carry a sword. The amused sergeant wants to send him home until he learns that Barna has no pension. Thereupon, he quickly draws up papers authorizing a pension of $18.20 a month for the old man for the rest of his life in recognition of his dedication.

In the stories of assimilation into the life of the new land, the contrast between the rural-agricultural background of the immigrants and the industrial society into which they were forced is a dominant theme. The best expression is found in *The Golden Village* by Joseph Anthony (1924). Anthony is not a Hungarian, but he wrote many similar romantic stories chronicling the lives of the immigrants who had become part of the American melting pot. The details of life are general, yet the thesis is valid. Árpád Romer, who had been unable to accompany his son and the younger men of the village to America twenty years previously, arrives to seek his family and the farming community they had intended to establish. He finds his eighteen-year-old grandson, now an orphan, who knows nothing of the others. After months of wandering, the two come on the families of the others almost by accident. But they are not farmers. When they arrived in America, they learned that work was to be had only in factories; they have since then become businessmen and some are even professionals. This picture is unrealistic in light of what we know about the first generation of immigrants, and the works of truly ethnic writers attest that only rarely were the first-generation Hungarians able to escape the cycle of hard work and low wages. The hope always was for the sons and daughters. In this story, however, the years are compressed, and the prosperous immigrants have moved into an ideal community where, though they are relatively recent immigrants, they can enjoy the fruits of their labors. Also, while keeping their ties to one another, they have formed friendships with the other immigrants of the town, and the portrayal here is reasonably accurate. These families welcome old Árpád Romer, yet they realize that Romer's dreams can never fit into the lives they have built for themselves and their children. Árpád, too, sees this, and he eventually returns to Hungary, but his grandson stays on as a newsman for the local paper and as the suitor of a French woman.

Restless Is the River by Anthony Derleth (1939) belongs in the same category. The hero is Count Brogmar, a political refugee from Metternich's Europe who hopes to establish vineyards in the Midwest. Like the story of the Romers, this story seems to be based on true experiences (the Ujházy settlements), but it is romanticized and politicized. Derleth's effort to add touches of realism through the use of names and other external details misfires; for example, the Brogmars' son is called "Gaza," a name that does not exist in Hungarian, instead of "Géza," the name of the father of Saint Stephen and a common Hungarian name. Similarly, in *Golden Village* when Stephen is addressed in Hungarian, he becomes "Stefan," a German name. The politicization of both works is apparent in the emphasis on complete assimilation into the melting pot. While these writers do not condemn the use of the Hungarian language by some of the characters or the continuation of some of the customs, they do concentrate on the young people who do not know these customs and who see little value in them.

With these conclusions in mind we can consider Teréz Stibran's *The Streets Are Not Paved with Gold* (1961). Stibran writes of what she knows; she came to the United States as a young girl and worked in the factories of Cleveland. In the story of Stephen Strohm and Terry Marianivsky, Stibran traces the struggles of the immigrants who came at the turn of the century as unskilled workers and of their children, who had to move into American society with little help from home. She also tells of newer immigrants, who are young and skilled and yet cannot find employment except as exploited laborers. Stibran's approach, however, is positive. Stephen's parents work as laborers, and his mother even takes in boarders for a while, but eventually they are able to open a grocery store and buy a farm. A combination of his father's naiveté and urban renewal takes their business from them and keeps them from prospering, yet they and their friends live better than do the workers in Szécskay's stories, partly because of the changed American economic system and the role of the unions in gaining a living wage for workers. Yet, in spite of its positive orientation, the novel is not blind to the many areas that needed reform.

Of more interest to the author than the changes in life in America, however, are the changes in life in Hungary and the rest of Europe as a result of World War I. Most of the characters in the novel came from the areas lost to Hungary in 1920, with the result that the younger immigrant families often have to provide for their parents, even if they are of non-Magyar extraction, because they are considered Hungarians by the new rulers, and as such they fare much worse in the new order of things than they did under the old. More important, Terry comes to America precisely because all opportunities are closed to her in the Czechoslovakia of which her native village has suddenly become a part. In fact, the weakness of the novel lies in the length of the digressions on the political situation in Europe, including one rather long episode in which Terry returns to Hungary to learn of the changes there and to help her decide to settle in the United States after all.

The most interesting part of the novel is the account of Terry's struggles in the labor market. Working as a seamstress, she knows she is being exploited, but she is determined to gain respect and to use her skill to improve her lot. She does move up, eventually becoming a buyer for a suburban department store. Stephen, meanwhile, pursues his studies in medical school with equal determination. Stibran does not minimize the hardships, and she draws a generally balanced picture of American life and the ethnic experience. She does not neglect the conflicts between the newcomers and the establishment, between labor and management, but her tone is not stridently critical. She gives ignorance, lack of sensitivity, differences in customs, and the general economic situation rather than malice as reasons for the workers' difficulties.

The anthology of writings for the socialist press, *A szocialista magyar irodalom dokumentumai az amerikai magyar sajtóban* (*Documents of Hungarian Socialist Literature in the American Hungarian Press* [Budapest: Akadémiai Kiadó, 1977]), collected by József Kovács, presents a more militant view of the workers' struggle. "Vera sztrájkba indul" ("Vera Goes on Strike"), by Klara Hollos, first published in *Kultúrharc* (1932), chronicles the beginnings of a strike in the New York garment industry and tells of the stirrings of labor consciousness in the mind of a young girl who works there, though she is better educated than most, because no other jobs are available for immigrant laborers. Agota Illés' account of a young woman looking for work as a governess or nursemaid in "Könnyebb a tevének..." ("It Is Easier for the Camel...") is a skillful account of the "Catch 22" situation faced by many immigrants who failed to get the jobs they could have qualified for if they had not needed those jobs — that is, if they had had connections with the rich.

While the works of Derleth and Anthony are not truly representative of ethnic literature because they are not really tuned into the immigrant experience, those of Lajos Fűry fail as ethnic literature because they are not true portrayals of the American component. Yet they are interesting in that they present the experience of the postwar generation and its perceptions of American life. His *Forgószél* (1958) purports to be the story of a Hungarian settlement gradually dying out as the younger members move into the city to find jobs. Only the young Calvinist minister, who was educated in Hungary at the expense of the community, tries to keep the settlement alive. What is unrealistic in this story is the portrayal of the Hungarian community as completely remote from American life, almost as if the community were a Hungarian village existing in a turn-of-the-century time warp. The city and American life intrude into this existence, but the community would hardly be threatened if the gulf portrayed actually existed between their mode of life and that of the American community. Fűry spins an interesting tale but fails in presenting the milieu of his piece or providing adequate motivation for events. The outlines of the story, however, do show some of the problems faced by the ethnic communities in adjusting to new ways while hoping to keep their old traditions alive. The final scenes, in which a reconciliation between the minister and his estranged wife is effective in bringing the community together again, build on the outpouring of help that the arrival of Hungarian refugees in 1956 elicited. *Az Arácsi csodakút* (*The Wonderwell of Arács,* 1970) is similar. The young daughter of Hungarian immigrants of the 1950s, thoroughly assimilated into American life, goes to Hungary to learn about the life of her parents. This work has some realistic touches on the assimilation of the 1950s immigration, but the emphasis is not on this subject. The work quickly becomes a romantic tale of the affair between the American-Hungarian girl and an older Hungarian neighbor on the shores of the Lake Balaton.

Tibor Florian (b. 1908), one of the best Hungarian-American poets, also belongs to the most recently emigrated group, and the poems he wrote in this country reflect the style and, to some extent, the themes that had already earned him recognition in Hungary.[7] Gradually, he wove his experiences in the United States and the imagery of his homes in New Jersey and Connecticut into the fabric of his verse. "A második holdraszállás" ("The Second Moon Landing") expresses the thrill and quiet sense of adventure shared by those who watched the moon shots on television. Florian's lyrics transcend time and place to become universal expressions of beauty. "Tavasz" ("Spring") uses the alternating short and long lines and the *aba* rhyme of much of the best Hungarian poetry. It is a richly musical poem worthy of inclusion in any anthology of American poetry. "New York szimfoniája" ("The Symphony of New York") is even closer to the American experience: in free verse it captures the sound of New York in a tribute to a side of the city not often seen in literature. The personal and lyrical response to American realities found in Florian's work is in many ways as important an aspect of ethnic literature as are the stories that chronicle the external events of life.

This personal response—expressed in a personal, modern and often cosmopolitan style—is also found in the works of writers who came to the United States after 1956. Most of them have become a part of American life, assimilating in some respects with a vigor not found in earlier immigrants, yet as poets they remain sensitive observers and commentators. They are in touch with both American literature and the literature of Hungary as well as the works of Hungarians writing in the West or in Eastern Europe. For example, Elemér Horváth and József Bakucz are avant-garde poets who belong to the Hungarian Workshop based in Paris but who live in New Jersey. Ferenc Mózsi of Chicago expresses his observations on American life in unusual associations and images, and Judit Ilosvay Selymes proceeds on the path of self-search and self-expression.[8]

Antonia Juhász Harangi's short stories have been collected under the title *Csendes csodák* (*Quiet Wonders,* 1956). The title is appropriate: she tells of the little wonders in the life of a mother and in "Bimbofakadas" ("Budding") expresses the bonds between all human beings. This is a short story of a Hungarian immigrant mother who goes to the hospital, feeling lonely and scared, to give birth to her first child, only to find the companionship of a black woman who is also there to give birth. The bond between the two women transcends the need for language, and the Hungarian girl's feeling of alienation is soon dispelled by the smile and encouraging nod of the more experienced woman.

Imre Sári Gál (b. 1923) is a traditionalist in style, but within the realistic tradition he is innovative. More talented than the turn-of-the-century writers, he is a representative of the new generation. His poems are personal, but few are love lyrics, philosophical expressions, or even nature poems; most are comments on life around him. Sári Gál settled in Cleveland upon coming to the United States after the revolution of 1956, and that city is the focus of many of his poems. Cars, highways, airplanes and airports, trade and commercialism — all are his topics; he appreciates their positive values but has some reservations about the materialism they symbolize. The poems in his two collections, *Ősember, esernyőnovel* (*Caveman with an Umbrella*) and *Toronycsordák* (*Tower Herds*), focus on American life.[9] "Jelentes napjainkról" ("Report on Our Days") is an emblem poem in the shape of a television set; "Amerika," written in the shape of a car, comments on our dependence on the automobile as a means of transportation. But he is also sensitive to natural values: "Húsz gyönyörű vadló" ("Twenty Beautiful Wild Horses") presents these noble beasts through the eyes of an Indian, emphasizing their value on the great plains of the United States, as well as their obvious aesthetic superiority to their mechanized replacements.

Sári Gál's striking use of images can illustrate the fresh perspective brought to a land by the new settler. "Himnusz a város-falukról" ("Hymn of the City-Villages") abounds in such images; high-rise buildings are masts of a ship, and "on them, the sky is stretched / and the city-villages sail." "Repülőgép a mezőn" ("Airplane on the Meadow") illustrates the attention that Sári Gál gives to things that others often take for granted. It is an admiring comment on the small plane parked by a farmhouse:

> Before Erie, to the North
> by the curve, there where
> the highway turns to the right,
> stands a farm-house,
> with its airport. And the plane

like a giant wild dove
alighted on the ground watches
the galloping
athlete cars.
In its beak
it holds a love letter:
the scene: a 3 dimensional
picture postcard. On it
the postal cancellation:
the setting sun.

(*Ösember,* p. 15)

In another poem the writer's admiration for the natural wonders of this land is obvious. "Mississippi" is a tribute to the river:

Who could say evil of her? Not even from envy
could any do her harm. And what sweet tales are told
of her, by those whom she carried on her back, or those
to whom she gave shelter on her banks.—The Mississippi
strings the States onto herself from Duluth down to her delta
and dreams of the sea, the hordes of fish, which, forming
huge banks, swim in her. Or perhaps
her two banks are reflected in her?

Sári Gál does not neglect the human quality of the river. Not only does this humaity dominate the imagery but it also finds concrete expression in the last stanza, where Sári Gál pays tribute to the other poet of the river, Mark Twain:

Mark Twain, too, listened to the gurgling of the water,
                                        the writer,
and his pseudonym, too: the two-knot mark, which was
on the ship's rope.—And they listened to the drawn-out
wailing of the ship's horn: We have arrived. Fragrant
woods and flowering meadows, here are men!

(*Ösember,* p. 61)

Sári Gál's appreciation for science is a welcome contrast to the hostility felt by many humaists. The harmony is a result of his unified view: humanity creates, and becomes part of, science and technology:

how can technology be praised?
Through man?

Would it be possible to separate them from each other?...
Is it possible to separate the microcosmos
from the macrocosmos?

Thus Sári Gál begins his "Leszállas a Holdra" ("Landing on the Moon"). The awe and glory of the moment are not lost on him. The speed with which pictures are transmitted to earth and the physical laws that had to be conquered to achieve the moon landing are a prelude to the lines of praise:

...And how sublime was the GLORIA: the picture
wholly shining like a pearl: the space ferry
bathing in pictures, and the instruments planted there where there is
no air, no atmosphere, there where all is pure
contrast. And when they planted the flag...

Yet, in spite of the sublimity of the moment, a homeyness pervades the scene, which is familiar, even while being remote. The stanza concludes with a reference to the telephone call to the President, full of informal exclamations:

Hey, Neil Armstrong and Edwin Aldrin, what's up? You
speak on the phone to the Earth? See what? with
the President! and above, in space, Collins drew
forced rings of honor with the mother-ship.
(*Ösember,* p. 24)

Wonderful as this feat is, however, the poem really concentrates on the spin-offs from this technological achievement. They will be of more benefit to mankind than the spectacular show of the moon landing — the technology to develop new plastics, new adhesives, new alloys; the many other achievements that already enable us to replace some human parts: today the heart valve, tommorrow the artificial heart.

In 1962 Leslie Konnyu published his *History of American Hungarian Literature: Presentation of American Hungarian Authors of the Last 100 Years and Selections from Their Writings,* an extensive survey of Hungarian-American literature. But this literature, like most other ethnic literatures, has yet to be acknowledged or dealt with in a traditional American literary history. Scholars should pay more attention to the literary responses to American life of America's European immigrants whose works often chronicle major steps in American social and economic history and scrutinize the problems and consequences of progress. Like the novels of Hemingway and Faulkner, these works comment on American life. In a multiethnic and multicultural society, all varied threads are essential parts of the fabric of literature. Unfortunately, not all the material is available in English. Of the truly ethnic Hungarian-American writers, Teréz Stibran is the only one who wrote in English, and she wrote only one book. Almost no translations exist of the others. But this need not be a permanent problem. The short stories of Szécskay or Illés could easily be translated. With the life and experiences it describes, its geographical settings and its social background, Hungarian-American literature deserves a place in American literature. A greater awareness of what is available should help uncover other neglected pieces, other works that must be recognized before a complete picture of American literature can develop or at least before the ever-changing and evolving organism that is literature can be accepted as complete for the moment.

Bibliographical Note

Among useful background and critical works are the following: József Gellen, "Immigrant Experiences in Hungarian-American Poetry before 1945," *Acta Litteraria Academiae Scientiarum Hungaricae*, 20, Nos. 1–2 (1978), 81–97; Leslie Konnyu, *A History of American Hungarian Literature: Presentation of American Hungarian Authors of the Last 100 Years and Selections from Their Writings* (St. Louis: Cooperative of American Writers, 1962) and *Amerikai magyar irodalomatörténet* (*American Hungarian Literary History*) (St. Louis: n.p., n.d.); Emil Lengyel, *Americans from Hungary* (Westport, Conn.: Greenwood, 1974); Ferenc Merő, *Emigrációs magyar irodalom lexikona* (*Lexicon of the Hungarian Literature in Exile*) (Köln: Amerikai Magyar Kiado, 1966); and Miklós Szántó, *Magyarok a nagyvilágban* (*Hungarians in the World*) (Budapest: Kossuth, 1970).

Notes

[1] *András Vas: Verses mese a vádormadarakról tizenkét részben* (n.p.: n.p., 1923), p. 166. The translations are mine and are essentially interlinear prose versions.

[2] *Élet könye [Book of Life], 1892–1942* (Detroit: n.p., 1944), pp. 33-34.

[3] *Idegen világban: Versek és dalok. A holt ország és egyébb elbeszélések* (New York: n.p. 1910), p. 32.

4 *Vándordalok, ujabb versek* (New York: n.p., 1920).

5 *Őszi tarlózás ötven éves mezőn* (Pittsburgh: n.p., 1947).

6 *Szécskay György harmadik könye: Baltimorei rapszódia, és más amerikai magyar versek* (Pittsburgh: n.p., 1938).

7 Tibor Florian, *Keserű gyökéren, versek* (New York: Pilvax, 1975).

8 Elemér Horváth, *Egy fehér néger naplójabol* (Paris: Magyar Mühely, 1976) and *A mindennapok arca: Versek, 1953–1962* (Roma: Anonymus, 1962); József Bakucz, *Kővesedö ég* (Paris: Magyar Műhely, 1973); Ferenc Mózsi, *A képzelet kertjeiben* (Los Angeles: Nemzetör Baráti Köre Kiadása, 1974); and Judit Ilosvay Selymes, *Félúton* (Center Square, Pa.: Alpha, 1975).

9 Imre Sári Gál *Ösember, esernyővel* (Cleveland: Amerikai Magyar Könyvtar, 1974) and *Toronycsordák* (Cleveland: Amerikai Magyar Könyvtar, 1971).

Italian-American Literature

Rose Basile Green

In March 1816 the Philadelphia *Aurora* carried an obituary for Philip Mazzei, companion and mentor to Thomas Jefferson and phraser of some of the most well-known rhetoric of the Declaration of Independence. The obituary read in part:

> ...he was possessed of a great ingenuity of character and simplicity of manner. He was profoundly adept in the science of human nature. Towards the United States his affections were entirely devoted. His principal consolation in the decline of his life was derived from seeing that county flourish, of which he was proud to consider himself an adopted citizen.[1]

This homage paid to the Italian who had helped so much to give verbal form to the spirit of the American Revolution stands also as a fitting preface to the contribution, long unsung, that many others from Italy were to make to our American literary patrimony. Representing some twenty to thirty million residents of the United States, Americans of Italian extraction have in every literary genre creatively documented their experiences with the larger society. The compilation of historical, bibliographical, and critical materials for *The Italian-American Novel* made it clear to me that (1) there is a distinctive quality in the writings of Italian Americans and (2) the quality of such writing evolved in tandem with the literary activities of the larger culture.[2]

Prose Fiction

Over seventy American writers of Italian ancestry have had novels published, not all of which qualify as Italian-American works. We may define the Italian-American novel as a long work of prose fiction written in English either by an Italian immigrant in the United States or by an American of Italian ancestry and dealing with the social and emotional effects of ethnic origins. Such a novel also consistently projects values that are uniquely Italian. While some of the novels discussed in this essay fall short of the highest literary standards, they merit study as examples of creative attempts to record experiences not examined elsewhere. Hence one must interpret them not only as literature but as literary renditions of sociological themes.

Like the writings of most pioneers, the first literary efforts of the Italians in America were expository — letters, diaries, news articles, brief histories, monographs, descriptions, biographies, political reports, and autobiographies. The titles often indicate their content: *The Story of Antonio the Galley Slave* (1911), by Antonio Arrighi; *Son of Italy* (1924), by Pascal D'Angelo; and *Americans by Choice* (1956), by Constantino Panunzio.

When later writers moved from simply recording to interpreting their experiences, their cultural concepts demonstrated the influence of the established American culture. This study concentrates, therefore, on the creative materials — the experiences — that underpin the development of Italian-American fiction. Its course, paralleling that of American literature as a whole,[3] went through five stages: (1) the early impact of the new environment, (2) the first attempts at assimilation, (3) the shift into non-Italian-American themes, (4) the return to old sources, and (5) the branching of an Italian culture rooted in American soil.

Ever since the turn of the century American literature has been preoccupied with the "common man." The schools of realism and naturalism were a reaction to the genteel concepts of the nineteenth century. The American dream as an odyssey from rags to riches fascinated the immigrant, as did the underprivileged who inhabited the fictionalizations of that dream. While native-born American schoolchildren were reading Horatio Alger tales, Italian immigrants were following their own pluck-and-luck models. As late as 1935, Garibaldi Marti Lapolla wrote *The Grand Gennaro*, in which an immigrant succeeds in America by ruthlessly exploiting his own people. More humane themes also appeared, in books like John Antonio Moroso's *The Stumbling Herd* (1923), which depicted Jews, Italians, and Irish living compassionately together.

The social isolation of ethnic clusters tends to make them fragment and congeal. Some novelists have attempted to relate the experiences of these groups to those of the larger society. In

Men of Silence (1928) and *The River Between* (1928), for example, Louis Forgione analyzed how violence can initially act as a powerful force in assimilation. Other writers, such as Bernard De Voto, Paul Gallico, Frances Winwar, and Hamilton Basso, moved into the mainstreams of American literature by rejecting the restrictions of their ethnicity. In *The Literary Fallacy* (1944) De Voto argued that American writers should represent more factually the complexion and the aspirations of the American people as a whole; he later embodied his arguments in the characters of his novels. Others used symbols as instruments of propaganda for minorities. Hamilton Basso, for example, uses the American South as a symbol of a cultural minority within the larger culture, especially in *The View from Pompey's Head* (1954), where he explores the rigidity of a society that worships its ancestors.

In response to this kind of external objectivity, a group of Italian-American novelists began to look back to their own ancestors and to resurrect old ethnic themes. These writers had mastered the national idiom and the literary style and knew the criteria of acceptance. We see, among others, Jo Pagano writing about his parents, in *Golden Wedding* (1943); Guido D'Agostino exploring the dual culture, in *Olives on the Apple Tree* (1942); and George Panetta dramatizing linguistic distortions, in *We Ride a White Donkey* (1944). Mari Tomasi in *Like Lesser Gods* (1949), a celebrative story about quarry workers, recorded the social integration of the Italians in Vermont. Perhaps one of the most enduring and popular of the novelists who regenerated the ethnic theme is Pietro DiDonato, who drew from his own experience to write *Christ in Concrete* (1939), the story of an exploited immigrant worker. DiDonato completed the story in *Three Circles of Light* (1960).

Inevitably, as these writers analytically focused on ethnic themes and backgrounds, they became preoccupied with the feeling of being "out of place" in America, and this sense of isolation led them, along with other contemporary novelists, into intense psychological probing. In their search for self-identity, ethnic writers often try to discover who and what their fathers were — a search taken up by Michael De Capite in *No Bright Banner* (1944), Rocco Fumente in *Tree of Dark Reflection* (1945), Charles Calitri in *Father* (1962), and Jerre Mangione in *Night Search* (1965). In the works of Niccolo Tucci, Robert Cenedella, Helen Barolini, and especially Robert Canzoneri, introspection expands to more universal themes; in *I Do So Politely* (1965), for example, Canzoneri integrates the Italian father into the family system of the Confederate South.

The attempt to overcome the "out-of-place" feeling is presented by Marion Benasutti in *No Steady Job for Papa* (1966), an honest and appealing account of the growth of a young girl to ethnic womanhood in the Philadelphia area. In *Love and Pasta* (1968), Joseph Vergara offers a virile contrast to Benasutti's reminiscing narrative. The theme of virility is intensified to metaphorical terms by Antonio Turzo, whose *La Strega, the Witch of South Philadelphia* (1975), tells the story of a sensitive man trapped in the conflict between being accepted and being rejected. Turzo's *poèta* eloquently symbolizes the Italian immigrant aesthete abandoned to the attic of American materialistic indifference. Much of the power of *La Strega* resides in its ethnic-oriented phrasing, a kind of speech that is currently surfacing as a type of authentic American-English.

Many of these ethnic writers chose themes that had special appeal for American readers. One attractive subject was the search for the American dream. Some writers, such as Ralph Corsel, Lucas Longo, and Ben Piazza stressed the impermanence of material things as contrasted with the enduring qualities of strong family ties. Frank Miceli, in *The Seventh Month* (1969) uses a metaphor to striking artistic effect depicting Italian immigrants as aborted in their dream of work and freedom in America. These ethnics, he says, cannot nurture their children to fulfillment within the body of the nation. Eugene Mirabelli argues for assimilation through young love in *The Burning Air* (1968) and *The Way In* (1968); he also shows knowledge of certain American mores in *No Resting Place* (1972), whose protagonist, an academic publisher, succumbs to the sexual advances of his secretary and consequently loses everything he values.

Italian-American fiction, viewed from its inception as an important artifact of ethnic thought and culture, eventually received acceptance for its artistic value. For example, critics praise the fiction of Mario Andrew Pei, well-known as a linguist and scholar, for its creative artistry, social comment, and intellectual perception. In *Swords of Anjou* (1953), Pei narrates the story of Juan and Thierry, two characters from the *Chanson de Roland*, dramatizing such themes as loyalty, steadfastness, and adherence to a personal code of honor. More originally, Pei explores fantasy in *The Sparrows of Paris* (1958), where he makes a connection between medieval demonology and the contemporary traffic in narcotics. His literary skill is also apparent in the rapidly paced plotting of the stories in *Tales of the Natural and Supernatural* (1971). Pei's works seek not only to confirm his readers' faith in America (an increasingly articulated Italian-American position) but also to emphasize the poetry of intellectual rhetoric.

Many Italian-American writers consciously strive to create the novel as a work of art. Among contemporary America's better novelists are Joseph Papaleo, Francis Pollini, and Mario Puzo. Such ethnic writers have used a variety of innovative structures in their works. Joseph Papaleo, for example, develops his plots by dramatizing poetic irony. In *All the Comforts* (1967), the characters are symbols of ideas, and the plot is a convenient device for creating a point of encounter between two ethnic groups. The ironic climax of his poetic treatment occurs when Vito, an Italian-American, identifies success in America with the status not of the established WASPs but Jewish Americans. Papaleo emphasizes the problem of the person who finds that the American dream is the pursuit of material success. He expands this theme in the significantly titled *Out of Place* (1970), which demonstrates that Italian Americans, though well established both economically and socially, are still strangers in their environment.

Two exemplary writers of well-constructed novels who have passionately imbibed the contemporary American scene are Francis Pollini and Mario Puzo. In both his plays and novels Pollini scrutinizes today's values. An original artist, he creates paradoxical heroes who personify both good and evil. He contends that everyone is a split personality, a hyphenated alien, and that American's seemingly smooth society is but an aggregate of imperfect fragments. His style — full of frenetic sharps, harsh disharmonies, and abrasive reprises — reflects his themes.

Pollini's first book, *Night* (1961), which takes place in a prison camp, relates to the Korean War as Hemingway's *A Farewell to Arms* relates to World War I. The central event, Marty Landi's nightmarish resistance to an inquisitor, is psychologically superimposed on Marty's recollection of his Italian-American family's resistance to a hostile neighborhood. Ching, the subtle interrogator, probes Marty's life history like an exquisite electrical instrument, bringing to the surface the boy who had once shared his mother's suffering. The inquisitor tortures the memory, showing Marty that being a soldier for America has not changed his role. The sequences dramatizing the "brainwashing" of the other soldiers are a terrorizing warning of the consequences of the manipulation of psychic power.

In *Glover* (1965), Pollini pursues the theme of a man's conscience fragmented by military training. While various characters dramatize different attitudes toward war, the protagonist embodies Pollini's idea of the dichotomy of the American character: outwardly a hero, inwardly a conditioned murderer.

Pollini's *Excursion* (1965) also uses a structured metaphor. The title refers to a pilgrimage that an ex-ballerina makes through Europe to the cities of her former dancing triumphs. Through her discovery of peace in Italy, Pollini emphasizes that Italian positivism provides respite for the Italian American and acts as a restorative against contemporary ills.

Pollini's protagonists become more defined with every book he writes. In *The Crown* (1967), the prizefighter Dave Stanley, his manager, Farn, and the prizefighter's mistress, Sheila Benton, are contending members of their own private sparring match. Dave embodies the duplicity of American society, its idealism and its intrigue — a duality that Pollini dramatizes by having Farn and Sheila narrate alternate chapters. Sheila's behavior shows how the creative instinct can become degraded into intrigue; Farn demonstrates how the values of the marketplace operate in the human psyche. As for Dave, his crowning achievement is to destroy illusions, remove distortions, and open the door to fair and honest competition.

In the popular *Pretty Maids All in a Row* (1968), Pollini extends this theme to academic circles. Outwardly attractive and much beloved, the protagonist, Tiger McDrew, is actually a double-edged source of good and evil, a monster of terror. Much of the tension of the novel is the product of Pollini's masterful exposition of established values, which encompass Italian concepts and attitudes. The immigrant's son, Ponce de Leon, symbolizes Italian-American aspiration, suggested by the romantic connotations of the boy's name. It is Ponce who insists on "doing the right thing" and reveals the crimes of Tiger. The author persuades us that we must reject rampant sex and conditioned violence; we must remove our masks and honor ourselves.

Interestingly, Italian Americans, as shown in these novels, are now identifying themselves with what was once inimical to them: the national American culture, which has come to accept them and is absorbing them. The most acclaimed literary representative of this emerging attitude is Mario Puzo, the author of short stories, numerous articles, and five novels.

Much has been written about crime and violence in America and about the alleged Italian-American association with lawlessness. While some Italian-American fiction has validly explored the social causes of crime — like Frank Canizio's account of underworld crime, Vincent Siciliano's realistic *Unless They Kill Me First* (1970), and George Cuomo's books, especially *Among Thieves* (1968) — the recent deluge of literary "mafiana" was triggered by Puzo. The Italian-American press and other groups have long decried the depiction of the Italian as a criminal in books, periodicals, newspapers, and broadcasting, but the stereotype persists more or less unchecked. Ironically, one reason this ethnic group has served as a scapegoat is that the traditionally self-sufficient, law-abiding Italians have disdained to unite into protest groups. Furthermore, in reporting the increased violence in the nation, the mass media have not always acknowledged that only a small fraction of Italian Americans engage in criminal activities.

Mario Puzo's first novel, *The Dark Arena* (1955), deals with the occupation of Germany after World War II. An exceedingly informative and thought-provoking book, it explores the extremities to which military occupation leads both the conquered and the conqueror. In the story, Walter Mosca, a twentieth-century centurion who has lost his idealism as a soldier, becomes involved in black-market activities through which the Army of Occupation allies itself to the starving German people. His personal problem evolves from our national psyche: he is a microcosm of our national military machinery. Standing midway in America's stratified society, with its stratified morality, Mosca functions symbolically, especially in such scenes as the one where he is struck still in a basement filled with headless corpses. This place of mindless darkness stands for our modern world — a place that holds no safety for us, where we are all blind with fear. In such darkness, we perpetrate evil, itself the universal dark arena. With this book, Puzo has made a significant contribution to American literature. His style has power, precision, and verisimilitude, and his depiction of mood and place is almost cinematic.

In his second novel, *The Fortunate Pilgrim* (1964), Puzo explores the stresses of life experienced by Italian Americans along New York City's Tenth Avenue during the 1930s. Through the story of one tenacious immigrant, Lucia Santa Angeluzzi-Corbo, Puzo universalizes the struggle of all immigrants to survive and to get ahead. Using all the familiar episodes of living in crowded rooms from which emanate the births, the children's conflicts, the family arguments, the weddings, the street scenes, the religious rituals, and death itself, Puzo creates a rich and unforgettable character. A typical Italian-American mother, Lucia Santa hounds her son, the resisting Gino, who escapes her to serve in the army. In the end, Lucia rides in her son's limousine to the new home on Long Island, reflecting on her good fortune and anticipating the better life ahead. A masterfully told story and one that Puzo himself thinks highly of, *The Fortunate Pilgrim* may well become acclaimed as the representative Italian-American novel.

In analyzing *The Godfather* (1969), one must emphasize the role played by crime in the achievement of socioeconomic success. One should also recognize that, historically, killing has been defined in pragmatic and paradoxical ways. It may be patriotic in times of war; it may be criminal when committed by a self-directed syndicate within the body of the nation. Also, in America's inclination to make literary heroes out of rebels — Huckleberry Finn, for example — there lies a logical connection to the acceptance of the matured, "reasonable" Don Corleone. In any event, Mario Puzo has sculptured an ice-coated snowball and hurled it into the face of American duplicity.

As a novel, *The Godfather* has been called everything from a staggering literary triumph to a calculated package for bestsellerdom. Out of a conceivable but exceedingly limited ethnic scenario, the author has fashioned an effective and convincing story. Puzo makes generally incredible episodes plausible and natural, while offering the prescription that law and order should be reformed. A social historian of American civilization, he explores the nation's sinister and powerful fraternity of crime and argues that its power stems from rebellion against corrupt law enforcement. Adding new terms like "makes his bones" to our literary lexicon, Puzo demonstrates the need for Italian-American writers to acquiesce in the use of unconventional and extreme themes in contemporary fiction—depravity, crime, lust, violence, bigotry, racism, and hate.

In his latest book, *Fools Die* (1978), Puzo seems deliberately less intent on creating a good story. While flirting with the menacing terror of treachery, the author of *The Godfather* now fills his action pell-mell with a mixture of characters caught hopelessly in the American pursuit of power at any price. He makes little attempt to foreshadow events, and the book suffers accordingly.

Puzo quickly informs the reader, however, that he is striking a blow at those in the higher reaches of power. When the power-mongers achieve success, he believes, they feel little satisfaction, because they know nothing about virtue's being its own reward. For this reason, the "fools die." As for the exploited victims — the average descendants of immigrants and the original settlers of housing projects — their virtues have enabled them to climb the economic scale and move to private homes. The author contends that we are now getting the "hard-core poor," those who could never make an honest living and do not want to do so. Therefore, he concludes, the magic of ideals also dies.

A mixture of related plots forms the structure of the novel. There is a "family" closeness in the friendship of the three "degenerate gamblers" who share the violence, the females, and the green baize world of Las Vegas. Their relationship embodies the "fools die" theme: the unhappy Jordan wins a half-million dollars and shoots himself; Cully, the undercover houseman, turns to treachery; and John Merlyn, a writer and also the narrator, makes a lucrative income by taking bribes in his job as an army recruitment worker, cheats on his wife, and eventually reforms. When Merlyn's novel proves a success, the rapidly paced and powerful narrative changes to tedious illiterate and underdeveloped reportage. The self-named writer who had identified himself with Merlin of the Arthurian legend tries to make magic with words and realities. The orphan-writer, the seeker of ideals, changes from a struggling novelist of virtue to a succesfully marketed literary figure.

Merlyn pins his hopes for success on Osano, a lionized literary figure whom publishing hucksters have chosen to write the future Nobel Prize-winning best-seller. After Osano's suicide, "hundreds of thousands of words were written about Osano as the first great Italian literary figure in our cultural history.... He never thought of himself as Italian-American. But one thing would have pleased him. All the critics said that if he had lived to publish his novel in progress, he would have surely won the Nobel Prize." For Puzo, every great hero must have a weakness that will destroy him. For this reason, Puzo has created a recognizable alter ego in Merlyn, who is convinced that he can rule his own life only by some sort of magic. About Jordan's death he says, "Life was too much for him. But not for me. Only fools die."

It may be true that Puzo's gambling casino is a convenient metaphor for the current state of American civilization. *Fools Die* is, likewise, a merchandised comment on the American way of life, a self-indulgent *mescolanza* of bits and pieces, of people and plots, the mass embodiment of what has been the tragic Italian-American situation. This is the dark setting where the dreamers and dealers cannot control the available elements of power and success. They have not been allowed to weave their magic spells, to find the Holy Grail of heroism, in the written story of the American experience. Hence Puzo's method is his message. He would let those fools die who sell their art to stereotypes.

As Italian-American writers integrate into the national society, they differ from other writers only in their personal, subtle, and almost unconscious attitudes toward their experiences. Some of them use plotlessness and formlessness, as Gilbert Sorrentino does in his books of word-pictures like *Steelwork* (1969) and *Imaginative Qualities of Actual Things* (1971). Most of the current Italian-American novelists use episodic progression to structure their works. Richard D'Ambrosio, for example, in *No Language but a Cry* (1970), tells a true-to-life story of his experiences in transforming a neglected, broken piece of "human refuse" to a functioning human being. Similarly, John Nicholas Iannuzzi brings to life the cases of a trial lawyer in the imaginative *What's Happening* and *Part 35* (1970).

Some writers, like Gay Talese and Julia Savarese, come from the mass media. Based on factual rather than imaginative materials, Talese's works may be classified as nonnovels with the power of novels. Especially well-concieved are his *The Kingdom and the Power* (1969) and *Honor Thy Father* (1971). Julia Savarese writes a conventional novel about the magazine business in *Final Proof* (1971). Her heroine exemplifies the ethnic American who finds herself — or himself — confused by the corporate intrigue. Joseph Sorrentino's *Up from Never* (1972), offers a candid and powerful portayal of personal survival and the conquest of the inimical environment as a breeding place of mob action and sexual casualness. Other current Italian-American writers using traditional plot structures include Joseph Pillitteri, Don De Lillo, Bill Pronzini, Paul Gillette, John Fante, and the ever fecund Paul Gallico.

Most Italian-American writers extol traditional democratic principles in setting forth their views about improving relationships among people. De Lillo, for example, astutely presents both the idealistic and materialistic situations and shows how characters succeed or fail in their pursuit of the American dream. His *Americana* (1971) received praise for its brilliance, as did his *End Zone* (1972), *Ratner's Star, Great Jones Street* (1973), *Players* (1977), and *Running Dog* (1978). In all these works De Lillo explores the secret terror of contemporary sensibility.

In *Americana*, De Lillo, a native New Yorker, restates the American myth of innocence and vitality. A young and successful former television executive in New York, David Bell attempts to discover himself by making a movie. Accompanied by three friends—a sculptor, a former fighter pilot, and an inebriate — he makes a journey into the "depths of America, wilderness dream of all poets and scoutmasters, westward to our manifest destiny, to sovereign red timber and painted sands, to the gold-transfigured hills, westward to match the shadows of my image and myself." After a variety of experiences with an assortment of strangers, he observes, "I felt it was literature I had been confronting these past days, the archetypes of the dismal mystery, sons and daughters of the archetypes, images that could not be certain which of two confusions held less terror, their own or what their own might become if it ever faced the truth." With an almost circular movement, beginning and ending in New York, De Lillo depicts the coastal towns, the small villages, and the wilderness that American writers have traditionally filled with myth and innocence. By using the process of film making to show David's growth, the author presents the story as though on a panoramic screen with a wide angle. David becomes contemporary youth seeking to find itself, his flight on the plane symbolizing his direct route to the core of the action.

When *End Zone* appeared, the *New York Times* judged De Lillo "among our best young writers." Referring to the author's metaphysical use of football as a demonstration of life, S. K.

Oberbeck of *Book World* wrote that "Don De Lillo had done for (or perhaps to) football what Nathanael West did for Hollywood." All have agreed that in this one particular story the author, like a good back, grinds out comic yardage and crisp, basic plays. The book established De Lillo as a major American writer of fiction.

In *Great Jones Street*, De Lillo focuses on the rock music scene. Bucky Wunderlick, a rock superstar, embodies the fragments of a shattered age — the rock music explosion of the 1960s in the fallout of the 1970s. Finding the pressure of his career too much, Bucky leaves his band, abandons a cross-country tour, and seeks sanctuary in a dismal apartment in New York City. Protected by the rumor that he is dead, he tries to have some privacy, but his solitude is interrupted by a string of visitors. The writer upstairs wanders in and out, talking about pornographic books for children. Others come and go, but the most persistent is Bucky's manager, Globke, who wants Bucky to make a comeback. It is not enough to betray a friend, Globke advises him; it is when "you betray a friend and then you brag about it. That's star quality." Globke's plan is to exploit the idea that the superstar has only one year to live. Evoking the style, design, and even the diction of Norman Mailer's *An American Dream*, De Lillo manifests a talent for inventive language and imagery. His dramatic verve, satiric caracature, and witty dialogue, however, mark him as an artist with distinctive qualities of his own.

For many readers, De Lillo's artistry is even more evident in *Players* (1977) and *Running Dog* (1978). *Running Dog* starts with the discovery of a man, dressed as a woman, who has been murdered in a deserted section of Manhattan. A search ensues for the "ultimate piece of decadence," the only copy of a pornographic film shot in Hitler's Berlin bunker during the final days of the Third Reich. Out of the elements of conventional thrillers — murder, espionage, pornography, a reporter who prostitues herself, a powerful United States senator with a taste for erotica, an investigative journalist, a well-dressed "hit" man, and an intelligence agency operating for profit — De Lillo composes a work with style, wit, and power. From the Lower East Side to the senator's home in Georgetown, wantons and intriguers arrange themselves into fatal parallel lines of action — a cross-country chase by car and helicopter and a quest for the evasive film. Underlying this figurative American nightmare are serious themes. One character says, "Tendency finds an outlet. I'm saying espionage is a language, an art, with sexual sources and coordinates," dramatizing the point that we live in an age of conspiracy and fantastic assassination schemes, of connections, and secret relationships. Another observes, "Before pop art, there was such a thing as bad taste. Now there's kitsch, schlock, camp and porn." A third complains that everything has become orgasmic; the question is, "What happened to normal?" For De Lillo normalcy is in the Italianism of Talerico, who yearns secretly for the familiar faces and voices — the mother, the sister, the cousins, the uncles, the nieces.

Italian-American writers have predominantly focused on those among the underpriviliged who have succeeded in the conflict with their environment. Most of these characters are consistently — and, as a fictional group, uniquely — optimistic in their attitudes toward life. As a result, writers who are not Italian Americans are depicting Italian-American characters not only sympathetically but even as protagonists. In *The Immigrants* (1977), for example, Howard Fast has created Dan Lavette as both the agent and the victim of what Fast sees as politicized capitalism. An ethnicized version of Horatio Alger, Lavette evolves as his own man. One might venture the opinion, however, that an Italian-American writer would have portayed Lavette with more particularity.

Italian-American writers have adopted a variety of forms. Joseph Pillitteri, for example, concentrates on neat, tight frames in *When the Giraffe Runs Down* (1970) and *Two Hours on Sunday* (1971). In the first novel, he intertwines the lives of three people through their interaction in a hospital. In the second novel, a professional football player's personal problems are set in counterpoint to his team's football strategies, showing the man as teammate in a tensely competitive activity and symbolizing the American corporate system.

For the many readers who still enjoy mysteries the most, there are the books of Bill Pronzini, including *The Stalker* (1971), *The Snatch* (1971), *The Vanished* (1973), *Undercurrent* (1973), *Snowbound* (1974), and *Games* (1978).

As observers of contemporary American society, new writers with Italian-rooted names appear constantly. Among these is Joseph DiMona, who, after collaborating with H. R. Haldeman in writing *The Ends of Power*, has written two successful mystery stories: *Last Man at Arlington* (1973) and *The Benedict Arnold*

Connection (1977). The latter has been hailed as an electrifying supershocker with "adrenalin-pumping suspense." It is the story of George Williams, who has received orders directly from the president to find a live nuclear warhead buried under three hundred feet of ocean. Williams has thiry-six hours before the bomb will explode, hurling a million tons of radioactive water over the Eastern seaboard and killing millions of people. A brittle staccato style keeps the narrative moving at a relentless pace. Other writers involve the reader with an absorbing tale. Among these are Mel Arrighi, Anthony Caputi, Vincent Crapanzano, Frank De Felitta, Arlene De Marco, Patricia Dizenzo, Len Giovannitti, Daniela Gioseffi, Joe Maggio, Iris Orego, Orlando R. Petrocelli, Martin Sampierre, Frank Scarpetta, Guido Edmond Schiavone, and Marco Vassi.

Good storytellers sometimes even become prophets of their times, and such can be said of the prolific Paul Gallico. The books of this major writer, who has constantly brought his own special zest and polish to celebrate the average person who aims for higher goals, always provide engrossing reading. In *The Zoo Gang* (1971), a new Gallico emerges — a classic writer who has abosrbed the contemporary scene. The five members of the bizarre menagerie called the Zoo Gang fight crime along the Côte D'Azur on the French Riviera. These contemporary Robin Hoods, survivors of a French resistance group who had plagued the Nazis, have individual pseudonyms that belie their personalities: Le Léopard, an obese and slothful electrical contractor, formerly an expert in communications; L'Eléphant, a slight figure trafficking in garlic and onions, once an expert in sabotage; Le Loup, a bar owner, a part-time aviator, and an expert locksmith; Le Tigre, a sad and gentle carnation grower and an expert assassin with a stiletto; and their leader, Le Renard, a blue-eyed and suave antiques dealer and the contact with the Riviera underground. The group advises, pursues, and avenges in giving assistance to the chief of detectives in four separate cases. The episodes involve the theft of twelve Renoir paintings from a local museum, the goal of their retrieval being to provide a new hospital with free beds for the poor; a hypothetical jewel robbery in which the group, finding themselves unwitting advisers of the local security men, are able to help forestall a real robbery plan they had presaged and preenacted; a double kidnapping involving an auto tycoon's child and the child of the kidnapper; and a battle with a drug syndicate that is smuggling narcotics into the Riviera. The drugs are transported during the Mardi Gras carnival on a float called "Snow White and the Seven Dwarfs" and are stored on the stage of an abandoned theater. In an old-time gang-style climax, the Zoo Gang shoots it out with the seven "dwarfs" of the narcotics ring, and the bodies are removed in the fashion of a "Dutch" Schultz melodrama.

Perhaps Gallico's most convincing work is *Matilda* (1970), in which he masterfully injects irony into the treatment of innocence. With the sure control of the director who also plays the role of the protagonist, he intrigues the reader with violence, conspiracy, and personal human involvement. The counterhero of the story is Matilda, an Australian kangaroo trained as a boxer. By making an animal the champion of a popular American sport, Gallico dramatizes Donald Heiney's statement that modern American literature is conventionally iconoclastic and verbally local.[4] A victim of two contending, illegally organized syndicates, the animal is exploited in direct proportion to its love for and its responses to the people around it.

Gallico's realistically narrated story contains overtones of philosophical significance. The Calvinist preoccupation with the struggle between good and evil here becomes a contemporary dialogue on what constitutes honesty. Billy Baker, a "limey" from Australia, has trained the kangaroo, and he knows what will make the animal succeed or fail — the human touch. The local promoter, "Bimmie" Bimstein, uses every possible ploy to turn Matilda into a million-dollar property and make himself a fortune. The powerful and widely admired sportswriter, Duke Parkhurst, is the controlling point of view, the narrator of the drama. He speaks of having an "irreconcilable distaste for baddies" but a soft spot for the "corney people, the concession operators, barkers, shills, pitchmen, grafters and cappers. . . ." To be sure, the world of professional boxing is one of calculations, contrivances, planned procedures, and agreed victories or failures, and it is presented as the necessary human condition for survival. The "flesh peddlers and merchants of injury" may eventually become powerful organized syndicates. In that case, a Parkhurst will have trouble "when Uncle Nono and his boys begin to operate." As for the common man (the kangaroo), the manager says that "as long as he thinks he's the greatest, he'll knock your brynes out. But once he finds out there's more to the game than just dishing it out, he folds up like an umbrella."

Gallico, like Puzo, admits that there is a Sicilian Mafia, but he argues that it is a business like any other. Once, people like the Goulds, the Astors, and the Vanderbilts held all the power; today the list of names includes people like "Nono" or di Angeletti, Matilda's owner. The author stresses the point that Gio diAngeletti had been the editor of the *Lampoon*, Harvard's comic magazine, and that, later, inheriting his father's importing business, he lost his comic sense. A graduate cum laude from Harvard, he also inherited the "overlordship of the Eastern seaboard family of Cosa Nostra" with its varied activities. Of course, he has to keep his two worlds apart. Society recognizes him for his wealth, the breeding farm in Westchester, the town house on Upper Fifth Avenue, the villa and marina on Biscayne Bay in Miami. Members of the Cosa Nostra view him in a different light, and, since one of their "varied activities" is the control of boxing, he eventually comes to own Matilda.

The problems created by this control of the sport reflect the current counterreaction to oranized enterprise. Comparing prizefighting to military operations among nations, Gallico writes that boxing is the "public torture of human beings" and Matilda a soldier in a tournament that is ostensibly a noble and democratic way of "getting the boys off the streets" and giving them a chance to make their way. In the end, two tangible embodiments of the renewed dream emerge: di Angeletti (the contemporary entrepreneur) and Matilda (the common man). It is up to the reader whether or not to believe, as "Nono" does, that nothing lasts, not even the current interpretation of good versus the forces of evil. For the time being, as Parkhurst is convinced, one must substitute an occasional gray for one's uncompromising blacks and whites.

Perhaps the time has come for writers of Italian ancestry to be concerned not only that their books reach the Italian-American community but also that they dramatize themes that relate the general condition of American culture. Italian-American writers will ultimately be judged as American writers. One thinks of critics like Michael Novak, who insist that America is not a melting pot because it has not confronted squarely the problem of preserving diversity, despite the Bill of Rights and a culture that permits everyone "to do his or her thing."[5] Certainly, to be critical and intelligent is not to be less ethnic, but the ethnic novel must reflect the whole evolving social order.

The novels written by Americans of Italian ancestry demonstrated that their authors have, on the whole, absorbed both the material and transcendental values of traditional American literature, while they have consistently maintained an endemic constructive and optimistic view of the future. That the Italian-American novel has been acclaimed finally through books of violence like *The Godfather* attests to a basic American belief that crime is as much an accepted method for gaining power as transgression is the occasion for the soul to gain salvation through repentance. In general, Italian-American writers reveal that the presence of any alien in American society inspires interest in the person who is isolated from but still a part of the culture. The presence of the Italian immigrant has helped to direct that interest to human relationships with a constructive attitude emanating from self-discipline. To explore the writings of this assimilated immigrant, therefore, is a step toward making American literature more representative of American civilization—a process of putting our literary index in order.

Drama

The increasing identification of the Italian American with the national literature has inevitably been reflected in drama. Recent years have seen the emergence of a powerful and influential dramatist, Albert Innaurato. His play *The Transfiguration of Benno Blimpie* appeared off Broadway, and he won critical praise for his first Broadway play, *Gemini*. As Eleanor Lester wrote in the *New York Times*, this dramatist has a passion for the outcast — a familiar theme also among Italian-American novelists. In creating the gargantuan Benno Blimpie, Innaurato champions the fat person, a primary outcast of a society "imprisoned by cosmetic values, by the notion that if you are not young, tall, slim, blond and WASP, you are all wrong. Our society is far from liberated. Everyone — not just fat people — is in a constant state of crisis, trying to be more manly or more womanly or younger, making desperate gestures to conform to ridiculous standards of beauty."

As William Collins of the *Philadelphia Inquirer* wrote, *Benno Blimpie*, which starred James Coco, allows for a performance of "terrific dramatic intensity." In the play Innaurato projects a harsh view of his Italian-American background as he uses the consumption of food to build the tension of the action. The pathetically obese Benno Blimpie, who has locked the windows of his rented room, is eating himself to death. Seated above the action, he ceaselessly consumes ice cream and soda as he recalls his suffering as an unloved child. He envisions a grim death, his body a feast for the rats of the tenement. Into one long act the playwright compresses the horror of a lifetime lived as an outcast.

In *Gemini* Innaurato displays his creative impulse to write opera. This full-length work has been praised for its intense feelings, operatic tumult, and "hilariously funny ethnic types." Clive Barnes judged the work "immensely likable" with "ethnic and social jokes of considerable vigor and good nature." In the play, Francis Geminiani, who has come home from Harvard to celebrate his twenty-first birthday, undergoes a crisis of sexual identity. He is attracted to a younger schoolmate as well as to a friend's sister, both of whom pitch a tent under a fig tree in the backyard. There Francis is embarrassed by Bunny Lowenstein and her asthmatic child. The homefolk present further trouble, especially the doting father, who has lost his wife to another man and taken on a sensible but rapacious mistress. This is a comedy of penetrating social observation sharpened by the author's general feeling for both the ecstasy and the pain of human existence.

The drama critic Walter Kerr has praised Innaurato's language as "atonally musical, taut and tough as piano wire." The playwright believes that an appreciation of his plays requires a sensitivity to rhetoric. At a time when, in Innaurato's words, "everyone is oriented to the visual, to movies and TV, and this has affected theater as well," his attention to diction may be his forte as a major contemporary dramatist.

His genius for adapting to the times helped Innaurato make the transition from Broadway to television through *Verna: U.S.O. Girl*. He considers television the principal hope for drama in the future. *Verna*, a single-draft adaptation of the short story by Paul Gallico, features a singer-dancer of little talent who must decide whether to perform for wounded troops in a dangerous combat area during World War II or accept a handsome young officer's offer of marriage and safety. The dramatization adheres to the original story, with much of the narration taken directly from Gallico.

Poetry

From the external presentation of the drama, literary expression moves to the ultimate internal synthesis and verbal tension of poetry. For the first Italian immigrants, versified expression was a calculated response to a hostile society. An early poetic voice was that of Arturo Giovannitti, whose *Arrows in the Gale* (1914) had an introduction by Helen Keller. Eventually his *Collected Poems* (1962) was published with an introduction by Norman Thomas. A socialist and erstwhile editor of *Il Proletario*, Giovannitti wrote poems that reflect the long-standing conflict between labor and management.

The few who expressed themselves in verse came to identify with antiestablishment forces, perhaps because their creative endeavors went largely unnoticed. One of them described his experiences in writing: *The Autobiography of Emanuel Carnevali* (1967), compiled by Kay Boyle, tells how the author arrived at the age of sixteen in the United States in 1914 and became an avant-garde poet.

The rebellious spirit of the new immigrants eventually produced famous poets like Lawrence Ferlinghetti (b. 1919) and Gregory Nunzio Corso (b. 1930). Ferlinghetti, a universally recognized poet of the "beat generation" and a writer of "colloquial verse," writes comic and satiric poems that show the influence of the French poet Jacques Prévert, whom he has translated. Ferlinghetti has traveled widely to read his poetry in public. Among his many works are *Pictures of a Gone World* (1955), *A Coney Island of the Mind* (1967), *The Secret Meaning of Things* (1968), *Back Roads to Far Places* (1971), *Open Eye, Open Heart* (1973), and *Who Are We Now?* (1974). His poetry manifests breadth of vision and range in both form and content. His poems are spoken and sung, are often concerned with popular and political subjects, and may be delivered in a personal and lyrical style to communicate their meditative and satiric qualities. In the tradition of Kenneth Rexroth and Kenneth Patchen, Ferlinghetti takes an anarchist-pacifist position, viewing the poet as a force for radical humanism. This perspective also imbues his surrealist novel *Her* (1960).

Gregory Nunzio Corso also believes in communicating poetry through readings. His appearances in the West and Midwest in the 1950s popularized four of his eight books of poetry, one of which — *Marriage* — won the Longview Foundation Award in 1959. His *Selected Poems* (1962) and *Elegiac Feelings* (1970) are particularly characteristic. He has also written a novel, *The American Express* (1961); a play, *The Hung-Up Age*; and a book of poetry, *Heirlooms from The Future* (1978).

The revived interest in ethnicity has won an audience for poems that treat the emotional problems created by cultural assimilation. An expression of personal solace achieved through evocation is *Incarnation* (1974) by Gerard Malanga, whose poems span the years 1965 to 1971 and make reference to the Italian past and present. Similar ethnic poems are offered in *Delano in America and Other Early Poems* (1974) by John J. Soldo.

The ethnic poet bridges the gap between cultures by exalting the human condition. Much Italian-American verse is devoted to God, family, and the people. One poet who focuses on these subjects is Maria Vecchione, who, after writing prose and poetry in Italian, published a lyrical collection in English, *Bits of Stars* (1975). Using a variety of short forms including haiku, dockette, cinquain, cinquo, and tanka, Vecchione proves that words can serve to bond cultures. Most often the words exemplify ties between the Italian and the American.

Inevitably, with the increased skill in verse technique and in the use of English, poets like Angelo DeLuca and Joseph Tusiani emerged. Using traditional forms to give voice to social protest, DeLuca treats such subjects as travesty, parody, nostalgia, philosophy, and disciplined word-writing. His privately printed works have appeared under the titles *Book I*, *Book II*, and *Book III*. Other works include *Intimate Portraits of Long Ago* (1965) and *Elegy for a Friend* (1975).

In responding to the tension created by a dual ethnic loyalty, Joseph Tusiani shows the intense perception of the scholar-poet. An expert in Italian literature and translator of many Italian masterworks, he has the intellecutal and emotional breadth required for a sensitive interpretation of the Italian-American experience. His books of poetry include *Rind and All* (1962), *The Fifth Season* (1964), and *Gente Mia* (1978). The poetry of Tusiani brings to mind many of the qualities that distinguish the major English and American poets.

Another Italian-American poet who merits study is Robert Sebastian. He has used Italian subjects to comment on universal social conditions in the tradition of T. S. Eliot. In *Memoirs of a*

Paid Mourner (1973), Sebastian presents a series of dramatically conceived, expertly drawn, and candidly detailed poetic vignettes infused with both realism and nostalgia. Exacting in his choice of words, Sebastian offers felicitous insights into a society that he makes intensely human. Using Venetian settings, he portrays Italians and Italian Americans everywhere in a timeless manner.

An Italian American unversally accepted among the nation's established poets, John Ciardi has produced volumes of creative works. He has served as a distinguished educator and a poetry editor of *Saturday Review* from 1956 to 1972 and has received many literary awards, including the Prix de Rome of the American Academy of Letters.

Miller Williams has written that the poems of John Ciardi are "introspective, iconoclastic, humanistic, and world affirming, as straightforward as poetry is likely to be." The poems also exhibit a self-conscious presence like that in Dante, except that Dante is supernal, Ciardi terrestrial. Ciardi obviously feels himself to be the son of a region, a nation with "cultural roots running down to invisible and ancient rivers."[6] In the poem "Fragments from Italy," he writes, "One day I went to look at the Mediterranean and found myself on an infected hill." In "Poem for My Thirty-Ninth Birthday," he extends the particular when he says, "all men are their fathers and their sons / in a haunted house of mirrors to the end." Continuing his autobiographical musings, he confesses in "Autobiography of a Comedian" that he does not understand "presidents, popes, kings / ministers, marshals, or policemen" and that he does not know the "invisible people I killed for wings / when I was a gunner for our tribe." Like Mario Puzo, he evokes, in the same poem, the all-American metaphor, the game of chance:

> What we all pray to is the dice, the wheel
> and the holy jackpot. Have you seen
> the grandmothers praying at those steel
> altars where the heaven-eyes blink and wink
> fruit, bells, and dominion? It's God they feel
> coming at the next click.

His conclusion, however, is that we must have enough mercy not to love ourselves too much.

Like other Italian-American writers, Ciardi feels a sense of loss and of alienation, the need to identify with what has gone before. In "Tree Trimming," he weeps for his son, "who has no history, no name / he knows long, no ritual from which he came / and no fathers but the forgotten." Yet he maintains that Italy matters in the recall of family, the language, and the land. He imagines the land of his origin "as, somewhere in a thicket like the mind / a gargoyle might stare at running water. / What the Roman sun says to the Romans / I have said to you in all the tongues of sleep" ("Fragments From Italy"). At the same time, he voices anger at America, at the breaking of so many idols: "I remember the United States of America / As a flag-draped box with Arthur in it" ("A Box Comes Home"). Further channeling his inner turmoil into contemporary social criticism, he writes, "Everyone in my tribe hates / everyone in your tribe . . ./ we . . . / shall all finally kick all of your / heads. We are united" ("My Tribe").

Perhaps the reason John Ciardi so well personifies the Italian American is that, surviving a loss of faith in society and its structure, he maintains his belief in the individual, a civilized member of an invisible state. As Miller Williams has said, the struggle that is within Ciardi is a struggle, not of the man against himself, but of the man against a void he seeks to fill (p.16). In writing about this struggle, Ciardi appeals to both the mind and the heart; he seeks confirmation of the family of people and of the relativity of things. He tells us that the world is a happy place where "A man can survive anything except not caring" ("Joshua on Eighth Avenue").

In recent years I have published numerous volumes of poetry dealing with the creative artist and the American ideal: *To Reason Why, The Violet and the Flame, Primo Vino, Seventy-Six for Philadelphia, Woman, The Second Coming, Lauding the American Dream, Songs of Ourselves, Century Four,* and *The Pennsylvania People.*

Italian-American creative writers substantiate the cultural isolation of the newcomer in America. Their ethnically oriented works, so many of which focus on their sense of being out of place, have manifested a constructive attitude toward human relationships emanating from a tradition of self-discipline. The Italian-American novelists, dramatists, and poets, performing with literary proficiency and social awareness, are beginning to receive an audience commensurate with their talents. Gallico, Puzo, Innaurato, and Ciardi are but a few of the current masters who serve as predecessors of and inspiration to the Italian-

American men and women who will add their voices to tomorrow's American literature.

Notes

[1] See Margherita Marchione, ed. and trans., *Philip Mazzei: Jefferson's "Zealous Whig"* (Rutherford, N.J.: Fairleigh Dickinson Univ. Press, 1976).

[2] Rose Basile Green, *The Italian-American Novel: A Document of the Interaction of Two Cultures* (Rutherford, N.J.: Fairleigh Dickinson Univ. Press, 1974).

[3] Robert E. Spiller et al., eds., *Literary History of the United States* (New York: Macmillan, 1948), 2 vols.

[4] Donald Heiney, *Recent American Literature* (Great Neck, N.Y.: Barron's, 1958), p.3.

[5] Michael Novak, *The Rise of the Unmeltable Ethnics* (New York: Macmillan, 1972).

[6] Miller Williams, *The Achievement of John Ciardi* (Glenview, Ill.: Scott, Foresman, 1969). pp. 1-2.

Jewish-American Literature

Richard Tuerk

In an essay entitled "The Jew as Modern American Writer" (1966), Alfred Kazin writes: "Definitely, it was now the thing to be Jewish."[1] And in a book published in 1969, Donald L. Kaufman writes that in America, "the new look in postwar writing is Jewish."[2] In an introduction published the next year, Charles Angoff and Meyer Levin declare: "To 'write Jewish' is in fashion."[3] When viewed in a historical perspective, these statements are startling. As recently as 1944, Lionel Trilling proclaimed that "as the Jewish community now exists, it can give no sustenance to the American artist or intellectual who is born a Jew." But as Irving Malin and Irwin Stark point out in the introduction to *Breakthrough* (1964), "circumstances have radically changed"; a group of Jewish-American authors has "broken through" into the mainstream of American literature and become "an important, possibly even a major reformative influence in American life and letters."[4] Yet, as Abraham Chapman observes in the introduction to his anthology, *Jewish-American Literature* (1974), until very recently in America, the Jewish author "has been viewed as an alien in the prevailing American culture unless the writing had nothing to do with Jews or anything Jewish."[5]

Of course, all these statements oversimplify somewhat. In addition, all contain problems of definition; for example, exactly what do these writers mean when they use the word "Jew," and what does "Jewish-American" mean in the phrase "Jewish-American literature"? Although these questions may appear trivial, they are of the utmost importance to those who write about and teach Jewish-American — and, indeed, American—literature.

Before discussing Jewish-American literature, we must try to arrive at a workable definition of the word "Jew." According to Orthodox Jewish tradition, a Jew is anyone born of a Jewish mother or anyone formally converted to Judaism. Yet even this definition presents problems for the teacher of literature. Are persons who have converted away from Judaism still Jews? Large segments of the Gentile world would consider them Jews, as great numbers of converts in Europe discovered during the Hitler era. In America in the last quarter of the twentieth century, however, where total assimilation seems possible, the old saying "Once a Jew, always a Jew" no longer seems true. Instead, the word "Jew" now seems for many people to imply conscious choice. Abraham Chapman classifies as a Jew anyone of Jewish descent or any person who considers himself or herself a Jew. In his anthology of Jewish-American literature Chapman includes works by Bret Harte and Denise Levertov, the former because he had a Jewish grandfather and the latter because her father converted from Judaism and became an Anglican priest. Harte's and Levertov's ancestry would undoubtedly lead many non-Jews to call those two writers Jews. For purposes of this essay, anyone is a Jew who, as a result of either birth or conversion, whether formal or informal, *considers* himself or herself a Jew. Although, as we shall see, in connection with literature this definition probably presents as many problems as any other definition, it does give us something to work with.

Next, how do we define "Jewish-American literature"? Essentially, it is, of course, literature written by American Jews; it does not have to deal specifically with the ethnic dimension. There are many writers like J. D. Salinger whose writings rarely reflect their Jewishness. But, given the limitations of space, I have concerned myself with those works by American Jews who seem particularly or consciously concerned with their Jewishness. I recognize that even this perspective is insufficient and troublesome, for what happens to a work like *An American Dream,* by Norman Mailer? Mailer is a Jew (in a series of reviews in *Commentary,* he calls himself a "non-Jewish Jew"), and his main character, Stephen Rojack, is "half Jewish," whatever that means. Rojack's ascendance over the Irish Catholic Kennedy involves a definite ethnic dimension, but, except for mentioning that he is "descended from peddlers," Rojack's Jewishness (or lack of Jewishness) is minimally developed.[6] Then again, even though essays have been written about, say, the Jewishness of Saul Bellow's novel *Henderson the Rain King,* the book still has no Jews in it. If we looked at Jewish-American literature as that which is in some way *consciously concerned* with the authors' Jewishness, recognizing that this is an abbreviated perspective, perhaps we can understand its success and examine the impact this extensive body of literature has made on American literary history and culture.

The works that fit into this category as we have defined it have certain tendencies in common. In their introduction to *Breakthrough,* Malin and Stark summarize these tendencies: "the American-Jewish writer has approached the divine by seeking to make his way to what is most human"; he searches "in the Old Country or New, in the image of the father or in the discoverable if unrecoverable past." Sometimes, "he violently assaults the corrupt values of his society, endeavors to mediate between the dualities which divide him from himself, recognizes suffering as the necessary condition of compassion, insists on the sanctity of life or—in the face of man's alienation from man as well as from God,—reasserts...the centrality of love, in the reconstruction of the social order."⁷ These, then, are some of the central concerns of the authors of Jewish-American literature.

Jews in America

During the second half of the twentieth century, a large proportion of the major authors in American literature have been Jewish Americans, and many of their books have dealt with explicitly Jewish concerns, but this, as I have indicated, was not always so. Although Jews have been present in this nation continuously since before the Revolution, only recently have they begun to have a great impact on American literature. The first identifiable Jew in North America, Elias Legardo, came to Virginia in 1621. The first group of Jews arrived in New Amsterdam in 1654. They were fleeing from Brazil, which had just been taken over by Portugal, and the Portuguese had followed their usual practice of expelling all Jews who would not convert to Christianity. Because the Jews had fled originally from Spain and Portugal to Holland and from there had gone to parts of Brazil then under Dutch control, they naturally sought refuge in Dutch possessions. Most moved to the Dutch West Indies, but twenty-three sailed to New Amsterdam. Although Peter Stuyvesant did not want Jews settling there, the directors of the Dutch West India Company allowed them to stay. Of course, Jews have been present in New Amsterdam, later New York, ever since.

By 1776 about 2,500 Jews lived in America. Until about 1729 most of the Jews in North America were of Sephardic—that is, Spanish and Portuguese—descent. And even in 1852, when Henry Wadsworth Longfellow wrote his poem, "The Jewish Cemetery at Newport," names like Abraham Alvares and Jacob Rivera were typical of American Jews. In 1830 there were only about 6,000 Jews in America, but by 1880 the number had grown to 250,000, largely as a result of large-scale immigration of German Jews. The defeat of Napoleon, who had done much to emancipate European Jewry, and the failure of the Revolution of 1848 caused many German Jews to come to this country and establish Jewish institutions here. The largest wave of immigrants, however, came between about 1881 and 1924, the period of the great migration, when approximately 2,750,000 Jews moved from Eastern Europe to the United States. Many fled from persecution, discrimination, and pogroms. Others sought economic and political equality and opportunity as well as religious freedom. Part of the group called the "new immigrants," these Eastern European Jews are the ancestors of about ninety percent of the Jews in America today.

The passage of restrictive immigration legislation in the early 1920s started to have a profound effect in 1924, and the waves of Jewish immigrants slowed to a trickle. Nonetheless, by 1924 the center of world Jewish culture had shifted from Europe to America.

Early Jewish-American Literature

No identifiable body of Jewish-American literature existed before the beginning of the twentieth century. Although several Jews wrote creative works, especially plays and poems, their writings are for the most part indistinguishable from works by non-Jews. Jewish authors before the twentieth century include Samuel B. H. Judah, Jonas B. Phillips, Isaac Harby, and Mordecai Manuel Noah. The most outstanding of these is Noah, who, although he tried to establish a Jewish state on Grand Island in the Niagara River, did not allow his plays to reflect his Jewishness. Penina Moise and Adah Isaacs Menken were nineteenth-century American Jews who wrote verse, and their verse did reflect their Jewishness. But even though Menken's verse reached a fairly large audience, she hardly achieved the distinction of Emma Lazarus, who was the only truly outstanding Jewish author before the turn of the century.

Lazarus was born in 1849. Her family traced its roots to pre-Revolutionary America. She avoided Jewish themes in her early work. But her meetings with Jewish immigrants who had fled persecution in Eastern Europe, her knowledge of the pogroms in Russia, and the publication of George Eliot's *Daniel Deronda* (1876) stirred Lazarus into asserting her Jewish identity in spite of her relatives' pleas that she not do so. As Sol Liptzin puts it, she was "shocked into dynamic activity by the suffering of Jews who had been victimized solely because of their Jewishness."[8] Her most famous poem is, of course, "The New Colossus" (1883), which is inscribed on the pedestal of the Statue of Liberty. Allen Guttmann considers Lazarus "Too derivative to be considered a major poet," but he says that "her passionate return to an identification with her ancestors makes her a forerunner of others who responded similarly to pogroms and. . .to the catastrophic exterminations of the 1940s." Guttman hails her volume of 1882, *Songs of a Semite,* as America's "first important work of Jewish poetry."[9]

It was, however, the new immigrants and their children who began what we today think of as Jewish-American literature.[10] In their accounts—both fiction and nonfiction—of their lives in the Old World, their journeys to the New World, and their problems adapting to life in America are to be found the material out of which modern Jewish-American literature grew. Most of these works remain period pieces, mere curiosities for the student of American literature or American culture. Several, however, give profound insight into the problems Jews faced in trying to adjust to the new culture they found in America. Some, like Mary Antin's autobiographical volume, *The Promised Land* (1912), may be read as songs in praise of assimilation. Others, like Abraham Cahan's classic immigrant novel, *The Rise of David Levinsky* (1917), seriously question the assimilationist ethic.

In *The Promised Land,* Antin explicitly uses the biblical Exodus as the structuring metaphor for her own journey from Russia to Boston. America is her promised land, and, to her, that promise lies in assimilation. In America, she was "made over"; as an American, she experienced a "second birth."[11] In the concluding paragraph of her book, she declares: "The endless ages have indeed throbbed through my blood, but a new rhythm dances in my veins," and she adds: "America is the youngest of the nations and inherits all that went before in history. And I am the youngest of America's children, and into my hands is given all her priceless heritage. . . . Mine is the whole majestic past, and mine is the shining future" (p. 364). She no longer feels that she is in exile; America is her Jerusalem. Just as she herself has, she thinks, become thoroughly assimilated into American life, she feels that all other immigrants can and should do the same.

But for many, the price of assimilation—giving up one's religion, one's language (usually Yiddish), and one's ties to one's point of origin—was too high. Many Jewish immigrants still felt themselves to be in exile even in America. And for them Antin's promised land was a place where they continued to eat the bread of affliction. One of those who seriously weighed the losses against the gains was Abraham Cahan. Born in 1860, just outside Vilna, Cahan received a secular education in Russia before he came to America in 1882, at the beginning of the waves of immigrants who were to change the face of Jewish America. He became active in union and socialist activities and helped organize the *Jewish Daily Forward,* a Yiddish-language news-paper begun in 1897; he became its editor in 1902 and held that position until his death in 1951. That he should have questioned the ethic of assimilation is ironic, for through his column, "A Bintel Brief," in the *Forward,* he hastened the Americanization and eventual assimilation of countless Jews. Even though he could hardly have been called religious, he expressed outrage at the idea of a Jewish family's having a Christmas tree, but he also assured worried Jewish parents that playing baseball would not hurt their sons. In fact, he praised this American sport because it got the children outdoors and helped keep them healthy. In "A Bintel Brief," Cahan obviously saw his role as trying to enable his fellow Jews to come to grips with the day-to-day problems that beset them in America, and for them, Americanization seemed the best answer. Nonetheless, in his more serious literary work— his fiction—Cahan made it clear that he was not so sure.

As early as 1896, when he published *Yekl: A Tale of the New York Ghetto,* Cahan questioned whether Jews gained more than they lost when they embraced the American ethic with its premium on material goods. Even this early in his career he wondered whether the Old Country ways might not have been better. In the title story of *The Imported Bridegroom and Other Stories of the New York Ghetto* (1898) Old and New World values clash directly; New World values win, but as a result, everyone is unhappy.

It is in his masterpiece, *The Rise of David Levinsky* (1917), that Cahan examines most thoroughly the effects of the desire for assimilation. Levinsky grows up in Antomir in Russia. His poor but pious mother wants nothing more than to see her son become a talmudic scholar. But when David comes home after an encounter in which some Gentile children rolling Easter eggs split his lip and tear off his cap, she runs into the street screaming that she is going to kill the boy who hurt her son. Fifteen minutes later she is carried home, mortally wounded; she dies the same evening. After continuing his talmudic studies and receiving board from various members of the community, David comes to America. Like Mary Antin, David says that his arrival in the New World was "like a second birth" in which he entered "a new world in the profoundest sense of the word."[12] In America, Levinsky quickly loses his devotion to Judaism: he shaves off his beard, cuts his sidelocks, stops studying the Talmud, and develops a desire, never fulfilled, to study at New York's City College. Instead, like so many real-life Jewish immigrants, he goes into the garment business, first as a worker and then as a manufacturer. He becomes tremendously successful, but he is unhappy. Accordingly, he concludes his narrative by confessing:

> I don't seem to be able to get accustomed to my luxurious life. I am always more or less conscious of my good clothes, of the high quality of my office furniture, of the power I wield over the men in my pay. . . . I still have a lurking fear of restaurant waiters.
>
> I can never forget the days of my misery. I cannot escape from my old self. My past and my present do not comport well. David, the poor lad swinging over a Talmud volume at the Preacher's synagogue, seems to have more in common with my inner identity than David Levinsky, the well-known cloak manufacturer. (p.530)

Neither wholly an American nor wholly a Jew, David ends in a kind of no-man's-land without any identity that he can understand.

Between the extremes of assimilation, as achieved by Antin and sought by Levinsky, and alienation, which involves total refusal to accommodate oneself in any way to one's new home, lies acculturation, a kind of middle ground that enables one to remain a Jew, even a "good" Jew, and still be an American. In *The Rise of David Levinsky,* the Kaplans represent this middle

position. Their American-born son Ruby studies the Talmud, and
when Ruby reads the Talmud in Hebrew and interprets it in
Yiddish, David is reminded of himself at age eleven when he read
the Talmud while his mother beamed exactly as Mrs. Kaplan
beams at Ruby. Mr. Kaplan even reminds David that "One has to
be a Jew," advice that David does not heed (pp. 396–98).

The drive for assimilation or even for acculturation becomes a central issue in Jewish-American literature during the
twentieth century. For some Jewish authors and Jewish characters, being a Jew seems to be unpleasant; they flee in horror
from their ethnic and religious identity, or they describe their
fellow Jews as crass, vulgar, materialistic, and ugly. Authors who
fit into this category are often labeled self-hating Jews or even
anti-Semitic Jews. Such labels, however, may often be misleading,
and their use by critics may be even more misleading. Among
authors who have perhaps rightfully been given these labels is
Montague Glass, whose *Potash and Perlmutter* (1910) humor-
ously treats two partners in the garment industry whose lives
consist of a series of shady deals and narrow escapes. Yet I doubt
that readers of this book in the second half of the twentieth
century find it nearly as offensive as Jewish readers of the first
half of the century found it. True, its characters are, for the most
part, unpleasant, and their desire to make deals and get money
plays on negative stereotypes. But a genuine friendship develops
between Potash and Perlmutter, with each for the most part
willing to take considerable risks for the other. Another author
who at least in one phase of his career seems to deserve these
labels is Ben Hecht, who in the beginning of his novel, *A Jew in
Love* (1931), wrote of "Jew faces in which race leers and burns
like some biological disease."[13] But Hecht later became an
outspoken Zionist and defender of the Jews.

In fact, the list of authors who have been accused of putting
their "Jewish self-hate" on paper at times reads like an honor roll
of Jewish-American authors: Abraham Cahan, Meyer Levin,
Ludwig Lewisohn, Herbert Gold, Irving Howe, Alfred Kazin,
Louis Untermeyer, Philip Roth, and even Isaac Bashevis Singer. As
many critics are now recognizing and as several recognized even
before 1920, whenever a Jewish writer describes Jews realistically, he or she is liable to be accused of being a Jewish anti-
Semite. The usual argument runs that it would be fine to write
realistic fiction in Yiddish and not allow it to be translated into
English, but to write in English or to permit such works to be

translated into English allows Gentiles to see them, thus making the author into an anti-Semite who wants to destroy the image of the Jew in the eyes of non-Jews. In *A Young Man in Search of Love* (1978), one of his autobiographical volumes, Singer presents a variation on this theme when he tells of his editor's saying to him:

> Why write about thieves and whores when there were so many decent Jewish men and devoted Jewish wives? If such a thing were translated into Polish and a gentile read it, he might conclude that all Jews were depraved. A Yiddish writer...was honor-bound to stress the good in our people, the lofty and sacred. He had to be an eloquent defender of the Jews, not their defamer.[14]

Similar questions have been asked of Jewish authors in America by their fellow Jews who possibly see in realistic accounts of Jews with both good and bad points a threat to their own precarious position in the United States. These attacks tend to have no relation to time and space; even though they may occur sixty years apart, the charges and the responses to them tend to be the same.[15]

The defenders of the realistic works point out that the Jewish author has just as much right as any other author to portray people in all of their complexity and that a treatment of an evil or bad Jewish character in fiction will make no one but the already committed anti-Semite think that all Jews are bad or evil. They also, at times, point out that the critics, by seeing the work as a condemnation of Judaism and Jews, are often misreading the piece of literature. Two fairly recent examples are Budd Schulberg's novel *What Makes Sammy Run?* (1941) and Philip Roth's short story "Defender of the Faith" (1959).[16] Both stories have been condemned because they have unpleasant characters: in the former, Sammy Glick, who among other things runs from his Jewishness; in the latter, Sheldon Grossbart, who uses his Jewishness to get special favors for himself. What the negative critics overlook is that neither Glick nor Grossbart sets the moral standards in the stories, and neither is necessarily the central character in the work. In fact, the moral standards are in each work set by the narrator: Al Manheim in Schulberg's book and Nathan Marx in Roth's story. Neither of these characters actively renounces his Judaism; in fact, Marx is reembracing it. And these two may be the central characters in these two works.

Another important aspect of early Jewish-American literature is Yiddish drama. Although Yiddish theater still exists in America, its heyday is long past. Though it served primarily to provide an escape for Jewish-American immigrants from their daily drudgery, Yiddish theater nonetheless helped introduce some to the ways and customs of America and provided to a limited extent some genuine works of art for its audiences. In spite of some American settings, however, the dramas for the most part, critics agree, lie in the tradition of European Yiddish theater rather than Jewish-American literature. In fact, one scholar asserts, "Yiddish literature in substance is *purely* Jewish" and adds, "Geographically, Yiddish literature is in two parts, Russian and American, but these two parts developed into one aim; even the plots and themes are from the old country; the aim was for Yiddish literature to stand independently and self-sustaining among the literatures of the world." This same scholar feels that when Yiddish literature became aware of "world struggles in politics, economics, problems of other religious and ethnic groups," when "an involvement with desolation in a world bereft of morality and justice, infiltrated Yiddish literature," it "became anemic."[17] Nonetheless, the Yiddish theater in America was so popular from before the turn of the century to World War I that something about it must be included here.

Abraham Goldfaden is regarded as the father of modern Yiddish theater. Born in the Ukraine in 1840, he began his acting career in the plays given at Purim time, performances believed to be descended from the simple plays that used to dramatize the Book of Esther. He later modeled the early shows he produced on his experiences in the Purim entertainments. For a while he worked with the Broder Singers in Romania, but soon engaged his own actors and singers and formed a troupe that toured Russia and Romania.

In 1883 a Russian edict prohibited the performance of Yiddish plays, so Yiddish theater companies moved, first to countries near Russia and eventually westward, often first to London and then to the United States, where they found large Yiddish-speaking communities eager for entertainment in their native tongue. In 1887 Goldfaden was invited by some of his actors to join them in New York City, but when he got there, he found such severe competition from established producers and scriptwriters that he went back to Europe. He returned to the

United States in 1903, however, and remained until his death in 1908.

In the meantime, Yiddish theater flourished in cities like Cleveland, Detroit, Chicago, Philadelphia, and especially New York. The first Yiddish production in New York was probably *The Selling of Joseph,* put on by an amateur group in the 1860s. In August 1882 the first professional performance of a Yiddish play in America probably took place. Among the actors was Boris Thomashefsky, born in the Ukraine in 1868. Even though he was young, he is supposed to have been instrumental in getting the players invited to America.[18] Before the turn of the century Thomashefsky was running the People's Theater. He wrote original plays and adapted others like *Hamlet* (1893) and *Richard III* (1895) for the Yiddish stage. In 1912 he built the National Theater in New York, where Yiddish drama flourished until after his death in 1939.

By the early years of the twentieth century the "golden epoch" of Yiddish theater in America had begun. At first, the Yiddish shows appealed to sentimentality. The plays depended on *zingen un tantsen* (singing and dancing); used stock comedy situations, often with American settings; and allowed the actors to improvise as they saw fit. Still, several producers tried to introduce artistry into Yiddish theater. They encouraged Yiddish writers and, like Thomashefsky, translated works from other languages, usually adapting them for the Yiddish stage. The most famous play of this sort is Jacob Gordin's *Yiddish King Lear,* produced in 1892 with Jacob Adler, the matinee idol, in the leading role.

In 1918 Ukrainian-born Maurice Schwartz started in New York City the Jewish Art Theater, dedicated to producing artistically excellent dramas. The Jewish Art Theater lasted until 1950. An attempt to revive it in 1955 failed. After trying unsuccessfully to make motion pictures, Schwartz went to Israel hoping to establish a Yiddish art center, but he died in 1960, two months after opening in *Yoshe Kalb,* a play that he had earlier adapted from I. J. Singer's novel of that name.

The most important figure in the American Yiddish theater and one of the most important figures in world Yiddish theater is Jacob Gordin. Born in the Ukraine in 1853, he fled Russia for political reasons and arrived in America in 1891. Although before he came to America he had never written in Yiddish and never written a play, during about eighteen years of activity he supplied the Yiddish theater with almost eighty plays. Most were adaptations and translations in which he introduced natural Yiddish in place of Germanized dialogue and demanded that his actors stick to the scripts. Several of his plays are considered of lasting value, including *God, Man and Devil* (1900) and the previously mentioned *Yiddish King Lear.*

Other prolific playwrights include Moshe Hurwitz and Joseph Lateiner, who between them wrote about 180 mostly sentimental plays. Leon Kobrin wrote over thirty plays, including realistic dramas that try to give a faithful picture of life in America at the turn of the century.

The most outstanding works of Yiddish literature for the stage were written not in America, however, but in Eastern Europe. Sholem Asch's *God of Vengeance* was first produced in 1907, before he came to America. And the most famous and probably best Yiddish play is *The Dybbuk* by S. An-Ski, a pseudonym for Solomon Zainwill Rapoport, who died thirty days before his play was first produced, on 9 December 1920 by the Vilna Troupe. Both these plays remain powerful on the stage today, and both are available in paperback.[19] With its emphasis on spirituality and its exorcism scene, *The Dybbuk* is especially moving.

By World War I the Jewish population of the Lower East Side of New York City was beginning to move away, and many younger Jews were unfamiliar with Yiddish. Thus, the Yiddish theaters in New York and elsewhere were losing their audiences. The theaters began to close. Even though Maurice Schwartz, as previously noted, kept his theater open until 1950, the golden epoch was past. Occasionally Yiddish plays are still produced in New York City and elsewhere, especially on university campuses, and as recently as 1968 Yiddish actors derived income from engagements at holiday resorts during the summers. But for the most part, Yiddish theater no longer functions as a living, vital force in America.

Jewish-American Literature between the Wars

During the 1920s and 1930s Jewish life in America became increasingly complex as various pressures, both internal and external, were exerted on the Jewish-American community. As Sol Liptzin puts it, "Jewish life increased in complexity and difficulty even while the environmental forces of assimilation kept nibbling away at Jewish essence." And he adds that anti-Semitism, "which could formerly be dismissed as a mild irritant, began to take on virile forms as poisonous Nazi doctrines drifted across the Atlantic" (p.172). Liptzin, of course, oversimplifies here. During the period before the Nazi takeover of Germany, many authors could not and did not dismiss anti-Semitism as a "mild irritant." Especially during the 1920s, many American authors responded with dismay to the anti-Semitism they found in America.

Born in Russia in 1882 and reared in the Midwest, Elias Tobenkin, a relatively minor author, questions the possibility of acculturation for Jews in an America that was, he felt, becoming increasingly anti-Semitic. Although in his first novel, *Witte Arrives* (1916), he espouses the ethic of the melting pot, in his third novel, *God of Might* (1925), he mirrors the bewilderment of a lot of American Jews who had begun to think that the doctrine of the melting pot involved not acculturation but complete assimilation, including giving up one's Jewishness altogether. In the first novel, Witte finally arrives when he decides that religious and ethnic differences are unimportant and that he will marry a Gentile of New England stock. In *God of Might*, the central character, Samuel Waterman, does marry a Gentile, only to discover that both small town America, where he lives, and big city America, in which he seeks refuge, demand either complete assimilation, including conversion, or total alienation of the Jew. In the course of his attempts to fulfill what he believes to be the American dream of individual freedom, Samuel discovers discrimination against Jews in banks, schools, universities, hotels, and apartment houses. He also becomes painfully aware of the anti-Semitism of Henry Ford and of the Ku Klux Klan.[20]

Ludwig Lewisohn is probably the foremost chronicler of American anti-Semitism before the 1930s. In his autobiographical volumes, *Up Stream* (1922) and *Mid-Channel* (1929), he describes his own struggles against anti-Semitism. Born in Berlin in 1882, Lewisohn came to America when he was seven years old. His family settled in South Carolina, where Lewisohn was brought up a Methodist. When he went to Columbia University to do graduate work, however, he discovered that the rest of the world did not care what he considered himself; the rest of the world considered him a Jew. Deprived of a graduate assistantship and of a job teaching English literature because he was a Jew (not until he was sixty did he get such a position, and that was at Brandeis University), Lewisohn found a job teaching German at a midwestern university. In his autobiographical volumes he describes his disillusionment with academic life, with the Midwest, and with American life in general; more important for our purposes, he describes his growing acceptance of and finally his love for his identity as a Jew.

In Jewishness Lewisohn eventually found all kinds of positive values. His final affirmation of his identity as a Jew was expressed through his espousal of Zionism; in his writing it is expressed in his novel *The Island Within* (1928), largely the story of Arthur Levy, a New York–born descendant of Jews who moved from Eastern Europe through Germany and eventually to America. Arthur and his sister Hazel experience repeated difficulties because of their lack of a firm Jewish identity, and in his profession as a psychiatrist, Arthur sees extreme examples of what Lewisohn believes can happen to Jews who lack a firm Jewish identity. After Arthur marries a Gentile and has a son, he starts to become more and more conscious of his inextricable ties to Judaism. His marriage falls apart, but he finally discovers "that Jews like himself who denied any tradition or character of their own were really trying to do a thing that was unhuman, that no one else was trying to do." For him, being a Jew and being human coincide.[21]

Another outstanding Jewish author of fiction about Jews was Anzia Yezierska. Born in the Russian Pale in 1885, she arrived in New York when she was sixteen; she was most active as a writer during the 1920s. In her fiction she gives voice to the feelings of the women immigrants who wanted to make a place for themselves in the New World. Her first collection of stories, *Hungry Hearts* (1920), contains the basic idea that runs through her other works: no matter how bad America may be, it still has possibilities of becoming, as Mary Antin puts it, the promised land. In her novel of 1925, *Bread Givers,* Yezierska's central character, Sara Smolinsky, has to break away from her domineering father, who spends his time, he claims, studying the Talmud, who demands that his daughters act as his bread givers—that is, support him—and who arranges terrible marriages for several of them. Sara finally leaves her home, gets a college education, and becomes a teacher, a road that many of her real-life contemporaries followed. At the end of the novel, she is even able to understand and accept her father.

The outstanding works of Jewish-American fiction to appear during the 1930s were Michael Gold's *Jews without Money* (1930), Henry Roth's *Call it Sleep* (1934), and Meyer Levin's *The Old Bunch* (1937). Many generalizations may be made about the Jewish-American literature of the Great Depression. For example, Angoff and Levin characterize the decade as one during which "writers" thought that "readers would not care to identify with Jewish fictional characters." Consequently, many Jewish "writers who had begun. . . by writing about people and backgrounds with which they were familiar soon abandoned Jewish material or falsified it." Others "tried to write honestly about the Jewish life they knew,. . . even attained critical acclaim," but "grew bitter over the lack of reader response and over publishing pressure to abandon such material" (pp. 10–11). Some, most notably Henry Roth, stopped writing. Guttmann writes of "the novels of generational conflict" of the 1930s and 1940s (p. 34). And Liptzin characterizes the 1930s as "the decade of the uprooted and estranged Jewish intellectuals," whom he calls "Jewish saplings that had wrested themselves loose from the cultural earth of their fathers and transplanted themselves in the rich soil of their adopted culture." Yet

> their roots were severely damaged and their healthy growth impaired. . . . Revolting against both American and Jewish realities, they took refuge in hedonism, aestheticism, communism and psychoanalytic self-dissection. (p. 180)

Obviously, Liptzin is far too emotional in his condemnation of the writers of the decade. And as the three works mentioned at the beginning of this paragraph attest, the 1930s did produce some outstanding Jewish-American literature.

Michael Gold was born as Irwin Granich in New York in 1893; he grew up on the Lower East Side. By 1930 he was editing the *New Masses* and trying, of course, to win people to communism. In *Jews without Money* he presents a sympathetic picture of the immigrants and their children. The novel is largely autobiographical, and the narrator is a thinly disguised version of Gold himself. Especially poignant are his recollections of his parents and their dismay with a New World that was certainly not their promised land. His father uses the by-then ubiquitous

words, "A curse on Columbus! A curse on America, the thief!"—
words repeated often in the Jewish-American literature of the
1920s and 1930s, usually in Yiddish. And his mother expresses
her nostalgia for the forests of her youth with the words, "Ach,
America, the thief, where children only see dry, dead mushrooms
in grocery stores."[22] In spite of his avowed antireligious, communist sympathies, Gold gives a touching, realistic description of
the poverty-stricken Jews living on the Lower East Side during
the first two decades of the twentieth century; only in the last
few pages does he give vent to his communist ideas. In spite of
its many flaws, which critics have examined extensively, Gold's
novel remains a touching, insightful description of the lives of
ghetto Jews in New York.

Call It Sleep, by Austrian-born Henry Roth, however, has
been justly hailed as a masterpiece. In Roth's story of the
conflicts between David Schaerl and his father, Albert, the critic
Daniel Walden, for example, finds re-created "the inner pain of
the second generation and its social and familial roots."[23] And
Guttmann hails the novel as the "classic study of second-
generation childhood" (p.49). David's attempts to come to grips
with his father's violence and his mother's overpowering love
lead him into a chain of deceit that culminates in his questioning
aloud something his father has been questioning in silence: is he
the child of Albert Schaerl or of a Gentile with whom his mother,
Genya, had an affair before she met Albert? Albert explodes, and
David flees to the streets in panic. In his misery, he thrusts a milk
dipper into the third rail of an electrified railway. After he almost
dies from the shock, he is taken home, where Albert, for the first
time in the story, shows true compassion for his son. Albert is
probably able to show this compassion because he has finally
spoken openly to Genya of his doubts and she has reassured him
that David is indeed his child. Numerous critics have recognized
Roth's debts to James Joyce and Sigmund Freud, but the overall
story is entirely original. The book, however, lapsed into
oblivion, to be resurrected in 1960, when it was reprinted and
recognized as a masterpiece.

Meyer Levin's *The Old Bunch* treats the generational
conflicts of twenty boys and girls who grew up on the West Side
of Chicago, Levin's native city. The novel moves from 1921 to
1934 as Levin evokes a lost era in America's history. The account
of the conflict between his bobby-soxers and their boyfriends,
on the one hand, and their immigrant parents with their old

country ways, on the other, enables Levin to investigate sympathetically the problems of adjusting to America. Although *The Old Bunch* was, as noted earlier, attacked as an example of Jewish anti-Semitism, Levin himself became a leader in the raising of Jewish consciousness and a strong supporter of Israel, where he spent most of his last days, and his novel is now regarded as one of the monuments of Jewish-American literature.

In a later story, "After All I Did for Israel" (1951), Levin illustrates the conflicting attitudes of many older American Jews toward the Jewish state, the desire to see to it that Israel continues to exist but also the hope that one's own children will not move to Israel. The central character in the story feels that he has been betrayed by the Jewish state, for which he worked so hard to raise funds, when he discovers that his son has decided to settle there.[24]

Other important Jewish-American works of the 1930s include Hecht's *A Jew in Love* and Jerome Weidman's *I Can Get It for You Wholesale* (1937), Daniel Fuch's Williamsburg Trilogy—*Summer in Williamsburg* (1934), *Homage to Blenholt* (1936), and *Low Company* (1937)—and Albert Halper's novel, *The Chute* (1937).

World War II and After

The 1940s were, of course, momentous for Jewish Americans and for Jewish-American authors. The defeat of Hitler and the founding of the state of Israel caused many Jews who had not previously been concerned with their identity as Jews to reassess their situations. A revivification of Jewish consciousness occurred as Hitler's racist policies convinced many Jews that they were only deluding themselves by believing that they could escape their Jewishness through total assimilation, including conversion to Christianity. On the more positive side, the founding of Israel in 1948 brought ethnic pride to many American Jews who felt that they had in a sense survived the Nazi attempts at genocide only through an accident of birth and that European Jews had been abandoned by most of the civilized world, including Britain and the United States. Nonetheless, in helping to found Israel, that same civilized world—especially the United States—acknowledged, many American Jews felt, that Jews too had a place in the universe. This feeling of ethnic pride was, of course, reinforced by the Sinai Campaign of 1956, the Six-Day War of 1967, and the Yom Kippur War of 1973. Many American Jews felt a new sense of Jewishness, and this sense quickly manifested itself in literature. A popular manifestation was *Gentleman's Agreement* (1947) by Laura Hobson, daughter of Michael Zametkin, a Yiddish writer. In spite of its shallowness and sentimentality, Hobson's book does explore some of the problems, especially social ones, that the Jew faces in America and does denounce people who practice even less virulent forms of anti-Semitism.

During the 1940s Sholem Asch published *East River* (1946), a sentimental view of first- and second-generation American Jews in their attempts to become acculturated or assimilated. He also treated this subject in several earlier works, most notably *Uncle Moses* (1917; English trans. 1920). Asch was constantly at the center of various controversies, especially following the publication of his "Christological Trilogy"—*The Nazarene* (1939), *The Apostle* (1943), and *Mary* (1950). He wrote these three novels in an attempt to bring together Jew and Gentile; they represent Asch's desire somehow to undo the horrors of the Hitler era. But they succeeded only in creating a rift between Asch and many of his fellow American Jews, a rift so wide that the Polish-born Asch finally left America (he had become a citizen in 1920) and settled in Israel in 1956.[25]

Probably the most important events in Jewish-American literature in the 1940s, however, were the publication of first novels by Norman Mailer and Saul Bellow. Mailer's explicit treatment of Judaism and Jewishness is limited. His own negative-positive identification of himself as a Jew (as we have seen, he calls himself "a non-Jewish Jew"), is reflected in his ambiguous attitude toward Jews in his works. In his first novel, *The Naked and the Dead* (1948), still considered his master-piece by many critics, two Jewish characters—Privates Roth and Goldstein—figure prominently; Roth revolts against being identified as a Jew whereas Goldstein quietly accepts his Jewishness. But these two are not the central figures in this novel. Instead, it centers on Sergeant Croft, Lieutenant Hearn, and General Cummings as they lead soldiers attempting to capture a Japanese-held island in the Pacific during World War II.

In his later novels. Mailer touches on the Jewish dimension but never fully explores it. As has been noted, Rojack in *An American Dream* says that he is "half Jewish." When Rojack is asked what the other half is, he responds, "Protestant. Nothing really," a remark that certainly contains explosive implications when delivered by a "half Jew" (p. 37). Rojack is placing himself in a category similar to Mailer himself as a non-Jewish Jew. In *Armies of the Night* (1968), Mailer's nonfiction novel about his participation in the march on the Pentagon in 1967 in protest over the Vietnam War, Mailer asserts that "the one personality he found absolutely insupportable" within himself was that of "the nice Jewish boy from Brooklyn," a personality that in this book he nonetheless seems to find inescapable. For when he is sentenced to a prison term as a result of his activities in the march, he gives a speech in which he says that he is not a Christian, but he is "married to one," and he especially admires "her unspoken love for Jesus Christ." He concludes his speech by saying:

> it is Sunday and we are burning the body and blood of Christ in Vietnam. Yes, we are burning him there, and as we do, we destroy the foundation of this Republic, which is its love and trust in Christ.

Then, he dutifully copies into his book an article that appeared in the *Washington Post* concerning his sentencing and his speech, including the ending of the article: "Mailer is a Jew."[26] Ultimately he is forced to come to grips with his identity as a Jew—an identity forced on him by others.

Canadian-born Saul Bellow, to be sure, does not deny that he is a Jew. And he is indeed very much a Jewish author. Even in a novel like *Henderson the Rain King* (1959), which lacks Jewish characters and explicit discussion of Jewishness, critics find a pervasive Jewishness.[27] But for Bellow, the Jew becomes a truly representative man, an Everyman who stands for all readers, both Jews and Gentiles. As Keith Michael Opdahl notes, "Bellow describes the Jewish experience in terms that make it representative of historical alienation and determinism." Nonetheless, Opdahl sees a true Jewishness at the heart of Bellow's vision; in his "celebration of the temporal world, his emphasis on community love, and his rejection of the formal for the spontaneous and individual" Opdahl finds elements of Hasidism. And Bellow's "love of the particular scene . . . even at the expense of larger form, conveying the sense that the particular may contain the larger mystery, may owe," Opdahl feels, "something not only to the Romantics but to the faith and the anecdotal, aphoristic literature of the Hasids."[28]

Beginning with *Dangling Man* (1944), Bellow explores the problems of marginality faced by the Jew in America during World War II and the postwar period. A list of his works with central Jewish characters reads like a roll call of the most important works of postwar American fiction: *Dangling Man*, *The Victim* (1949), *The Adventures of Augie March* (1953), *Seize the Day* (1956), *Herzog* (1964), *Mr. Sammler's Planet* (1970), *Humboldt's Gift* (1975), and *The Dean's December* (1982). These works have been widely acclaimed as literary masterpieces, so much so that Bellow was awarded the Nobel Prize for Literature in 1976. His works show that Bellow is, as Guttmann rightly says, *"par excellence* the explorer of marginality, concerned with men situated somewhere between old and new, with comic and tragic characters in quest of their uncertain identities" (p.178). As numerous critics have noticed, in his later works, especially from *Herzog* on, Bellow's central characters often break out of their alienation as they find their true identities.[29]

Perhaps Bellow's explorations of marginality in part help explain his popularity and his importance for readers in the second half of the twentieth century. In explaining the willingness of post–World War II readers to accept fiction by and about Jews, Chapman writes that those readers are responding to "themes of alienation, human suffering, social criticism, the multidirectional quests for identity and meaning in a dehumanizing and irrational age." But the readers are also attracted by

> the validity of an underlying attitude to life that derives somehow from the core of the Jewish experience: learning how to live and cope with the continuous expectation of uncertainty, contradictions, the unpredictable, the unanticipated, and the unfathomable, with the realization that adversity, trouble, grief, and sorrow...are the normal conditions of life. (pp. xlvii–xlviii)

This attitude is similar to the one Max Schulz in *Radical Sophistication* (1969) finds at the center of modern Jewish-American fiction. In his excellent study, Schulz writes that the "capacity for belief in the face of 'uncertainties, mysteries, doubts' is a radical sophistication that the Jew, with a culture historically of long standing, is currently giving to a century convinced in its existential isolation of the incoherence of existence.[30] It is as though these two critics are writing most particularly of Bellow, who exemplifies in work after work the very traits they mention.

As I indicated, the 1950s saw the Jewish author move to the center of—and possibly become the dominant force in—American literature. During this decade, in addition to Bellow and Mailer, major figures who were explicitly concerned with Jewishness and with Jews include Bernard Malamud, Philip Roth, Alfred Kazin, and even the poet Allen Ginsberg. Among popular novelists whose works had an appeal that went far beyond Jewish readers were Herman Wouk, author of *The Caine Mutiny* (1951) and *Marjorie Morningstar* (1955), and Leon Uris, author of *Exodus* (1958). Although problems of Jewish identity hardly lie at the center of *The Caine Mutiny*, they are central to the story of Marjorie Morningstar, born Morgenstern, who initially rebels against her Jewishness but eventually returns to a middle-class, suburban, conservative position and even starts to attend synagogue regularly. Uris' novel depicts the Jews and non-Jews who helped found Israel as larger-than-life heroes with few, if any, flaws. Even though *Exodus* is the most popular Zionist novel ever written in America, it can hardly be taken seriously as a literary work. Like *The Caine Mutiny* and *Marjorie Morningstar*, it too readily slips into cliché and oversimplification. Nonetheless, these three works demonstrate the kind of popular appeal Jewish authors writing about Jewish characters had in America during the 1950s.

Among the more serious authors, Bernard Malamud is outstanding. Repeatedly in his novels and short stories, he explores the role of Judaism and Jews in the modern world. In *The Assistant* (1957) he reverses the age-old theme of conversion of the Jew to Christianity and shows a Christian, Frank Alpine, who goes through a formal conversion to Judaism. Malamud uses the grocer Morris Bober to explore the meaning of Jewishness in a secular age. Morris explains to Frank that Morris is indeed a Jew:

> Nobody will tell me that I am not Jewish because I put in my mouth once in a while, when my tongue is dry, a piece ham. But they will tell me, and I will believe them, if I forget the Law. This means to do what is right, to be honest, to be good. This means to other people. Our life is hard enough. Why should we hurt somebody else? For everybody should be the best, not only for you or me. We ain't animals. This is why we need the Law. This is what a Jew believes.

Although Frank replies, "I think other religions have those ideas too," he nonetheless finds Judaism tremendously attractive.[31]

Frank is especially concerned with what he considers Jewish suffering. When he asks Morris "why it is that the Jews suffer so damn much," Morris replies, "They suffer because they are Jews." Then Frank says, "they suffer more than they have to," and Morris responds, "If you live, you suffer. Some people suffer more, but not because they want to. But I think if a Jew don't suffer for the Law, he will suffer for nothing."Not content with generalities, Frank asks Morris why *he* suffers, and Morris replies, "I suffer for you" (pp. 124–25).

The need to define a Jew runs through *The Assistant*. It surfaces at Morris' funeral, for example, when the rabbi says:

> When a Jew dies, who asks if he is a Jew? He is a Jew, we don't ask. There are many ways to be a Jew. So if somebody comes to me and says, "Rabbi, shall we call such a man Jewish who lived and worked among the gentiles and sold them pig meat, trayfe, that we don't eat it, and not once in twenty years comes inside a synagogue, is such a man a Jew, rabbi?" To him I will say, "Yes, Morris Bober was to me a true Jew because he lived in the Jewish experience, which he remembered, and with the Jewish heart." Maybe not to our formal tradition—for this I don't excuse him—but he was true to the spirit of our life—to want for others that which he wants also for himself. (p. 229)

Three more works by Malamud in which Jewish identity is of the utmost importance are the short stories "The Lady of the Lake" and "The Last Mohican," both collected in *The Magic Barrel* (1958), and the novel *The Fixer* (1966). In "The Lady of the Lake," Henry Levin travels to Europe after World War II. "In Paris, for no reason he was sure of, except that he was tired of the past—tired of the limitations it had imposed upon him," he decides to call himself Henry Freeman and to deny that he is Jewish. In Italy he meets and falls in love with Isabella del Dongo, who repeatedly asks him whether he is Jewish. Suspecting that she is an anti-Semite, he insists that he is not. Ironically, when he asks her to marry him, she refuses because she thinks that he is not Jewish. She reveals that she is tattooed as a result of having been sent to Buchenwald, and she replies to Henry's proposal: "I can't marry you. We are Jews. My past is meaningful to me. I treasure what I suffered for."[32] In "The Last Mohican" Arthur Fidelman, who is also in flight from his Jewishness, is forced by Shimon Susskind to acknowledge his relation to his fellow Jews after Susskind steals Fidelman's suit and burns a chapter of a book on art that Fidelman is writing.[33]

In *The Fixer* Yakov Bok, living in prerevolutionary Russia, intitially passes as a Gentile and denies that he is a Jew. He even goes to work for an outspoken anti-Semite. When a boy is murdered and Bok is accused, he admits that he is a Jew. The long tale of his imprisonment follows, a period during which he finds himself more and more isolated. Consistently refusing to acknowledge faith in the God of the Jews, he nonetheless finds himself labeled a Jew, and even he realizes that he cannot escape from his Jewishness. Toward the end of the novel, Bok thinks: "One thing I've learned, . . . there's no such thing as an unpolitical man, especially a Jew. . . . You can't sit still and see yourself destroyed." And he adds, "If the state acts in ways that are abhorrent to human nature, it's the lesser evil to destroy it. Death to the anti-Semites! Long live revolution! Long live liberty!" By this time Bok has become a kind of national hero for the Jews and revolutionaries, who try unsuccessfully to release him from the carriage in which he rides to trial. The carriage continues along streets lined with crowds, among whom are "Jews of the Plossky District. Some, as the carrriage clattered by and they glimpsed the fixer, were openly weeping, wringing their hands. One thinly bearded man clawed his face. One or two waved at Yakov. Some shouted his name."[34]

Another treatment of the return to a Jewish identity occurs in Alfred Kazin's autobiographical volume, *A Walker in the City* (1951). In this work, Kazin, an eminent critic of American literature, returns to his roots in Brownsville, roots from which, earlier in his career, he had tried hard to escape. Guttmann places Kazin's book in a larger context. "Once the mythic voyage from Antomir to New York was successfully completed," Guttmann writes, "David Levinsky was able to look back upon his youth and articulate his doubts." Similarly, "Once the children and grandchildren of the immigrant generation had moved from the urban *shtetls* of Chicago and New York to America's wider world, they too were able to indulge themselves in memories of community and in moments of regret." And he adds, "The most poignant and complex literary statement of these second thoughts is probably Alfred Kazin's memoir, *A Walker in the City*" (pp. 88–89).

A *shtetl* is a small, rural community in Eastern Europe; a large percentage of the new immigrants came to America not from ghettos in large cities but from *shtetlach* (to use the Yiddish plural). Guttmann implies that they reproduced these *shtetlach* in the big cities in America, only to escape from them again and then to return to them in memory, as Kazin does in *A Walker in the City.*

Kazin tells a tale of "making it" (to borrow Norman Podhoretz' phrase) in the New World. He leaves his Jewish neighborhood to enter the mainstream of American life, but he chooses in this book to make the mental excursion into the past, back to his roots, just as he at times makes the physical trip by subway back to Brownsville and moves "From the Subway to the Synagogue," as he entitles his first chapter.

During the 1950s at least two other writers of importance appeared, Philip Roth and Allen Ginsberg. Ginsberg is another figure who is uncomfortable with his Jewishness, even going to the point of appearing to renounce it. In a passage strongly reminiscent of Walt Whitman's "Chanting the Square Deific," Ginsberg calls himself in "Kral Majales" (1967)

> a Buddhist Jew
> who worships the Sacred Heart of Christ the
>   blue body of Krishna the straight back of Ram
> the beads of Chango the Nigerian singing Shiva
>   Shiva in a manner which I have invented.[35]

Exactly what a Buddhist Jew may be is, of course, unclear, but, like Mailer, Ginsberg at least admits here that he realizes he cannot entirely escape his Jewish identity.

In his earlier works, *Howl, and Other Poems* (1956) and especially *Kaddish and Other Poems: 1958–1960* (1961), almost in spite of himself Ginsberg acknowledges his Jewishness, especially in *Kaddish*, his largely autobiographical lament for the death of his mother. Kaddish is, of course, the Jewish prayer for the dead, and although his parents did not bring Ginsberg up in a Jewish religious context, it is interesting that he places his entire poem in that context by means of its title.

As has been noted, Philip Roth's fiction has been the center of repeated controversy about Roth's relation to his fellow Jews. He has often been accused of being anti-Semitic. In a scathing attack on Roth, Irving Howe even goes so far as to write, "I think it clear that Roth, despite his concentration on Jewish settings and his acerbity of tone, has not really been involved in this tradition [of Jewish self-criticism and satire]. For he is one of the first American-Jewish writers who finds that it yields him no sustenance, no norms or values from which to launch his attacks on middle-class complacence."[36] Thus, Howe dismisses those critics who place Roth in the tradition of the prophets of old.

Nonetheless, Roth is a powerful force in modern American literature, and repeatedly he creates characters who are consciously aware of and concerned with their Jewishness. In "Eli the Fanatic" in *Goodbye, Columbus and Five Short Stories* (1959), for example, when confronted by the Yeshiva of Woodenton, Eli becomes intensely aware of his Jewish heritage and vows that he will pass it on to his son. And even a Jew as notorious as Alexander Portnoy, who tries to escape from his Jewish past by making love with *shikses* (Gentile women), feels himself strangely moved when he goes to Israel; his landing in "the land of Israel, where the Jewish people first came into being," causes him to be "impaled upon a memory of Sunday morning softball games in Newark."[37] In novels like *Goodbye, Columbus* (1959), *My Life as a Man* (1974), *The Professor of Desire* (1977), and *Zuckerman Unbound* (1981), Roth explores characters involved in love-hate relationships with their own Jewishness, people who, like Portnoy, often begrudgingly admit that in their own personal histories they can find miniature versions of the history of the Jewish people. In his baseball story, *The Great American Novel* (1973), Roth parodies the whole idea of writing "the great American novel." In this book, which Roth places solidly inside American literary tradition by his use not only of baseball but also of parodies of major works of American literature and of American literary traditions, Jews and Jewishness are by no means central, so Roth's discussion of "Jewish Wheaties" and the "seventeen-year-old Jewish genius" who makes them seem out of place;[38] the whole idea of Jewishness seems irrelevant.

During the 1960s, several writers seemed to move in slightly different directions. They returned to exploring fictional worlds that are almost exclusively Jewish, and often the Jews in those worlds are Orthodox. The foremost example is Chaim Potok, whose novels tend to center on tensions, not between Jews and non-Jews, but among various Orthodox Jews. *The Chosen* (1967) and *The Promise* (1969) treat the lives of Danny

Saunders and Reuven Malter as these characters try to reconcile their traditional beliefs with modern reality. The novels are rich in description of Hasidic and non-Hasidic Orthodox life in New York City during and especially after World War II. Potok continues to treat traditional forms of Judaism in *My Name Is Asher Lev* (1972), the story of a Hasidic Jew who becomes a painter.

Other writers of the 1960s and 1970s have returned to similar themes, treating Jews, often in connection with Orthodox concerns, even though Orthodox Judaism continues to attract a smaller and smaller percentage of America's Jews. Cynthia Ozick, for example, in the title story of *The Pagan Rabbi and Other Stories* (1971), tells the tale of Isaac Kornfeld, a brilliant Talmudist and a respected, promising young rabbi who studies pagan nature religions and becomes convinced of their validity. He deserts his wife Sheindel after falling in love with a tree nymph. When he is no longer able to have sexual relations with the nymph, he uses his *tallis* (prayer shawl) to hang himself from the nymph's tree. Hugh Nissenson, on the other hand, tends to set his stories in Israel, and in his novel *My Own Ground* (1976) he returns to the almost exclusively Jewish Lower East Side of turn-of-the-century New York. Even when his narrator, Jacob Brody, leaves New York City in the last few pages of the book, he comments almost exclusively on his relation with other Jews.

In an essay entitled "American Jewish Writing, Act II" (1976), Ruth R. Wisse examines trends in this literature during the 1970s. She concludes that:

> ...it is Philip Roth and not Cynthia Ozick, or Hugh Nissenson, who can best afford to write about the American Jewish reality. For American Jews today in their numbers live not on Nissenson's Lower East Side or in Ozick's hasidic *shtetl* [a reference to the short story, "Bloodshed"] but in "Woodentown," the home of Eli Peck [of Roth's "Eli the Fanatic"].

Wisse writes that for those who, unlike Roth,

> ...take Judaism seriously as a cultural alternative, and wish to weave brilliant cloth from its ancient threads, the sociological reality of the present-day American Jewish community would seem to present an almost insurmountable obstacle.[39]

Of course, no general study of Jewish-American literature can even approach completeness without some discussion of Isaac Bashevis Singer, who even though he supervises and even helps translate his works, still writes in Yiddish and treats for the most part the now destroyed Jewish communities of his native Poland. His few stories set in America, as well as his numerous novels, stories, and autobiographical volumes written in America, testify to his growing importance in the American literary tradition. That he received the Nobel Prize for Literature in 1978 testifies to his international importance and to the vitality of the Yiddish language, even though few people now consider it their native tongue. Singer's treatment of a lost culture in such works as *The Magician of Lublin* (1960), *The Spinoza of Market Street and Other Stories* (1961), *The Manor* (1967), and *Shosha* (1973), as well as in his three autobiographical volumes—*In My Father's Court* (1966), *A Little Boy in Search of God* (1976) and *A Young Man in Search of Love* (1978)—provides Americans living in the second half of the twentieth century with a panoramic view of the Eastern Europe from which the ancestors of most of America's Jews came. And his stories set in America, some of which are collected in *Passions* (1975) and *Old Love* (1979), show his extraordinary sensitivity to the lives of Jews, especially Jews who escaped from the Nazi terror, in the New World. Although his works really stand outside the mainstream of present-day Jewish-American literature, they will probably have a profound effect on Jewish-American works to come.

Notable because of its absence from this discussion is poetry by American Jews about Jewish themes. There are, of course, many Jewish-American poets besides Emma Lazarus and Allen Ginsberg who write about Jewish themes. Their works, however, are really not as consistently good as are works of Jewish-American prose writers. I agree with Harold Bloom, who, in "The Sorrows of American-Jewish Poetry" (1972), asserts that "though it causes me real grief to say this, the achievement of American-Jewish poets down to the present moment remains a modest and mixed one. There are no Bellows or Malamuds among them, though there are a few signs that this melancholy estimate some day may need to be revised upward." As promising Jewish-American poets who have produced at least some verse "of considerable distinction," Bloom mentions Allen Grossman, Alvin Feinman, Robert Mezey, and Geoffrey Hartman.[40]

It is then in prose, especially prose fiction and autobiography, that Jewish-American authors have excelled up to now. Jewish-American literature has emerged as one of the central forces in the literature of the American nation. Although before and during World War II a Jewish-American author was often urged to change his name and write about non-Jews and non-Jewish themes, today his works about Jews and Jewishness are read repeatedly by numerous non-Jews who see themselves mirrored in the trials and tribulations of which they read. Guttmann theorizes that modern Jewish-American authors are so popular in part because "many of them are only nominally Jewish and present fictional worlds all but indistinguishable from those presented by other writers of their generation" (p. 86). This criticism, however, clearly cannot apply to the fictional worlds of writers like Ozick, Nissenson, and especially Potok, whose characters can exist only in a Jewish milieu and only as Jews. Yet these authors, too, enjoy widespread popularity. As we have seen, there is indeed a good deal of truth to the statements with which we began this essay, for Jewish authors and Jewish writing are indeed a predominant force, if not the dominant force, in American literature during the second half of the twentieth century.

Notes

[1] Alfred Kazin, "Introduction: The Jew as Modern American Writer," in *The Commentary Reader: Two Decades of Articles and Stories*, ed. Norman Podhoretz (New York: Atheneum, 1966), p. xxiv. Throughout this essay, whenever dates, such as the birthdate of Ludwig Lewisohn, are in dispute, if possible I arbitrarily use the date given in *Encyclopedic Dictionary of Judaica*, ed. Geoffrey Wigoder (New York: Leon Amiel, 1974).

[2] Donald L. Kaufman, *Norman Mailer: The Countdown (The First Twenty Years)* (Carbondale: Southern Illinois Univ. Press, 1969), p. 99.

[3] Charles Angoff and Meyer Levin, Introd., *The Rise of American Jewish Literature: An Anthology of Selections from the Major Novels*, ed. Charles Angoff and Meyer Levin (New York: Simon, 1970), p. 15.

[4] Irving Malin and Irwin Stark, Introd., *Breakthrough: A Treasury of Contemporary American-Jewish Literature*, ed. Irving Malin and Irwin Stark (New York: McGraw-Hill, 1964), p. 1. Malin and Stark quote Trilling.

[5] Abraham Chapman, Introd., *Jewish-American Literature: An Anthology of Fiction, Poetry, Autobiography, and Criticism*, ed. Abraham Chapman (New York: New American Library, 1974), p. xxviii.

[6] Norman Mailer, "Responses and Reactions, I," *Commentary*, Dec. 1962, p. 506; *An American Dream* (New York: Dell, 1965), pp. 37, 29.

[7] Malin and Stark, p. 24. See also Malin's introduction to his book, *Jews and Americans* (Carbondale: Southern Illinois Univ. Press, 1965), pp. 3–12.

[8] Sol Liptzin, *The Jew in American Literature* (New York: Bloch, 1966), pp. 60–61.

[9] Allen Guttmann, *The Jewish Writer in America: Assimilation and the Crisis of Identity* (New York: Oxford Univ. Press, 1971), pp. 25, 21; Emma Lazarus, *Songs of a Semite, The Dance to Death, and Other Poems* (New York: American Hebrew, 1882).

[10] In *The Jew in the American Novel*, Herzl Institute Pamphlet 10 (New York: Herzl Inst., 1959), Leslie A. Fiedler rather ingeniously argues that the Jewish-American novel was, in fact, "created" by Henry Harland, who most likely was not a Jew (pp. 9–16).

[11] Mary Antin, *The Promised Land* (Boston: Houghton, 1912), p. xi.

[12] Abraham Cahan, *The Rise of David Levinsky* (New York: Harper, 1917), pp. 86–87.

[13] Ben Hecht, *A Jew in Love* (New York: Covici, Freide, 1931), p. 3.

[14] Isaac Bashevis Singer, *A Young Man in Search of Love*, trans. Joseph Singer (Garden City, N.Y.: Doubleday, 1978), p. 109.

[15] See, for example, such widely separated but similar works as Bernard G. Richards, "The Attitude of the Jews towards Jewish Fiction," *Reader*, 1 (Nov. 1903), 43–50, and Philip Roth, "Writing about Jews," *Commentary*, Dec. 1963, pp. 446–52. In his most recent novels, *The Ghost Writer* (1979) and *Zuckerman Unbound* (1981), Roth deals explicitly with this problem.

[16] Included in Philip Roth, *Goodbye, Columbus and Five Short Stories* (1959; rpt. New York: Bantam, 1963), pp. 115–43.

[17] David S. Lifson, *The Yiddish Theater in America* (New York: Yoseloff, 1965), pp. 29–30.

[18] The dating here is uncertain. In his article "Theater: Yiddish Theater" in *Encylopedia Judaica*, 1971 ed., Joseph Leftwich gives the date 18 Aug. 1882. In *World of Our Fathers* (New York: Harcourt, 1976), Irving Howe gives 12 Aug. 1882 but says that Thomashefsky was sixteen (pp. 461–62). In *The Downtown Jews: Portraits of an Immigrant Generation* (New York: New American Library, 1976), Ronald Sanders says 1884, a date that would make Thomashefsky sixteen. In *Vagabond Stars: A World History of Yiddish Theater* (New York: Harper, 1977), Nahma Sandrow says that the performance occurred in 1882 and that Thomashefsky was then thirteen (p. 72). Sandrow's excellent study traces Yiddish theater from its theoretical beginnings in the Purim plays of the fifth century into the 1970s.

[19] For example, both are included in *The Great Yiddish Plays*, trans. Joseph C. Landis (New York: Avon, 1972).

[20] Elias Tobenkin, *God of Might* (New York: Minton, Balch, 1925); see especially the conclusion of the novel, pp. 268–72.

[21] Ludwig Lewisohn, *The Island Within* (Philadelphia: Jewish Publication Soc. of America, 1968), p. 219. This work was first published in book form in 1928 by Harper.

[22] Michael Gold, *Jews without Money* (1930; rpt. New York: Avon, 1965), pp. 79, 109.

[23] Daniel Walden, Introd., *On Being Jewish: American Jewish Writers from Cahan to Bellow*, ed. Walden (Greenwich, Conn.: Fawcett, 1974), p. 18.

[24] See Meyer Levin, "After All I Did for Israel," *Commentary*, July 1951, pp. 57–62.

[25] For a sensitive study of these novels and the furor they created, see Ben Siegel, *The Controversial Sholem Asch: An Introduction to His Fiction* (Bowling Green, Ohio: Bowling Green Univ. Popular Press, 1976), pp. 140–87.

[26] Norman Mailer, *The Armies of the Night: History as a Novel, the Novel as History* (New York: New American Library, 1968), pp. 153, 238–40.

[27] See, for example, Steven Gould Axelrod, "The Jewishness of Bellow's Henderson," *American Literature*, 47 (1975), 439–43.

[28] Keith Michael Opdahl, *The Novels of Saul Bellow: An Introduction* (University Park: Pennsylvania State Univ. Press, 1967), p. 25.

[29] See, for example, Bernard Sherman's discussion of *Herzog* in *The Invention of the Jew: Jewish-American Education Novels (1916–1964)* (New York: Yoseloff, 1969), p. 133.

[30] Max F. Schulz, *Radical Sophistication: Studies in Contemporary Jewish-American Novelists* (Athens: Ohio Univ. Press, 1969), p. 22.

[31] Bernard Malamud, *The Assistant* (New York: Farrar, 1957), p. 124.

[32] Bernard Malamud, *The Magic Barrel* (New York: Farrar, 1958), pp. 105, 132.

[33] Malamud, *The Magic Barrel*, pp. 155–82. Later Malamud used this story as the first chapter of *Pictures of Fidelman: An Exibition* (1969).

[34] Bernard Malamud, *The Fixer* (1968; rpt. New York: Dell, 1968), p. 271.

[35] Allen Ginsberg, *Planet News: 1961–1967* (San Francisco: City Lights, 1968), p. 90.

[36] Irving Howe, *The Critical Point* (New York: Horizon, 1973), p. 146. The essay was originally published in *Commentary*, Dec. 1972, pp. 69–77.

[37] Philip Roth, *Portnoy's Complaint* (New York: Random, 1969), p. 244.

[38] Philip Roth, *The Great American Novel* (New York: Holt, 1973), pp. 291, 286.

[39] Ruth R. Wisse, "American Jewish Writing, Act II," *Commentary*, June 1976, p. 45.

[40] Harold Bloom, "The Sorrows of American-Jewish Poetry," *Commentary*, March 1972, pp. 69, 73–74.

Polish-American Literature*

Jerzy J. Maciuszko

Literature has a special place in the hearts of Poles. They regard it as more than adornment of life and certainly as much more than mere entertainment. When Poland was wiped off the map of Europe in 1795, literature assumed the role of guardian of the Polish identity. After the country was divided politically among three neighboring powers, literature became for Poles the very soul of the nation. Great Polish poets, like Adam Mickiewicz, were accepted almost as prophets. Henryk Sienkiewicz wrote his trilogy not merely to entertain but also to lift up the spirit of the nation and to show how Poland, after the wars and invasions of the seventeenth century and particularly after the Swedish "flood," had risen triumphantly to its former greatness.

The first ties between Polish literature and America can be traced to the Colonial period. They go back to Wawrzyniec Goślicki, senator and chancellor of Poland and author of the famous political treatise *De Optimo Senatore* (1568). Mieczysław Haiman states:

> Its first English edition appeared in 1598; a second edition was published in 1607, and though both issues were suppressed by the British authorities, nevertheless, this book greatly influenced the English revolution of 1648. Indirectly, Goślicki's work was not without its influence on the American Declaration of Independence.[1]

Polish literature has made and still makes a special contribution on this continent. Polish literature in English translation — and this is how it is largely known — persistently affirms that literature is the mirror of a nation's soul and that the nation's mission is reflected in its literature. It would not be an exaggeration to say that Polish literature has helped this nation find its own identity. Is there anything more important that a literature can contribute? In my examination of the Polish-American scene, I include some discussion of translations from the Polish, but I deal mainly with works published in the United States in English by Polish-American authors, and I discuss the image of Poles in American fiction. I conclude with a brief discussion of periodicals featuring pertinent articles and reviews and a few remarks on the Polish-American press.

The Novel

When we speak of the novel, Henryk Sienkiewicz (1846–1916) comes to mind first. Translations of his fiction were popular in America until 1915, and Sienkiewicz visited the United States in 1876–78.[2] All his major works have been translated into English. One of his short stories, "After Bread," has appeared in six different English translations. Sienkiewicz' first novel, translated by Jeremiah Curtin, was *With Fire and Sword* (*Ogniem i mieczem*, 1884), the first volume of the historical trilogy. The novel appeared in English in 1890, and others followed. Sienkiewicz, however, owes his fame in this country not to the trilogy but to his novel set in ancient Rome, *Quo Vadis* (1896), which led to his receiving the Nobel Prize in 1905.

A Polish novelist from the next generation who made a contribution to American letters is Władysław Stanisław Reymont (1867–1925). His *The Peasants* (*Chłopi*, 1904–09) brought him the Nobel Prize in 1924. Although the novel describes a peasant community somewhere in central Poland, its appeal has proved universal. In spite of the difficulty presented by its somewhat stylized dialect, the work has been widely translated.

Coming closer to our own times, we cannot overlook a writer whose literary contribution extends beyond the United States to the Americas, both South and North: the eminent Polish author, Witold Gombrowicz (1904–69). Gombrowicz happened to reach Buenos Aires a week before the beginning of World War II. He remained in Argentina as a Polish émigré. Perhaps the most characteristic of Gombrowicz's works is his excellent novel *Ferdydurke* (1937). When the French translation appeared in 1959, *Ferdydurke* was compared to Sartre's *La Nausée*. It was first translated into English in 1961. Within this cleverly knit story, the author analyzes such concepts as traditional and modern education, modernism in general, liberalism, and traditionalism. Ten years after *Ferdydurke's* publication, Gombrowicz, in cooperation with a Committee of South American Writers, translated it into Spanish. Gombrowicz' other works of fiction that have been translated into English include *The Marriage (Ślub,* 1953), *Pornografia* (Polish original, 1960), and *A Kind of Testament (Rozmowy z Gombrowiczem,* 1969). Through the daring originality of his thought and form, Gombrowicz made a clear impact on American letters.

Maria Kuncewiczowa (b. 1897) was the founder of the International P.E.N. Club Centre for Writers in Exile in England after World War II. When two volumes of the anthology *The Pen in Exile* were published in London (1954, 1956), she was the P.E.N. president. Many of her novels have been translated. *The Stranger (Cudzoziemka,* 1936) appeared in English in 1945. *The Conspiracy of the Absent (Zmowa nieobecnych)* was published in 1950, while *The Forester* (1954) is the English translation of her *Leśnik* (1952). Her novel *The Olive Grove* (1963) was written originally in English. From 1962 to 1968, the author was visiting professor of Polish literature at the University of Chicago. She now resides and continues to write in Poland.

Like Kuncewiczowa, Józef Wittlin (1896–1976) belongs to the small group of Polish writers who found themselves in America as a result of World War II. His *Salt of the Earth (Sól ziemi,* 1936) in Pauline de Chary's translation has been published by various houses in several editions. A fragment from the book appears in the anthology *Heart of Europe* under the title "The Emperor and the Devil."[3]

A resident of New York until his death, Józef Wittlin was a colorful spokesman for Polish authors and Polish literature. He was invariably present whenever Polish literature was discussed at any meeting in New York. His last such appearance was at the inauguration of the reactivated Literary Section of the Polish Institute of Arts and Sciences in America, when he movingly and lovingly introduced the guest author, Zofia Romanowiczowa, on 15 March 1975. Wittlin's speech was carefully recorded in the chronicles of the Literary Section, making him in a sense the godfather of that active and successful group. In gratitude and recognition of his status, the section organized a literary evening in his honor on 6 November 1976, following his death earlier that year.

His namesake, Tadeusz Wittlin, born in Warsaw in 1909, now resides in Washington, D.C. Tadeusz Wittlin's *Reluctant Traveller in Russia* (1952) is based on the author's own experiences in Soviet labor camps. The book was translated into French,

Spanish, Dutch, and Japanese. His documentary work about the Katyń massacre, *Time Stopped at 6:30* (1965), was highly acclaimed by critics. Wittlin's latest work, written in English and titled *Commissar* (1972), reflects the author's personal experiences in the Soviet Union and deals with the ill-famed Lavrenty Pavlovich Beria.

When we turn our attention to authors of Polish descent who write exclusively or predominantly in English, we encounter a major writer who has recently been compared with Joseph Conrad; he is Jerzy Kosinski. As Ivan Sanders has pointed out,

> When one thinks of Jerzy Kosinski, Joseph Conrad comes to mind. Both Kosinski and Conrad were in their twenties when they began to learn English (Kosinski was twenty-four when he arrived in the United States in 1957), yet both chose to write only in their adopted language, disproving the widespread notion that one cannot ever make a second language, its nuances, its soul, completely one's own. Against formidable cultural and linguistic odds, "by some miracle of training," as Irving Howe has said, both of them became brilliant English stylists. . . . One could easily imagine Kosinski adopting Conrad's famous *ars poetica,* as expressed in the Preface to *The Nigger of the Narcissus* ("My task which I am trying to achieve is, by the power of the word, to make you hear, to make you feel—it is, before all, to make you *see*"), for his prose, though terse and unadorned, is also stunningly vivid.[4]

Kosinski has, so far, produced seven works of fiction: *The Painted Bird, Steps, Being There, The Devil Tree, Cockpit, Blind Date,* and *Passion Play.* He came to the public eye soon after publication of his first novel, *The Painted Bird* (1965), which has a Polish setting. When war breaks out in 1939, a boy is sent by his parents to a village far from his home. All the atrocities that the boy goes through are vividly described. The novel, however, is much more than a study of horror. The boy suffers because he appears to his tormentors to be "different." Beneath the mask of horror, *The Painted Bird* presents a study in alienation. *Steps* (1968), for which the author received the National Book Award, eludes any simple classification. *Being There* (1970) is also, in a sense, a psychological study of an outsider, pursuing the theme of alienation. *The Devil Tree* (1973) seems to be the weakest of the first four works. In *Cockpit* (1975), Tarden is a former agent of the powerful security system of the government; he refers to it as "the service." To fill the vacuum, he seeks adventure and intrigue. This is, of course, a superficial view of his actions. The publisher tells us on the dust jacket that

> Before we know it, Tarden has peeled off our illusions of security layer by layer, leaving us alone on a barren lunar meadow scattered with the wreckage of our most vital support systems: family, friendship, sex, love, career, sports, art, medicine, possessions and justice. Stripped of our defenses, we at last perceive the significance of his penetration: since our fortifications are crumbling facades, our strength must rise within us.

Blind Date (1977) centers on George Levanter, a mysterious businessman. His parents emigrated from Russia and settled in Eastern Europe shortly before he was born. We meet him first in a Swiss resort as a free-wheeling world traveler in free enterprise. The theme of alienation takes a different form here. Levanter has no home; he explores the whole world and meets people from all walks of life. His world of moral choices is equally far from conformity. When the author shows his protagonist as a lover, even the reader who has already experienced emotional shocks in reading Kosinski's previous novels is likely to be terrified.

When we come to the latest novel, *Passion Play* (1979), we cannot help thinking of what Jonathan Baumbach said of *Cockpit* as compared with Kosinki's other works of fiction:

> All of Kosinski's novels are extremely similar in method and impulse and extend into one another as if they were a long, fantastic autobiographical nightmare, manipulations in slightly varied forms of the same obsessive materials. . . . he moves through the void of a self-created world changing roles as the seasons of vengeance or survival demand.[5]

In *Passion Play,* Fabian, a knight-errant driving his VanHome across the North American continent, is another version of George Levanter of *Blind Date.* Fabian earns his livelihood in a special kind of polo, that is, in the one-on-one contest. The scenes of his polo encounters and of his passion for women whom he had once met as girls are the open plains and cities of America. The similarities in the structure of this novel and that of *Blind Date* are striking.

Jerzy Kosinski was the recipient of the Prix du Meilleur Livre Etranger (France) for *The Painted Bird* in 1966. He has received awards in literature from the National Institute of Arts and Letters and the National Academy of Arts and Letters. He was awarded the Brith Sholom Humanitarian Freedom Award in 1974. Since 1973 Kosinski has served as president of the American Center of P.E.N. He received the Perspectives Achievement Award for 1980.

There is no question about Kosinski's great literary talent and his uncommon abilities. Born in Lodz, Poland, in 1933, he came to the United States in 1957 without knowing a word of English. Three years later, he published under the pseudonym Joseph Novak his first work in English, *The Future Is Ours, Comrade* (1960). After his arrival in America, he worked as a paint scraper on excursion boats, a truck driver, and a photographer. In 1970 Kosinski became professor of English prose and criticism at the School of Drama of Yale University; he is also a fellow of Davenport College.

Another writer who comes to mind when we speak of Joseph Conrad and other authors who use English, their adopted language, in their creative works is Wiesław S. Kuniczak. The author of *The Thousand Hour Day* (1966), a novel about the first thousand hours of World War II, was born in 1930 in Lvov.

Frank Mocha, in his review article titled "History as Literature," states:

> *The Thousand Hour Day,* the fictionalized story of the fall of Poland in September 1939, written by Wiesław S. Kuniczak, a young expatriate Pole now living in America, is an unusual book. . . . the Book of-the-Month Club. . . selection for June of 1967. . . was followed by a series of reviews running the gamut from objectively enthusiastic by Thomas Lask of *The New York Times* and mockingly incredulous by Frederick Morton in the *New York Times Book Review* to an offensively biased account by a reviewer of Long Island's *Newsday.* In between these extremes, the reviews were, on the whole, positive and sympathetic. . . . the dilemma of a critic faced with such a depressing novel as *The Thousand Hour Day* is that to recommend it to others is to feel restricted to those with a liking for real, raw war stuff. And yet, to deny the book's power would be to perform a disservice to the author. In its own way, this is a perfect book, if not a great one. For those who feel the need to submit themselves to this experience, who feel, perhaps, that if we relive it often enough in literature we

can keep both alive and forever dead the events of that "Day," *The Thousand Hour Day* is required reading.[6]

After the publication of this novel, the author studied Eastern philosophy in India, endured imprisonment and torture by the Greek government when it was run by the junta of the colonels, experienced the death of his wife, lost his home and all his possessions, and suffered two heart attacks. He descended into the lowest abyss of the human experience of pain. He emerged not as a broken man but as a person with a song of victory on his lips. Hope saved him, and it is hope that he is holding out to the world now. His new book, *The March* (1979), paints in vivid colors the nightmare of the Polish people after the invasion of Poland by the Nazis and the Russians in 1939. Kuniczak describes the fate of the thousands who were deported to Soviet work camps and the millions who were arrested and murdered. He blames the Russians for the ghastly death of thousands of Polish officers in the Katyń Forest. "It is a story about the agony of betrayal, about the uses of hope and courage, and the redemptive power of love. Written in rich, powerful prose, it is a celebration of the human spirit worthy to stand with the greatest novels of our time." This is what the publisher tells us on the dust jacket, and this is what we are ready to accept in the context of the Gehenna of the author's life and his victory. *The March* is the second volume of the trilogy that began with *The Thousand Hour Day.* The author is now completing the final volume of this monumental work. Kuniczak also published *The Sempinski Affair* (1969), which deals with Eastern Europe in a radically different manner, and *My Name Is Million,* subtitled *An Illustrated History of the Poles in America* (1978). Kuniczak considers the trilogy his *opus magnum.* The author's unquestionable talent holds a promise of more great works to come.

Richard Bankowsky (b. 1928) grew up in New Jersey. He is famous for his widely acclaimed tetralogy *The Glass Rose* (1958), *After Pentecost* (1961), *On a Dark Night* (1964), and *The Pale Criminals* (1967). All his stories realistically portray poverty-stricken families in Anderson, New Jersey. In the works of Bankowsky, human values rather than specifically Polish elements seem to prevail. The stream-of-consciousness technique in which the stories are told raises the artistic level of the novels above their ethnic connotations. Bankowsky now lives in California and teaches at Sacramento State College.

One important Polish-American author now residing in this country is Maia Wojciechowska, who writes children's books in English. She won the Newberry Medal for her *Shadow of a Bull* (1965), which was judged "the most distinguished contribution to American Literature for Children." The author's other titles include *Odyssey of Courage* (1965), *Kingdom in a Horse* (1966), *The Hollywood Kid* (1967), *A Single Light* (1968), *Tuned Out* (1968), and *Winter Tales from Poland* (1970).

Maia Wojciechowska was born in Warsaw in 1927 and came to the United States in 1942. One brief quotation will, perhaps, suffice to reveal her character: "What I deplore most in my world. . . is how much fear there is all around. We have let the liars tell us that we should not trust each other and we believed them."⁷ Through her books, she teaches children otherwise.

Polish-American literature has been enriched by the contributions of a group of war-time émigrés and by a continuous stream of postwar arrivals from Poland. These authors write almost exclusively in Polish, but their works are becoming known in English-speaking literary and academic circles. A typical representative of this group was Aleksander Janta (1908– 74), journalist, novelist, poet, essayist, and bibliophile. Unlike most Polish émigrés, Janta moved beyond the narrow émigré world into Polish-American and American cultural and academic circles. As a result, many of his works have been translated,⁸ and he began to write in English quite early. His articles in the *Polish Review* and, more recently, the *Queens Slavic Papers* show not only a good grasp of the English language but also erudition and an intimate knowledge of Polish literature and culture in America.⁹ The Literary Section of the Polish Institute of Arts and Sciences paid tribute to Janta's versatility and generic richness at a literary evening in his memory on 1 November 1975.¹⁰

A slightly younger writer who belonged to the same group was Paweł Łysek (1914–78), whose folkloristic stories and novels set in the Silesian Beskids are becoming known in literary circles. Two of them—a collection of stories, *Przy granicy (At the Border,* 1966), and a novel, *Twarde żywobycie Jury Odcesty (The Hard Life of Jerry from Across the Road,* 1970)—have been translated or are being translated into English. Like Janta, Łysek was a man of many talents and accomplishments. A writer, educator, and librarian, he was also, according to his bibliographer, "well known to students of literature for his regular chronicle and analysis of belletristic production of today's

Polonia in the pages of *Books Abroad*."[11] As a professor of Polish literature at the City University of New York, Łysek gained acceptance in academic circles, and the general public in New York became acquainted with his writings through popular author's evenings organized for him by the Literary Section of the Polish Institute. His position as an émigré writer was probably best summarized by Florian Śmieja of Canada in an excellent article, "The Writer in Exile as Custodian of Folklore."[12]

Poetry

With regard to poetry, the link between Poland and America goes back to the seventeenth century. Mieczysław Haiman writes:

> The poetry of Casimir Sarbiewski, the celebrated "Polish Horace" of the 17th century, was probably the earliest cultural tie between the American colonies and Poland. His *Odes of Casimir* translated into English and in their original Latin langugage, were quite popular in colonial America.[13]

The earliest Polish poem to mention America appeared a century earlier. *The Boatman (Flis)*, written in 1595 by Sebastian Klonowicz (c. 1545–1602) but only recently translated into English by Marion M. Coleman, speaks of the newly discovered land as a "heroic paradise."

The great Polish Romantic Adam Mickiewicz (1798–1855) was the first Polish poet to attract attention in America in his own time. We know that he met James Fenimore Cooper in Paris, but we cannot say how much this meeting contributed to America's awareness of Mickiewicz, who was translated into English in America about the same time. It seems that James Gates Percival (1795–1856), the New England poet, was the first to translate one of Mickiewicz's poems when he rendered into English the "Crimean Sonnet" (XVII), "Ruiny Zamku w Bałakławie" ("The Ruins of the Castle at Balaclava"), and published it in the *New England Magazine* in April 1835. Percival's interest in Mickiewicz continued, and he later translated more of his poems. These early translations, however, did not seem to lead to any lasting popularity for Mickiewicz in America.

The book that made Mickiewicz popular among American readers, more than any other single volume, is *Poems by Adam Mickiewicz* (1944), edited by George Rapall Noyes. "Translated by various hands" and furnished with a lengthy and informative introduction by the editor, the volume includes a few early ballads, *Forefathers' Eve* (Parts II and III), *Grażyna*, "Crimean Sonnets," *Konrad Wallenrod*, "Faris" and some other later poems, and *The Books of the Polish Nation and of the Polish Pilgrims*. Even though the quality of the translations is uneven, one cannot overestimate the value of this volume.

Noyes also did a highly successful prose translation (1917) of Mickiewicz' masterpiece, *Pan Tadeusz, or the Last Foray in Lithuania*. For a long time it was the only English translation of this great epic poem, but today two fairly recent translations of *Pan Tadeusz* exist. One, by Watson Kirkconnell, with an introductory essay by William J. Rose and notes by Harold B. Segel, was published by the Polish Institute of Arts and Sciences in 1962, and the other, by Kenneth Mackenzie, appeared over the imprint of the Polish Cultural Foundation in London in 1964. Watson Kirkconnell's translation began as a joint venture with George Rapall Noyes. The original intention was that Kirkconnell would be responsible for the prosody. Noyes died in 1952, when only two of the twelve books had been completed, and Kirkconnell finished the task on his own. Although Mackenzie's translation may read more smoothly, there is no question that Kirkconnell's text is also valuable.

Kazimierz Wierzyński (1894–1969), a poet of the interwar period, made his literary debut in 1913. One of the five leading lyric poets between the wars, he exemplified the ideas of the so-called Skamander group, of which he was a prominent member. He gained international repute in 1928, when he won first prize at the Olympic Games for his poem "The Olympic Laurel" ("Laur Olimpijski"). His first collection of poetry, *Spring and Wine (Wiosna i wino)* appeared in 1919, followed by *Sparrows on the Roof (Wróble na dachu)* in 1920. His early poems sang of pure joy, but around 1930 his poetry began to show a return to the Polish Romantic heritage. At the outbreak of World War II, Wierzyński emigrated to France. He reached the United States, where he settled, by way of Portugal and Brazil. His best-known prose work is *The Life and Death of Chopin* (1949), which has a foreword by Artur Rubinstein.

In 1965 an anthology of Polish poetry translated and edited by Czesław Miłosz was published.[14] In his Preface, Miłosz shares with the reader the philosophy behind his selections: "I wish to explain in a few words why and how I made this anthology. The underlying motive, as I see it, was my distrust of poetry which indulges in negation and in sterile anger at the world" (p. v). The basis is broad, and thus the anthology includes selections from the works of all important Polish contemporary poets such as Leopold Staff, Antoni Słonimski, Jarosław Iwaszkiewicz, Kazimierz Wierzyński, Aleksander Wat, Julian Przyboś, Mieczysław Jastruń, Adam Ważyk, Tadeusz Różewicz, Zbigniew Herbert, Stanisław Grochowiak, and others. From his own works, Miłosz has included his short and ironic "A Song on the End of the World."

Born in 1911, Czesław Miłosz made his debut as a poet in the early 1930s. He was soon acknowledged as one of the leaders of the Second Vanguard. In his own words, "a movement turning away from both 'Skamander' and the First Vanguard, the Second Vanguard was a reaction against the narrowness of quarrels centered around form" (p. 49). Miłosz found strength to write under all circumstances. He once said, "The act of writing a poem is an act of faith; yet if the screams of the tortured are audible in the poet's room, is not his activity an offense to human suffering."[15] He edited an anthology of anti-Nazi poems in Warsaw during the Nazi occupation and managed to have it clandestinely printed. He left Poland in 1951. For ten years he lived in Paris, where he published his important prose work, *The Captive Mind* (*Umysł zniewolony*), which was translated into several languages, including English.[16] He is currently professor of Slavic Literatures at the University of California, Berkeley.

In 1973 Miłosz published his *Selected Poems,* a collection that focuses primarily on the last ten years, although it goes back several decades and includes poems written in Nazi-occupied Poland. The volume consists of fity-one poems divided into four parts. His next contribution was a translation (1977) of Aleksander Wat's *Mediterranean Poems.* The year 1978 marked the appearance of his *Bells in Winter.* On the pages of *Choice* (April 1979) I had this to say, in part, about the book: "*Bells in Winter* appears in print when Miłosz has been recognized as what he has always been, one of the greatest poets of our time. The book is a collection of his poetry translated jointly by the author and Lillian Vallee. . . . He is teaching us to look at reality not only with the eyes of a poet but also with the eyes of a philosopher" (pp. 230–31). In April 1978 the poet was awarded the Neustadt International Prize for Literature.[17] In 1980 he received the Nobel Prize.

Several Polish poets of a younger generation are active in America now. Tadeusz Chabrowski, Edward L. Dusza, and Anna Frajlich-Zając are known for their published collections of poetry as well as for poems in Polish-language periodicals in New York and London. They are also gaining recognition through their poetry recitals, particularly those organized by the Literary Section of the Polish Institute of Arts and Sciences, of which they are members and through which they become known to non-Polish audiences.

We do not want to leave the reader with the impression that no poetry is being written in English by Polish Americans. Two collections of poems on a variety of subjects may serve as examples of the poetry written on American soil in English and bearing clear traces of the authors' Polish origin. They are *"Nature Smiles"* (1947) by John H. Drechney and *Star Hunger* (1943) by Victoria Janda, who is also the author of two more collections, *Walls of Space* (1945) and *Singing Furrows* (1953). Janda's works were all published by the Polanie Press in Minneapolis. Although none of those collections contains great poetry, each has its charm, and many of the shorter poems by both authors can touch the reader's heart.

Charles Bukowski (b. 1920) was born in Germany but was brought to the United States when he was two. Called "the only Polish-American literary beatnik," he has written unconventional, untraditional poetry, including *Mockingbird, Wish Me Luck* (1972), *Love Poem to Marina* (1973), and *Life and Death in the Charity Ward* (1974).

Before we close this rapid glimpse at Polish-American poetry, we should note the thoughtfully prepared *Anthology of Polish American Poetry,* edited by Tadeusz Mitana.[18] Part I collects poems written in Polish by various authors in America, whereas Part II presents short poems written originally in English by Polish Americans. All these examples testify that poetry, as well as prose, is a means of literary expression for Americans of Polish descent.

The Short Story[19]

The first Polish short story to appear in English was the work of Henryk Sienkiewicz, the exclusive representative of the Polish short story in America from 1884, when his "Paul" ("Z pamiętnika poznańskiego nauczyciela") was translated by W. R. Thompson, until as late as 1915. That year an anthology of translations of Polish short stories appeared that for the first time included authors other than Sienkiewicz. Thus, Sienkiewicz dominated the Polish-American short story for over thirty years.

The first collection of Sienkiewicz's short stories was published by Little, Brown in 1893 as *Yanko the Musician, and Other Stories*. It was followed by *Lillian Morris, and Other Stories* in 1894. "Lillian Morris" is the English title of Sienkiewicz's "Przez stepy."

In 1915 *Tales by Polish Authors*, translated by Else C. M. Benecke, appeared in England.[20] Sienkiewicz was represented in this volume by one story, "Bartek the Conqueror," which had been translated twice before. In the following year Benecke joined Marie Busch, and the two as joint translators published *More Tales by Polish Authors*.[21] Welcome new names in this volume included Polish Nobel Prize-winning author Władysław Stanisław Reymont (Sienkiewicz was absent from this collection) and Bolesław Prus (the pseudonym of Aleksander Głowacki). There were two stories by Adam Szymański and one by Wacław Sieroszewski. The two translators actively and most fruitfully collaborated on this volume, and the quality of the translations is the best of any book in which Benecke had a hand.

Throughout the twentieth century other anthologists have published Polish short stories in English translations, but not until 1958, in *10 Contemporary Polish Stories*, edited by Edmund Ordon, did a collection include émigré authors in America. The editor followed the best tradition in the selection of the stories; he brought in new stories by authors already known in translation, such as Maria Dabrowska and Kazimierz Wierzyński, and he also introduced some new authors, such as Marek Hłasko. Olga Scherer-Virski introduces the volume.

One Polish-American short story writer deserves mention. Monica Krawczyk is the author of *If the Branch Blossoms and Other Stories* (1950), a highly regarded collection among Polish Americans. The dozen stories demonstrate the author's great warmth of feeling toward her compatriots and her great understanding and sympathy for their struggles in the new land. Many stories also introduce the reader to Polish-American customs. Krawczyk grew up in Winowa, Minnesota, steeped in her heritage. A second generation Polish American, social worker, and teacher, she organized the Polanie Club before her death in 1954. A lesser-known writer is John Zebrowski, now director of the University of Puerto Rico Press. He published a collection of short stories based on one character: Uncle Bruno. *Uncle Bruno* (1972) contains eight humorous stories about Polish-American life.

Polish Americans in American Fiction

Another important aspect of Polish letters in America is the characterization of Poles (or, strictly speaking, Polish Americans) in American fiction. Neither a comprehensive study nor a complete bibliography on the subject has been published, although this matter has already received some attention from scholars.[22]

We cannot discuss Poles in American fiction until we have taken a broader look at the American scene. Traditionally, the United States was seen as a land of equal opportunities for all and as a melting pot of all nationalities. Ethnic awareness has come to America only in the last decades. Its application to literature has been aptly expressed by Eric P. Kelly in his Foreword to Monica Krawczyk's *If the Branch Blossoms and Other Stories*:

> A greater expansion perhaps than that which allowed women a more important place in American letters was the extension of American thought through all the intellectual fields of its people. Almost mute hitherto, and indeed discounted blindly by those who could see nothing but Anglo-Saxon culture in our literary outcroppings, there came voices, broken at first and almost deprecatory, from great groups of people who were finding a new form of expression in a new land. At the beginning these voices were scattered and suffering from dissonance when heard separately, but as the years went on, there came unifying elements that seemed to foretell the basis for a new American expression.

Briefly then, the scope of literature in this country has increased so enormously in fifty years that it includes the culture that has gone to make all of its citizens what they are, and he who interprets America today must be familiar with every racial background that one finds here.[23]

Glad as we are to see Poles enter the pages of American fiction, we must remember that Polish-American protagonists are often idealized or exaggerated. To make his point in *After Bread* that emigration agents in Europe misrepresent facts about life in America, Henryk Sienkiewicz consciously exaggerated, and he purposely painted a more tragic picture than we would have been likely to encounter in life. In many instances, the humanity of the protagonists is underplayed, whereas their specifically Polish qualities are pushed to the fore.

It would be a rather crude oversimplification to say that authors of Polish descent always portray Poles in America in a favorable light, while non-Polish writers tend to do the opposite. In *American Beauty* (1931) Edna Ferber tells with genuine warmth and understanding the story of Polish-American families on Connecticut farms. She gives Poles credit for making a contribution to the community as she points out that Polish families increase the prosperity of the state. Edna Ferber is not alone in this respect. Other American authors of non-Polish descent take a similar attitude.

When we come to Nelson Algren and his novels *Never Came Morning* (1942) and *The Man with the Golden Arm* (1949), we find a brutal presentation of poverty and crime among Poles in the underworld of the Chicago's West Side. The presentation of his protagonists has little to do with the author's pro-Polish or anti-Polish feelings. This is how Chester E. Eisinger sees Nelson Algren:

> He is the poet of the jail and the whorehouse; he has made a close study of the cockroach, the drunkard, and the pimp, the garbage in the street and the spittle on the chin. He has a truly cloacal vision of the American experience.... The poetic quality of his writing comes in part from the impressionistic way in which he sees reality. He has an acutely developed feeling for mood.[24]

We should view Nelson Algren's characters against this background. Although we can understand how this author's creative imagination works, we may still regret that his protagonists happen to be Polish.

Ruth Tabrah's *Pulaski Place* (1950) examines the ethnic prejudice Steve Kowalski faces. He has joined the town's police force, and, though his struggles are specific, they all spring from the same source. Another version of this theme permeates Joseph Vogel's *Man's Courage* (1938). Adam Wolak's dream of owning his own farm in America is shattered when he faces the harsh realities of life, and his valiant struggle ends in defeat.

Edith Miniter, in *Our Natupski Neighbors* (1916), brings some humor to the story of a Polish family who try to gain the acceptance of their neighbors in West Holly, Massachusetts. The social and human conflict between improverished New Englanders and Polish newcomers is presented by Cornelia James Cannon in *Heirs* (1930). The story of how prejudice against Poles is overcome in a village in the Connecticut Valley is aptly told in *The Invaders* (1913) by Frances Newton Symmes Allen. *The Invaders* and *The Doctor's Wooing* (1926) by Charles Phillips are early examples of works that present Poles in American fiction, and they are listed in Eleanor E. Ledbetter's pioneering bibliography.[25]

The portrayal of Poles in American fiction varies with the author's approach, style, and personal prejudices, and it might or might not depend on whether Polish blood flows in his or her veins. Equally important are the social climate and the way in which the ethnic problem is generally viewed at the time the work was written. The only fair way to study the image of Poles in American fiction is to take into account all the views and all the factors contributing to them and then try to build as complete a picture as possible. This picture should include a variety of authors, whether their portrayals of Poles are favorable or unfavorable, and it should also include writers from the early waves of Polish immigration as well as those who reached American shores after World War II. Thus I fervently believe and strongly hope that, with the idea of the melting pot gone (one hopes forever) and with ethnic awareness on the rise, American literature will reflect the contribution that Polish Americans have made and are now making to the culture of this country.

Other Writing

Although many Polish plays have been translated, few relate directly to Polish-American letters. One exception is a contemporary playwright whose works are in the tradition of the theater of the absurd. An émigré writer Sławomir Mrożek (b. 1930) has been widely translated and produced. Six of his plays were translated into English and published in 1967: *The Police* (*Policja*), *The Martyrdom of Peter Ohey* (*Męczeństwo Piotra Ohey'a*), *Out At Sea* (*Na pełnym morzu*), *Charlie* (*Karol*), *The Party* (*Zabawa*), and *Enchanted Night* (*Czarowna noc*). The volume does not include *Tango*, his first full-length play, which had its premiere in Warsaw in 1965. The following year *Tango* opened the Summer Season of the Royal Shakespeare Company at the Aldwych Theatre in London. One of Mrozek's more recent plays, *The Blessed Event*, was produced at Pennsylvania State University in 1974, where the author was then an artist in residence.

The *Polish Review*, published by the Polish Institute of Arts and Sciences in America under the editorship of Ludwik Krzyżanowski, is the only periodical in English devoted entirely to Polish history, economics, philosophy, and so forth, as well as to literature. As such, and because it frequently publishes translations of Polish literature, the *Polish Review* represents an important contribution to Polish letters in America. In its relatively long existence, approaching a quarter of a century, the *Polish Review* has published literary articles and reviews, some of them penned by the best scholars in the field. Articles on Polish language and literature, as well as occasional reviews of books on these topics, may also be found in such journals as the *Slavic and East European Journal* and the *Slavic Review* (formerly *American Slavic and East European Review*).

The subject of the Polish press in America is too vast to be tackled within this outline. Jan Kowalik reports that

The origins of the Polish American press go back to 1842 when a group of political refugees in New York started an English language publication entitled *Poland — Historical, Literary, Monumental and Picturesque.* Paul Sobolewski and Eustachy Wyszyński, the editor-publisher team of this periodical, intended to acquaint Americans with the history and culture of Poland and to evoke sympathy toward the partitioned country. Despite favorable publicity (*The New World*, New York, issue from May 28, 1842), an evident lack of support compelled the *Polish Literary Society in America*, which had un-officially endorsed the enterprise, to terminate the publication after a few issues....

...By the late seventies, newspapers were mushrooming in Polish immigrant communities in Milwaukee, Buffalo, Detroit, Winona, Manitowoc, Toledo, Elba, Philadelphia and Pittsburgh. The Polish American journalism became an integral part of the settlers' daily life. When the first historian of the Polish American press, Henryk Nagiel, surveyed the crop in 1893, he counted 105 Polish periodicals appearing in the last thirty years in twelve states of the Union; half of them still being published in 1893.[26]

Kowalik's study deals with the history of the Polish-American press and gives information on the contemporary state of the Polish press in the United States. It is a source not only for the names of Polish-American journals, newspapers, and so forth but also for statistics concerning their circulation. The work also places the Polish press in the context of other ethnic publications.

The reader who is interested in the historical aspect of the Polish-American press should be directed to the essay "An Historical Outline of the Polish Press in America," in which Bernard Pacyniak describes his goal: "The present inquiry is concerned with tracing the history of the Polish press in the United States and, through the benefit of hindsight as well as close observation of *status quo*, determining whether indeed the Polish American press is headed for extinction."[27] He reaches the conclusion that the future of the Polish-American press will largely depend on "how successful Polonia will become as an emerging ethnic group in America's multi-cultural society" (p. 528).

There is no clear-cut place on these pages for a discussion of Julian Ursyn Niemcewicz (1757–1841), the great Polish patriot and writer. His place in this chapter has been secured through his special association with the United States. He is probably the most logical Polish literary figure with whom to conclude.

According to Miłosz: "Niemcewicz is one of the most colorful personalities of Polish letters, and his long life allowed him to live through radically different phases of history" (*The*

History of Polish Literature, p. 170). Through these phases he never ceased writing and became, as a result, one of the most prolific writers in the history of Polish literature. A poet, novelist, translator, playwright, and memorialist, he is known in this country through English translations, particularly for works dealing with America and its heroes, such as George Washington, whom he knew personally.

Niemcewicz accompanied Tadeusz Kościuszko to America as an aide-de-camp on Kościuszko's second visit here in 1797. After Kościuszko's sudden departure for France the following year, Niemcewicz stayed on, settled in New Jersey, married an American woman, and left only when Napoleon created the Duchy of Warsaw in 1807.

Niemcewicz' stay in America and his extensive travels here, including visits to Mount Vernon, resulted in a valuable book, *Travels in America*, which presents a perceptive view of this country as seen through the eyes of a Polish writer. Niemcewicz' book had to wait a century and a half for a translator and found one a dozen or so years ago in America. Rendered as *Under Their Vine and Fig Tree*, and subtitled *Travels through America in 1797-1799 and 1805*, with some further account of life in New Jersey, Niemcewicz' original text was translated and edited with an introduction and notes by Metchie J. E. Budka.[28] This work, by an indefatigable Polish-American scholar, reaching back to the beginnings of America, can serve as a symbol of the literary ties between the two countries that last to this day.

Notes

* Based on my essay in *Poles in America: Bicentennial Essays*, ed. Frank Mocha (Stevens Point, Wis.: Worzalla Publishing, 1978).

[1] Miecislaus [Mieczysław] Haiman, *Polish Past in America, 1608-1865* (Chicago: Polish Museum of America, 1974), p. 27.

[2] A major portion of Sienkiewicz's "Letters from America," which he wrote for Warsaw newspapers, was published in 1959 as *Portrait of America*, trans. Charles Morley (New York: Columbia Univ. Press. 1959).

[3] For an account of Wittlin's life and work, see Zoya Yurieff, *Joseph Wittlin* (New York: Twayne, 1973).

[4] Ivan Sanders, "The Gifts of Strangeness: Alienation and Creation in Jerzy Kosinski's Fiction," *Polish Review*, 19, Nos. 3–4 (1974), 171.

[5] Quoted in Clare D. Kinsman, ed., *Contemporary Authors*, XVII–XX, rev. ed. (Detroit: Gale, 1976), 417.

[6] Frank Mocha, "History as Literature," *Polish Review*, 12, No. 4 (1967), 78, 83.

[7] Quoted in Anne Commire, *Something about the Author* (Detroit: Gale, 1971), p. 228.

[8] *I Lied to Live*, pref. Rex Stout (New York: Roy, 1944); *Bound with Two Chains* (New York: Roy, 1945); and *Psalms of Captivity*, trans. G. White (New York: Pocahontas, 1947).

[9] Aleksander Janta, "Polish Exile Prose," *Queens Slavic Papers* (Flushing, N.Y.: Queens Coll. Press, 1973), I, 8–24.

[10] "Pamięci Aleksandra Janty," *Nowy Dziennik*, 20 Nov. 1975.

[11] Thomas E. Bird, "A Bibliography of the Writings of Paweł Łsek," *Queens Slavic Papers*, I, 93–101.

[12] Florian Śmieja, "The Writer in Exile as Custodian of Folklore," *Queens Slavic Papers*, I, 80–92.

[13] Haiman, *Polish Past in America*, p. 26-27.

[14] *Post-War Polish Poetry: An Anthology*, ed. and trans. Czesław Miłosz (Garden City, N.Y.: Doubleday, 1965).

[15] Czesław Miłosz, *The History of Polish Literature* (New York: Macmillan, 1969), p. 458.

[16] Miłosz is also the author of the autobiographical account *The Native Realm: A Search for Self-Definition* (1968) and the novels *The Seizure of Power* (Eng. trans. 1955) and *The Issa Valley* (Engl. trans. 1981).

[17] A "Selected Bibliography" of all the works of Miłosz can be found in *World Literature Today*, 52 (1978), 373–76.

[18] Tadeusz Mitana, ed., *Anthology of Polish-American Poetry* (Chicago: Polish Arts Club, 1937).

[19] For more information, see Jerzy (George) J. Maciuszko, *The Polish Short Story in English* (Detroit: Wayne State Univ. Press, 1968).

[20] *Tales by Polish Authors*, trans. Else C. M. Benecke (Oxford: Blackwell, 1915).

[21] *More Tales by Polish Authors*, trans. Else C.M. Benecke and Marie Busch (Oxford: Blackwell, 1916).

[22] Apart from selected bibliographies, the following essays, all published in *Polish American Studies*, deal with Poles in American fiction: Walter Zebrowski, "Polish Americans in Fiction," 16, Nos. 1–2 (1959), 62–64; 'Critical Appreciation of Ruth Tabrah's *Pulaski Place*," 16, Nos. 3–4 (1959), 120–28; "Poles in Gladys Hasty Carroll's *As the Earth Turns*," 20, No. 1 (1963), 17–20; and John W. Petras, "Polish Americans in Sociology and Fiction," 21, No. 1 (1964), 16–22.

[23] Monica Krawczyk, *If the Branch Blossoms and Other Stories* (Minneapolis: Polanie, 1950), pp. v–vi.

[24] Quoted in Clare D. Kinsman, ed., *Contemporary Authors*, XIII-XVI (Detroit: Gale, 1975), 18–19.

[25] *Polish Literature in English Translation* (New York: Wilson, 1932).

[26] Jan Kowalik, *The Polish Press in America* (San Francisco: R and E Research, 1978), pp. 2–3.

[27] *Poles in America*, ed. Frank Mocha (Stevens Point, Wis.: Worzalla, 1978), p. 509.

[28] Published in 1965 as Vol. XIV in the Collections of the New Jersey Historical Society in Newark.

Portuguese-American Literature

Leo Pap

Portuguese-American literature cannot compare in bulk with the Hispanic literature of the United States or with that of the Italians or Germans or Poles. Portugal is a small country, and the Portuguese population of North America, even if we include Canada, has never reached the million mark (if we limit ourselves to the foreign-born and the second generation). Portuguese ethnics have settled rather compactly in southeastern New England, metropolitan New York, and New Jersey as well as in central California. At an earlier stage many Portuguese settled in Hawaii, and since World War II many have moved to southeastern Canada. If we disregard a very sporadic Portuguese presence from the early sixteenth to the midnineteenth century, we may place the onset of the Portuguese mass immigration into the United States in the last third of the nineteenth century. This movement was first triggered in New England by whaling-industry contacts and then later by a demand for textile labor. Most Portuguese in New England and, more recently, in parts of Canada have been mill workers, whereas the Portuguese in California have veered toward dairying and intensive farming. Those who went to Hawaii originally worked as contract laborers on the sugar plantations.

Two other facts stand out. First, most Portuguese came from *insular* Portugal, that is, chiefly from the Azores but also from the Madeira and Cape Verde islands. The so-called Continentals, from mainland Portugal, started arriving half a century after the islanders, with some exceptions, and they still represent only a small part of the group. Second, the earlier Portuguese immigrants, those who came before World War I, included a higher percentage of illiterates than did almost any other immigrant nationality, and they were generally of peasant background. Since the late 1950s, however, the heavy influx of Portuguese immigrants, chiefly into southeastern New England, has been of a different ilk: generally literate and largely from urban backgrounds.[1]

What, then, exists in the way of literature produced by Portuguese immigrants and their children? There isn't any to speak of, I was bluntly told by various literate Portuguese Americans when I first became interested in this population group in the 1940s. (By contrast, French-Canadian literature in New England, not counting works by residents of Canada, was then said to comprise at least four hundred titles.)[2] By the 1970s Francis M. Rogers reported having unearthed "only" fourteen published books of what might be called creative Portuguese-American literature written in the United States (five volumes of verse, two autobiographies, seven novels).[3] What follows is a brief but, I hope, reasonably complete and up-to-date account of this minor, yet always interesting, literature.

I begin with a few Portuguese who, while residing in the United States during the second half of the nineteenth century, were actually diplomatic representatives of Portugal at least part of the time, but with relatively close ties to the American Republic. Frederico Francesco Stuart de Figanière e Morão was born in New York in 1827, the son of a native Portuguese who had become Portugal's minister to Washington and in 1825 had married an American woman of Scottish descent. Frederico himself entered Portugal's diplomatic service as a young man, serving in Washington, under his father, for a number of years after 1847 and later in other world capitals. In 1848 he married the daughter of U.S. General Henry Jackson Hunt. He combined diplomacy with an interest in scholarship and in writing. Works of nonfiction by Figanière e Morão include, in English, a chronological table of European emperors, kings, popes, and so on, from the year 800 to his day (1850); a travel account, *Notes Taken during a Trip to Santarem, Batalha and Alcobaça* (1852); and, in Portuguese, *Memorias das rainhas de Portugal* (1859). In 1861, in the weekly magazine *New York Ledger*, there appeared two tales entitled "The Shoemaker of Seville" and "The Phantom's Cave." Both were published anonymously with the notation, "Translated from the Portuguese," but they may nevertheless be original stories by Figanière.

Later that year, the same literary journal published a third tale entitled "A Millionaire's Revenge," to which Figanière, now coming halfway out of his anonymity, appended the initials "F.F.F."

And finally, also in 1861 and still in the same *New York Ledger*, Figanière published a short novel, "Vasco Peres, the Cooper of Alcobaça," eighteen brief chapters spread over eight installments, again under the cloak of anonymity.[4] The first two stories are set in Spain, the third in France, the fourth in Portugal; all of them have a historical base and an archaic-romantic style typical of the magazine fiction of the period. It would appear, from the documents at hand, that Figanière's writing career ended after 1861, probably because of his transfer to other diplomatic posts with greater responsibilities.

Two Portuguese consular officials stationed in the United States in the 1860s and 1870s in a sense complemented each other as authors, one interpreting the United States to the Portuguese back home, the other describing his Azorean home to New Englanders. The former, Antonio da Cunha Pereira de Sotto Maior, lived in New York from 1861 to 1866 and in Washington from 1869 to 1872, first in the capacity of consul general, then with the rank of chargé d'affaires of the Portuguese delegation. During those years he compiled a three-volume history of the United States, based largely on the works of George Bancroft and Benson Lossing. *Os Estados Unidos: Esboço histórico desde a descoberta da América até à presidência de Johnson (1492–1865)*, published in Lisbon (1877–78, 1881), attracted considerable attention, for as Cunha Pereira explained in his "Prólogo" and as critical press reviews soon confirmed, the Portuguese of that period knew little about the United States; in effect this was the first history of the United States to be published in Portugal.

The other author, Manuel Borges de Freitas Henriques, wrote a handsome travel narrative entitled *A Trip to the Azores or Western Islands* (1867) to acquaint Yankees with the homeland of the several hundred Portuguese immigrants — soon to number in the thousands — who had begun to settle around Boston and New Bedford. These early settlers were almost exclusively from the western Azores (the islands of Faial and Flores). Borges himself was born on Flores in the 1830s, emigrated to the United States in 1848, and eventually became the Portuguese consul in Boston and ran a small shipping business. His little book, written in impeccable English, offers lively alternation between objective description and sensitive personal comment.[5]

A fascinating personality was Manuel Garcia Monteiro, one of the relatively few early Portuguese immigrants of the intelligentsia who in some measure succeeded. Born in the western Azorean town of Horta in 1859, Garcia Monteiro showed a literary bent in his early years, publishing poems in local newspapers, seeing one or two of his one-act comedies performed, briefly even floating his own newspaper. In 1884, after publishing *Versos*, a small volume of nineteen poems, he sailed for the United States and settled in New Bedford. In a series of letters written by Garcia Monteiro to a friend back in Portugal between 1884 and 1890 and subsequently published by Henrique das Neves in a volume entitled *Individualidades*, we learn of the young intellectual's struggle against poverty and of his short-lived attempt to get another newspaper going, among a readership of semiliterate factory workers whom he unceremoniously described as a bunch of "hippopotamuses...." Finally forced into poorly paid factory jobs himself, he fought off a bout with tuberculosis and ultimately managed to work his way through medical school in Boston (which was tuition-free at that time!). After his graduation in 1890, he married a woman from upstate New York, herself a writer, and he practiced as a physician in the Boston area until his death in 1913.[6] In 1896 he published his second little volume of poems, *Rimas de ironia alegre*.[7] Written in a vein of social satire somewhat reminiscent of Eça de Queiroz and Voltaire, the poems mainly are about conditions in Portugal.

Another member of the small Portuguese immigrant intelligentsia in New England early in this century and, if we disregard purely journalistic efforts, probably one of the most prolific and genuinely gifted authors was Quirino de Souza. A native of Lisbon, he attended the Escola Politecnica there, married, founded a dramatic group, and with it toured the Cape Verde Islands. From Brava, Quirino de Souza emigrated with his wife to the United States in 1894, settling in New Bedford, where he remained until his death in about 1930. The picture of him that emerges from various sources is that of a melancholy Bohemian who wrote a great many plays, poems, and so on but who seldom bothered to collect them for publication. He worked in factories and at the same time wrote for several Portuguese immigrant weeklies and for limited periods filled the position of editor. Some of his plays, of either one act or three acts, were perfomed by dramatic groups he directed under the pseudonym "Zig-Zag." In the daily *Alvorada Diária* for the year 1920, for example, at least one poem by de Souza appears in each issue! Some of his earlier poems were printed as a volume entitled *Estilhaços* (1900). Another book of his poems appeared under the title *As ilhas em audiência*. The transatlantic flight by Sacadura Cabral and Gago Coutinho in 1922 was an occasion for a long poem by de Souza, "Os herois do ar." The *Alvorada Diária*, in the early 1920s, contained short stories of his, such as "O papagaio da fábrica," and even a full-blown adventure novel entitled "Aventuras de dois gemeos," besides almost daily satirical comments on the news.[8]

Characteristically, the great bulk of Portuguese immigrant writing, in the narrower sense of this term, is buried in the (often lost) back files of Portuguese immigrant newspapers, most of which appeared weekly or less frequently. One major exception was a daily newspaper that was published in New Bedford from the early twenties until just a few years ago. There have also been some, usually short-lived, Portuguese immigrant magazines or journals with belletristic-intellectual ambitions. All in all, since the 1880s until this day, in New England and central California primarily but also in Hawaii, metropolitan New York, and more recently in southeastern Canada, there have been literally scores of Portuguese immigrant newspapers, some of them surviving for several decades, others giving up the ghost after a few months or a few years. How much of their contents can be called immigrant literature is a matter of definition. In this brief survey, I must necessarily disregard most of the journalistic output and single out primarily those individuals who have published some material in book or pamphlet form.

During World War I and the 1920s, once more two Portuguese consular officials in the United States (long-term visitors rather than immigrants) wrote about the American scene, more or less critically from the Portuguese point of view. Alfredo Mesquita, who had been consul in New York earlier in the century, published in 1916 a volume entitled *A America do Norte*. Eduardo de Carvalho, a consul in Boston from 1922 to 1925, was unusually active in trying to "educate" New England's Portuguese "colony" and to strengthen its members' loyalty to the old country. Carvalho's book, *Os Portugueses na Nova Inglaterra*, published in Rio de Janeiro around 1930, in an intelligent and informative, though biased, account of many aspects of Portuguese immigrant life of the period.[9] Another

Portuguese, Alfredo Amado, wrote a travel account covering American life in general and life in New York and Boston in particular, under the title *Vida Americana* in 1918.

Among the relatively few Portuguese immigrants who have shown strong political consciousness and activist commitment over the past hundred years or so, one of the most vocal was Porfirio Bessone, who was especially active during World War I and well into the twenties. Born in 1874 at Ponta Delgada, the largest city in the Azores, of aristocratic ancestry but from the low white-collar class, Bessone strongly espoused the antiroyalist and anticlerical cause, and after his immigration into the United States in 1905 wrote vehemently against what he called "reactionaries," particularly against Jesuits and the Catholic church in general. His interests, it seems, remained focused on the old country; he never became an American citizen. In Cambridge, Massachusetts, where he lived until his death in 1948, he made a modest living as a printer and piano tuner. His volume of satires, *Espontâneos,* appeared shortly before the outbreak of World War I. This work was followed in 1914 by an anticlerical volume of over 400 pages entitled *Abusos cristãos.* A year later, Bessone published *Autopsia ao "Piloto,"* a critical analysis of the Jesuit organ of the Boston archdiocese. *Liberais e reaccionários* (1919) was the title of a two-volume collection of articles that Porfirio Bessone had written for two Portuguese immigrant newspapers.

Bessone's journalistic output seems to have waned in the 1920s. He turned instead to writing little skits, duets, monologues, and miscellaneous comical short pieces with or without music, in the vein of Azorean popular entertainment, for performance at club affairs and various social events in the New England Portuguese communities. During the 1930s Bessone wrote several one- or two-act comedies, and a more substantial three-act drama entitled *A vingança dum negro.* In 1932, on the occasion of the five hundredth anniversary of the discovery of the Azores, he compiled a *Dicionário cronológico dos Açores,* a long series of chronological tables rather awkwardly arranged by alphabetized cue words or subject categories. All these writings appeared as author's editions in Cambridge.

A different kind of Portuguese immigrant laboring in industrial New England during the interwar period is represented by Antonio Luiz Marques and by Joaquim de Oliveira. The former poured out his frustrations and miscellaneous criticisms — not so much of America as of his fellow immigrants — in a 1924 volume of mostly journalistic pieces entitled *Gente sem pátria* (*People without a Homeland*). Oliveira — a native of continental Portugal who settled in Danbury Connecticut, some time after World War I—gathered a dozen or so nostalgic poems under the title *Do meu coração ao vosso* (*From My Heart to Yours*), published around 1934.

S. Cardoso de Silva, born on the small island of Pico in the western Azores, reached Martha's Vineyard off the New England coast at a tender age, perhaps as a stowaway on a Yankee vessel — as did quite a few Azorean boys in the early days of Portuguese immigration. Cardoso de Silva spent his school years and much of his adult life on Martha's Vineyard, in an environment much like that of his early boyhood, unlike most other Azoreans who had to adjust to the drabness of New England's textile mills and tenements. Most fittingly, two published works of his, both in English, are a three-act musical comedy-drama entitled *The Azorean* (1933) and a volume of twenty-five exquisite, superbly wrought poems, bearing the title *Songs of the Vineyard* (1932). *The Azorean*, which may be partly autobiographical, tells of an orphaned Azorean youngster of relatively wealthy parentage who arrives in New Bedford, where he is adopted by (and eventually marries into) a Yankee family; he ultimately returns to the Azores to claim his rightful heritage from greedy relatives. In a letter addressed to me some thrity years ago, Cardoso de Silva, then principal of the Boston School of Self Expression, wrote, without false modesty: "There is so much that I have done [i.e., his writings] that it would hardly be possible to gather it and send it to you." His other plays, as of 1945, included *The Cosmopolitans* and *The Song of Italy.* They, as well as *The Azorean*, were repeatedly performed. Moreover, Cardoso de Silva was successful on the lecture circuit with inspirational and self-improvement talks. For ten years, he was in charge of the Little Art Theatre on Martha's Vineyard, where he wrote and produced many plays. There, before setting up his school in Boston, he conducted the Vineyard School, and in the Midwest he founded De Silva College, and Psychean School in Philadelphia.

Most of the writings mentioned so far originated in the Portuguese settlements of New England and adjoining parts of the northeastern seaboard, but there was also a second major area of Portuguese settlement: California.

Guilherme Silveira da Gloria, born on Pico in the Azores in 1863, did not publish a major volume of poetry until the 1930s. When he had nearly completed his studies for the priesthood, Gloria left the Azores for California, where he was ordained. He did mission work in various Portuguese immigrant communities and became a pastor in Oakland in 1896. After a few years in that post, he abandoned the priesthood to marry a native of Santa Ana and threw himself into journalism, a career he had pursued part-time while he was still a priest. In 1900 he founded the weekly *A Liberdade*, which he was to direct until its demise in 1936. Many of his poems originally appeared in that newspaper. The volume entitled *Poesias*, published by the author in 1935, contains a selection of these and earlier pieces, some on religious or lyrical themes but most in commemoration or celebration of some community event. In addition this volume contains the lengthy epic poem "Cabrilho," which honors the Portuguese discoverer of California and resembles somewhat the *Lusiadas* by Camões. A second, much briefer volume of occasional poetry appeared in 1940 under the title *Harpejos*. In the course of his long journalistic career, Gloria also translated (and published in his newspaper) several French and English novels. He died in 1943.

Starting in 1930 and for nearly three decades thereafter, Arthur V. Avila and his wife Celeste conducted a Portuguése-language radio program in California. To this program Avila himself contributed many poems over the years, usually quatrains dealing with love, with memories of Portugal, and the like. Avila, born in 1888 on Pico in the Azores, had come to California in 1909 and spent years working for immigrant newspapers in that area before switching to broadcasting. Some of his best poems were first published in Oakland's *Jornal Português*. In 1961, a year before his death, he gathered much of his poetry in two volumes, *Rimas de um imigrante* and *Desafio radiofónico*.[10]

Probably the only Portuguese immigrant author ever to make the book review section of the *New York Times* was Alfred Lewis, who in 1951 published his largely autobiographical novel *Home Is an Island.* Lewis (Luiz before he Anglicized his name) hailed from the Azorean island of Flores. He arrived in California penniless in 1922 at age nineteen, held a variety of jobs, including one as a typesetter for a Portuguese immigrant newpaper finally studied law and eventually became a judge. When I interviewed him in Los Banos in 1962, he was operating a real estate office. In his novel, Lewis recreated his childhood years on Flores, writing, as the *Times* book reviewer put it , with simple directness and tender feeling; the book is a slight exercise in nostalgia, without any real plot.[11] Until his recent death, Lewis also tried his hand at plays and short stories as well as poetry.

Apart from Alfred Lewis, at least four recent authors of Portuguese birth or extraction may be described as novelists. Fausto Lage, a physician who immigrated from Portugal in 1925 and who practiced medicine in New Bedford and Lowell, Massachusetts, for many years before moving to San Leandro, California, first tried his hand at writing a historical novel in Portuguese entitled *Joana d'Arc*, published in Lisbon; it deals with the heroine of Orléans. This was followed by *Fantastic Dilemma* (1951). Written in English and set partly in the Cape Verde islands, it is a strange mixture of romantic mysticism and science fiction. Elvira Osorio Roll, a second- or third-generation Portuguese-Hawaiian, wrote *Hawaii's Kohala Breezes* (1964), a novel about a girl of Portuguese descent in Hawaii who is in love with a "haole," a white Anglo, and who gets caught in interethnic tensions. James Carvalho, a radio announcer of Portuguese extraction, also in Hawaii, wrote a short novel entitled *Haole Come Back!* (1975) under the name Oaktree Carvalho. The story involves a Portuguese family that resists eviction by native Hawaiians by retreating to a secluded mountain sanctuary.

Another novel is *Aventuras no Eldorado*, by João J. Vieira Jr., a Protestant minister in Oakland. The book, published in Portugal in 1966, has been called overly romantic in style and religious and moralistic in theme. The plot includes a Dantean journey under California's Sierra Nevada. Vieira has also written an autobiography, *Eu falo por mim mesmo* (1963).

Two recent autobiographical accounts written in English by Portuguese immigrants who have synthesized the Portuguese and American experience deserve mention here. Lawrence Oliver (Lourenço Oliveira), born on Pico in the Azores in 1887, arrived in California in 1903 and worked his way up to a position as a leading businessman in San Diego, where he died in 1978. His engrossing life history was published in 1972 under the significant title *Never Backward*. Equally well chosen is the title of the autobiography of Laurinda C. Andrade, *The Open Door* (1968). Andrade crossed the Atlantic from Terceira, Azores, in 1917 as a young woman emigrating on her own. She started out as a cotton mill worker like most of New Bedford's Portuguese, but she found America's door open enough to allow her to get through college and become a high school teacher of Portuguese.

None of the authors mentioned so far has ever been known to a wide public; nor could any of them be described as a professional writer, although some of them made a living as journalists. The next two names, however, do belong to professional literary men of some renown: José Rodrigues Migueis and John Dos Passos. I mention Dos Passos with hesitation and only in passing, for despite his Portuguese name, he was a native American whose Portuguese ancestry was limited to one Portuguese-born grandfather — a Madeiran who had setted in Philadelphia as a shoemaker about 1830. In his later years, however, Dos Passos manifested a strong interest (not atypical of second- or third-generation ethnics) in his one-fourth Portuguese descent. In 1969, one year before his death, he published *The Portugal Story: Three Centuries of Exploration and Discovery*, an overall history of Portugal for the general public. Some years earlier, in 1961, Dos Passos had accepted the Peter Francisco prize offered him by the Portuguese Continental Union of the United States.[12] Francis M. Rogers, in a recent booklet assembling many interesting details about this celebrated American writer's awareness of his Portuguese heritage, concludes that this heritage had an "extraordinary impact" on Dos Passos and on his literary production.[13]

José Rodrigues Migueis was born in 1901 in Lisbon, where he went through law school. After a few years in legal practice and a brief period of high school teaching, Migueis left Portugal (which had meanwhile come under the fascist rule of Salazar) in 1929 and spent most of the next four years as a graduate student of education in Brussels. He published his first novel, *Páscoa feliz*, in 1932. In 1935, unable to reconcile his leftist liberal views with life under Salazar's leadership, he emigrated to the United States and subsequently spent the greater part of his adult life in New York City as a translator, a magazine editor, and ultimately a free-lance writer. He briefly resumed residence in Portugal several times after the war but always returned to New York, where he continued to live until his death in November 1980. Although he was an American citizen and fluent in English, Migueis did most of his professional writing in Portuguese, thus sharply curtailing his chances of becoming better known in the United States and at the same time getting little recognition in his native country. (The new Portuguese regime, however, did award him a high decoration in 1979.)

The writings of Rodrigues Migueis most relevant to the Portuguese immigrant experience and to the American scene are all in the form of short stories, most of them closely based on actual occurrences and some of them only thinly fictionalized. A thread of deep concern for social justice and a mixture of more sadness than humor are woven into most of these pieces, which are generally written in a fairly simple and straightforward style. Many first appeared in Portuguese-language newspapers or magazines; they have been collected in five volumes so far, published at different times in Portugal or Brazil. This output is in addition to several full-length novels and at least two volumes of essays. Actually Migueis published little in the 1940s and early 1950s, partly because of illness; the bulk of his work dates from about 1956 to the mid-1970s.

Space does not permit more than a brief summary of the most characteristic stories. In the volume entitled *Gente da terceira classe* (1964), we find an autobiographical story of the same title that describes a voyage from Lisbon to the United States, via Southampton, with Portuguese and Spanish emigrants constituting "third-class people." "O Cosme de Riba Douro," in the same volume, revolves around an illegal Portuguese immigrant on Manhattan's waterfront during World War II who is willing to fight and die for democracy. "Natal branco," also set in Manhattan, sketches the life-style of a Portuguese-born window washer. In "O viajante clandestino," we find a Portuguese stowaway being let into the country at Baltimore by a kindly policeman who is willing to look the other way. In *Onde a noite se acaba* (Rio de Janeiro, 1946), the story "Beleza orgulhosa" (this one also published in an English version elsewhere) tells of the murder of a nightclub dancer, daughter of an immigrant janitor, in a building where the author was living at the time.

In a third volume entitled *Leah e outras histórias* (1958), Migueis provides perceptive glimpses of New York City in a rather funny piece entitled "Pouca sorte com barbeiros." This is the only story Migueis ever wrote in English and then rewrote in Portuguese. "O natal do Dr. Crosby," in the same collection, also treats life in the United States. In the fairly recent volume, *O espelho poliédrico* (1972), Migueis recalls a holdup in New York in "Linóleo 36," tells of the tribulations of yet another illegal New York resident in "Com visto de visitante," and recounts the ill fate of an Azorean family in Queens beset by illness and death in "Uma casa portuguesa". Several more episodes or vignettes of the same type are "Na casa-de-bordo," on the life of some Portuguese boarding together near Manhattan's waterfront; "Bowery '64," a compassionate sketch of the Manhattan district frequented by derelicts; and "Sua majestade o automóvel," reflections on the motorization of American life. The latest volume of stories, *Comércio com o inimigo* (1973), describes a New York shopping crowd on Chirstmas eve ("O conto alegre de natal que não escrevi"), relations between members of a Portuguese immigrant club ("A inauguração"), and the like. Although I have concentrated on stories set in the United States, many other narratives by Rodrigues Migueis, ranging from brief sketches to full-length novels, are set in Portugal and other parts of Europe.[14]

The published work of this important Portuguese immigrant author spans half a century; thus it reaches from the older period of Portuguese settlement in the United States to the large new wave of immigration that began about 1960. As indicated at the beginning of this essay, these newer immigrants have a higher average level of literacy than did the earlier arrivals. From their ranks may well arise a number of worthwhile writers in coming years. To conclude this survey, at least three of these newer names warrant brief mention here.

Jorge de Sena, who was already a recognized poet in his native Portugal when he came to the United States, taught Luso-Brazilian literature at American universities until his untimely death in 1978. In 1972, while at the University of California at Santa Barbara, he composed a series of eight meditative poems referring to the nearby "semi-deserted Pacific shores," *Sobre esta praia: oito meditações à beira do Pacífico.* They were first published at Santa Barbara in 1977 and reprinted two years later together with a translation by Jonathan Griffin. Another collection of de Sena's poems had appeared in Portugal in 1974. José Brites, born in continental Portugal in 1945, was an airline mechanic at the time of his emigration to the United States in 1970. In this country, while employed as a steelworker in Bethlehem, Pennsylvania, he published a book of his poems in 1975 under the title *Poemas sem poesia;* they deal in part with the immigrant's experience. Brites has continued to produce poetry while embarking on an academic career. Onesimo T. Almeida, a native of São Miguel in the Azores and currently on the faculty of Brown University, published a volume of essays in

1975; under the title *A vida quotidiana na Lusalândia*, they constitute a critical analysis of Portuguese immigrant life. This was followed in 1978 by the play, *Ah! Monim dum corisco*, which is actually a series of skits satirizing the immigrant community.

To sum up, the published literature of Portuguese-American authors — most of them immigrants but a few of them Portuguese residents of the United States who did not consider themselves immigrants, and two or three of them native Americans close to their Portuguese heritage — has been modest so far. It cannot be termed entirely negligible, however, if we consider the numerical and educational limitations of this ethnic group. Much of the material cited, the greater part written in Portuguese rather than in English, does reflect the typical immigrant experience, often nostalgically harking back to Portugal, but just as often revealing a growing concern with and for America.

Notes

[1] For a complete account of Portuguese immigration, see Leo Pap, *The Portuguese-Americans* (Boston: Twayne, 1981). I describe language conditions among these immigrants in my earlier *Portuguese-American Speech* (New York: King's Crown, 1949).

[2] Jacques Ducharme, *The Shadows of the Trees: The Story of French Canadians in New England* (New York: Harper, 1943), p. 134.

[3] Francis M. Rodgers, "The Portuguese Experience in the United States: Double Melt or Minority Group?" *Journal of the American Portuguese Society* 10 (Spring 1976), 1–16.

[4] See the biographical sketch in Esteves Pereira and Guilherme Rodrigues, eds., *Portugal: Diccionário histórico, chorográfico, biográphico...* (Lisbon: Torres, 1904–15), III, 456.

[5] For comments on and by Borges, see *The North End Mission Magazine*, 2, No. 3 (1873), 65–66, 71–72, 73–74.

[6] Henrique das Neves, *Individualidades: Traço característicos, episódios e anécdotas authênticas de indivíduos que se evidenciaram* (Lisbon: Pereira, 1910), esp. "O dr. Garcia Monteiro," pp. 57–81. See also excerpts from two letters in Eduardo de Carvalho, *Os Portugueses na Nova Inglaterra* (Rio de Janeiro: A Leitura Colonial, 1931), pp. 153–54.

[7] Of the thirty-five poems in the collection, which was privately printed in Boston, only sixteen carry a Boston dateline; the rest are from Horta or Lisbon. In a note the author explains that these poems (all of them? or only those not showing the Boston dateline?) were in manuscript in Portugal by 1884; a friend sent them to Garcia Monteiro in Boston a few years later, and he ultimately revised them for publlication. Some poems by Garcia Monteiro were published in Lisbon in the *Diário da Manhã*, 4 May 1885. Others appeared in Porfirio Bessone, *Almanach luso-americano 1910*, p. 15, and in *Portugal-America*, Sept. 1928, p. 17.

[8] Some plays by Quirino de Souza are *O filho das ondas* (three acts, performed in New Bedford in 1922); *Beldemónio; Os guisos do trenó* (three acts, performed in 1935 as well as earlier); *O violino encantado* (three acts, based on a novel by H. P. Escrich); *Sem tirar nem pôr* (one act); *A morgadinha de Tavira* (written in 1908); and *Thomá Thomé & Ca.* (one-act musical, written in 1895).

[9] Using various pseudonyms, Carvalho also wrote several shorter pamphlets in which he criticized his "flock." They include *Problemas da nossa colónia, Palestras coloniais,* and *Falar e escrever,* all privately printed in Boston in 1924.

[10] In a vein somewhat similar to Avila's, Manuel J. Nunes contributed several dozen popular poems of great charm to the *Jornal Português,* but they never appeared in volume form. Nunes, too, had been born on Pico Island, in 1874, and upon settling in California, worked himself up from fisherman to boatbuilder. He attributed his knowledge of metrics to Guilherme Gloria.

[11] See *New York Times,* 9 Feb. 1951. For a more recent review see Nelson H. Vieira in *Gávea-Brown* (a "bilingual journal of Portuguese-American letters and studies," Brown Univ.), 1, No. 1 (Jan.–June 1980), 18–25. In this review, Vieira also mentions two short stories by Lewis, "Box-Maker DeLuxe" and "Fame, Fortune and Tequila," published in *Prairie Schooner,* 23 (1949), 374, and 24 (1950), 388.

[12] The Portuguese Continental Union is the leading mutual aid society, or fraternal insurance company, of the Portuguese Americans in the eastern United States. The name of Peter Francisco, who was a powerful soldier in George Washington's army and reputedly of Portuguese birth, has become an ethnic rallying symbol for the New England Portuguese since World War II.

[13] Francis M. Rogers, *The Portuguese Heritage of John Dos Passos* (Boston: Portuguese Continental Union, 1976).

[14] See the comprehensive bio-bibliographical monograph by John Austin Kerr, Jr., *Migueis: To the Seventh Decade* (University: Univ. Press of Mississippi, 1977), which covers Migueis' publications to 1973. Kerr's bibliography is an updated extract from his doctoral dissertation (Univ. of Wisconsin, Madison, 1970). Other portions of his dissertation, with later elaborations, have been published as articles in *Estudios Ibero-Americanos,* 2, No. 2 (1976), 261–68, and 3, No. 2 (1977), 273–81; *Modern Languages,* 59, No. 3 (1978), 146–50; *Kentucky Romance Quarterly,* 25 (1978), 225–41; *Journal of the American Portuguese Society,* 13 (1979), 19–27; *Romance Notes,* 19, No. 3 (1979), 1–6; *University of South Florida Language Quarterly,* 17, Nos. 3–4 (1979), 31–33, 40; and *Revista Lingua e Literatura,* No. 5 (1976), 169–207.

Romanian-American Literature

Alexandra Roceric

Romanians belong to the so-called new immigration to the United States, the wave that started in the 1800s, reached its peak in the years before World War I, and included people chiefly from Southern and Eastern Europe. This community has been little studied as a distinct group within the larger context of the American nation and culture. It is, however, a clearly identifiable minority that has exhibited over the last seventy years a surprising ability to preserve its cultural identity and attachment to ethnic roots, while integrating itself increasingly into the American society.

The first Romanians are reported in America in 1748. Subsequently, the presence of a small group of Romanians was noted in 1849, immigrants having been attracted by the gold rush in California. More Romanians came to this country between 1850 and 1880, when they are reported for the first time in the Annual Report of the Immigration and Naturalization Service. Large-scale immigration from Romania developed around 1900, when large groups from the Romanian provinces of Transylvania, Banat, Bucovina, Moldavia, and Macedonia entered the United States. By 1901 the newly arrived people had settled in or around large industrial centers, including New York, Philadelphia, Chicago, Detroit, Cleveland, Pittsburgh, Minneapolis, Youngstown, Saint Louis, Los Angeles, and San Francisco. Many of the émigrés were underprivileged Romanians who had been driven from their homeland primarily by precarious economic, social, and political conditions.

The first ten years after the turn of the century saw the growth of a host of secular and religious organizations of Romanian Americans. In 1902 the first mutual aid and cultural societies were founded: Vulturul, Homestead, Carpatina, Cleveland. The first Romanian churches were built in 1904 (Saint Mary's, Cleveland) and in 1905 (Saint Helen's, eastern Cleveland); both churches still exist. Romanian parochial schools began to open in 1911, the first one in Scalp Level, Pennsylvania. Romanian newspapers and periodicals had their beginnings in Cleveland: *Tribuna* (*The Tribune*, 1903), *Românul* (*The Romanian*, 1905), and *America*, 1906; the last of these significantly is still in print.

Immediately after World War I, a second large wave of immigrants arrived and settled around the centers of the older Romanian enclaves. Community efforts expanded to absorb and assist the newcomers. New newspapers were published; a diversification of organizations and professional groups occurred; Romanian women and young people organized their own clubs and societies. In 1928 at a convention in Cleveland, an umbrella association for all these organizations was created— the Union and League of the Romanian Societies of America. This helped expand and give structure to cultural, artistic, and political activities intended to help maintain identity and to promote mutual assistance among Americans of Romanian origin.

The post–World War II period was marked by still another wave of immigration, consisting this time of representatives of the middle and upper classes, the educated strata of Romanian society. Among the lay and religious publications these new immigrants have started are *Credinţa* (*The Faith*, Detroit, 1950–), *Micromagazin* (New York, 1972–), *Comuniunea Românească* (*Romanian Communion*, Detroit, 1973–), and *Romanian Sources* (Pittsburgh, 1975). New organizations include AROY (1961), for American-Romanian orthodox youth, and ARCAYD (1971), for Catholic youth. Continuing efforts have been made to maintain Romanian language and culture by means of radio programs in Detroit, Cleveland, and Chicago and since 1976, a special television program in Detroit.

The Romanian population in the United States is presently estimated at about 200,000, representing basically three generations. Small numbers of new immigrants continue to arrive, though slowly, from Romania.

A recent development bearing on the maintenance of the native culture in Romanian-American communities is an increase in travel by members of this minority group to the land of their forebears. Personal and group contacts have developed in the last eight to ten years; many older Romanian immigrants, who are now naturalized Americans, and their offspring travel to Romania to visit family homes and relatives. Family members living in Romania in turn are invited for visits to this country. Printed materials, records, and other materials flow in more regularly and complement the publications in Romanian that continue to be produced in the United States.

The number of studies dealing with Romanian immigrants in the United States is quite limited. This literature on Romanian-American communities is for the most part essayistic. Serban Drutzu and Andrei Popovici's *Românii în America* (1926) outlined aspects of Romanian life in America. Nicolae Iorga's *America şi Românii din America: Note de drum şi conferinţe* (1930) described the author's travel impressions after he met with Romanian Americans on a trip to the United States. Constantin C. Giurescu adopted the same approach in his tourist notes *Jurnal de călătorie* (1977).

The only comprehensive sociological account that covers the period up to 1929 is Christine Avghi Galitizi's scholarly monograph on assimilation of Romanians in the United States, *A Study of Assimilations among the Romanians in the United States* (1929). *Peasants and Strangers: Italians, Rumanians, and Slovaks in an American City* (1975) by Josef S. Barton compares the particular experiences of three immigrant groups—Italians, Romanians, and Slovaks—in an industrial metropolis and comes to the conclusion that ethnicity is a differentiating factor in career mobility. Recently, Vladimir Wertsman published *The Romanians in America* (1975), a chronological fact book that covers the years 1748 to 1974 and includes reprints of a few articles written in English by Romanian Americans in the last fifty years. Şerban Andronescu compiled *Who's Who in Romanian America* for those Americans who claim any kind of relation with Romania (birth, language, activity, or interest). Radu Toma's *Românii din America* (1978) is an annotated bibliography in Romanian on Romanian-American literature. Eli Popa's *Romania Is a Song: A Sample in Translation* (1967) contains some information on Romanian-American literature. Popa presents a few classic Romanian and Romanian-American poets and provides short biographies of the translated poets.

The first Romanian-American authors were not professional writers. Generally, they were peasants before they came to the United States. After arriving in the new country, these people started working hard, most of them in mines and factories, and they had little time in which to indulge in the pleasures of literature. They composed songs and poems to unburden their souls and to express enthusiasm and disappointment, tenderness and homesickness, solidarity and protest, good nature and anger. The poets showed a certain lyricism in their approach to their new realities, and their perceptions probably became sharper because they were aliens in a foreign land. They had also brought along from the homeland the necessary Romanian folkloric style for expressing their feeling about various situations, even if sometimes their subjects were prosaic. And when they met in boardinghouses (*bortul*) or in saloons (*salonul*) and later at festivals organized by the Romanian cultural societies, they shared not only the same language but also the same heritage. By singing, reciting, or reading Romanian newspapers and magazines, they managed to preserve part of their former common experience very well and they kept enriching it steadily. New songs and stories resulted in a new Romanian-American folklore. Most of the rhyming songs and literary texts in verse from the turn of the century were written in Romanian and published in the Romanian-American press after 1900.

Among the many popular artists, Dumitru Banciu and Nick Beldean are the best-known poets. While their works are in Romanian and therefore not accessible to the American readers, some young American researchers have now started to collect and analyze the early Romanian-American folklore. In *Folklore and Ethnicity in the Lives of Romanian-Americans* (1973), Kenneth Thigpen wrote on the importance of ethnicity in the lives of Romanian Americans, as reflected in folklore generated by the immigration experience. Thigpen's study is based on a large number of interviews with older Romanian Americans, whose folk narratives he has transcribed. Gretchen Buehler in the forthcoming *Romanian-American Plaintes and Other Romanian Folk Songs, with Spoken Reminiscences of Migrating to America in 1912 from Zaharesti (Suceava) Romania by Irimie Fartais* has studied the *doine*, diverse plaintive rhyming songs and literary texts in verse, describing the experiences of the Romanian workers in America and their earliest contacts with the American culture. These works, in English translation, include numerous samples of Romanian-American folklore. Several volumes of prose in English tell the history of Romanian-born Americans of Jewish background on their way to being Americanized. Of an autobiographical nature are Marcus Eli Ravage's *An American in the Making* (1917) and Konrad Bercovici's *It's The Gypsy in Me* (1941);[1] Myron Brining approaches the same theme in fiction in his *Singerman* (1929).

The most talented and prolific Romanian fiction writer in English is Peter Neagoe, who was born in Transylvania in 1881. At first, Neagoe was a student in painting at the Academia de Belle Arte and in philosophy at the College of Letters in Bucharest. In 1901 he came to the United States, settled in New York City, and continued to study painting at the National Academy. Gradually he began to devote himself to writing, and English became his language of expression. He went to Paris in 1926 and met some American writers who called themselves expatriates—Ezra Pound, Gertrude Stein, and Henry Miller. In 1928 Neagoe published his first works in *transitions*, an avant-garde magazine that he edited. Later on, he also edited an anthology of the works of expatriate writers and poets, *Americans Abroad* (1932). The short stories he published in the volume *Storm*, in the same period in Paris, were banned in puritanical America. In 1933 Neagoe returned to the United States, and in 1934 he published his first novel, *Easter Sun*, followed in 1936 by *There Is My Heart*. A visit to Romania in 1937 renewed his inspiration. During World War II Neagoe served as a translator for the Office of War Information. In 1949 *A Time to Keep* was published, followed in 1958 by *No Time for Tears*. After his death in 1960, *The Saint of Montparnasse* appeared.

Peter Neagoe's work is an important contribution to American literature, because it describes typical Romanian peasant characters and the Romanian way of life and customs. Folklore and legends occupy a prominent place in his writings. His heroes are passionate; their speech is picturesque. In *Easter Sun* he describes everyday Romanian peasant life in the Transylvanian village of Aciliu. The plot centers on the ardent and beautiful Ileana, who is seduced by the rich and handsome Serafim. At the same time, she is the object of Tedescu's love. Tedescu is the teacher in the village, a hunchback whom everybody respects for his wisdom. Ileana's father, One-Eyed John, is, like everybody in the village, obsessed with the notion that his daughter's soul is possessed by the devil. On Easter night, he tries to kill her in order to banish the devil, and he eventually loses his mind. Since the climax of the novel occurs on Easter, Neagoe describes all the rituals revolving around that holiday. He also introduces the reader to other Romanian customs: "At the age of sixteen, the village girls make their debut, so to say, at the Sunday dance"; "They had breakfast, warm milk and cold mamaliga"; "When he [the peasant] spoke to a boyer he used high words."[2]

The bridge between Romania and America appears in the novel *There Is My Heart*, a love story about the peasant John Codreanu, who leaves his homeland for the New World. On his way he falls in love with Ileana and decides to delay his trip. While delivering a child fathered by John, Ileana dies. Only then does John feel free again to continue his great adventure since "there [in America] is his heart." Woven into this plot are abundant descriptions of Romanian life. Neagoe explains the beautiful Christmas and New Year customs (Chapters XXIII-XXIV) and contrasts the folk costumes of Romanians with those of Saxons (Chapter XII). He analyzes the relations among Romanians, Hungarians, and Saxons in Transylvania and notes that "such tales are told by the Romanian peasants about the Hungarians and they tell similar derisive stories about the Saxons, for they need such tales as an anodyne for their hurt pride, because both Saxons and Hungarians consider the Romanian peasant inferior to themselves."[3] There are also interesting insights into the psyche of the Romanian peasant: "The Transylvanian peasant is industrious. He loves the earth and lives with the seasons"(p. 163); "Truly, the peasant is fashioned in the image and likeness of his earth. The soil he is rooted in he calls 'my earth.' His soul is earth-essence" (p. 202). Neagoe devotes several paragraphs to the Romanian emigration to the United States: "They [Romanian peasants] leave home and fatherland. They go to the new world, where dogs run about with buns in their tails" (p. 36); "John learned from Starevitch that conditions in America were not as bright as the stories of the tax burdened peasants painted them. 'These stories are made up out of the poor man's dream,' Starevitch told him" (p. 134).

In *A Time to Keep*, the author reminisces about his boyhood in a Transylvanian village. Many of the people of the countryside will later become Americans. The narrator is a boy whose story about the village in which he grew up contains many lyrical passages. The main character is old Moş Gherasim, a wonderful combination of industriousness, intelligence, kindness, and wisdom.

Neagoe also wrote a novel on Jewish emigration, *No Time for Tears*. His *The Saint of Montparnasse* is situated in France and based on the life of the famous Romanian sculptor Constantin Brancusi. Neagoe had known Brancusi personally; in fact, the two had shared a room in Munich when they were students in fine arts.

A word should be said about Anişoara Stan, one of the earlier immigrants. She was quite prominent in Romanian-American cultural life between the two wars, lecturing on Romanian folk art on radio, at universities, and before large groups. She exhibited her remarkable private collection of Romanian folk art in many American cities. She recalled her homeland with love and national pride, and she wrote about it in *They Crossed Mountains and Oceans* (1947), providing information about Romanian folklore, customs, costumes, and holidays, along with some notes about her experience as an immigrant in America.

After World War II, a new Romanian-American literature developed. Many new arrivals had come from Romanian cities and from the middle and upper classes, as we have pointed out. They belonged to the more educated and professional strata in Romania. Some of them knew English or at least other foreign languages (most often French), which aided their adjustment. Some of them had been writers in Romania and continued to write after they came to America.

The most famous name among the Romanians who came to America during this period is Mircea Eliade. Eliade was born in 1907 in Bucharest and came to the United States in 1956. As a young student, he went to India in 1929, where he studied Sanskrit and yoga and decided to write his Ph.D. dissertation on the historical comparison of yoga techniques; he received his doctorate in 1933 in Romania. Continuing his early interest in literature, he published in Romanian his first novel, *Maitreyi*, which won a literary prize in 1933 and met with great critical and popular success. He taught philosphy at the University of Bucharest between 1933 and 1940. After 1940 Eliade lived outside Romania, first as a cultural attaché of the Romanian legation in London, then as cultural counselor in Lisbon during the war. Between 1945 and 1956, when Eliade lived in Paris, he became a noted scholar and taught at universities in Paris, Rome, Padua, Strasbourg, Munich, Lund, and Uppsala. Between 1951 and 1955, he obtained a research scholarship from the Bollingen Foundation in New York and in 1956 was appointed to the faculty of the University of Chicago, where he has remained as professor of history of religions. Among the many awards and distinctions he has received during a brilliant academic career, the title of Honoris Causa of the University of Paris-Sorbonne, given in 1976, is one of the most important.

Eliade has published numerous books on the nature of religion, Zen Buddhism, and mythology, which have made him a world-renowned scholar. His work has been translated into many languages, including French, English, German, Spanish, Italian, Portuguese, Scandinavian, Japanese, and Korean. During recent years, several monographs , as well as an impressive number of dissertations, both in the United States and in Europe, have been devoted to the analysis of his work.

While Eliade's scholarly and philosophical writings are well known, his narratives have enjoyed less popularity, since only a limited number have been translated. In the preface to his journal, *No Souvenirs*, Eliade explains, "I continued to write literary pieces only in Romanian for I considered myself to be a Romanian author belonging with the organic whole of Romanian literature."[4]

The short stories and novels of Eliade cannot be summarized. His characters are, in fact, projections of his many possible selves. Many of his heroes are young people in search of their identities. Often they strive to overcome their human condition, to understand the meaning of death, and to step into a world beyond time. Eliade's comments on his short story "With the Gypsy Girls" (1973) throw light on the universe in which his characters belong: "I have the impression that the essential has not been grasped; this story does not symbolize anything, it does not transform immediate reality by a cipher. The story *founds* a world, a universe independent of the geography and the sociology [of the Bucharest of 1930–40]" (*No Souvenirs*, p. 307.)

Mircea Eliade synthesizes his experiences in *Forbidden Forest* (1977). This novel, a fantasy, has a special place among Eliade's literary works. The plot is complicated and the characters are numerous and varied. Stefan Viziru, the hero, is tortured by the feeling that humanity is enclosed in a labyrinth, as inside a whale. He hopes to be able to withdraw from time as well as from the profane space, to live in Sambo, the privileged space, a kind of paradise or nirvana, striving toward the absolute. The story takes place in Romania, and it is a historical-social account of the years between 1936 and 1948: the war, fascism, and the beginning of the postwar period. Eliade realistically describes the vicissitude and oppression, and yet he approaches .the spiritual life of his characters from a mystical angle, from a folkloric perspective, that allows for suffering and permits a quest for a psychic ideal. The forbidden forest of the novel can also be seen as an eternal plane to replace the historical plane on which the action unfolds.

For the English edition of his journal, *No Souvenirs*, Eliade selected only the notes he wrote after he started a new cycle of his life, in the United States. This book contains comments on his experiences and discoveries in America. Here, everything was different from all his previous experiences. He is interested in the aggressiveness of the young American intelligentsia. He meditates on the origins of American democracy. He points out the American lack of history and roots, saying that Americans are still pioneers and immigrants from the cultural point of view. He falls under the spell of the hippies, thinking they have found a real meaning of life. The journal also contains his recollections of Romania, from happy childhood to adolescence and, later on, his first intellectual revelations, his discovery of Oriental philosophy, and his interest in the history of religions. He writes about storms on the Black Sea, adventures in the Carpathians, the forests around Bucharest, and the beauty of Romanian monasteries. He comments on Romanian history and art, on the Latin origin of the Romanian language, on folk culture as a source of Romanian creativity. He discusses the major political changes that occurred after World War II, as they were described to him by friends from Romania.

In 1959 he still perceived his constant traveling from one place to another as a risk: "I suddenly realize I risk losing myself in this perpetual vagabondage. I no longer have a refuge; I mean that I no longer have any place that I can call home, a universe of my own, in direct possession, but private, with the memories that constitute 'my history.' I perceive this risk, and I am afraid of succumbing to it" (p. 63). Also, the breaking of a pair of glasses he had worn since he was young, in Bucharest, has a special meaning for him, since they were "the last object I still have from *my own country.* I don't have anything else" (p. 70). At the same time, he sees his departure from Romania as the event that saved his life and freedom: "This departure [in 1940 from Romania] saved my life to begin with, then my freedom, and finally allowed me to become what I am: a writer who can write and publish what he thinks. That would have been impossible had I stayed." (p. 31).

The most recently translated work by Eliade is his play *The Endless Column,* which was performed at a conference on this work of Mircea Eliade, at the University of Notre Dame in April 1978.[5]

Among the immigrants who arrived after World War II, we distinguish a specific group of poets and writers—the exiles or displaced persons. They are people of strong political beliefs, most of them refugees from the communist regime. The literature they have produced, generally written in Romanian, is nationalistic and openly anticommunist. Representatives of this literary trend are Aron Cotruş, Vasile Posteucă, Nicolae Novac, Ion Cârja, and Eglantina Daschievici. Cotruş, born in 1891, emigrated to America after World War II and died in 1961. In 1956 he published a volume of poems, *Intre Volga şi Mississippi (Between Volga and Mississippi)*. Vasile Posteucă (1912–72) spent the last four years of his life in the United States. His best known collection of poems is *Cîntece de Fluer (Songs of the Flute)*.

Nicolae Novac (b. 1916) published his poems in *Ultimul Învins (The Last of the Vanquished)*. Most are in Romanian, but a few are translated into English and German. In "I" he recalls his Romanian background: "Within me surges, sparkling, vitalizing / The native sap of my Romanian soil."[6] In "Exile" the poet dreams of returning to the country but worries that the exiles may be accused of not doing anything while they were away (pp. 89–90).

Ion Cârja was born in the United States in 1922 and went with his parents to Romania in 1927. There he received his education, which explains why Romanian remained for a long while his language of expression. He was a political prisoner in 1943, during the Antonescu regime, and again from 1949 to 1964. He came back to America in 1965 and died here in 1977. Cârja wrote about his suffering in communist prisons in three consecutive volumes: *Întoarcerea din Infern (Return from Inferno)* I and II, and *Canalul Morţii (The Channel of Death)*. This last volume was recently translated into English and will be published soon. While these books are of a documentary nature, in 1977 Cârja wrote *Tom, Emperor of the Mountains*, a story for children.

Eglantina Daschievici (b. 1903 in Romania), who emigrated to the United States in 1956, also considers herself an exile, as expressed in the poem "L'Exile" ("The Exile"). She writes nationalist poems and songs, with fond recollections of her homeland. Some of these are available on records and tapes. In

1978 she published *Ma Patrie (My Homeland)* in both a Romanian *(Patria Mea)* and a German *(Meine Heimat)* version. Other Romanian-American authors tend toward a literature without political impact, one that blends into the general stream of American literature. Mircea Vasiliu, who was a diplomat, is a relative newcomer whose writing career started in the 1960s. In 1963 Vasiliu published *The Pleasure Is Mine* and *Which Way to the Melting Pot.* He writes, with a remarkable sense of humor, about his efforts to learn English and to adjust to America. By 1969 he had become a well-known writer and illustrator of juvenile books, having publishing approximately a dozen titles, including *What's Happening?*, *Mortimer, The Friendly Dragon,* and *Do You Remember?*[7]

G. Floran was also born in Romania, where he was a journalist. He came to the United States in 1969. Two of his books have been translated into English: *Good Morning, America* (1969), a poem dedicated to former President Nixon, on the occasion of his inauguration, and *Pierre Larousse* (1971), a play for children, about the famous French publisher.

Another native of Romania, Nicholas Catanoy, writes in four languages, including English. He has published four volumes. *Hic et Nunc* (1968) is particularly interesting for the language Catanoy shapes to express a broad range of feelings. He is "bitter / between the sky and nothingness" ("Expectation")[8] and he creates words, names, and structures to name his suffering.

Cornelia Damian-Tait is an American-born writer of Romanian descent whose native language is English. Born in Philadelphia of Romanian parents, she is a painter, designer, sculptor, weaver, teacher-lecturer, photographer, and amateur musician. Some of the poems in her *Spirals* (1976) are in both English and Romanian, while others are in English and Spanish. She describes her environment, her dreams, and her fears, trying to interpret the sights and sounds of the world around her. She challenges the world: "Let us meet the challenge, / or die in the attempt" ("Challenge to the World"), and she questions her own identity: "I seem to have lost the sense / Of the ego-person called C." ("Who am I?"—with Spanish translation).[9] In a poem like "hora să [sic!] joacă" ("The Hora Is Being Danced," pp. 42–43), she evokes the Romanian folk dance and treats it as a symbol for joy and optimism: "Hora să joacă acum vioaie; Să vede în fețe bucurie!" ("The Hora is being danced / Joyfully: faces now are gay!"). Damian-Tait approaches the condition of the immigrant with some fear of the unknown and with an awareness of the future and the knowledge that there is no possible return: "Across the precipice before me lies the future. / I will and cannot turn back!" ("The Immigrant," p. 18).

In a volume of essays on art, *Art in Its Fourth Dimension* (1976), Cornelia Tait-Damian writes: "My visits to Romania in 1971 and 1972 retraced for me my ancestral root—the heritage my parents had wished me to take pride in and understand."[10]

Michael Veshia (b. 1942) is a first-generation American of Romanian descent. His book *Monodies of a Troglodyte* (1969) carries the message expressed in the poem with the same title: "Still he sings hoping to be understood. / Until that day comes, / These songs of woe remain disregarded—MONODIES OF A TROGLODYTE" ("Monodies of a Troglodyte").[11] As an emigrant, he hears a voice calling him always: "His shout echoes throughout the hills / A voice forever calling me; / Someday I will answer" ("The Emigrant," p. 53). The contemporary world is an industrialized society, and Veshia seems to cry for the saving of the human soul: "Factories deal in mass production; / God is a mass producer; / God is a general motors factory" ("Mechanix Illustrated" p. 12).

This discussion of American literature through 1979 produced by poets and writers of Romanian background is, of course, not exhaustive. First of all, I have deliberately limited my study to authors published in the United States (the inclusion of Canada would require another study) and to those who have published books. Second, I have emphasized works written in or translated into English and available to readers in this country. Seldom did I compromise and mention literary works in Romanian, such as the Romanian-American literature. I did, however, mention briefly the works of post–World War II exiles, who, as a group, did not write in the language of their adoptive country.

My presentation may be somewhat partial in the way I comment on authors and their works. This is not, however, a history of Romanian literature but, rather, an introduction to the Romanian contribution to American literature. Therefore, I have emphasized Romanian consciousness and memories to highlight the Romanian heritage brought along to the New World.

I have also tried to include as much information as possible. This explains why, along with Peter Neagoe, a writer of traditional literature, and Mircea Eliade, the dialectician of the sacred and the profane, I also mentioned less famous poets and writers. Some of the beginners of today, the "young hopes," may become renowned authors. My study has been not an evaluation but a documentation.

Notes

[1] Bercovici also wrote *Around the World in New York* (1924), a book about immigrants from all countries who settled in New York; Romanians are described in the chapter "In the Balkan Coutnries."

[2] *Easter Sun* (New York: Coward, McCann, 1934), pp. 14, 56, 83.

[3] *There Is My Heart* (New York: Coward, McCann, 1936), p. 163.

[4] Mircea Eliade, *No Souvenirs* (New York: Harper, 1977).

[5] See *Romanian Bulletin,* Aug. 1978, p. 9.

[6] *Ultimul Învins* (Cleveland: Colecţia Culturală ULSRA 1965), p. 83.

[7] See Barbara Harte et al., eds., *Contemporary Authors,* XXII–XXIV (Detroit: Gale, 1970), 425.

[8] *Hic et Nunc* (New York: Exposition, 1968), p. 18.

[9] *Spirals* (Philadelphia: Dorrance, 1976), pp. 1, 52.

[10] *Art in Its Fourth Dimension* (New York: Philosophical Library, 1976), p. 53.

[11] *Monodies of a Troglodyte* (Philadelphia: Dorrance, 1969), p. 1.

Russian-American Literature

Carol Bachman and Edward Ifkovic

We begin with a problem that has plagued immigration officials, social commentators, and even the Russian immigrants themselves: who among those who leave the vast reaches of Russia is actually a Russian? Of the millions who streamed into America after 1880—the time of the great migration from Eastern Europe—how many were really ethnic Russians? In truth, only a minority, for most were Russian Jews (the largest percentage) escaping czarist pogroms. Large numbers of Poles, Finns, Lithuanians, and Germans also left during the final desperate decades of the czarist regime. Perhaps only three percent were ethnic Russians, and thus the Russians remain the "smallest of the Slavic groups of immigrants."[1] In fact, many Russians who chose to move went somewhere inside their own borders. Siberia was that vast untapped region, the unknown territory. As Arthur Ruhl stated, "They had no need to go abroad when they had their own frontier and their own 'wild west' at home."[2] Until the aborted 1905 revolution only small numbers of ethnic Russians came, and they were often members of religious groups like the Mennonites, Molokans, or Doukhobors. After 1905, however, the numbers drastically increased and continued to do so through World War I. Strangely, then, unlike most of the millions who came from Eastern and Southern Europe for economic security, those from Russia were often motivated by political or religious reasons (Balch, p. 277). The situation has remained the same throughout the twentieth century.

For the purpose of this survey of Russian-American literature, we need to define "ethnic Russian." Our focus is largely on two branches of the Slavonic peoples: the Great Russians, who constitute about half of the population of Russia, and the Byelorussians (also called White Russians, White Ruthenians, or Kryviches), who make up about four percent. The one ethnic Slavic people we omit from this consideration of Russia proper are the Ukrainians (the Little Russians, Rusins, Ruthenians,

Carpatho-Russians), a group who emigrated in record numbers from Russia proper and from the Austro-Hungarian Empire. The term "Ukrainian" was not used by the U.S. Census Bureau until 1930, but it has now replaced the older, more common "Ruthenian." Lacking a separate country, Ukrainians have often been discussed as one more rich tangent of Russian culture. They have a long, varied culture and literature, however, both in the old country and in America, distinct from both the Great Russians and the Byelorussians, and American-Ukrainian authors clearly define and demand the separation.

Despite the proportionately small numbers of ethnic Russians who emigrated, the American-Russian connection goes back to twenty-five years before the American Revolution, for in 1741 a group of Russians, led by Captain Alexei Chirikoff, entered what is now Alaska and established the first Russian settlement on the island of Kodiak. By the end of the eighteenth century a Russian-American company had coordinated the expanding commercial ventures in the Aleutians and Alaska. Eventually the colonies moved down into northern California, where Fort Ross became a thriving Russian-American community. In 1867 Russia sold Alaska to America, and settlement ceased. In 1872 the Orthodox See moved from Sitka to San Francisco. And out of this exotic piece of American history the turn-of-the-century romance writer Gertrude Atherton fashioned a novel about the tragic love affair of Count Nikolai Resanoff, governor of "Russia-America," who, on a trip to California in 1805 to meet Spanish authorities, fell in love with Dona Conchita Arguello. Resanoff died after returning to Russia, but Conchita, unaware of his death, waited all her life for his return.

A more sober reality informs the significant Russian immigration to the East Coast after 1880. Most of these Russians were peasants, land-poor and often illiterate. They were escaping economic deprivation, persecution at the hands of oppressive landlords, and an unyielding Russian Orthodox church that dictated law to all peoples, Orthodox or not. In addition, there was the awesome threat of czarist persecution. Like their Slavic brethren throughout Eastern Europe, the immigrants came from an agrarian subsistence into America's industrial urban life. They "were among the most unskilled and economically insecure of all the newer arrivals"[3] as a result of life in a backward country. They came with "patience to endure suffering,"[4] and this characteristic served them well in a land that used them to fuel its bustling industrial machine, which subjected them to intolerable working and living conditions. Toiling in mines and mills, they went unnoticed by America. Isolated from other Americans, they hid in their ghettos ("The peasant is naturally suspicious of strangers, the inevitable and bitter result of a long experience with those whom he regards as superiors.... The impress of an autocratic Tsar's regime lies heavy upon these people")[5] and many continued to use the Russian language at all costs—an important factor in the production of literature here, for many writers (including the political émigrés of the twentieth century) have persisted in using Russian instead of English. While this survey will touch on Russian-language materials, the main focus is on available English-language literature.

The year 1914 stemmed the flood tide of immigration to America, but once again the Russian pattern differed from that of other peoples. Beginning with the revolution of 1905 and continuing through the Bolshevik Revolution and the subsequent Soviet regime, the numbers of political refugees greatly increased. Fewer impoverished peasants came now; instead America became a haven for political dissidents of various ideologies—at first anticzarist professionals, then former czarist officials, members of the propertied classes, and the disenfranchised bourgeoisie: "princes and princesses, counts and barons, feudal lords, big industrialists, engineers, professors, army officers, aristocrats, and officeholders." Together, said Louis Adamic, "about forty thousand came as refugee-immigrants to the United States."[6] Emigration was largely terminated by U.S. government legislation in 1920-21, although a smattering of European émigrés filtered in during the 1920s and 1930s. Struggling to maintain the old aristocratic life, the Russian immigrants found that they had to work, and many "generals of the Old Imperial Army became hotel and apartment-house doormen. Princesses took to writing books and selling gloves and perfume over department store counters" (Adamic, p. 155). Throughout the 1920s and 1930s they were the exotic people in America, these former gentry now become working class (as in the Broadway hit *Tovarich*). But such exoticism ended with the rise of Hitler and Nazism. Once again, during and after World War II, many Russians came to America, entering under the relaxed quotas of displaced persons legislation. And from the cold war down to the present period of detente, the political refugees still look to America for salvation. Many of the exiled dissidents are Jews in flight from Soviet anti-Semitism, of course, but ethnic Russians leave as well. Often they are artists like Aleksandr Solzhenitsyn who seek unfettered freedom to write as they wish. So the twentieth century has seen Russian immigration that has been largely political and religious rather than, as earlier, economic in motivation. It is difficult to establish the size of the Russian-American population (estimates run as high as one million, including descendants), but one observation is pertinent to our survey of the Russian-American literature these people produced: the political orientation of the ethnic Russians, coupled with their usual nonpeasant or "privileged" status, has left its mark on Russian-American literature—from the numerous memoirs of displaced royalty and officials to the émigré fiction and poetry of the latest refugees.

Inevitably, the roots of Russian-American literature are found in the pages of newspapers produced by and for the Russian immigrants of the pre-1917 period. In the late 1800s immigrants struggled to issue newspapers as vehicles for both news and belles lettres: fiction, poetry, memoirs. Two newspapers appeared in 1887, six in 1897, eight in 1907, twenty-four in 1917, and so forth, until, one scholar estimates, over 150 such periodicals existed.[7] Nearly all began in the large Russian-American colonies in Chicago or New York City. Most, of course, lasted only a year, if that long. But archives of such newspapers are replete with early attempts at literary expression, often crude and unsophisticated but nevertheless valuable as honest responses to the new life in America. Understandably, much of the content has been political in nature, ranging from far left to far right. Unlike many other immigrant papers, the Russian journals were not characterized by often weak and groping attempts at expression. Because many Russian immigrants were well-educated political émigrés, a high level of articulation has always marked certain Russian-American journals and newspapers. The history of these newspapers, to be sure, has been "checkered," to use Jerome Davis' word (p. 123). Davis cites the example of *Novi Mir* (*New World*), which was suppressed by the U.S. government in 1920 because of its affiliations with the Community party. Another, however, an IWW weekly, the *Golos Trushenka*, was allowed to publish. During its publication days *Novi Mir* went from Menshevik to Bolshevik hands. Leon Trotsky was on the staff from 15 January 1917 to 27 March 1917. At the other extreme were papers that represented fraternal or religious organizations—for example, *Svyet*, the organ of the Russian Orthodox and Mutual Aid Society, and *Pravda*, organ of the Russian Brotherhood Society. Ivan K. Okuntsov estimates that over eighty periodicals were political, thirty religious, and fifteen literary and scholarly (p. 344). Admittedly most belles lettres in such papers were ephemeral, but often writers who had established reputations at home were represented in the American-Russian papers. A few almanacs also appeared; for example, the Russian Literary Artistic Circle published three: *Dymnyi sled* (1925), *Kaliforniiski sbornik* (1934), and *U Zolotykh vorot* (1957).

Current publications include the oldest Russian periodical in the world, *Novoe russkoe slovo* (*New Russian Word*), published in New York City. Begun in 1910, it was edited for fifty years (1923-73) by Mark Efimovich Veinbaum. He was followed by Andrei Sedykh, long connected with the periodical and known for both his journalism and his fiction. The paper, long the grandfather of Russian-American letters, has published work by virtually every distinguished émigré, from the widely touted Solzhenitsyn to writers such as V. E. Muksimov who are unknown to most Americans. Short stories, poetry, and novels have appeared, and a special Sunday supplement, "Literatura i iskusstvo" ("Literature and Art"), expands the Russian and Russian-American perspective. Of course, the most prominent showcase for belles lettres was the literary review, but its audience was usually small and sophisticated. Thus, any such journal was destined for a short run. Most of these appeared much later than the turn-of-the-century migrations—only after the huge influx of educated political émigrés. (There were earlier—and often uneven—collections of stories, poems, and reminiscence, like *Dosug*, edited by N. Sergievsky in 1918 for the New York-based First Russian Publishing House in America. Such volumes preceded the formal literary reviews that began to appear in the 1940s.) *Novosel'e* ran from 1942 to 1950, first in New York City and then in Paris. *Opyty*, edited by Maria Tsetlina in New York City, ran from 1953 to 1958. The most venerable, to be sure, is the long-standing and still-published *Novyi zhurnal* (*New Journal*), started by expatriots Mikhail Osipovich Tsetlin and Mark Alexandrovich Aldanov in 1942. The review has published work by every important émigré and by many Russian writers still in the homeland: I. Bunin, V. Nabokov, N. Berberova, G. Glinka, and

M. Demin, to name only a few. The review, which published part of Boris Pasternak's *Doctor Zhivago*, has been the most useful and artistic compendium of Russian émigré literature. Its contents, of course, are in Russian and are thus inaccessible to many. The *Russian Review,* however, is in English. Started in 1941 in New York City as a nonpartisan journal (but excluding works with a totalitarian outlook), it is now published by the Hoover Institute. The review is a valuable source of English-language materials relating to Russian and Russian-American culture.

American curiosity about the quixotic events of czarist and Soviet Russia has resulted in a long tradition of popular memoir and reminiscence, the one genre widely represented in English-language publication. While most impressive and important poetry and fiction remains untranslated, the memoirs of exiled royalty or of recent political refugees have been issued by the large commercial houses. In the pre-1917 period, when virtually nothing appeared in English by Russian-American authors, one slim volume presaged what was to become a twentieth-century literary phenomenon; Vladimir de Bogory Mokrievitch's *When I Was a Boy in Russia* (1916), a book aimed at young American readers, capitalizing on the exoticism that many Americans once associated with czarist Russia. Born in 1848 Mokrievitch came from a distinguished and noble family ("My father was a Colonel of Hussars in one of the Tsar's regiments"),[8] and he relates with childlike wonder the joys of childhood under the old regime— playing in the cherry orchard, watching the serfs. The family estate was in the Ukraine, and he enjoyed the "picturesque expressions" of the Ukrainian peasants (p. 38). He recalls the romantic Christmases in the icebound Ukraine, and he rhapsodizes about "Holy Russia": "The words are the keynote to every Russian life, and through them, memories of childhood bring back clearly some of the most wonderful of all my happy days" (p. 47). He chronicles the oppressive tactics of his tutors in the gymnasium. He was thirteen when Alexander II freed the serfs (the "Great Change") in 1861. After becoming a student at the University of Kiev, he began to absorb "revolutionary" ideas after he came up against censorship of his personal library. Sympathetic to the struggling, illiterate peasants, he gradually was drawn more and more into antigovernment postures, eventually doing manual labor and being hunted by the police. Captured after engaging in terrorist activity, he was sentenced to nearly fifteen years of hard labor in Siberia. After his adventurous escape, he returned to Moscow but no longer sympathized with the political ideologies that resulted in the assassination of Alexander II. He escaped to Switzerland, then went to America, England, and finally Bulgaria.

Another pre-1917 immigrant, Marya Zaturenska, is a more visible (and more distinguished) writer whose work has become part of mainstream American literature. Born in Kiev in 1903, she came to America in 1907. A precocious child, she nevertheless spent her early years working in factories until, driven by her own poetic fervor, she entered Valparaiso University. She later attended the University of Wisconsin. With her husband, Horace Gregory, a noted poet and critic, she edited several anthologies. Zaturenska was at the height of her powers and poetic reputation in the 1930s when her second book of poetry, *Cold Morning Sky,* won the Pulitzer Prize in 1938 as the best volume of poetry for that year. Other volumes include *Threshold and Hearth* (1935), *The Listening Landscape* (1941), and *The Golden Mirror* (1944). Her poetry was reissued in collected editions in the 1950s, but today she is largely unknown, the reputation she acquired is now gone, and her role as an American poet has been relegated to a footnote in standard literary histories.

In her poetry she touched on her experiences in Russia and, as well, her "ethnic" life in America—themes she abandoned as she became Americanized and moved into the mainstream. One searches the volumes, especially *Cold Morning Light,* for intimations of the Russian-American spirit and heart, but one would never guess her origins, for she chose to skirt autobiographical reflection and avoid the use of ethnic life as metaphor. Early poems appearing in *Poetry* magazine show her at her most ethnic (when she was Zaturensky, not -ska). In "Memories" she looks back to her Russian days, nostalgically, longing to hear the "noise" that was so different from that of the "alien crowd" she now encounters:

> There is a noise, and then the crowded herd
> Of noon-time workers flows into the street.
> My soul, bewildered and without retreat,
> Closes its wings and shrinks, a frightened bird.
>
> Oh, I have known a peace, once I have known
> The joy that could have touched a heart of stone—

> The heart of holy Russia beating still,
> Over a snow-cold steppe and on a hill:
> One day in Kiev I heard a great church-bell
> Crying a strange farewell.
>
> . . . .
> Here in this alien crowd I walk apart,
> Clapping remembered beauty to my heart![9]

In "Song of a Factory Girl," a less successful poem than "Memories" because of its overly familiar images, she deals with the life of the immigrant girl in America:

> It's hard to breathe in a tenement hall,
> So I ran to the little park,
> As a lover runs from a crowded ball
> To the moonlit dark.
>
> I drank in clear air as one will
> Who is doomed to die,
> Wistfully watching from a hill
> The unmarred sky.
>
> And the great trees bowed in their gold and red
> Till my heart caught flame;
> And my soul, that I thought was crushed or dead,
> Uttered a name.
> I hadn't called the name of God
> For a long time;
> But it stirred in me as the seed in sod,
> Or a broken rhyme.[10]

Although her later poetry occasionally touched on her Russian soul ("To walk fur-wrapped, cheeks glowing, feet on Russian snow, / The melancholy steppe from which my inner longings grow"),[11] most poems employ familiar abstraction ("Recall O Time each son, each daughter"),[12] vague imagery ("Sweet the unnamed Presence everywhere"),[13] and much classical metaphor (Grecian nymphs, Aurora's golden hair, Cytherea, Helen and Paris). Derivative and often mechanical, the later poetry is deservedly forgotten. We can idly speculate on the strange turns of Zaturenska's career: what would have happened had she not become a mainstream author, a prize winner, an anthologizer with Gregory? What would have happened had she continued to nourish the ethnic roots that gave her early poetry its verve? But she chose another path—she became no Anzia Yezierska—and her few ethnic poems remain her only moving testimony to the rich, vital tradition she carried with her to America.

Actress-writer Olga Petrova, while very much a part of 1920s New York theater—a glamorous star who enjoyed her celebrity—strangely kept her sense of Russian heritage. In the 1920s she was often a star attraction at the Broad Street theater in Newark, and she participated in the first broadcast of radio station WJRZ of Newark.[14] She wrote *The White Peacock*, a play, and her *Hurricane* opened at the Frolic Theatre in New York on 26 December 1923; it was published in 1924.

Hurricane shows Petrova's use of Russian-American experience in what is supposedly a 1920s hard-boiled "realistic" drama. It is the story of the blind, feverish ambition that propels the daughter of Russian immigrants to wealth and success — a Slavic *Sister Carrie*. We see the benighted life on the isolated Texas farm where Marya and Stephen Leshoff and their daughters Illyena and Masha struggle to survive. Petrova draws a vivid picture of that demoralized family: the mother is "flabby, blowsy, rather than fat, and she is as sordid as the room."[15] Her husband is cruel, brutal, a miserable man. The daughter Illyena, at twenty, is "exuberantly healthy; beautiful in atmosphere and coloring" (p. 11), and she refuses to allow the degradation in the new country to overwhelm her; she will escape. With the help of a creaky deus ex machina—the appearance of young John Arkwright from New York City, wealthy, unmarried, and out of gas in front of their shack—she begins her ascent up America's shaky ladder to success. First, she leaves for Saint Louis with a flashy two-bit con man, Joe Jennings, after she physically attacks her father. Eventually she falls victim to the city; she becomes a prostitute to survive ("her hair a vivid pink. It stands straight on end, a curious aureole about her head," p. 48). She no longer says "nuthin," or "pertaters," but what she gains in standard (if stilted) English-language fluency is matched by a decrease in self-respect and self-worth. In Florida she meets Arkwright again; a mad passion erupts, but the specter of her scarlet past intrudes. And when she does tell him ("Do you remember that day you offered me a fifty dollar bill?...Well, that fifty dollars was the first money and the last that I refused from a man from that day on....My business was men," p. 81), John, though stunned, vows his love. The play's expected happy ending does not materialize. In the final moments Illyena, vaguely ill for some time, learns she is dying from venereal disease. She commits suicide and dies in John's arms. Sensational for its time, *Hurricane* has a certain dramatic power, although ultimately it fails because of its lack of structure and language appropriate to its theme and because of its wooden and stereotyped characters and plot. Petrova retired from the stage in 1926 and published her autobiography, *Butter with My Bread*, in 1934. A collection of short stories, *The Black Virgin and Other Stories* (1926), features international characters and themes, only one of which—the title story—uses the horrifying events of the 1917 revolution as background.

Petrova's autobiography is in the tradition of reminiscence and memoir. From the late 1930s to the 1950s such works were the most prominent form of Russian-American literature in English. Perhaps the volatile atmosphere in the old country and America's own confused relations with Soviet Russia led Americans to turn to accounts written by émigrés. The personal dimension lent a certain authority to the dark headlines. One of the most delightful and popular autobiographers, and an all-around Russian-American man of letters, was M. K. Argus, pseudonym of Mikhail Konstantinovich Jeleznov (1900–70), who was born in Minsk and came to America in 1924, settling in New York City in 1934. For nearly forty years he was a satirist on the staff of *Novoe russkoe slovo*. He wrote two books in Russian, produced poetry, and wrote a humorous autobiography, *Moscow-on-the-Hudson* (1951), and a novel, *A Rogue with Ease* (1953). *Moscow-on-the-Hudson* is a collection of personal narratives about life in America. Although the book is laced with wit, humor, and startlingly effective satire, it has an underlying seriousness: "We were not pioneers setting out to conquer new land and discover new horizons. We were fugitives, the first Displaced Persons of the twentieth century, to be followed by multitudes of others driven by the great holocaust that has not yet abated."[16] Life among the exiled Russians in New York was exciting, if insane: "We brought with us our own language; our own traditions, habits, prejudices, and samovars; our own writers, artists, and poets; even our own nursemaids of peasant stock to nurse our future babies" (p. 3). Painstakingly avoiding the "natives," they huddled in the Russian colony and tried to be Russian. The same political structures were reinstituted, and the internal wars began. But:

We arrived in New York without any money, clad in tattered clothes, hungry and destitute, but with our brief cases intact.

A Russian will part with his home, his estates, his wife, his children, even his own life, but not with his briefcase.

We take it to work and play, to funerals and weddings, to theatres and concerts. We go to visit friends carrying it, and we take a Sunday stroll with a brief case under the arm. The brief case is our national emblem. It is to us what long hair was to Samson, the source of our wisdom and strength. It is proof that we are an earnest people, preoccupied with weighty matters, and not flighty or scatter-brained or unsubstantial as the natives are.

Armed with a brief case a Russian fears no exile.

(pp. 14–15)

Argus reveled in meeting "Russian old-timers" who "knew" America:

Boris knew everything about American literature: "There is no American literature." He knew everything about American art: "There is no American art." He knew everything about American foreign and domestic politics: "They don't know what they are doing." (p. 4)

He enjoyed putting down the pretensions of his people: "Almost every Russian who came to the United States, and had not declared himself to be a singer or a nobleman, became a former actor of the Moscow Art Theater and a personal friend of Stanislavsky. The number of actresses and actors the Moscow Art Theater must have employed and Stanislavsky befriended exceeded the number of places where Washington slept in this country" (p. 61).

Eventually Argus married an American woman, to the horror of his emigré friends, and began the process of Americanization. He learned not to leave the spoon in his tea glass, not to wave his arms during dinner, and not to disagree with anyone. The book ends with Argus' description of the new immigrants— not from czarist Russia, as he was, but from the Soviet Union. Different from him, suspicious, uncertain of the liberty they now have, they are removed from even the old-timers like Argus. Responding to the new immigrants' criticism of America, Argus makes an interesting observation: he has become an American: "We tell them that there is, incredible as it may sound, an American literature, and an American heritage, and an American culture, yes, even an American culture. We are, after all, Americans and deep in our hearts proud of it" (p. 182).

Argus also cast his satirical eyes on the Russian immigrant as poseur: the new royalty in America. In his spirited novel, *A Rogue with Ease* (1953), he deals again with Russians in New York—in particular, the Russian colonies on the Upper West Side around 137th Street. Argus realized that Americans were giddy with royalty fever: titled foreigners looked for American heiresses; American heiresses looked for titled foreigners. So Argus satirized the cultural phenomenon by telling the story of Prince Basil Saratov (a Russian, but not a prince) and Count Andrei Simsky (not a count, not a Russian, and in fact, from Liverpool, Ohio). The prince sells heirlooms of the Imperial family (from a shop on Third Avenue). Madcap adventure follows, accompanied by Argus' own sardonic, worldly observations on the foibles of human beings:

> Basil Saratov was the product of a war and a revolution. The war had taught him how to be cruel to people he did not know. The revolution had taught him how to be cruel to people he knew. He was born in a small town in southern Russia. His father was a physician, his mother a feminist. It was incongruous for his mother to be a fighter for women's rights when men had none, but in Russia everything begins from the end.[17]

Most personal stories by other authors are not as spirited and humorous as those of Argus. Dealing with political flight from czarist and Soviet Russia, the other stories emerge as somber testimony to the iron will of humanity—the need to stand up and declare, the need to assert one's dignity, the pursuit of freedom, the struggle to adapt to an alien society. Michael Fyodrov's *Death My Generation* (1946) chronicles the life of a young man born of mixed parentage who lived in several countries:

> They talk about half-breeds but if you really want to make life difficult for a man let his father be a Russian nobleman of ancient lineage and his mother a descendant of puritanical American pioneers. A billion atoms of sensuality and superstition wedded to another billion of steadfastness and ruthless independence, myriads of particles whirling blindly through the centuries generation after generation, groping and fusing until one day they clash in the darkness of the womb.
> Let his childhood be nurtured in luxury redolent with Byzantine mysticism. At the age of awakening consciousness fill his

nostrils with the smell of blood and his ears with the rattle of machine-guns in a land racked by revolution. At puberty throw him on the granite streets of New York and make him like it. And after trailing him around Europe, torn up by the roots, spew him out into the world and let him fend for himself. Then see what he makes of life.[18]

So opens his work, and these two paragraphs outline a life of search, speculation, and often tiresome pursuit of serenity. Born in 1910 near Saint Petersburg to a mother originally from San Francisco and a father of the nobility, he seemed to have the charmed life. His description of the revolution of 1917 (he was only seven) is vivid and not a little horrifying. His knowledgeable father got his wife and two sons out of Russia, and he himself stayed behind: "Russia is ill too—much more than I am. And she will need all the help she can get to become well again. . . . I want my sons to have a chance to start life in security and without starving. Take them to America" (p. 22). They never saw him again. Fyodrov then chronicles the life in America, emphasizing the value-thin veneer of the 1920s, when so many Russian émigrés were floundering: "By the time I was fifteen, I had been factory apprentice, delivery-van boy, office messenger, I wore long trousers, smoked cigarettes, carried a hip-flask and was as hard-boiled as any New York boy of my age" (p. 63). He found himself shuttled back and forth between France and England, until in his twenty-fifth year (1939) he discovered his Russian roots: "I had forgotten the Russian language, read none of its literature and knew of its history only as much as the average schoolboy knows" (pp. 173–74). But suddenly he was inspired to write a short story about Russian peasants, and the return to the source began. That moment led to a building of Russian ethnic consciousness, an awareness that carried into his professional and personal life. Fyodrov's book, one of the better-written autobiographies, is filled with drama and color; it is reflective, intelligent, and characterized by a rich use of language. His life is an appropriate metaphor for the individual who searches for an intelligent balance between two disparate worlds.

Other autobiographies include Victor A. Yakhontoff's *Over the Divide* (1939). Yakhontoff, author of standard works like *Russia and the Soviet Union in the Far East*, reflects on the old czarist regime of his youth, the problem of "wealth and egotism" in the privileged world he knew, his important positions with the government, the coming of war, travels to Japan and America, the decision to stay in America ("There was no way home for me"), [19] and the creation of a new life here. Nicholas Wreden's *The Unmaking of a Russian* (1935) is another story of a man born into the privileged class (his father was a major general in the medical corps) who found his world overturned by revolution. Much of the book is a detailed account of World War I and the revolution, and only in the final pages does he deal with his departure to America in 1920. He was forced "to throw my heritage and my future into the melting pot, and in so doing to link myself with America."[20] Eugene Da Savitsch's *In the Absence of Caviar* (1940) tells of a physician who left Russia as a teenager, studied medicine in Paris and America, and practiced in the Belgian Congo. Princess Catharine Radziwill's *It Really Happened* (1932) is the story of a Russian aristocrat in the United States. Kyra Govitzina's book *Service Entrance: Memoirs of a Park Avenue Cook* (1939) tells of a more specific American experience: she, an alumna of the Institute for Noble Young Ladies in Saint Petersburg, and her husband, an ex-officer of the Imperial Guards, arrived in New York in 1923 and became cook and butler for the most exclusive American families. A popular, lightly written volume, it is far away from the intriguing autobiographies written by later Russian émigrés. One of the most fascinating is Nina Berberova's *The Italics Are Mine* (1969). Published first in English and later republished in Russian (*Kursiv moi*, 1972), it is a gold mine of rich observation and anecdote. Berberova shows us life in the intellectual émigré colony, giving vivid portraits of Nabokov, Bunin, Kerensky, Anna Akhmatova, Ehrenburg, and others who were distinguished in the old country and the new. Deeply involved with literature, she seems to have met all the important literati at just the right moment. She was involved with Russian émigré life in Paris in the 1920s, and she chronicles the changes in the colony in France during World War II. She came to America after the war.

Although very little poetry has been written in English—a great deal was (and is) composed in Russian, some translated in Vladimir Markov's *Modern Russian Poetry* (1966), and in Russian with adjoining English translation in Valentina Sinkevich's own collection *The Coming of Day*—the same cannot be said for fiction. Many volumes have been published for English-speaking audiences. But despite some reference to America and the life of the Russian émigré here, most novels deal with matters in Russia, especially political and social intrigue. Few writers so far have chosen to deal with the Russian-American experience. One who did was V. S. Yanovsky in *No Man's Time* (1967), the story of Cornelius Yamb, who was born in Russia and emigrated to Chicago. He is hired to find Bruno, heir to a fortune, and we follow Yamb's adventures in Chicago and New York. An intriguing, suspenseful work, it is also a commentary on the second generation in America. The fathers are the heroes, the men of action; the sons have the heroism but the ideals are gone. They act for profit alone. The novel was highly praised by W. H. Auden. Russian-born Irina Kirk deals with the tragedy of self-exile in her novel *Born with the Dead* (1963). She fled to Manchuria after the revolution, received her Ph.D. at Indiana University, and now teaches at the University of Connecticut. She has received a number of awards for her fiction. Other works dealing with Russian (Soviet) intrigue include N. Narokov's *The Chains of Fear* (1958), Mikhail Soloviev's *When the Gods Are Silent* (1952), and Vladimir Yuvasov's *Parallax* (1966). *Parallax* was first published in English and later serialized in Russian in *Novoe russkoe slovo*. Soloviev's work was also published first in English and later in Russian (1963). All three novels explore the complexities of terror in the Soviet Union, although *Parallax* ends with a central character living in America.

One other novelist needs mentioning. Nina Fedorova, a White Russian born there in 1895, studied at the University of Petrograd before the revolution. In 1919 she and her family moved eastward into Manchuria and then into China. Later, driven out by the Japanese, she eventually, in 1938, came to America with her husband and two sons, settling in Eugene, Oregon. Her novel *The Family* (1940) won the Atlantic $10,000 Prize. It was later republished in Russian (*Sem'ia*, 1952). Set in China during the Japanese invasion of 1937, it deals with a White Russian family—Granny, Mother, and the third-generation children—trying to survive. She continued the story in *The Children* (1942; in Russian, *Deti*, 1958).

The most distinguished White Russian émigré—and one of the few Russian-American writers to enter mainstream American literature as one of the acknowledged masters of language and stylistic innovation—is, of course, Vladimir Nabokov. His long journey to America began in 1899 in Saint Petersburg, where his childhood was a privileged one: he grew up in a worldly, wealthy environment. His family's sophisticated taste and political liberalism exposed him early to the energies of philosophical commitment. Nabokov's father—a jurist, an editor, and a statesman—was an articulate spokesman for the the ideals of the provisional government, established between the February and October revolutions in 1917. Opposed to the despotism of the czar, he believed in fair play, civil rights, and the individual's right to express openly his or her political philosophy. Attending school in Saint Petersburg, the young boy cultivated his father's reformist zeal. In 1916 the seventeen-year-old Nabokov inherited from his Uncle Ruka an estate of some two thousand acres; his place in the Russian world of reformers thus seemed secure. In 1919, however, the Bolsheviks seized his land, and Nabokov and his family began their life of voluntary exile. This was the first in a series of moves that took him at once farther from his native land and deeper into its mythical life stream. In the substance of his long migratory experience, Nabokov found the material for a dominant theme in his work, the theme of exile.

He graduated from Cambridge with an honors degree in foreign languages. From England he made his way to Berlin to pursue a career as a writer. But in 1937 he fled to Paris to escape the horrors of the Nazis, only to have to flee again in 1940 when they invaded France. Nabokov was, from the outset, an émigré writer whose audience was initially made up of other Russians who, like himself, had left behind more than estates and wealth. In *Speak, Memory*, a reminiscence, he tells of the strangely disembodied state of the exile, particularly of those Russians with whom he spent so much time in Paris and Berlin:

> As I look back at those years of exile, I see myself, and thousands of other Russians, leading an odd, but by no means unpleasant existence, in material indigence and intellectual luxury, among perfectly unimportant strangers, special Germans and Frenchmen in whose more or less illusory cities we, emigres, happened to dwell.[22]

His rootless existence resulted in a twofold response: he felt nostalgic for the home of his childhood, for its warmth, its laughter, its civility; at the same time he found liberation from the facticity of time and place. He wrote to Edmund Wilson (an early supporter) in 1941, stating that part of him still yearned for a transfigured Russia:

> For almost twenty-five years Russians in exile have craved for
> something—anything—to happen that would destroy the Bol-
> sheviks—for instance a good bloody war. Now comes this tragic
> farce. My desire that Russia, in spite of everything, may defeat or
> rather utterly abolish Germany—so that not a German be left in the
> world, is putting the cart before the horse, but the horse is so
> disgusting that I prefer doing so. First of all I want England to win
> the war. *Then* I want Hit[ler] and Stal[in] despatched to Christmas
> Island and kept there together in close and constant proximity to
> each other. And then—I quite realize that everything will happen in
> some ridiculously different way—just as an automobile advertise-
> ment juicily interrupts the accent of hideously dramatic events.[23]

But his journey from home had awakened more than fruitless
desires and political disaffection; his paradigmatic comment
closing the letter is of a piece with his thematic preoccupations.
His is an ironic recognition—humorous, sardonic, detached—of
the absurdity of our efforts to shape our world in the face of
circumstances that do not yield to our will. Perception such as
his gives rise to a definition of humanity that places it in the role
of exile in the world, alienated, "itinerant" and "dramatic," to be
sure, but also free to create an interior world. Nabokov observes
in *Speak, Memory*:

> What the Tsars have never been able to achieve, namely the
> complete curbing of minds to the government's will, was achieved
> by the Bolsheviks in no time after the main contingent of
> intellectuals had escaped abroad or been destroyed. The lucky
> group of expatriots could now follow their pursuits with such utter
> impunity that, in fact, they sometimes asked themselves if the sense
> of enjoying absolute mental freedom was not due to their working
> in an absolute void. (pp. 280–81)

The void, for Nabokov, is the landscape his dislocated heroes
occupy.

The void that is the immediate world emptied of security
and a sense of home is partially annihilated through memory and
artistic sensibility. These internal, creative forces allow Nabokov's lonely itinerants momentarily to reshape their lives.
Characeristically, the past haunts the present, often surfacing in
the instant when painful, isolating, or threatening experience
mingles with a re-creation of an earlier, less rootless life. Not
surprisingly Nabokov himself chose to remain permanently

"uncountried." In 1938 he discarded Russian as his literary language, turning to English, which he had read as a child even before he learned Russian. In 1960 he moved from America to neutral Switzerland and became a citizen of the absurd world of space and time, but a free citizen of the void, too. He never owned a home, preferring to move from place to place, picking up pieces of the lives that inhabited the space before him, which he then transmuted into art.

Perhaps because in Nabokov's work the pervasive figure of the exile is symbolic of his vision of reality, he turns only once to the specifically American experience of a Russian immigrant. *Pnin* (1957) is a tragicomic parody of a Russian exile's life in American academe. At the level of simple biography the story of Pnin's difficulties with the strange language and unintelligible customs is not unlike other depictions in this genre. The significant difference, however, is that Nabokov weaves throughout the story a more universal consideration of the disparity between external reality, external appearance, and the private reality of the creative perceiver: his victim-émigrés are not merely figures of comic misapprehension of the new world; they are tragic victims of cruelty or mockery in America that suggests the very conditions they thought to leave behind. Through his wanderers Nabokov suggests the ultimate isolation of all individuals.

Pnin, like Nabokov, comes to the United States by way of Europe, drawn here not so much by his bright faith in American freedom and democracy as by his absolute need to flee the horrors of political Europe and the muddle of his personal life. He was born in 1898 into a respectable, well-to-do family in Russia; he leaves his homeland as a result of the revolution. In Western Europe he lives within the community of Russian exiles, where he becomes known as the "erudite young author of several admirable papers on Russian culture."[24] There he meets and eventually marries lovely, treacherous Liza Bogolepov, who soon divorces him, although she has no scruples about continuing to use him. At the start of World War II Pnin comes to America and, in 1945, starts to teach at Waindell College, "a somewhat provincial institution" (p. 363). Because the school has no regular Russian department Pnin's position depends on the goodwill of the German department, "a university within a university" (p. 364), ironically suggesting his outcast state professionally, politically, and personally. He deals with his colleagues with a kind of distracted detachment, revealing that he and they do not understand one another. Yet, serene in their academic incompetence, Pnin's associates, beneath their thin facade of camaraderie, barely conceal their contempt for Pninian language and style. They offer him neither sympathy nor respect for the rootlessness of his life. He is merely a "cracked ping-pong ball. Russian"(p. 382). Pnin moves frequently, about once every semester, during his nine years at Waindell, in search of perfect silence, an "impossible isolation" (p. 405) from the cacophonous din of the immediate American world. Of course he never finds silence. He takes his only vacation in 1954, risking his life by erratically assaulting the New England landscape with his car, on his way to join his fellow Russian émigrés at The Pines, home of his old friend, Alexander Petrovich Kukolnikov. The following year, at a party he has given for his colleagues, he confides to the head of the German department that he will make his commitment to America: he will buy the small, inconvenient house he currently inhabits. "The sense of living in a discrete building all by himself was to Pnin something singularly delightful and amazingly satisfying to a weary old want of his innermost self, battered and stunned by thirty-five years of homelessness" (p. 473). Filled with enthusiasm for his decision, he launches into his plans for new courses whose focus will be the issue of tyranny, for, he declares, "the history of man is the history of pain!" (p. 493). Only then does he learn that he is to be exiled once more; he is being fired. It is too much of a financial burden to retain the scantily populated courses he teaches. His German department "protector" tells him, "Political trends in America, as we all know, discourage interest in things Russian" (p. 494). Timofey Pnin leaves Waindell College without specifying his destination.

While such a summary suggests the kinds of incidents that mark Pnin's journey from Russia to America and then toward the unknown, it misses the qualities of parody and seriousness that distinguish the Pninian-Nabokovian style that makes Nabokov's work unique in Russian-American literature. Certainly a summary cannot convey the humorous absurdity of poltergeist Timofey in the mysterious world of American machinery or untenured Professor Pnin's college lectures on Russian literature that dissolve into merriment at recollections from his past: "He was beloved not only for any essential ability but for those unforgettable digressions of his, when he would remove his glasses to beam at the past while massaging the lenses of the present" (p. 365). Nor can it reveal his profound hatred for political systems in their broadest definition. Memories of their horrors have haunted his life as much as the reassuring memories have. They contribute to Nabokov's habit of finding correspondences between past and present events, people, language, and tyrannies. For instance, when Pnin joins his fellow exiles at The Pines, in the soft light of evening he experiences a familiar, terrible feeling of melting into his surroundings. His mind moves back to a time of similar light, on the Baltic long ago, and to Mira, his love. Mira is dead now, but not Pnin's memories of her or of the Nazi mentality that killed her and continues to kill her in his mind.

Pnin ends where it began: with the story of Timofey Pnin's journey from Waindell to Cremona to deliver a lecture to the Women's Club, "Are the Russian People Communists?" The version that closes the novel is told by Pninian mimic, Jack Cockerell, who will, according to his own lights, reshape the event to reflect his mockery of Pnin. The version that opens the novel is (if one leaves the narrator's intrusions aside) Pnin's own: he is lost. In his desire to save twelve insignificant minutes of travel time, he boards a train that has not stopped in Cremona for two years; his timetable is obsolete. But he will arrive on time and deliver his lecture on a subject far from his heart. He will speak in English — although a "special danger area in Pnin's case was the English language" (p. 367). He will find no more sympathetic understanding with the Cremona ladies than he has with most of his academic associates. The episode alludes to themes the novel explores. Pnin is as lost in the frenetic, confusing landscape of America as he once was in revolutionary Russia. His vague navigation through train and bus depots merely exemplifies his passage through an alien world. Pnin is momentarily seized by an eerie feeling of unreality, not for the first time and certainly not for the last. Such moments occur when the past informs and nourishes the present for this persistently resilient man. Through his shaping, responsive memory, he deals with the conflict between the world of circumstance and the transcendent world of imagination. The narrator observes that "one of the main characteristics of life is discreteness. Unless a film of flesh envelops us, we die. Man exists only insofar as he is separated from his surroundings. The cranium is a space-traveler's helmet. Stay inside or you perish" (p. 372). Nabokov's personal voice in *Speak, Memory* reflects the same sense of exile:

> I have to make a rapid inventory of the universe, just as a man in a dream tries to condone the absurdity of his position by making sure he is dreaming. I have to have all space and all time participate in my emotion, in my mortal love, so that the edge of its mortality is taken off, thus helping me to fight the utter degradation, ridicule, and horror of having developed an infinity of sensation and thought within a finite existence. (p. 297)

The events surrounding Pnin's present life takes place within the context of his American experience. But naturalization is impossible for him. His real life is in the past, in the library that is "intimately and securely connected with Pnin's heart." In "his scriptorium in the stacks" he is transported to his "paradise of Russian lore" (p. 415). Here he can live as he chooses, with Pushkin and Gogol and the history of nineteenth-century romantic Russia; in an important way this is the history of his childhood and of his life.

Nabokov's reputation in America is securely established among the major writers of the twentieth century. His richly complex opus has brought praise from such diverse critics as John Updike and Alfred Kazin. Perhaps one tribute would be appropriate to close both this account of Nabokov and the larger discussion of the Russian-American literary experience. This from Kazin:

> Ours is an age so dominated by politics, historical "necessity," the seeming total reality of social and racial conflict, that Nabokov stands out just now because he has no country but himself. He is the only refugee who could have turned statelessness into absolute strength. The penniless have-not fleeing the Crimea in 1919 has turned out to be, in his blessedly unconventional terms, the true possessor. . . . And Nabokov's imaginary realm puts his own readers to shame, for *they* are still in bondage to actual states and cruel political abstractions.[25]

So, too, the countless other Russian immigrants and émigrés who preceded Nabokov turned their peculiar "statelessness" into "absolute strength." If Nabokov has outshone their literary contributions, it remains true, nevertheless, that men and women like Zaturenska, Jeleznov, Fyodrov, and Fedorova are emphatic, and enduring, footnotes in the long chronology of Russian-American letters.

Notes

[1] Emily G. Balch, *Our Slavic Fellow Citizens* (New York: Charities, 1910), p. 277.

[2] Quoted in Maurice Davie, *World Immigration* (New York: Macmillan, 1936), p. 136.

[3] Carl Wittke, *We Who Built America* (Englewood Cliffs, N.J.: Prentice-Hall, 1939), p. 422.

[4] Stephen Graham, *With Poor Immigrants to America* (New York: Macmillan, 1914), p. 285.

[5] Jerome Davis, *The Russian Immigrant* (New York: Macmillan, 1922), pp. 212–213.

[6] *A Nation of Nations* (New York: Harper, 1945), p. 155.

[7] Ivan K. Oksuntsov, *Russkaia emigratsiia v Severnoi i Iuzhnoi Amerike* (Buenos Aires: Seiatel', 1967), pp. 311–12.

[8] *When I Was a Boy in Russia* (Boston: Lothrop, Lee, 1916), p. 11.

[9] *Poetry,* April 1920, p. 15; rpt. in Harriet Monroe and Alice Corbin Henderson, eds., *The New Poetry* (New York: Macmillan, 1923), pp. 609–10.

[10] *Poetry,* Sept. 1921, p. 118; rpt in Monroe and Henderson, pp. 610–11.

[11] "The Vision of Marie Bashkirseff, *The Golden Mirror* (New York: Macmillan, 1944), p. 53.

[12] "Silent Pursuit," *Golden Mirror,* p. 4.

[13] "The Old House," *Golden Mirror,* p. 2.

[14] Gemady Klimenko, "Russians in New Jersey," in Barbara Cunnigham, ed., *The New Jersey Ethnic Experience* (Union City, N.J.: Wise, 1977), p. 391.

[15] *Hurricane* (New York: Four Seas, 1924), p. 9.

[16] *Moscow-on-the-Hudson* (New York: Harper, 1951), p. 2.

[17] *A Rogue with Ease* (New York: Harper, 1953), p. 10.

[18] Mikhail Fyodrov, *Death My Generation* (New York: Roy, 1946), p. 1.

[19] Victor Yakhontoff, *Over the Divide* (New York: Coward, McCann, 1939), p. 232.

[20] Nicholas Wreden, *The Unmaking of a Russian* (New York: Norton, 1935).

[21] Foreword, *No Man's Time* (New York: Vanguard, 1967), pp. 7–13.

[22] Vladimir Nabokov, *Speak, Memory: An Autobiography Revisited,* rev. ed. (New York: Putnam's, 1966), p. 276.

[23] Simon Karlinsky, ed., *The Nabokov-Wilson Letters: Correspondence between Vladimir Nabokov and Edmund Wilson, 1940–1971* (New York: Harper, 1979), p. 46.

[24] Vladimir Nabokov, *Pnin,* in *The Portable Nabokov,* ed. Page Stegner (New York: Viking, 1968), p. 502.

[25] Quoted in Alfred Appel, Jr., and Charles Newman, eds., *Nabokov: Criticism, Reminiscences, Translations, and Tributes* (New York: Simon, 1970), pp. 364–65.

Scandinavian-American Literature

Dorothy Burton Skårdal

The question of whether or not there is a Scandinavian-American literature has long been in dispute. Certainly there were many Norwegian, Danish, and Swedish immigrants in the United States who wrote a great deal, but most of them, like most critics and historians of their work, have considered themselves Norwegians, Danes, or Swedes rather than members of a single ethnic group.

Norway, Denmark, and Sweden are, of course, separate sovereign nations with distinct though similar histories. Close-knit cultural, economic, and political interrelationships among them have developed over centuries, but each nation has its own distinctive language and dialects and its own literary tradition. Yet Norwegians, Danes, and Swedes can communicate with one another with little difficulty when each speaks or writes his or her own tongue; they know quite a bit about one another's leading authors, whose influences reach easily across national boundaries; and all three national literatures have developed in concert from neoclassicism through Romanticism, realism, naturalism, and various stages of modernism in interaction with one another and the larger literary movements of the rest of Europe.

These similarities among the three nations have so strongly marked their people that when some emigrated to the United States the host society could hardly tell them apart. Incidents in which a Norwegian is taken for a Swede, or a Swede for a Dane, are common in the immigrant fiction (and the misclassified Scandinavian is always annoyed). Life in America, so different from that in the homeland, highlighted the likenesses shared by Scandinavians and gradually dissipated both their provincial and their national differences, so that the term "Scandinavian" came to denote even greater ethnic unity when used in reference to immigrants in the New World than when applied to natives in the Old. The literary record shows that Norwegians, Danes, and Swedes responded to the immigrant experience in ways that were nearly identical, while their three branches of literature underwent parallel development in the same way at the same time. In this sense a Scandinavian-American literature most definitely does exist.

Yet because this literature was written in different languages, we must remember that Scandinavian-American literature has three distinct branches. Two of them are more closely related to each other than to the third. Although very different in spoken form, Danish and Norwegian were almost identical in written form throughout the nineteenth century and even longer in the United States, where immigrants tended to go on using their mother tongue in the form it had reached when they emigrated. This similarity in language enabled Danes and Norwegians to read and publish in one another's ethnic newspapers and magazines, and they did, but since the Norwegians were a much larger group and had more periodicals and publishers, it seems the Danes knew more about the Norwegians than the Norwegians did about the Danes. Swedish is much different from the other two languages in written form, however, although spoken Swedish is close to Norwegian. As a result, Swedish-American literature remained little noticed by the other Scandinavians. It is in fact surprising how little attention most cultural leaders of these closely related groups paid to one another's activities in America. As late as 1922, for example, Ole Rølvaag, the best author of them all, claimed that the Norwegians were the only immigrants in the United States who had created their own non-English literature.[1] This volume on American ethnic literatures is proof of how wrong he was. As a major Norwegian leader he ought at least to have known about the rich literary achievement of both Danes and Swedes by that date. Thus when we discuss specific authors and their works, we must arrange them in three distinct but closely related groups by nation of origin; that is the way they defined themselves in their own time. Looking back from our day, however, we see clearly their common characteristics and shared experiences as Scandinavians in America. Therefore we can consider the history of their ethnic literature as a whole.

A *Survey of Scandinavian-American Literary History*

In spite of their small numbers as compared with other immigrant groups,[2] Scandinavians in the United States published an amazing amount of native-language material in a multitude of forms. In addition to the journalistic writing in hundreds of newspapers, we can list short stories and novels; poems and plays; literary, cultural, and social criticism; memoirs, biographies, letters, and diaries; travel essays, informal historical accounts, religious homilies, and meditations; compilations of jokes and yarns; juveniles and mysteries; even comic strips. All these forms are to be found in books, pamphlets, and periodicals printed by Scandinavian-language presses in the United States. A few first-generation authors also wrote and published in English, as did most of the second generation. We shall here deal only with belles lettres, but one should not overlook the broad publishing activity that created and maintained a tradition of writing for publication and a potential reading public for Scandinavian writers of fiction, poetry, and autobiography whose book publication began in the 1870s.

Long before then, however, the first belles lettres appeared in the Scandinavian-language newspapers that began to emerge around the middle of the nineteenth century and were soon popping up like toadstools, with most of them dying just as fast. Many were primarily organs for political or religious views, though some were cultural; several developed a national readership and became important institutions for ethnic identity. The first magazines were church-sponsored, but secular ones began to appear after the Civil War, as did more specialized periodicals for families, for women, for those who enjoyed humor, for socialists. Organs of fraternal organizations followed, along with technical journals. These ethnic newspapers and magazines varied greatly in size, duration, and content, but nearly all printed some belles lettres.

Verse was the first form of literature to appear in early newspapers, often on festive occasions like Christmas and patriotic holidays. Gradually sketches and tales, reminiscences, essays, and serialized novels were added, the last reprinted from sources in the old country for the most part but later also in translation from other European and American publications. A number of immigrant journalists were also authors, and they contributed literary efforts along with their regular writing.

Letters to the editor had early become a prominent feature of this press, and readers also sent in immense amounts of their own verse and fiction. Scandinavians were almost all literate when they arrived; they seem to have rapidly developed a widespread writer's itch.

By no means were all such unsolicited contributions bad. On the contrary, much of the best poetry and fiction by Scandinavians in America was first printed in ethnic newspapers. Introductions to collections of verse and tales usually acknowledged previous publication in newspapers much more often than in magazines. Some major papers instituted literary supplements in which they published the most significant stories and novels by members of this immigrant group. Almost all the journals printed vast amounts of fiction, running at least one serialized novel all the time, not infrequently two or even three at once. Much of this was low-level popular fiction from various sources, but many classics of both European and American literature were introduced in translation to Scandinavian readers in this way, as were novels by fellow immigrants.

Publication of Scandinavian-American books began only when this ethnic group had established a firm footing in the Midwest and after its key institutions—churches, schools, and periodicals—had begun to flourish. The first books at the beginning of the 1870s were small volumes of poetry. The Norwegians produced the first novels shortly afterward. Strangely enough, the first real novel by a Scandinavian immigrant was in English. Hjalmar Boyesen's *Gunnar* appeared in *Atlantic Monthly* as a serial in 1873 and in book form the following year. It was a romantic tale of peasants in Norway, written for Americans, and had nothing to do with immigrant life. In 1874 came the first novels about Norwegians in America, published as two connected serials in a magazine called *For Hjemmet* (*For the Home*). Dealing with a pioneer settlement in Minnesota before and during the Indian uprising of 1862, the stories were extremely moralistic, pious tales of no literary value, and they never came out as books. They did, however, introduce a number of themes from immigrant life that became standard in Scandinavian-American fiction, and incidentally they revealed one of the few examples in ethnic fiction of sympathetic understanding for the displaced and mistreated Indians. Norwegians also, immediately after this, wrote the first Scandinavian-language novels to appear as books: Bernt Askevold's *Hun*

Ragnhild, eller billeder fra Søndfjord (*Ragnhild, or Scenes from Søndfjord*) in 1876 and Tellef Grundysen's *Fra begge sider af havet* (*From Both Sides of the Sea*) in 1877. The first was set in Norway, the second moved to America, and both settings continued to be popular with immigrant writers. Danes and Swedes first got under way with comparable novels in the following decade. Norwegians continued to lead in the production of fiction as long as this ethnic literature lasted. Swedes wrote the most poetry and much of the best, while the many fewer Danes published about equal amounts of equally good prose and verse.

By the end of the 1880s all three branches of Scandinavian-American literature were growing strongly. Both periodical and book publication reached full flower between the turn of the century and World War I, when antiforeign hysteria drastically cut back all Scandinavian-language activity. The newspapers and the literature revived after the war, but by then most of the best Danish and Swedish fiction writers had done their major work. The Scandinavian reading public was melting away. Immigration from Scandinavia had declined far below its peak in the 1880s when the quota acts of the 1920s slammed shut America's doors. Without a steady stream of newcomers to renew the foreign-born stock and as the children and grandchildren of older immigrants abandoned their ancestral tongue, there were fewer and fewer left who could read the Scandinavian languages.

In this twilight of decline the Norwegian branch of the literature reached its highest achievement in the novels of Ole E. Rølvaag. His masterpiece, *Giants in the Earth*, was published in Norwegian in 1924 and in English translation in 1927. An immediate best-seller in both Norway and the United States, it has become a classic in both countries. Rølvaag wrote two sequels that were immediately translated into English, and he revised two of his earlier works for translation as well. After his premature death in 1931, a few other ethnic authors continued to write in all three Scandinavian languages. But the Great Depression of the 1930s killed so many of the foreign language newspapers and publishing houses that this ethnic literature rapidly withered away. Since World War II only a handful of non-English books has appeared, and the few elderly first-generation authors still writing publish their work mainly in the small number of struggling Scandinavian newspapers that survive today. For all practical purposes the history of this immigrant literature is over.

It may be argued, however, that Scandinavian-American literature in English has continued as a subdivision of American literature written by the descendants of Scandinavian immigrants about the life of their group. Some of these books are pleasant and informative, but none is significant. In the 1950s, for example, well before the current ethnic revival began, there was a spate of nostalgic domestic novels by second-generation women recounting their growing up in Scandinavian immigrant families. We shall return to the English-language portion of this literature later, including what has been translated, but since the main body and all the major works of Scandinavian literature were written in the Scandinavian languages, we should first consider the special problems and themes of the ethnic literature proper and look briefly at its major figures.

Special Problems of Non-English Authors

Scandinavian-language literature in the United States reproduced in miniature practically all the levels, genres, and interests of the national literature but with special emphases and at a lower level of competence. The reading public was too small to support professional authors. The majority, who were of lower-class origin, subscribed faithfully to newspapers but bought few books, while the better-educated minority preferred to read the national literature of their homeland. Lutheran ministers were the main cultural leaders of the group, along with some newspaper editors and teachers; many clergymen ignored or rejected imaginative literature, while those who did not tended to insist that it should primarily teach the Ten Commandments. The conventional piety and widespread conservatism of much of the immigrant reading public thus limited most authors' choice and treatment of subject and necessitated the didactic intent and strongly religious tone of most of their books, although there were a few fiery radicals and atheistic socialists on the fringes of the literature from the 1890s on.

Such a limited reading public meant that creative writing had to be a spare-time activity. To the last man and woman, the Scandinavian-language authors were all amateurs. This is perhaps the main reason that, with the sole exception of Rølvaag, they must be judged minor figures when compared with the major writers of any nation. Students of this ethnic literature must realize that none of the Norwegian-, Danish-, or Swedish-American authors can be considered great. Rølvaag is the best of them, but only his *Giants in the Earth* is a masterpiece. All his other works, however interesting they may be otherwise, have artistic flaws. The best of the other writers are second-rate, and the rest range downward to the perfectly awful.

This discouraging judgment, it should be noted, is based solely on artistic standards applicable to national literatures. These standards alone cannot be used in evaluating ethnic literature not only because they are manifestly unfair, given the towering special problems of immigrant writers, but also because they would eliminate from our consideration many interesting, moving, and enlightening books. We must add other standards to artistic ones in determining who are the major authors of an ethnic literature: first, the seriousness of their intent in writing; second, how many works they published, and where (in the United States or in the homeland, which took only the best), by a major firm or a minor one, or all too often at the writer's own expense; third, the evaluation of these works by their authors' contemporaries; and fourth, the extent and accuracy of the authors' insight into the life of their group. This last criterion is the most difficult to apply because to do so we must compare a work to those of a large number of similar authors and to history, and we must also assume (in working with Scandinavians, at least) that the major authors were primarily concerned with the life of their own group.

The applicability of these criteria differs from one writer to another with the amount of evidence that we can marshal on each point. Since research into Scandinavian-American literature has barely begun, our judgments can only be tentative. I have selected the authors to be discussed on the basis of these five criteria, however, the fifth—artistic ability—being the one we started with. We should not abandon this standard, but, rather, we should use it to measure Scandinavian immigrant writers against one another and against the authors of other ethnic groups, not against the great writers of any national literature. When we then turn to read the best of these ethnic works, we must forgive, if not forget, their artistic weaknesses if we are to appreciate their strengths.

These weaknesses were caused by overwhelming problems faced by all immigrant authors, major and minor. Most serious was the problem of language. Here the different class origins of the Scandinavian Americans played an important part, as did their age at the time of immigration and the place in which they settled in the United States—a tightly knit colony of their own kind who still spoke the mother tongue or an English-speaking or a mixed community. Writers who came from the upper classes, particularly those who had received some higher education in the old country, spoke and wrote the formal "book language," while the lower classes, particularly those of rural origin, spoke dialects that had no written form and learned a formal version of the "book language." When with little practice they tried to write in the "book language," the results were often stylistically disastrous.

Norwegians had a special problem because of the "New Norwegian" language movement in their homeland in the latter part of the nineteenth century, a movement that has lasted until today. This change involved the creation out of the ancient dialects of a new written language to replace the Dano-Norwegian that reminded them of the centuries during which Norway had been only a province of the Danish kingdom. Most immigrants rejected this movement, having enough trouble trying to keep their native tongue alive in America without dividing their efforts. However, the new language was much closer to the immigrants' dialectal speech, and a few authors adopted it in the New World. In addition, this movement rapidly pulled the homeland's "book language" away from Dano-Norwegian, so that all forms of written Norwegian in the homeland changed too fast for the immigrants in distant America. Danish and Swedish also developed rapidly during this period back home, so that the style of most immigrant authors, cut off from this evolution, tended to be at best old-fashioned and at worst stiff and awkward. Also the steady admixture of English terms gradually created in the United States new hybrid dialects that writers with a good ear sometimes used to great comic effect but that often crept into printed texts and caused unintended or misplaced humor or just poor style. Some books written in or translated into English by first-generation authors and published privately or by ethnic presses were marked by unbelievably bad English. The style of these books illustrates a major language problem for all first-generation Scandinavian immigrants and a towering one for writers: the gradual undermining of their native tongue and their difficulties in learning English.

The lack of an audience for serious literature was a most discouraging problem for the major ethnic writers. The news-papers were eager markets for shallow popular writing, espe-cially humorous or sentimental stuff. The church presses would subsidize moralistic and religious stories and poetry, but the chance of publication was much smaller for critical and realistic works. As one major Norwegian author complained, the church and politics were his fellow immigrants' sole cultural concerns above and beyond the price of wheat and hogs; nobody wanted or missed books:

> What on earth was the good of fiction and poetry? Would it bring taxes down or land prices up? And so they smothered the brat [literature] or nearly so...those who had something to say soon learned to address themselves to themselves. It is characteristic of our most gifted authors that they have worked under the convic-tion that they have no audience.[3]

For limited periods, editors made a difference, individuals of good taste and education heading publishing houses or influen-tial periodicals. Some major writers were themselves newspaper or magazine editors who published their own works, and a number of newspapers printed and bound as books fiction that they had carried as serials.

Naturally there was not much of a literary milieu within the Scandinavian immigrant groups. Only in a few cities with the largest concentration of this ethnic population—like Chicago, Minneapolis, or New York—might a handful of authors gather. The rest lived in artistic isolation, spread out over the entire Midwest or, after the turn of the century, on the two coasts. Writers also lacked the stimulus of effective criticism. Most of their efforts were ignored or viewed with contempt by writers and critics in the homeland, where little of their work was considered good enough to print anyway. Fellow immigrant writers who reviewed their works in ethnic journals were well aware of the overwhelming odds these writers had had to overcome to appear in print at all and tended to be too gentle. Thus most of the best authors were those who had learned to write in other, related professions: journalism, the ministry, teaching. At least this was true of prose writers, although many second-rate writers earned their living in other ways. Most of the best writers of fiction were also much better educated than the average immigrant, though some were self-taught. Poets, however, came from all professions and social classes. The best were Julius Baumann, a Norwegian-American small-town businessman and politician in Wisconsin and Minnesota; Anton Kvist, a Danish-American bricklayer in Chicago; and Arthur Landfors, Swedish-American housepainter in Rosindale and Sharon, Massachusetts.

The wonder is that so many perservered in writing at such length against such odds. Hundreds of minor writers published only a book or two, often at their own expense, or wrote solely for newspapers; two or three dozen of some talent were known only to compatriots in their own lifetime, but their books are now valuable to social historians; and a few can be regarded as major writers within their own ethnic tradition. One of these dedicated souls described this compulsion to write:

> I know one who in stolen hours, preferably when bad weather hindered work outdoors, sat in a cold room and with numb fingers scrawled stories and poems about his people in this land. I know one who the whole day long—and it was not a mere eight-hour day, either—followed his plow and harrow and composed verses which he tried to memorize until in a pause for rest he could scribble them down on a piece of wrapping paper. I know one who sat in a jolting mail wagon on the prairies of South Dakota and tried to set lines of verse on paper. The sun burned, the wind howled, storms broke loose—but this man wrote poetry. In the end he died of tuberculosis.[4]

Major Themes

The great theme that runs through all Scandinavian-American literature is change, the radical and painful change in individual and group identity required for adjustment to a new society when one has left the old. Scandinavian-American authors dealt with this theme as the problem of assimilation. They recognized that the host society expected them to become Americanized and to conform to Anglo ways, and they felt that they were required to become full-fledged, unhyphenated Americans—or, if they could not, that their children were. In most books

Americans were assumed to be Yankees: white, Anglo-Saxon Protestants of New England background.

The immigrant authors of the three Scandinavian nationalities were divided in their attitudes toward assimilation. All agreed that they had to adapt to American economic and political life, learn English, become citizens, compete with Americans in work and politics.

In spite of their agreement on this issue, however, they split into three schools. One thought they should, insofar as they could, adopt American ways in all aspects, abandoning everything they had brought from Europe in order to achieve full assimilation as rapidly as possible. Authors who wrote in English belonged to this school. The bilingual writers sometimes embraced the second school of thought: they accepted the melting pot in which all groups would be melted down together into something new. They believed in and worked for the preservation of their ethnic heritage as long as possible but recognized that ultimately it was doomed to disappear. The best they could hope for was to add some positive ingredients to the final blend. The third school overlapped with the second to the extent that its members, too, were preservationists. They argued, however, for the permanent continuation of their heritage in a nation of cultural pluralism. A few thought they should fence themselves off from the host society to keep their Scandinavian heritage pure, but most realized this was impossible and argued that they should develop their own unique bilingual subculture, drawing elements from both sides of the Atlantic. Some thought they would inevitably lose their language but might preserve other cultural characteristics, especially their Lutheranism, forever. All schools recognized, however, that the tide of change was flooding strongly toward a full Americanization that threatened to wash all their European heritage away. Some English-language authors approved of this assimilation, but most others regretted it, and many saw in it the basic tragedy of immigrant life: the loss of their Scandinavian identity.

Whether they opposed or approved of assimilation, however they defined that term, Scandinavian immigrant authors agreed on the way it took place. Each writer's description is, of course, molded by its time and geographical setting, but most authors of fiction and autobiography agree in their accounts of the ocean journey under sail or steam, the paralyzing shock of the tumultuous landing, the trials of being a greenhorn. The

Swedish novelists used a special term for the most painful period of adjustment: "the dog years." This period lasted until the immigrants had learned enough English and enough about American institutions and ways to fight exploitation and stand on their own feet.

Success, defined as social and economic betterment, is a major theme in this literature. Many characters who came from the peasant and working classes in the Old World are shown rising to middle-class status in their own lifetimes, most as farmers or small businessmen in the Midwest. This was especially so in stories set before the 1890s. From then on, the closing of the frontier, recurrent depressions, and exploitative capitalism darkened the picture. Most authors agreed, however, that hard, honest work was much better paid in the United States than in Europe and that, because the cost of living and taxes were lower, most workers were better off in the New World. After the turn of the century, however, there was a definite increase in the number of characters who went under in the struggle for survival. This gradual change toward more pessimistic plots could have come about because economic opportunity for individuals was declining as industrial capitalism developed and because realism was belatedly entering this ethnic literature from both Scandinavian and American sources. Scandinavian-American literature began at a time when Romanticism had gone to seed, but until after the turn of the century most of its novels remained in that mode, although enlightened by touches of naive realism when the unskilled authors described the daily life of their group.

Most Scandinavian-American authors agreed that America offered a whole series of benefits: democracy, greater respect as human beings, personal freedom, the possibility of improving one's status through individual achievement, and opportunity for advancement impossible in the class-bound Old World. For a great many characters of lower-class origin the American dream defined in these terms came true, but the authors also agreed that social and personal betterment was won in America at great cost.

One price to be paid was the physical strain of strenuous work in a difficult climate, work that prematurely aged many characters or brought them to an early grave. Another price they paid in the struggle for survival was the loss of Old World culture, not only the pleasant folk customs that had colored the dullness of their workaday lives but also the higher values like personal honor, family solidarity, cooperation with and responsibility for one's neighbors, contentment with comparatively little material wealth. Many authors pictured individualism and competition in the American spirit unleashing destructive forces of greed and materialism within the group, resulting in dishonest business ethics, conspicuous consumption, and open-ended ambition that could never be satisfied. As a character in a Norwegian-American novel complained,

> It's as though the people were over-eating! They came here, over-hungry, and now one chance after another opens before them, and they can't stand it, after being starved so long.[5]

A common figure in this ethnic literature is the character who wins success but loses his or her own soul.

Sometimes stories showed immigrants losing their children, too. By working their children so hard to pay off the farm mortgage, parents often drove the next generation off the land or taught only materialism. Or the children completed the family's assimilation process by moving into American society and leaving the parents behind. Shame over immigrant parents' broken English and ignorance of American ways was a frequent theme in both fiction and autobiography, though it was often countered by filial loyalty and love presented as an Old World value.

Certainly the parental role of preparing children for entrance into society was extremely difficult for immigrants who had been socialized in a different culture. Many stories showed that the inevitable generation gap between immigrant parents and their children led to rapid breakdown in the Scandinavian pattern of father-dominated families, while American mobility undermined both the extended family and generational continuity on the family farm. Some of the saddest stories are of grandparents who sold their homestead to strangers and retired to town:

> The evenings were long and the days too, and they slept poorly at night. Somewhere in Canada and on the West Coast there were children they were grandparents to, but they didn't know how many and weren't certain of their names. It was seldom they heard anything from them, and no invitation for a visit ever came. That's

the way things go in a big country—the young leave, as they themselves had once left, and now they sat alone just as their own parents had also been left alone long ago.[6]

Since most authors regarded love of the land and family loyalty as the highest values of their group, the two being connected through the concept of the farm as the family seat, many felt that the social betterment of their group in America had been bought at too high a price.

If materialism was portrayed as the worst sin of the Scandinavian-Americans, alcoholism was their greatest social problem. The collision between ancient Nordic drinking customs—to imbibe only on festive occasions but then to drink oneself into a stupor—and the omnipresent American saloon brought disaster to so many fictional families that prohibition books of both fiction and poetry made up almost a separate genre. Only the men drank, but the women and children suffered. Those from pietistic circles in the homeland soon found support in American prohibition movements and founded innumerable societies to fight the demon rum within their ranks. Both in fact and in fiction Scandinavian immigrants played a significant role in passing laws to ban liquor first from midwestern states and then from the nation. This issue absorbed much of their political energy until the battle was won, perhaps partially explaining why ordinary party politics appeared comparatively rarely in their ethnic literature.

Since education was accorded a high place in the Scandinavian system of values, it was a frequent theme in the fiction. An actual attempt by conservative high-church ministers to found Norwegian parochial schools was reflected in some of the earliest novels. Public schools in all three homelands were originally designed to teach mainly the Lutheran faith, and they still instruct in that subject. Therefore immigrants in many stories condemned American public schools as godless and deliberately and needlessly destructive of their European heritage. Parochial schools proved too expensive to maintain, but religious schools during summer vacations became common and appeared constantly in the fiction. The Lutheran academies, seminaries, and colleges founded by people of all three nationalities, as well as special Danish "folk high schools," were mirrored too in the literature. Many stories sent immigrant children to high school and then to college or university as proof of family advancement beyond the peasant- and working-class status they had escaped in the old country.

The central institution of the immigrant Lutheran church, along with native piety pictured as the group norm, appeared as one of the most common themes throughout the literature. Conflict between high- and low-church factions in the state churches of the homelands developed into bitter wars within all three groups in America and led to multiple schisms that severely damaged ethnic-group solidarity until after the turn of the century. The authors paid little attention to the theological arguments behind this uproar, focusing instead on the human causes and effects. In his novel *Peder Victorious* Rølvaag gives a superb picture of Dakota pietists who—shaken by the local tragedy of an unwed mother who murdered her baby and then killed herself—withdrew from the local church that accepted all as members and formed their own exclusive congregation of the truly righteous. The result was long-lasting division of the local community into enemy factions, as summarized in a minor novel laid in Kansas, where antagonism between formalistic and "separatist" Swedish Lutherans "carried over into the social and economic life of the community. Stores owned by Lutherans employed clerks of like faith. Separatists did the same. People patronized those of their own creed, and lines were closely drawn. Intermarriage between young people of the two factions was unthinkable."[7]

Even after such bitter controversy over dogma had subsided, conflict inevitably remained between those (usually first generation) who wanted to keep the church language, ceremony, and customs as they had been in the old country and those (usually the second) who wanted to adopt American customs—no graves around the church, a kitchen in the basement, and frequent social functions, for example. The long-drawn-out fights in each congregation about the change to the use of English appeared in many stories at various stages, but Americanization always won out. Although some were shown as godless, ignoring or opposing religion out of indifference or atheism, the authors, to make clear their own piety, saw to it that such characters came to a bad end. This pattern held at least until the first decade of this century. From then on, complaints increased about declining faith among later immigrants and the second generation, but church membership and attendance remained pictured in the literature as the group norm.

Homesickness was a constant theme throughout all genres in Scandinavian-American literature, reflecting the pain of those who were caught between two cultures. This literature is evidence that the trauma of cultural shock, rejection by the host society, language difficulties, and incomplete acculturation left large numbers of immigrants with a marginal identity and a divided heart. Coming from a deep-rooted, comparatively stable society, most loved their native country and regretted having to leave it for economic reasons. Putting aside their memories of the repressive class structure and lack of economic opportunity that had motivated their departure, they expressed, in poetry and fiction, their longing for the beautiful landscapes, the familiar ways, and their beloved homes, friends, and family. Immigrant life invariably turned out to be more difficult than expected, and over and over again the writers asked themselves whether the benefits they had won by migrating to America were really worth the cost. After long deliberation some answered yes, some answered no, and some could never make up their minds.

Scandinavian-American literature is an invaluable source for studying both the mental and the emotional aspects of the immigration experience. Immigrants' intellectual life is preserved in these books in the authors' assumptions, basic concepts, value judgments, and choices. Their writings reveal the way in which they viewed the many facets of their group's life in America and what they considered typical of it. Many aspects of their emotional life are recorded too: their distinctive humor; their strong sense of honesty and honor; their concepts of religion, loyalty, duty, love; their frequent disillusionment with what they found in America. They had not expected immigration to be so painful.

The psychohistory mirrored in this literature indicates that varying combinations of two main factors determined where each writer stood on the scale stretching from those who were glad they had immigrated to those who regretted having done so. The first factor was the degree of betterment each felt that he or she had won by coming to America, measured against the kind of life the author had lived in the old country. This factor varied greatly from one writer to another. The second and more constant factor was the robustness and adaptability of the individual writer's temperament. Invariably the sensitive, the introverted, the tenderhearted, and the thin-skinned were the most discontented immigrants, while the strong and ambitious fared reasonably well. Rølvaag's *Giants in the Earth* pitted these two types against each other: Per Hansa, the born pioneer, rejoiced in the challenge of frontier life in Dakota, but his wife, Beret, so feared the naked plain where there was nothing to hide behind that she went insane. Only then did the husband, living for the future, finally realize that his wife could not escape her ties to the past:

> "She has never felt at home here in America. There are some people, I know now, who never should emigrate, because, you see, they can't take pleasure in that which is to come—they simply can't see it!"[8]

Per Hansa and Beret stand at the two extreme ends of this character scale. Most authors, together with the characters they created, seemed to fall somewhere in between. But none of them completely escaped pain; all expressed homesickness and regret for the loss of what they had left behind them and fear of the strange new life they faced. This aspect of the immigrant experience is least represented in the ethnic literature written in English, however. These works clearly show that the second generation could not understand or share their parents' longing for a life and society they had never known. Therefore to read only books written in English is to miss the most central theme of this literary tradition, its very heart. Translated works should be included in every syllabus. Unfortunately, however, only a few works and very few poems have as yet been translated into English. As we shall see from comparing the major works written in a Scandinavian language with what is available in English, at present no syllabus limited to works in English can do justice to Scandinavian-American literature. We must, then, proceed on the theory that half a loaf is better than none.

Major Scandinavian-Language Writers

Norwegian

Ole Rølvaag is clearly the most important and the best Scandinavian-American author, and at least three of his books should dominate any syllabus. *Giants in the Earth*, however, is more of an epic than an ethnic novel. The theme of humanity against the wilderness pervades the long story, set on the Dakota frontier in the 1870s. Among the secondary ethnic elements, perhaps the most important is the theme of the growing materialism of the ambitious men contrasted with Beret's old-country sense of honor and righteousness. The importance of education and religion to these peasant people is another theme, as is the deep respect they feel for their spiritual leader, the minister. Norwegian folklore is woven into the imagery: Per Hansa as the fairy-tale Ash Lad (a male Cinderella), who through his cleverness always manages to do the impossible and win the princess and half the kingdom; the threatening Irish as stupid but dangerous trolls; the primeval plain as a huge giant, a symbol of the dark powers of nature. Immigrant themes also appear in the passages about language problems, name changing, unfamilarity with American law and conditions, and the Norwegian peasant's deep love of the soil.

The two sequels to *Giants* are primarily ethnic novels: *Peder Victorious* (Norwegian ed. 1928, English trans. 1929) and *Their Fathers' God* (1931). *Peder Victorious* begins some time after *Giants* had ended with the death of Per Hansa in a blizzard. Its great strength is its portrayal of the youngest son Peder growing up torn between two worlds: his mother's isolated world of strict Norwegian piety and the exciting world of American life at school and with his Irish friends. The novel tells part of the same story twice, first from Peder's point of view and then from his mother, Beret's. This technique slows down the plot but succeeds in communicating the boy's impatience to break free from Beret's version of Norwegian culture, a negative pietism that denies life. It also makes clear the mother's despair as all her children drift away to where she cannot follow. When she realizes that she will lose the last and youngest, too, if she does not accept Peder's marriage to an Irish Catholic, she gives up her lifelong conviction that "you can't keep wheat and potatoes in the same bin," and the book ends on a note of hope for cultural compromise.

Peder is packed with vivid ethnic details: church fights, immigrant customs and mores, conflict between parents trying to preserve their European culture and the Americanizing force of the public school. It is probably the best ethnic novel in Scandinavian-American literature, although artistically it fails to reach the level of *Giants*.

Their Fathers' God, the third novel in the trilogy, is a disappointment. It traces the long, dull breakdown of Peder's marriage to Susie. Rølvaag means to demonstrate that Beret was right in believing that potatoes and wheat can't be kept in the same bin: cultural incompatibility will destroy sexual love. His moral is unconvincing, however, because he stacks the cards: Peder and Susie are more incompatible as individuals than as representatives of different cultures. As long as Beret lives, she holds them together; marriage and family are sacred to her peasant heart. But after her death the marriage is doomed. The books ends with Susie taking their little son and leaving Peder forever.

Rølvaag planned to write a fourth novel in which the dilemma of the second generation caught between two worlds would be resolved by Peder's discovery of the rich cultural heritage of Norway in art, literature, and history, which his parents had never known. But the author died at the age of 55 before beginning it. He had spent his life as professor of Norwegian language and literature at Saint Olaf College in Minnesota, teaching the children and grandchildren of immigrants the formal culture of their ancestors' homeland, and he believed that those of Norwegian descent could and should preserve their cultural heritage forever in the United States. Part of this heritage was the people's history as immigrants, and Rølvaag devoted much time and effort to the Norwegian-American Historical Society, which he helped found in 1925. As its first secretary he wrote hundreds of letters in an attempt to gather materials for its archives. In preparation for his trilogy he had collected much oral history about pioneering days and growing up as the second generation. He had immigrated in 1896, too late to experience life on the frontier.

His first novel, *Amerika-breve* (*Letters from America*), however, is an excellent record of what it was like to arrive as a greenhorn then. Based on the letters he sent home after his arrival, this epistolary novel has no plot except the young immigrant's gradual taking root in the new land. He had come only to earn money and then return, but the book ends with his family coming to join him instead. It is packed with ethnic themes: immigrants' firsthand positive and negative responses to America, for example, and the many and greater opportunities— for higher education, for instance—as compared with the loss of the fatherland, a loss too deeply felt to be expressed. This book belongs on every syllabus of this ethnic literature, for although it was first published in 1912, it was translated into English as *The Third Life of Per Smevik* in 1971 by Rølvaag's daughter and granddaughter.

Two other earlier novels by Rølvaag have also been translated into English. *Pure Gold* (Norwegian ed. 1920; English trans. 1930) is a satirical attack on the materialism of a second-generation couple who have lost every shred of their Norwegian cultural heritage and who have learned only love of money from their American surroundings. The exaggerated plot is not convincing, but the novel contains interesting scenes of farm and small-town life in the Midwest, particularly during the anti-foreign hysteria against hyphenated Americans during World War I. *The Boat of Longing* (Norwegian ed. 1921, English trans. 1933) is much better written; it contains some of Rølvaag's most poetic descriptions of Norway. His only novel set in a city, it follows the young dreamer, Nils Vaag, from Norway to Minneapolis and loses him in the maelstrom of American life, but not before he has met several interesting working-class immigrants in the slums.

Other works of Rølvaag have never been translated; they are of interest only to specialists, except for some marvelously humorous short stories originally published in a Lutheran Christmas annual but collected in a posthumous book in 1937. Some of these should be published in English, for they deserve to be better known.

Waldemar Ager (1869–1941) is widely recognized as the Norwegian-American author who ranks next after Rølvaag. A lifelong newspaper editor, he began his writing career with didactic prohibition stories, but his sharp observation and personal style soon made him a leading realist. His first novel, *Kristus for Pilatus* (1910), was published in English as *Christ before Pilate* in 1924 by a synodal press. His last novel, *I Sit Alone*, came out in Oslo in 1929 and in New York two years later. Rølvaag and Ager were the only two Norwegian-language immigrant authors to break through into mainstream American literature.

Christ before Pilate is a poor novel by artistic standards but unique in this ethnic literature for its description of an established immigrant community in a small city of the Midwest with its own sharply divided class structure. The hero is a young second-generation Lutheran minister of upper-class origin who tries to live like Christ but manages only to alienate every group in his own congregation and those in the low-class pietistic Norwegian church as well. His parishioners destroy him in the end.

I Sit Alone is a much better novel and deserves to be included on any syllabus of Scandinavian-American literature. Its main focus is not ethnic but moral: the narrator, Christian Peterson, sitting in a lonely shack on the Dakota plain, looks back over his wasted life and wonders how it went awry. Many ethnic themes enter into the description of his boyhood in Norway, his family's immigration and early years of struggle in Chicago, and their participation in the many activities of their ethnic group there. Always well meaning and afraid of hurting others, Christian gradually works his way up in business, winning material success but drifting away from religious and cultural values, for which he has no time. His selfish wife ruins his reputation and his career and drives him to saloons for solace. Finally, Christian leaves for Dakota and a long, painful settling of accounts with himself over his failure. The resolution is not entirely satisfactory, but the novel is interesting for both its psychological complexity and its reflection of Norwegian-American urban life.

Two other novels by Ager are his best ethnic works: *Paa veien til smeltepotten* (*On the Road to the Melting Pot*, 1917) and *Gamlelandets sønner* (*Sons of the Old Country*, 1926). The former is a marvelous satire on the foibles of Norwegian immigrants who try to make themselves over into WASP Americans by speaking broken English, spending all their money on conspicuous consumption, and spoiling their children. *Gamlelandets sønner* follows a group of varied Norwegian background through difficult early years in a Wisconsin sawmill town and a lumbering camp in the north woods, down to the close of the Civil War. It gives a convincing picture of the experiences of a wide range of typical immigrants, most of whom make good in a modest way. This novel may appear in English translation shortly.

Ager also wrote many first-rate short stories that contain brilliant flashes of insight into the life of both the first and second generation. Poignant, humorous, and scathing by turns, these stories should be published in English translation. They would make a permanent contribution to American literature.

Ager devoted his life to a passionate struggle for three major causes: the prohibition of alcoholic beverages, the preservation of a permanent Norwegian-American subculture, and the development of ethnic art, especially literature in the Norwegian language. When he died in 1941, all three causes were lost, and he felt that he had outlived his time. Yet his writings on ethnicity have been revived in a wider context today and can be read in translation: *Cultural Pluralism versus Assimilation: The Views of Waldemar Ager* (ed. Odd S. Lovoll, 1977). This is so central an issue for all ethnic literature that the book deserves to be widely read.

Johannes B. Wist (1864–1923) was a leading Norwegian-American journalist for nearly forty years. His trilogy of satiric novels makes him the Sinclair Lewis of this national group and the third of its major authors. *Nykommerbilleder* (*Newcomer Scenes*, 1920), *Hjemmet paa prærien* (*The Home on the Prairie*, 1921), and *Jonasville* (1922) are small masterpieces of sharply observed description and sharply etched criticism of both city and small-town immigrant life. Wist also published some short stories, one of which recently appeared in English.[9]

Simon Johnson (1874–1970) was also a lifelong journalist and a prolific writer of fiction. His early immigration (at the age of seven) and lack of formal education prevented him from perfecting his command of the Norwegian language, however, and his literary style remained inadequate to express his deep insight and broad experience in the life of his group. He continued to write until the end of his long life, but he had difficulty finding a publisher, and he left a legacy of many manuscripts. Of the six novels he published in the first quarter of this century, only one was translated into English: *From Fjord to Prairie* (Norwegian ed. 1914, English trans. 1916). This may be the worst English translation of any kind in print, but with all its flaws the little book contains so much of ethnic value that it is worth reading. Recently revived interest in Johnson's work resulted in a special issue of *Free Passage*, a literary journal in Fargo, North Dakota, that reprinted five of his short stories.[10] Johnson saw as clearly as Rølvaag both the triumphs and the tragedy of immigrant life, but he lacked the ability to turn his insights into books of artistic merit.

One must say the same of many other Norwegian-American authors: Jon Norstog, poet, dramatist, novelist, and social critic who wrote in a version of New Norwegian so strongly influenced by his dialect that almost no one could read him; Ole Buslett, poet and masterly storyteller when he kept his feet on the ground but all too inclined to go floating off into clouds of would-be philosophy; Kristofer Janson, a rare professional author (and even rarer Episcopalian minister) who after many years returned to Norway. The works of these writers contain much that is of value, but little has been good enough for publication in English translation.[11]

A few other secondary writers produced a book or two in English that one might recommend for additional reading, perhaps for special reports. H. A. Foss, for example, published the all-time best-seller in the popular, dime-novel tradition in 1884: *Husmandsgutten*, published as *The Cotter's Son* in 1963. This hopelessly bad novel went through innumerable editions in both the United States and Norway and has been described as the *Uncle Tom's Cabin* of Norwegian rental farmers. It applies the Horatio Alger formula to immigrants. A poor but honest cotter's son who has fallen in love with his landlord's daughter comes to the United States to make his fortune. Of course he returns in the nick of time to buy the farm at forced auction and marry his beloved. The main value in the book is not money but honor and piety defined in Scandinavian terms. (The book was also popular in Sweden and Denmark.) This reflection of widespread peasant ideas of the good life on both sides of the Atlantic is of interest to the history of ideas. In his long lifetime Foss published three other novels that contain sharp social and political criticism and therefore were much less popular. None of these has been translated into English.

Peer Strømme and Nils Rønning both had unpretentious but popular stories translated into English: Strømme's *Halvor: A Story of Pioneer Youth* (Norwegian ed. 1893, English trans. 1936, rev. ed. 1960), and Rønning's *Lars Lee, The Boy from Norway* (Norwegian ed. 1924, English trans. 1928) and *The Boy from Telemark* (1933). These tales were largely autobiographical.[12] Dorthea Dahl, the best woman writer of the group, was brought to America at the age of two. She published two books in Norwegian, one in English. Her innumerable short stories in both languages appeared in periodicals. *Returning Home* (1920) contains some of her best short stories in English.

Some historical works in Norwegian have considerable literary value. A considerable number have been published in English and might be used effectively in classroom study for special reports. Perhaps the best for its wide scope and personal immediacy is Hjalmar Rued Holand's *Norwegians in America:*

The Last Migration. Subtitled *Bits of Saga from Pioneer Life* and based on oral history, this was originally published in Norwegian in 1930, condensed from a much larger volume that had appeared in 1908. It was published in English translation in 1978 and thus is readily available. Holand wrote at least a dozen nonfiction books, including his autobiography, *My First Eighty Years* (1957). The Norwegian-American Historical Association has also published several books of letters and diaries in English translation.

Norwegian immigrant poets were not so good as Swedish and Danish ones. A number of them tried their hand at English-language verse now and then, but without much success. More interesting than this formal poetry are the many folk ballads about emigration and immigration, collected and translated in Theodore Blegen and Martin Ruud's *Norwegian Emigrant Songs and Ballads* (1936). Clearly the Norwegian Americans excelled in writing prose, especially fiction. Their branch of Scandinavian-American literature is by far the largest and the best of the three.

Danish

Danish-American literature produced only three or four major fiction authors, half a dozen of secondary rank, and a couple of excellent poets. There are several dozen minor writers, however, and two of the best Scandinavian Americans who wrote in English were of Danish birth. None of the top-quality work in Danish has yet appeared in English.

Adam Dan (1848–1931) was the grand old man of Danish ethnic culture in the United States and its first author. In addition to many religious works (he was a minister), he published between 1882 and 1903 seven volumes of fiction and poetry and an enormous number of contributions to periodicals. He remained an old-fashioned Romantic writer, but even the worst of his stories contain marvelous descriptive passages, realistic details of great value to social historians, profound insight into immigrant problems, serious concern with ideas, and the saving grace of humor.

Kristian Østergaard (1855–1931) was the most prolific Danish-American writer. Through a long career as teacher, editor, minister, and author he steadily developed his writing ability and published much work in Denmark. Many of his religious poems have been used as the texts of hymns in several languages. His fiction set in America is packed with fascinating material about Danish immigrant life in small-town and rural settings of the Midwest.

Carl Hansen (1860–1916) followed a varied career as teacher, postmaster, druggist, magazine editor, lecturer, author, and ethnic leader in Minnesota and Washington. He was a master of the short sketch, creating vivid snapshots of Danish immigrant life with realistic wit and ironic understanding. Undoubtedly the most skilled of all Danish-American writers, Hansen nevertheless failed to fulfill his contemporaries' expectation that he would produce a masterwork. He found time to write only one novel, but published several volumes of short stories and large amounts of material in periodicals. A volume of his best stories is now being translated for publication by Donald K. Watkins of the University of Kansas. It should be added to every syllabus of Scandinavian-American literature. One of the best Danish-American authors is still alive. Enok Mortensen (b. 1902) came to the United States with his family in 1919 and has had a long career as minister, historian, and author of outstanding novels and short stories in Danish. One story, "The Wayfarer," appeared in English translation in 1979 in the *Bridge*, journal of the Danish American Heritage Society, and in 1981 Mortensen published a charming memoir of his youth entitled *A Danish Boyhood.* He also completed a novel in English, *Plough to the Setting Sun,* and is seeking a publisher.

Although Danish literary production was the smallest of the three branches of this ethnic literature, a number of novels and the best of the ethnic poetry certainly deserve to be published in English translation.

Swedish

Most of the energy devoted to literature by first-generation Swedes went into verse forms influenced by various leading poets and poetic schools of the old country. Swedish-language verse flowered most fully between about 1890 and 1910, although the best poet of them all, Arthur Landfors (1888–1973), came later at the end of the tradition.

The only memorable poems in English by a Swedish-born immigrant were radical protest songs written by a labor organizer for IWW who had been born in Sweden in 1879. Joel Hägglund immigrated in 1902 and called himself Joseph Hillström, soon shortened to Joe Hill. After he was executed in 1914 for a murder he probably did not commit, he became a martyr, and he is still remembered in radical circles in the United States. In 1969, as part of an upsurge of interest in Joe Hill, *Joe Hills sånger: The Complete Joe Hill Song Book* was published in Sweden with Swedish translations of the English texts. There is also a collection of Swedish folk songs and ballads about emigration in translation: Robert L. Wright's *Swedish Emigrant Ballads* (1965).

The Swedes produced only a handful of major fiction authors. None was as good as the Norwegians, and only one was translated to English. Ernst Skarstedt (1857–1929) wrote prodigiously, but mainly nonfiction; he published only two volumes of stories. An outstanding and widely read journalist, he became the main critic and literary historian of the group, and his two volumes of accounts of Swedish-American writers are indispensable.

Anna Olsson (1866–1946) was one of the best writers of the Scandinavian-American group. Brought to America at the age of three, she was the daughter of a Lutheran leader and educator in the midwestern heart of Swedish America. Short stories were her forte, humorous but sharp observations of the foibles of her group, many written in a marvelous Swedish-American dialect the only drawback of which is its incomprehensibility to readers not conversant with both Swedish and English. Translation completely into either language deprives her work of much of its charm. Olsson wrote widely for periodicals, especially stories for children; she published seven volumes of the best of these as well as a book of her childhood recollections from Kansas (1917), which has been reprinted in Sweden two or three times and appeared in English in 1927 under the title *I'm Scairt: Childhood Days on the Prairie.* In 1978 the book was retranslated and privately printed in Lindsborg, Kansas, as Anna Olsson, *"A Child of the Prairie"* (sic). This version is much better than the earlier one and has the great advantage of being in print. It successfully presents a child's view of the special quality of Swedish pioneer life, and it is worthy of inclusion in a course on Scandinavian-American literature to represent the special problems of children.

Only three other major authors are worth brief mention: Vilhelm Berger (1867–1938), Johan Person (1867–1921), and Gustav Malm (1869–1928). Berger and Person, like most other

Swedish-American writers, were newspapermen, and both wrote short stories that portrayed the hardship and homesickness of their countrymen in America, although Berger's plots tended to have happy endings. Gustaf Malm, a painter and decorator, left a more optimistic record in two books and many short stories. His characters often succeed as midwestern farmers and businessmen; one even becomes a Kansas oil millionaire. All respect and preserve their cultural heritage but accept that it must ultimately disappear in the melting pot to make a better America. Malm was concerned about the low opinion most Swedes in the homeland held of emigrants, and he took pains to have his newly arrived characters learn proper respect for all that Swedish immigrants had accomplished in the New World.

The Swedes, like the other two national groups, had a larger collection of secondary than of major authors and a great number of minor authors. Leonard Strömberg (1871–1941) belongs in the secondary group, although most of his forty-odd novels are extremely poorly written. Strömberg was a Methodist minister in Nebraska whose prolific writings clearly echoed the platitudes that were dear to the hearts of large numbers of Scandinavian readers on both sides of the Atlantic. He is little remembered in America now, but in Scandinavia some of his books are still in print, and some are reprinted from time to time as serials in edifying magazines.

At least two nonfiction works should be mentioned: the two-volume translation of the memoirs of Gustaf Unonius, *A Pioneer in Northwest America 1841–1858* (ed. William Nils Olsson, 1958 and 1960), and H. Arnold Barton's *Letters from the Promised Land: Swedes in America, 1840–1914* (1975). Such raw materials of history can throw light on aspects of the immigrant experience. Their immediacy and authenticity are of great value when used in comparison with literary accounts.

English-Language Authors

English-language literature produced by Scandinavian immigrants in the United States was written for an American audience. It therefore escaped most of the problems of a foreign-language belles lettres and can be judged by stricter artistic standards. It is ethnic only by virtue of the authors' ancestry and choice of subject, characteristics not usually considered essential to literary worth. We are here mainly concerned with success in describing and communicating ethnic experience, defined as consciousness of one's specific cultural origin, in this case Scandinavian; for although the characters in these books are normally specified as Norwegian, Danish, or Swedish, there are no observable cultural differences among them. This is ethnic literature of a single type.

It begins with the works of first-generation authors who published exclusively in English. Hjalmar H. Boyesen (1848–95) is the most striking among them. Born into an upper-class Norwegian family, Boyesen had an excellent education and became professor of Germanic languages at Cornell and Columbia universities. He was accepted into the highest American social and intellectual circles, married an upper-class American woman, and wrote prodigiously to earn enough money to support her. His earliest novels were in the Romantic mode, but he soon adopted the tenets of realism and wrote most of his novels about contemporary American life. Boyesen was an ardent assimilationist, at least until late in life. He published two books about his fellow immigrants: *Tales of Two Hemispheres* (1877) and *Falconberg* (1879), both old-fashioned and mediocre. *Falconberg*, however, should be read in a course on Scandinavian-American literature because it is the only source in English that describes the great power of the clergy and the struggle over parochial schools in early Norwegian-American settlements. Its attack on ethnicity and Norwegian "clannishness" is an interesting contrast with Rølvaag's cultural pluralism.

The Danes produced the most famous of all Scandinavian-born writers in English: Jacob A. Riis (1849–1914), reporter, reformer, and author of early muckraking books, of which the best known is the shocking *How the Other Half Lives* (1890) about New York City slums. His autobiography, *The Making of an American* (1901), is seldom out of print and a classic of ethnic literature because Riis was an immigrant who became an outstanding success in his adopted country. One will look in vain for ethnic themes in it, however, except love for the old country.

The best-known novelist in English among the Scandinavians was also a Dane. Sophus Keith Winther (b.1893) came to the United States as a baby, grew up on a Nebraska farm, and became a college professor of English. His trilogy about the harsh life of a Danish farm family in Nebraska who came too late to get cheap land gives an excellent picture of this late phase of the rural experience of Scandinavian immigrants. Realist, in mode and critical in economic ideology, these novels are highly recommended: *Take All to Nebraska* (1936), *Mortgage Your Heart* (1937), and *This Passion Never Dies* (1938). The first two have recently been reprinted.

Probably the best Swedish-born writer was Gösta Larsson (1900–58), who came to the United States in 1922. *Our Daily Bread* (1934) and *Fatherland, Farewell!* (1938) are vivid and moving accounts of daily life among poor working-class families in Göteborg, Sweden, including their suffering during the general strike of 1910. These novels are the most successful attempts in American literature to describe the conditions that drove so many lower-class Scandinavians to emigrate. Neither these nor Larsson's later novels, however, dealt with immigrant life. Other Swedish-born novelists published in English mainly between the 1920s and the 1940s—Edwin Björkman, Edita Morris, Flora Sandström—but their work was mediocre and lacking in ethnic themes.

When we turn to second-generation writers of Scandinavian background the list grows endless, but most are second- or third-rate. The one major figure of Scandinavian background is of course the poet Carl Sandburg, but his Swedish immigrant origin plays no role in his work except in the early pages of his autobiography, *Always the Young Strangers* (1952). Anthony M. Rud's *The Second Generation* (1923), though second-rate in artistry, contains real insight into generational conflict between the dominating Norwegian immigrant father and his rebellious son. A number of other ethnic themes are also present. Although Kathlyn Forbes's *Mama's Bank Account* (1943) lacks depth, it is a well-written account of a Norwegian family in San Francisco that illustrates another kind of immigrant experience: the characters are totally isolated from their ethnic group; they are rapidly assimilated into American life, but they maintain their basic values. Norman Matson's *Day of Fortune* (1928) is a fascinating account of a boy's growing up in an immigrant family. His difficult father frequently loses his job and keeps moving the family from one city to another until they lose all roots, both Norwegian and American. After the death of the mother the family break up and are spread on the four winds. This book records the total loss of all ethnicity in a single generation, a frequent variant of ethnic experience. All these novels merit inclusion in an English-language course on Scandinavian ethnic literature.

In contrast, four other novels give excellent pictures of genuine ethnicity long preserved in strong Scandinavian communities. These are all fictional memoirs by women who grew up as immigrant children and who record with skill and charm how their lives derived meaning and direction by their ethnic background.

Skulda Banér's *Latchstring Out* (1944) positively glows with the color and joy that Swedish traditions brought to her childhood in a Michigan mining town. Life in this immigrant enclave is shown to be harsh and difficult in many ways, but vital ethnic values unite the community and redeem its hardships, even in the constant presence of death. Borghild Dahl's *Homecoming* (1953) is the best of her several books about second-generation girls in the Midwest. In order to be accepted as fully American, the heroine rejects her Norwegian heritage while growing up in Minneapolis, but she rediscovers its value during her first year as a teacher in a small Norwegian-American town. The conflict between loyalty to her family on one hand and loyalty to America on the other is convincingly portrayed and provides an excellent comparison with Rølvaag's *Peder Victorious*. Margarethe Erdahl Shank's *The Coffee Train* (1954, 2nd ed. 1968) records the experience of an orphaned girl growing up with her immigrant grandparents in a Dakota town that has preserved much of its Norwegian ethnicity, symbolized by the coffee train, so called because its approaching whistle announces the traditional time for afternoon coffee every day. Norwegian ways and values are here recorded in a multitude of ethnic themes. Helga Skogsbergh's *From These Shores* was first published as the middle novel of a trilogy focused on her Swedish immigrant mother: *Comes the Day, Comes a Way* (1960), *From These Shores* (1963), and *That Was Then* (1969). The current paperback edition of *From These Shores* (1975), however, is an abridged edition of all three novels, with the author's own experience bringing the story close to the present day. The whole sweep of Scandinavian pioneering experience is thus recounted in a late version as the working-class Swedish family struggles to make a decent farm out of cheap cut-over wilderness land in northern Wisconsin. This last book is artistically inferior to the preceding three, but its record of Scandinavian values permeating the daily lives of its simple, pious characters is of considerable value. All these four novels are recommended for their reliable accounts of genuine ethnicity.

A multitude of second-rate books by writers of Scandinavian background have appeared in the past half century and are still appearing. These are second-rate for one or more of a number of reasons. First, many were written for an adolescent or popular audience, mainly to entertain or to teach simple morals or religious faith. These may contain some genuine ethnic elements, but their level of conception bars them from serious consideration. They offer too little in return for the time it would take to read them. Examples of this type are the several novels of Thrya Ferré Bjorn and Ellen Turngren. Second, the artistry of many such works is mediocre, however serious their intent. A host of minor novels not worth mentioning fall into this category, including some—such as those of Lillian Budd and Martha Ostenso—not recommended for yet a third reason. Novels in this final category are unsatisfactory ethnically—that is, their ethnic elements are too shallow or misunderstood or downright wrong. The failure to convey the ethnic culture is a great danger in all second-generation fiction, although not necessarily the fault of the author. Of course the original ethnic culture underwent constant change in America, developing in many directions as a result of the personal choices of members of the group. Culturally hybrid conditions resulted, and only an expert can recognize the elements that are genuinely Scandinavian survivals in the general confusion. What a purist might call corruption of the original heritage interests the social historian for its own sake, as evidence of cultural interaction and its power to modify human behavior and ideas. Students reading such books for the first time, however, cannot separate genuine ethnicity from what the author may erroneously present as Scandinavian. For this reason only the second-generation novels identified above as best are recommended for an introductory course in Scandinavian-American literature. After all, the purpose of such a course is to teach what the Scandinavian heritage really was.

Instead of reading poor novels, one might turn to good second-generation autobiographies, such as those published by ethnic historical associations, whose imprint is proof of the genuine ethnicity of the contents. For example, Laurence M. Larson's *The Log Book of a Young Immigrant* (1939) and Birger Osland's *A Long Pull from Stavanger* (1945) are available from the Norwegian-American Historical Association, while *Farm, Forge, and Philosophy* by Adolph B. Benson can be ordered from the Swedish Pioneer Historical Society. These excellent accounts make interesting contrasts with the better second-generation fiction. A recent book might be of special interest to some: H. Arnold Barton's *The Search for Ancestors: A Swedish-American Family Saga* (1979). This is partly autobiography that traces the author's search for and discovery of his Swedish and Swedish-American family, partly the story of a Swedish-American family and the ethnic heritage it preserved, partly the history of Swedish emigration and immigration, and partly a handbook on how to find one's own ancestors and relatives in Scandinavia.

In addition, because of the paucity of immigrant materials in English, a few works by Scandinavian authors in English translation might well be included in courses on Scandinavian-American literature. Classic novels in their own national literatures are Norwegian Johan Boyer's *The Emigrants* (1925) and Swedish Vilhelm Moberg's tetralogy, *The Emigrants* (1951), *Unto a Good Land* (1954), *The Settlers* (1956), and *Last Letter Home* (1959). These works are frequently reprinted in the United States and thus are widely available. They are excellent novels by professional writers who visited the United States to study their emigrated countrymen. Their presentation of Scandinavian ethnicity is totally reliable and can be used as a standard against which to measure the authenticity of second-generation novels.

An outstanding recent book is Erik Bye's *Blow, Silver Wind: A Story of Norwegian Immigration to America* (1978), a beautifully illustrated selection of poetic materials used in a 1975 program and television broadcast on both sides of the Atlantic to celebrate the sesquicentennial of the arrival of the first shipload of immigrants from Norway to America in 1825. Erik Bye was born in the United States and is almost as much American as Norwegian in loyalty and interest, but he has made his career as a popular television personality in Norway. He is also widely known for his ballads, of which this volume contains an excellent selection of those written about Norwegians in America.

Finally, any course on Scandinavian-American literature must use a brief and excellent new literary history by Christer Lennart Mossberg: *Scandinavian Immigrant Literature* (Boise State Univ., Idaho: Western Writers Series No. 47, 1981). Although this account is largely limited to writing about midwestern farm life, it is by far the best brief survey of the field to date. It starts with the nineteenth-century letters and guide-books that first established a tradition of writing by and for immigrants, traces the development of literary genres in popular and serious fiction written in both English and the Scandinavian languages, and gives a brilliant analysis of the complex themes preserved in this ethnic literature. A number of the authors I have mentioned receive much fuller treatment here, while others I have omitted are given their due. The short bibliography of both primary and secondary sources is also excellent. This book is indispensable for any course in Scandinavian-American literature.

In conclusion it must be reiterated that comparatively little of the true wealth of Scandinavian-American literture is available in English. The best books of Swedish- and Danish-American belles lettres have not yet been translated, and all too few Norwegian works have appeared in English-language versions. Indeed, only half a loaf is available to the American reader instead of the rich smorgasbord of offerings available in the original languages. Perhaps the current ethnic revival will stimulate more translation, at least in anthology form. If it does, we will be able not only to assess accurately the impressive achievement of Scandinavian-American authors but also to enjoy and appreciate a unique contribution to American letters.

Notes

[1] O. E. Rølvaag, *Omkring fædrearven* (Northfield, Minn.: St. Olaf Coll. Press, 1922), p. 57.

[2] American immigration figures for the period 1820 to 1975 estimate that 1,270,000 Swedish immigrants, 855,000 Norwegians, and 363,000 Danes came to America. Almost all arrivied before 1930, with the peak in the 1880s.

[3] Waldemar Ager, "Norsk-amerikansk skjønliteratur" ("Norwegian-American Belles Lettres"), in *Norskamerikanernes festskrift 1914*, ed. Johannes B. Wist (Decorah, Iowa: Symra, 1914), p. 294.

[4] Simon Johnson, "Skjønlitterære sysler blandt norsk-amerikanerne" ("Literary Activities among Norwegian-Americans"), *Decorah-Posten*, 24 Feb. 1939.

[5] Simon Johnson, *From Fjord to Prairie* (Minneapolis: Augsburg, 1916), pp. 295–96.

[6] Simon Johnson, "Jon og Ragnhild," *Jul i Vesterheimen (Christmas in the Western Home)*, a Norwegian-American Christmas annual (n.p.: n.p., 1935); my trans.

[7] Anna M. Carlson, *The Heritage of the Bluestem* (Kansas City, Mo.: Burton, 1930), p. 44.

[8] O. E. Rølvaag, *Giants in the Earth* (New York: Harper, 1929), p. 385.

⁹ Johannes B. Wist, "When Bjornson Came to LaCrosse," *Dakota Arts Quarterly* [Fargo, N.D.], No. 12 (Summer 1981), pp. 14-21.

¹⁰ Simon Johnson, "Inga from the Grove," "Jim's Last Day," "from [sic] Diggings," Louis Alfred & John Otto," and "The Quarantine," *Free Passage, a Journal of Prose and Poetry,* No. 9 (Spring 1980), pp. 1-14.

¹¹ One long and one short story by Buslett have recently been published in English translation for the first time in *The Road to the Golden Gate,* Winchester Academy Ethnic Heritage Monograph No. 4 (Larsen, Wisc.; 1978).

¹² Two selections of writings by Peer Strømme have recently been published in English translation as monographs: *Memoirs of a Winchester Childhood,* Winchester Academy Ethnic Heritage Monograph No. 1 (n.d.), and *Noraville Stories,* Winchester Academy Ethnic Heritage Monograph No. 2 (n.d.).

Three South Slavic-American Literatures

Edward Ifkovic

Background: The Slovenians, Croatians, and Serbians in America

America, you dewy flower,
everybody desires you:
a child of two years,
or a man of hundred years.[1]

So goes one stanza of a Montenegrin folk song. The rhapsodic lyrics, typical of the many folksongs that sprang up in the villages of Montenegro and other South Slavic lands, reflect the people's intoxication with and passion for the New World and the hope that America represented for the millions of struggling peasants. As devastating poverty spread from northern Europe down through the Balkan lands around 1880, the great migration to America began. Fed by exaggerated descriptions of gold-paved streets, money from the blue, and cloudless skies, peasants in Croatia, Serbia, and Slovenia — oppressed by centuries-old misrule by Austria-Hungary and Turkey — found in the mythic image of America the hope of surcease from poverty, political oppression, and social immobility. If you were a Croat, Slovene, or Serb, you had to come to America: here you could speak your native language (forbidden in parts of Europe), here you could own your own land, here you could pass on to your children the precious legends that had come down from the Middle Ages, legends of Marko Kraljevic and the magnificent heroism of the battle of Kosovo: "Mi ideme trazeti ima in jos pravice na svieto" ("We go to see if there is still justice in the world").[2] Of course, the South Slavs did not reckon with the uncanny forces of America — its hypnotic power over them and especially their children. It only mattered that they came "across the pond" *trbuhom za kruhom* ("belly after bread"). Here, at the turn of the century, the long haphazard immigration of South Slavs to America suddenly became a flood tide: whole villages were virtually emptied, and the villagers often resettled together in some American city. Here, suddenly, men and women who were long used to a life on the barren soil found themselves in dark factories, mills, or mines in Pittsburgh, Cleveland, Chicago: "My people do not live in America, they live underneath America. America goes on over their heads."[3] Poor, often illiterate, knowing little or no English, they hid in their tenements, found comfort only in the company of other South Slavs, and emerged only on Sunday afternoons to sing the old songs, drink the fiery *sljivovica*, and feast on the barbecued lamb. Between 1880 and 1914 millions came, unheralded and often unnoted by the Americans.

But South Slavs had been journeying to America since the early Colonial days, albeit never before in such numbers as at the turn of the century. In their own way they created, and then entered, the mythic fabric that emerged as "America" and, inevitably, infiltrated its literature. Slovene-American Louis Adamic noted, "Little doubt exists that on Columbus' ships were cosmopolitan Croatians from the famous Dalmatian city-republic of Ragusa (Dubrovnik)."[4] Ragusa was a powerful maritime state, then at the height of its influence. And legend persists that a Ragusan ship visited the mysterious Roanoke "lost colony" in the seventeenth century — hence the word "Croatan" carved on a tree. Ragusa sent many trading vessels to the New World. Before the great migration many other South Slavs entered America, but most left little record of their presence and contributed nothing to South Slavic-American literature.

The earliest documented influences resulted from the work of South Slavic missionaries, many of whom left publications that suggest the beginning of a South Slavic-American literary tradition. Bringing God and the Bible to the American Indian, these clergymen left their mark in ways the nomadic South Slavic sailors and adventurers never could. One of the earliest was Baron Ivan Ratkay (Ratkaj), a rich Croatian nobleman and a Jesuit who arrived in 1673 and worked with the Taramuhara Indians of the Southwest. Driven by an insatiable intellectual curiosity, he studied the geography of the region and chronicled his extensive travels. He died at thirty-six at the hands of hostile Indians. His letters—like the "America" letters that later generations sent home inspiring so many others to come here—are vital records (certainly equal to John Smith's more famous letters back to England from the Jamestown colony) describing the land, the natives, and the progress of missionary work. One such letter, translated from the Latin, is included in H. E. Bolton's *Rim of Christendom* (1936). Another Croatian missionary, Ferdinand Konscak (Consag) arrived in 1733 at the San Ignacio mission in Baja California and eventually discovered that Baja California was not an island but a peninsula. Like Ratkaj he contributed to the beginnings of American literature: he wrote an authoritative history of the missions of California and, more important, his own personal story, *Diaria de California*.

Like the Croatians, the Slovenes had their distinguished missionaries, men like Mark Anton Kapus, Francis X. Pierz (Pirc), and Frederick Baraga. Baraga, arriving in Cincinnati in 1831, made contributions not only to Slovenian-American literature but to that of the American Indian as well. In 1835 he began working with the Chippewa Indians at La Pointe, Wisconsin, and stayed there eight years. He quickly became conversant with the Chippewa language and translated numerous books. He respected the long tradition of the Indians, but he believed that they would have to adapt to the white culture or die. He taught them agricultural skills and carpentry, and he recorded and described their traditions on paper. He also did revolutionary work in Indian linguistics. He produced a Chippewa dictionary and grammar, conscious of the need to give them a written language as a vehicle for preserving their heritage. His own book of poetry in the Ottawa language, *Life and Manners of the North American Indians*, is replete with curious lore and keen observation—a document precious in its literary and historical reflection. Widely beloved, he died in 1868 at seventy-one, and today Baraga County is named in his honor. He has been called the father of Indian literature.[5]

These scattered writings by missionaries remain isolated documents that are in no way part of any coherent body of South Slavic-American literature. Only after 1880 would there be sufficient numbers of South Slavs in America to precipitate a literary outpouring, however uneven in quality. From the 1880s until the restrictive legislation of 1924, South Slavs came to

America in unprecedented numbers as part of the "new immigration" (Immigration Commissioner Edward Corsi's term to distinguish the new influx of Slavs, Italians, and East European Jews from the "old" northwestern immigrants from England, Ireland, Scandinavia, and Germany). For centuries the South Slavic villages had remained static, with families clustered in communal homesteads called *zadrugas*. Gnawing poverty, declining infant mortality, depleted soil, and oppressive political conditions in the Austro-Hungarian Empire propelled the parochial peasant toward America. Many young men came for only a short time, intending to remain only as long as it took to amass the money they needed. Of those who came, some forty percent returned to the old country. "Many Yugoslavs were birds of passage, rather impassive and patient marginal laborers, unskilled and poor," said one immigration historian.[6]

It is difficult to estimate the number of Slovenians, Serbians, and Croatians who arrived. Poor statistics, coupled with American ignorance about South Slavic lands, made estimates uncertain. By calling themselves Austrians, Hungarians, and Slavonians, the immigrants contributed to the confusion. By the 1930s, Ivan Mladineo calculated, there were roughly one million Yugoslavs of the first and second generations in America: 500,000 Croatians, 300,000 Slovenians, and 200,000 Serbians.[7] Today there are probably three to four million, most in the Midwest and the West. At one point there were over one thousand South Slavic settlements throughout America, most clustered around factories and mines. Here thousands of men and women helped usher in America's technological and industrial twentieth century. Men often lived in cooperative boardinghouses called *drustvos*, as on New York City's West Side. Often they struggled in the worst working conditions. Many were maimed for life, and many were killed. The world of Little Slovenia, Little Serbia, or Little Croatia was a tapestry of material success and happiness alternating with scarred hopes and bitter experiences before the fact of native exploitation and blatant discrimination. As one unsympathetic observer remarked, "The phlegmatic Slavs seem to possess the nervous stability needed for the dangerous and toilsome work of the steel mill."[8] Phlegmatic or not, the South Slavs used their brawn and intellect to help build modern America, and their own indigenous spirit and strength helped them survive untoward and frightening experiences in this new promised land.

They brought with them various qualities and allegiances that helped them survive—and, more to the point, that contributed to the foundation of a literary expression. First, they formed benevolent fraternal societies, designed to provide insurance and other protection, and these organizations became focal points for all types of activity: social, educational, economic. In the pages of yellowing fraternal newspapers we find the beginnings of a literature: popular poetry, hesitant memoirs, melodramatic fiction. Examples of such organizations are the First Serbian Benevolent Society (1880) in San Francisco; the Independent Society of Saint Joseph (1882), a Slovenian organization in Calumet, Michigan; and the Croatian Fraternal Union (1894) in Pittsburgh. Second, the immigrant churches provided similar community. Most Slovenians and Croatians are Roman Catholic; most Serbians are Eastern Orthodox. In the early religious documents, almanacs, and anniversary publications, we find the same tentative groping toward a literature: homiletic poems (*pjesme*), vivid anecdotes, impassioned letters detailing both hard and beautiful experiences in America. And third, the role of the ethnic newspaper and magazine cannot be underestimated. Not only did such publications help interpret America—the laws, the employment opportunities—but they also provided the fertile ground in which the seeds of creative expression flourished. Newspapers like the Croatian *Slavonian Harmony* (1884), *American Slovene* (1891), and *United Serbdom* (1905) registered the heartbeat of an entire ethnic subculture often far removed from mainstream America.

Yet another influence bears mention: the elaborate, rich folk culture carried by the peasants to America. A centuries-old tradition of music and legend has sustained both Old and New World South Slavs through times of darkness. This vital repository of folk wisdom often reflects preeminent cultural values such as those involving male and female roles ("A man is worth more than ten women"; "A man of straw is worth more than a woman of gold"), and the folk legends and epic poetry, embedded in the people's memory, permeate all South Slavic literary expression to the present time. The old stories of the Jugović brothers, the heroism at the battle of Kosovo, the adventures of Marko Kraljevic reflect the soul of a long-oppressed people; only naturally such legend touched the South Slav even in the American factory. The melodic folk music (*narodne pjesme*) and the dance (the *kolo*, the circle dance, for example), accompanied by the mandolinlike *tamburitsa*, linked the life in America with that of the homeland. Through music the peasants remembered the past and relived the daily activities of the old days: harvesting the wheat, marrying, burying the dead. Such lyrics suggest the fiber of the peasant life; marrow deep, this intricate, stunning oral tradition prepared the way for written creative expression. By the 1920s, then, such an oral tradition was firmly implanted and already integrated into popular poetry, fiction, autobiography, and travel literature.

Throughout the twentieth century, South Slavs arrived, but—stifled by the discriminatory legislation of 1921 and 1924—in reduced numbers. Never again would the golden gates be completely open to the South Slav. In fact, during the depression deportation was more common than immigration. Only in the years after the ravages of World War II was there renewed influx. Because of special legislation passed by Congress, displaced persons were allowed in, and thousands of South Slavs came. Since the quota system was abolished in 1965, two to three thousand Yugoslavs have entered each year. And the nature of these immigrants has had a demonstrable influence on South Slavic culture here, for these new people are largely educated men and women, professionals and intellectuals who are far removed from the illiterate peasants. Artists, writers, businessmen, clergy, the products of a solid European education, they have brought a new perspective to America. Since 1945 over sixty thousand have come here.

As a result, there exists today in America an extensive émigré literature, a literature that, while sophisticated and often profound, bears allegiance more to old country sensibilities than to the popular traditions cultivated by the peasants who arrived after 1880. What has emerged, then, is a fascinating dichotomy: on the one hand, a loosely coherent body of South Slavic-American literature reflects the Americanization of the peasant during the first half of the century; on the other hand, a highly evolved intellectual literature, most of it in the old language, often ignores American experience and dwells instead on old country culture, frequently dealing with the politics of communist Yugoslavia. Of course, both groups are intricately bound by their heritage and language. It remains to be seen whether the émigré literature will finally tap the traditions already established by the earlier immigrants and produce a vital, contemporary American literature born of a South Slavic sensibility. A dazzling literature could result: the Slavic heart and soul born again in the rich American earth.

Croatian-American Literature

Despite the scattered diaries, travel essays, and religious tracts that the early Croatians in America produced, there was hardly a viable Croatian-American literature until the great migration. Then for the first time sufficient numbers emigrated, founded colonies, and thus created a foundation from which literature could evolve. Though often unlettered, these peasants possessed a rich oral tradition, and out of this Old World folk wisdom and New World dream and nightmare came the first attempts to transcribe experience on paper, to distill out of the new land a coherent sense of time and place. Those who could write were concerned lest the old poetry be lost. These were the journalists who provided not only reportage but also popular poetry and melodramatic fiction. They were South Slavs of various education who communicated American life to the immigrant in newspapers, journals, broadsides, almanacs, and dictionaries. Literate, often zealously political, and always passionately committed to the immigrant, they appropriately laid the basis for a Croatian-American literature. The first Croatian newspaper *Dalmatinska Zora* (*Dalmatian Dawn*), though short-lived, appeared in San Francisco in 1892. A more enduring paper was *Danica—The Morning Star*, founded in 1894 by Zdravko Mužina and Petar Pavlinac. The first newspaper on the East Coast was *Napredak* (1891) in Hoboken. Nikola Polić's *Chicago* (1892) was a typical immigrant journal, containing stories of American life, old country politics, and literary jottings. Most papers were sloppily printed, filled with errors, and marked by often irrational bias. Strangely, the best papers often represented steamship lines and immigrant banks. One such publication was Frank Zotti's *Narodni List* (1898). The most widely read paper, a New York weekly and later daily, *Narodni List* was chatty, informal, newsy—the kind of popular journal that was easily available and attractive to the barely literate working person. The organ of the Croatian Fraternal Union, *Zajedničar*, first appeared in 1904; it is still a successful newspaper whose files contain literally volumes of memoirs, letters, popular poetry, and so forth. Approximately sixteen Croatian papers were published before World War I.[9] The number declined after the war, but one journalist in particular, Ivan Mladineo, emerged as an important figure. His *Hrvatski Narod* (1909 in Saint Louis and later in New York) was permeated by a passion to save not only the history of his people but also the remnants of literary expression. Mladineo believed that the Croatian-American experience should be written down, especially "in the twilight of our immigrant racial existence in America" (p. xi). As the immigrants became Americanized, too much was lost. When Croatian scholar A. Trešić-Pavičić visited America in 1905 he sadly and repeatedly observed that too many Croatians were forgetting their heritage.[10] Mladineo and others worked to preserve the precious remnants. His *Žetva* (*Harvest*) was his one attempt at fiction.

Like the newspaper, the popular almanac (*kalendar* or *koledar*) was the repository of much creative literature—a tradition dating back to the old villages where the almanac was often the only available volume. Filled with popular poetry written in the ever-present decameter, these almanacs thrived in America and really are untapped anthologies of untranslated belles lettres. The earliest was Mužina's *Hrvatsko-Amerikanska Danica za Godinu 1895*, followed by Josip Marohnic's *Hrvatska Vila Kalendar* (1898). Many more followed. As George Prpić notes, "The editors encouraged contributions by immigrants, who usually offered descriptions of the colonies where they lived, or poems, short sketches, stories and recollections about the old days of their immigrant life" (*Croatian Immigrants*, p. 326).

Prpić also regards Marohnic as "the founder of popular Croatian literature in America" (p. 326) because of his stupendous outpouring of almanacs, books, grammars, pamphlets, and newspapers. He published the first book of Croatian poetry in America, *Amerikanke*. His 1913 *Velika Narodna Hrvatska Pjesmarica* is the first anthology of Croatian poetry in America. In these pre–World War I years, encouraged by the newspapers and almanac editors, the first writers of belles lettres appeared — none, however, in English. Matija Sojat, owner of a Croatian bookstore in Calumet, Michigan, published a book of poetry, *Sto Uzdisaja*, in 1910. Many of Sojat's poems were traditional sonnets. Some early works were anonymous, like *Osvetnici s Jadrana* (1914), a story about early immigrants. Victor Vojvodic published *Sabrane pjesme*, a collection of poetry (n.d.) based on the experiences of Croatians in America. This popular poetry —

often sentimental if not maudlin, usually poor in quality — was of course the written version of the oral folk tradition. The themes were the same. War predominates, both the conflicts of earlier centuries and those as recent as the Balkan Wars. Domesticity is commonplace: life in the old village, the harvest, the perilous voyage to America, life in the factories and in the mines. A nonliterary melodramatic account of the voyage, for example, is found in *Od Novigrada do Amerike* by Šime Sinovčič and Josip Mikečin (1914). Even Croatian writers who never visited America reflected the obsession with the New World. Dragutin Domjanič, for example, wrote "U Rudniku" ("In the Mine"), a perennially popular and often reprinted piece that describes the brutal death of a Croatian miner in America. Drago Gervais in "Bog Domovina" ("Farewell to the Homeland") lamented the flight to America. Such themes were familiar in the reams of popular verse found in newspapers, almanacs, and privately printed books. Strangely, in this prewar period, popular poetry was commonplace; fiction was not. Only two works of fiction stand out: S. R. Danevski's widely printed *Pripovijesti* (*Short Stories*, 1911), stories about Croatians here and in the old country, which were praised in Zagreb as the beginning of Croatian literature in America;[11] and Medo Krašić's 1904 novel *Zapisci* (*Notes*), the story of an ill-starred Croatian immigrant girl. Far removed from the formal and academic literary traditions of Zagreb, all this poetry and fiction was the stuff of the peasant, the folk tradition encasing American experience and groping for the printed word to interpret it.

Croatian-American literature in the post–World War I years was different: less cheap journalism, more conscious art, and increased publication in English. Publication in Croatian did not end, of course. In fact, Croatian-language books showed more conscious art. Grgo Turkalj, author of *Hrvatske narodne ratne pjesme* (*Croatian Popular War Poetry*, 1930), traveled back and forth to Croatia, fought in World War I, and described the horrors of war with vitality and sensitivity. His 220-page poem is epic in proportion, but that is not surprising when we realize that Turkalj was a *guslar*, a singer of folk legends on the one-stringed instrument, before coming to America. Another postwar writer was Stjepko Brozovic, author of a collection of short stories, *Sabrane Pripovijesti iz Americkog Hrvatskog Zivota* (*Collected Stories from American Croatian Life*, c. 1920).

But during these years Americanized Croatians began to tell their own stories in English, and the variety of their experiences (from pursuit of Indians to Lutheran missionary work to a fictionalized account of a Croatian-American physician's life) suggests the disjointed, fragmented literary endeavor then in evidence. There was no coherent literary progression, and to this day no tradition exists to nourish successive generations of writers. Croatian-American literature is, at best, a hodgepodge of disparate experience, often charming, often sensational or trivial, occasionally beautiful and profound.

Three autobiographies reflect this various experience. Anton Mazzanovich, son of a San Francisco musician, enlisted at age eleven in the band of the 21st U. S. Infantry in 1870 and later was part of the 6th U.S. Calvary. He assisted in the pursuit of the Apache Indians in 1881 and met their famed chief Geronimo. His autobiographical account, *Trailing Geronimo* (1926), is filled with the adventure and color of the Old West. His book, fragmented and largely unstructured, is a document valuable not only for its insight into the conflict in the Old West but for its revelation of character, for Mazzanovich deals with himself as a South Slav, as an Indian fighter, and as a restless, nomadic American frontiersman. He captures the feeling of an era — the braggadocio, the search for excitement, the rootless American content only with new experience. He roamed from one occupation to another: saloonkeeper, cowboy, stage performer. While the style of the book is often pedestrian, especially in his account of his private life and in the honorific tributes to his superior officers, Mazzanovich does rise to eloquence when he touches on some of the more adventurous activities. His style is deadpan, matter-of-fact, but often his account contains much of the almost stereotyped flavor of a yellow-back dime-novel western:

The day of the hanging Skitashe was so weak he could not stand. The Indian scouts were lined up, facing the scaffold. Dead Shot and Dandy Jim walked up unassisted, but Skitashe had to be carried up on the platform. Here he said to the sergeant of the guard: "No veno; commandanta give Indian clean clothes one day; hang him next day; what for?" The provost sergeant adjusted the nooses over their heads. The trap was sprung by a prisoner in the guardhouse who had been promised his freedom if he would perform the gruesome task. This ended the uprising and Indian raid in Arizona in the year 1881.[12]

Over a decade later another Croatian-American auto-biography appeared, as far removed from Mazzanovich's as can be imagined. Louis Sanjek's *In Silence* (1938) deals with the experiences of a Croatian-Lutheran minister in the Slavic set-tlements of the Northeast. Born in Croatia, Sanjek converted from Roman Catholicism to Lutheranism while in a Zagreb seminary and came to America to minister to his Slav brethren. As laborious in style as Mazzanovich's, Sanjek's book fails where we most want it to succeed: in his pictures of immigrant life in America. He often simply lists the parishes in which he served, and the book becomes more catalog than autobiography. While putting his life in order (he had been hospitalized after losing his voice, hence the title), he does manage to describe some old country traditions. Imbued with the folk legends, the stories, and the epic narratives of Marko Kraljevic — Sanjek talks of the "rich and beautiful folklore" and the "comfort and inspiration" these "war songs of old" provided[13] — he found that their idealism sustained him in America. Thus the early sections of the autobiography suggest the strong hold of the Croatian past — especially the Mariology so common in South Slavic autobiog-raphy. Only when Sanjek relates his American experience does he falter. Arriving in Hoboken in 1911, he found himself immersed in the life of the poor. His first response was to compare the filthy American cities with the spotless towns and cities of Croatia. He steeped himself in the mining and industrial settlements of Pennsylvania and New York. His book tells about the hard life of the working class in an unsympathetic America: the strikes, the mangled bodies he prayed over, the deaths of the blackened miners. But while these "discouragements" in the promised land evoked his compassion and charity, they did not awaken his social conscience. He remained the objective social worker, duly chronicling events as they happened. His autobiog-raphy thus becomes humdrum and not a little tedious, the mechanical jottings of an uninspired missionary.

The best autobiographer never fulfilled his early promise. In 1937 Gabro Karabin, a young Croatian American born in 1912 in McKeesport, Pennsylvania, published "Honorable Escape" in *Scribner's Magazine*. The account of the death of Karabin's father and brother in industrial accidents and of his own psychological difficulty in leaving behind the steel mill that served as home to so many Croatians won the thousand-dollar first prize in the magazine's Life in the United States series. Depressing in its depiction of the harsh brutality of factory life ("a man stumbling back from his job against a hot pipe that seared his legs off in a screaming fraction of time—hoarse bellowing from the booming mill where a drowsy assistant had been sucked into the rollers and mashed to pulp. These things were my nightly fears"),[14] the story also gives a bittersweet, often poetic image of life in the Croatian-American community:

> July was a relentless month—hot and steaming. After my three-o'clock shift release I would go back to the settlement and sit on the back porch that faced the hillside and the rivers and the mills. The Croatian church held a memorial service one evening for the two settlement boys who had been burned to death in the fueling pit at the airport. And after supper, the old women sat together and painted tin buttons which were to be sold sometime in September for the benefit of the St. Barnabas Home. The parched grass on the slopes above the mills grew wiry and tufted, and the shrubbery growing in the shale layers of the hillside turned yellow and gritty. (p. 42)

After leaving behind the steel mill and finding a job as a clerk, he feels guilty. How far is he removing himself from his people? How honorable is his escape? He seeks the world of ideas, the realm of literature ("to make Croat and Slavish art and literature and customs more than mere mill energy," p. 7).

> There was, to be sure, the intense feeling in me that in a way I would always be alien to the settlement and its beefy, meek living—that somewhere, perhaps not miles away, there was a future, a work for me, not allied with the omnipresent mills. And yet, as I have said, I was not lying boldly to myself. That restless, seeking urge had been with me since childhood when I would sit on the ragged edge of the settlement bluff and feel a loneliness growing within me, greater than I could explain or understand. But that was not all—I was afraid! (p. 42)

Karabin's eloquent statement epitomizes the common problem of the generations born in America: the tension between the Old World customs and the new American present, the breaking off of allegiances in an attempt to discover self, and the anguish and guilt that result. At age twenty-seven Karabin wrote perhaps the most beautiful and artful account of Croatian-American life, but he was never heard from again. The *Scribner's* editors spoke of the "qualities of a great artist" (p. 6), but Karabin never again published.

In 1931 Victor G. Vecki published a novel, *Threatening Shadows*, the only Croatian-American fiction written in English during the pre-World War II period. Vecki, a gynecologist, emigrated from Croatia, then set up medical practice in San Francisco. He published various medical tracts before he attempted fiction. His novel, a failure in the marketplace and as literature, tells how the innocent Victoria saves the profligate Croatian-American doctor Ivan Nemir from the nemesis of his family curse:

> The Nemirs all make their women exceedingly happy at first but always end by making them utterably miserable. But there is a law of retribution and an avenging God. They themselves can never be happy and, whenever they really and desperately love, the Nemesis follows them and the ending must be tragic. The curse of too many a woman's tear is upon them, upon every one of them![15]

The novel is marked by stylistic weaknesses ("the best physician in the city, the kindest fellow who ever lived," p. 3) and a lack of any realistic motivation for its psychological turns. Verisimilitude is an alien concept to Vecki. He chronicles Nemir's various love affairs, as well as Victoria's journey to happiness. Vecki is emphatically anticlerical and spends much time lambasting Roman Catholic dogma. His characters are stereotypes, and Vecki—ever the physician—clutters the novel with psychological and physiological terms. At one point he gives extensive information on glaucoma. The book is really a case study, perhaps showing the influence of Dreiserian naturalism—an accumulation of clinical detail. Vecki, however, has little understanding of human behavior and motivation; what results is reportage without the larger human and social perspective that gave dimension to the naturalists. Vecki has taken their technique but not their commitment to real human behavior, however degraded or sordid. Women are "perfect and beautiful," (p. 30) and the platitudes overwhelm: "love could not be a sin"

(p. 207). The ending, however, is hardly naturalistic. The errant Victoria and the obsessed Nemir discover in each other the stuff of salvation (she is his "light and sunshine," p. 262), and Nemir is saved from the family curse. Or is he? "Nemesis Conquered" is the final chapter heading, but why should we believe it? We have seen no evolution of his character, no altered perception as a result of his experiences. The novel concludes with a melodramatic flourish: "If you go to hell, to hell I go with you!" (p. 262). The reader is left wanting. Vecki has given us little—a smattering of Croatian-American life and even less of the workings of human behavior.

One important piece of anonymous oral tradition must be mentioned: the Croatian-American contribution to American folk culture, the heroic Joe Magarac. Ironically, this legend has emerged as the Croatians' most enduring literary contribution. *Magarac* means "jackass" and, as Prpić notes, was often "used as a nickname by which Croatian mill-workers and miners teasingly called each other" (*Croatian Immigrants*, p. 377). Joe Magarac, a Paul Bunyan type, evolved at the turn of the century in the Pittsburgh steel-mill regions; he was the larger-than-life man of steel. This mythic character, now part of our folkloric tradition, was supposedly born inside an iron-ore mountain. Made of steel, over seven feet tall, good-looking, this American Joe is clearly the descendant of another Joe, Veli Jože (Mighty Joe), a character in Croatian folk legend who could lift a fifty-ton ladle and hold molten metal in his bare hands. In America, Veli Jože evolved into Joe Magarac, who became an ironic symbol of the Croatian worker, whom the ruling social class considered all brawn and a *magarac*.

Many legends surrounding Joe doubtless are now lost, but a few have survived. In one story Steve Mestrovich, a steel worker, wants his daughter to wed the strongest man around. He gives a party at which the young men have to lift three weights—one 350 pounds, one 500, the third more than the two combined. Mary's beloved Pete Pusić lifts the second but not the third. A stranger appears, his back bigger than a door, handsome, tall. He lifts the bars with one hand. He will not marry, however; his work is his life. He gives Mary to Peter. Another story tells of the lights going out in the mills whenever Joe laughs. Typically, there are different versions of how he meets his end: in one story he dissolves himself into molten steel ("symbolic of the workers' own lives, which were sacrificed to the voracious steel mills")[16]; in another he is still alive, sleeping in a cave in the Allegheny Mountains (this version is close to the Croatian and Slovenian stories of the heroic Good King Mathias, who sleeps in a mountain and who will return some day to bring justice to his people).

The saga of Joe Magarac might have been lost had not Francis Owen, a steelworker, published it in *Scribner's Magazine* in 1931. B. A. Botkin reprinted it in his *Treasury of American Folklore* (1944). Owen's version is in dialect, supposedly told by a "hunkie" worker. Strangely, Owen and subsequent folklorists persisted in using the derogatory term "hunkie," which was commonly applied to Slavic workers. Few writers, except for South Slavic specialists like George Prpić, have referred to the Croatian origins of the legend. Owen noted that the "hunkies" called one another "magarac," but never "used the word derisively."[17] Acknowledging that Joe "belongs to the mills as do the furnaces and the rolling-mills," Owens added, curiously, that he has "no tangible connection...with the folklore of any of the countries which sent the Hunkies to the United States" (p. 505). Apparently, Owen's knowledge of South Slavic folk tradition was inadequate. He seemed content, also, to use a feeble, unrealistic dialect in his attempt to capture Croatian-American speech: "Dats all right, dats good business for me. Me, I was born inside one mountain many year ago. Today I comit down from mountain in ore train and was over in one pile by blast furnace" (p. 505). Such shortcomings aside, Owen did preserve a rich folk tradition in America. We can only regret that a Croatian-American in those early days did not provide a version more in concert with the stories told in the Croatian-American community. In any event, the presence of Joe Magarac in the immigrant imagination does tell us much about the Croatian steelworkers. The mighty Joe, made of steel, was the average working man writ large, the proletarian who transformed his powerlessness before the fact of American industry into that power itself. If the worker saw himself as a tool of industry, pure and expendable brawn, someone whose lifeblood entered the steel itself, then Joe was the appropriate apotheosis of this attitude: he gave dignity and pride to men who were daily stripped of both; he was steel, just as they were steel. He was a force in America, not a slavish nonentity. He entered the dreams and spirit of the South Slavic miner and steelworker.

In the post-World War II period the most significant Croatian-American novelist appeared but chose not to deal with the Croatian-American ethnic experience. After the last war, Joseph Hitrec emigrated to America, after a sojourn in India. Already a recognized poet in Yugoslavia (*Lirika*, 1932), he stayed in India until 1946. In America he became friends with Louis Adamic, who helped get Hitrec's first book, *Ruler's Morning and Other Stories* (1946), published. This work, like his later ones—*Son of the Moon* (1948) and *Angel of Gaiety* (1951)—dealt exclusively with India. Widely praised—the New York *Sun* said, "*Ruler's Morning* is perhaps the best fiction we have had about India since E. M. Forster's *Passage to India*"[18]—Hitrec's fiction, at once removed from both his Croatian past and his new American life, remains an exotic footnote to American literary history.

Other American-born Croatians have also produced fiction. Phillip M. Basvic (whose pseudonym was Barton Michael Phillips) wrote *And the Angels Won't Blame Him* (1955), a story of Chicago life, loosely based on his early years in the slums of that city. Thomas Raste's *The Destroyers* (1968) has nothing ethnic in it. Anthony V. Mandelic published a strange concoction in 1979. His *Mr. Has and Mr. Is* was advertised as a "modern epic," a "romance," a "political drama," "science fiction," all kept "vivacious by a mind stimulated with 'sljivovica.' " One autobiography became a best-seller: *The Dave Kopay Story*, written by Kopay with Perry Deane Young (1977). Kopay, a running back for ten years with the San Francisco 'Forty-Niners, New Orleans Saints, and Green Bay Packers, became a cause célèbre in 1975 when he announced his homosexuality. His autobiography is thus not an ethnic chronicle. The book might have been a fascinating psychological portrait had he amplified the sparse references to his Croatian childhood: "Father, Anton Kopay (the name was originally Kopaytich), was a first generation Croatian. He was proud of being Croatian, and sometimes would take us to a Croatian wedding or dinner."[19] We can only regret Kopay's failure to give a detailed glimpse of his youth.

In 1980 Edward Ifkovic published *Anna Marinkovich*, a novel about a young girl growing into adolescence on a Connecticut farm during the depression. Part of the novel was published as a short story under the same title in the *Journal of Ethnic Studies*. The story shows the hardships endured by a family of Croatian immigrants who are doubly isolated: from their native Croatia and from the midwestern Croatian colonies in America. It is partly the story of confrontation with America by a mother embittered by her new life and a father saddened by his experience. But it is mainly the story of Anna, the American-born child who finds herself caught between Old World restraints and the troublesome new American life. Quiet and lonely, she hides in a world of imagination and fantasy that allows entry only to her beloved older brother Joey. She watches as the fun-loving, good-hearted, but totally irresponsible Joey falters before a life he cannot contend with. She sees him spiral downward until the family becomes irrevocably enmeshed in his deterioration, a situation that threatens to destroy them all. Anna tells the story, relating through her child's eye the trauma and the joy of her life in America. The author attempts to present the rich Croatian traditions in conflict with the newer American customs and to provide a psychological portrait of a family in decline.

After World War II, the influx of disillusioned immigrants from the communist Yugoslav state brought many writers here who had already acquired reputations in their native Croatia. As in the first period of Croatian-American literature, at the turn of the century, the writing was in Croatian and often concerned the homeland. Were it not for the sophistication and polish of these new émigré writers, Croatian-American literature would seem to have come full circle back to the early roots. Many of these writers chose not to write in English even when dealing with American life. These authors continued to tap the rich culture of their past, and what results is a highly accomplished literature whose production rarely touches the ethnic American experience. The exceptions are noteworthy: Vinko Nikolic's anthology of Croatian poetry written in exile, *Pod Tudjim Nebom* (*Under Foreign Skies,* 1957), contains works dealing with the Croatian in America, poems by writers like Antun Bonifačić, Antun Nizeteo, and Nada Kesterčanek-Vujica. Bonifačić, the dean of Croatian émigré writers, had an enviable reputation in Croatia before coming here. His works on the immigrant are distinguished by a consciously refined literary style, mannered prose, and keen philosophical observation. His American poetry appeared in *Sabrane pjesme (Collected Poems,* 1974). Antun Nizeteo, a librarian at Cornell University, published a collection of short stories, *Bez povratka (Without Return,* 1957). Often concerned with the problems of immigrants—not only in

America but also in the old country to which many of them return—Nizeteo's stories revolve around a real ethnic dilemma. Traditional in style, almost contemptuous of modern innovation, and smacking more of the works of nineteenth-century masters, they nevertheless capture the spirit and verve of the Croatian immigrant, a quality seldom seen in émigré writing.

Other émigré writers are Nada Kesterčanek-Vujica, the author of *Short Stories* (1959) and *Koluti vremena (Circles of Time,* 1969), and Zlata Ivezić, who wrote *Srebrne suze (Silver Tears,* 1974). These, of course, are just a few of the émigré writers who deal with Croatian-American ethnicity. It remains to be seen whether or not the émigré writers will tackle American experience. The longer they are here and the more completely they are severed from their linguistic and cultural roots, the better the odds become that their literary production will grow stale and repetitive. Writers need the contact with their people; they must be part of their nation's evolving language and literature. To divorce themselves from the old country and to persist in identifying themselves solely with the old country is to guarantee their failure as writers and to become cultural anachronisms. One hope exists: if the émigré writers, once they are solidly entrenched in America, can turn their literary vision to the Croatian-American experience—either that of the old immigrant or that of the newer émigré—profound, meaningful Croatian-American literature might result, a literature that could approach the mainstream, that uses Croatian-American life to reflect the dilemmas of all humanity. Such a challenge, met by these already sophisticated writers, could not only galvanize the attention of the literary establishment here but, as well, could validate the careers of all those obscure Croatian-American writers who have struggled in isolation and neglect. Croatian-American literature could come of age.

Slovenian-American Literature

Like the Croatians, the Slovenians did not begin to produce a wide-ranging Slovenian-American literature until after the great migration. A small (1.8 million people), colorful nation in northern Yugoslavia, which sent perhaps half a million immigrants to America, Slovenia has been one of the most progressive European lands. It has long had a high level of literacy and a passionate devotion to art and literature. Oppressed by the Austro-Hungarian empire, Slovenia sent its people throughout the world, and these immigrants, largely from the peasant class, were often literate and advanced. Not surprisingly, then, the contribution of Slovenian-Americans to literature in this country is greatly out of proportion to their comparatively small numbers here. The level of culture that marked the early missionaries here—Baraga, for example—also informed the average peasant. Like the Bohemian immigrants to the north, the Slovenes came to America with a higher level of education than the average peasants from other lands. Indeed, the Slovenian-American immigrant was already influencing American literature in the nineteenth century. For example, Henry W. Longfellow's *Hyperion: A Romance* includes "The Story of Brother Bernardus," an account of a quixotic immigrant Bernard Smolnikar, a strange visionary writer who called for universal religion and government. Smolnikar, writing at the time of the Civil War, may have seemed a slightly maddened fringe character, the founder of many utopian communities, but such works as the *Proclamation of the True Union* (1862) and *The Great Encyclic Epistle* (1865) remain curious footnotes to American literary history.

The beginnings of a popular Slovenian-American literature are found in the early newspapers, almanacs, and journals. The files of early newspapers like *American Slovene* (Chicago, 1891), *Voice of the People* (New York, 1893), and *Prosveta (Enlightenment,* 1906), the organ of the Slovene National Benevolent Society in Chicago, are rich repositories of immigrant creative writing. In 1914 *The American Family Almanac (Ameriški Družinski Koledar)* appeared, the first issue of what was to become a long-lived publication. Socialist in political ideology, the almanac attracted a variety of readers because it contained some of the best Slovenian-American writing. It flourished under the editorship of socialist writer Frank Zaitz. Published by the Yugoslav Workman's Publishing Company and the Fraternal Slovenian National Benefit Society, it occasionally contained perceptive, informative assessments of the Slovenian in America. The editors were conscious of its ethnic mission and deeply committed to preserving the Slovenian soul in America, and so they sought and printed immigrants' writing. The almanac's influence led to the 1926 history, *Ameriški Slovenci (American Slovenians)* by Joseph Zavertnik, a book that sold over six thousand copies. Other early newspapers included

Novo Doba (New Era, 1924) and the long-lived *Amerikanski Slovenec,* which appeared from 1891 through the 1930s. Other papers in the 1930s were *Ameriška Domovina (American Homeland), Enakopravnost (Equality), Prosveta (Enlightenment),* and the long-standing *Glas naroda (People's Voice).* Socialists published *Proletarec* from a Chicago base at the Slovenian Workers' Center. The publication of this prolific Slovenian press—Prpić calls it "the most active of all South Slavic presses" *(South Slavic Immigration,* p. 162)—ranged from pure religious tracts to works of extreme ideological bias, either left or right. Often the antagonism between the presses was heated with the Socialist weeklies haranguing the Catholic press, or vice versa. Interestingly, these tensions and rivalries, laid bare in the editorial columns, point to a cultural dichotomy that marks Slovenian-American literature; the camps are often clearly delineated. Here an ethnic tension existed within the larger tension of Slovenian culture versus American culture. This double-edged tension informs some of the most important Slovenian-American writing, particularly that of Louis Adamic.

Many writers made the journey from the newspapers and almanacs to the printed book of popular verse or prose during the pre–World War I years and throughout the 1920s. With the proliferation of Slovenian publishing houses and eager editors, volumes were ground out. Most were mediocre but occasionally a work appeared that was a cut above the mass-produced verse that lauded mother and homeland or bemoaned death in unabashedly maudlin or puerile terms. Slovenian-born missionaries, like Oton Skola (b. 1833), wrote religious poetry. Andrew Smrekar, a poet at his peak in the 1920s, translated Shakespeare into Slovenian. Writing in the 1890s, Ivan Čebul was one of the few Slovenians who wrote poetry in English and French. Vital Vodusek published various collections of poetry, *Pesmi (Poems,* 1928) and *Poezije (Poetry,* 1937) among them. Nonclerical poets include Ivan Zupan, who wrote *Iz življenja za življenje (From Life to Life,* 1935), Frank Kerže, Janko Rogelj, and Etbin Kristan. The most distinguished Slovenian-American poet is Ivan Zorman (1889–1957), author of *Poezije (Poetry,* 1919), *Pesmi (Poems,* 1922), *Slovene Poetry* (1928), and *Iz novega sveta (From the New World,* 1938). Often provincial in tone and limited in artistry, these poets nevertheless represented the best of Slovenian-American verse. Nostalgic for the homeland, fearful of the new America, devoted to their heritage and their people, they transcribed the immigrant and ethnic dilemma onto the page, distilling their elation and anguish into popular poetic images that were at once comprehensible to their Slovenian-American readers. Their points of reference were the familiar ones: the harvest, the perilous voyage to America, the dark factory or mine, the obsession with God and the Blessed Virgin as icons of salvation, or the mills and the mines as icons of class struggle. This outpouring of popular poetry rivals that of the Croatians and doubtless reflects the same influence of the old folk and oral traditions. But the Slovenian-American writers also produced an impressive amount of fiction, both short stories and novels. Kazimir Zakrajšek was a prolific writer of short stories and plays, as were Bernard Ambrožić and Frank Kreže.[20] Andrew Kobal wrote numerous short stories and fifteen plays.

The most famous Slovenian-American writer is, of course, Louis Adamic, who began to write in the 1920s and emerged in the 1930s as an important American essayist, novelist, and social commentator. Until his mysterious death in 1951, Adamic was the most famous—some would say infamous—South Slavic writer in this country. His contribution to American ethnic awareness was farsighted and vital. He familiarized America with the agony and the ecstasy of the immigrant, and his writing had a profound impact on American political decisions. Adamic very early chose the immigrant as his vehicle to explore the far reaches of America. In *A Nation of Nations* (1945) he countered the prevailing sentiment of the time ("the United States is an Anglo-Saxon country with a White-Protestant-Anglo-Saxon civilization struggling to preserve itself against infiltration and adulteration by other civilizations brought here by Negroes and hordes of 'foreigners' ") with his own expansive, cosmopolitan definition:

> The United States is a new civilization, owing a great deal to the Anglo-Saxon strain, owing much to the other elements in its heritage and growth, owing much to the unique qualities and strong impetuses which stem from this continent, from the sweep of its land between two oceans, the mixture and interplay of its peoples, the plentitude of its resources, and the skills which we all of us have brought here or developed here in the past three centuries. (p. 6)

"Diversity itself," he said, "is the pattern of America" (p. 11). What we need to do, he maintained, is to transplant this diversity "from obscurity into the American imagination" (p. 13). Out of this diversit could evolve a freer, more democratic people. From 1940 to 1941 he edited *Common Ground,* a journal whose purpose was to encourage understanding of our multiethnic land. Just before his death, he was chosen by Lippincott to edit a series of books on immigration in America. A number of volumes of varying quality were issued as a fitting tribute to his lifelong commitment to the immigrant in American society. "The melting pot," he said when he undertook the series, "is used to fry the good out of a lot of people who get into it."[21]

Adamic was born in the Slovenian village of Blato in 1899. His parents had groomed him for the priesthood, but Adamic, a spirited boy, was attracted by two compelling forces: the revolutionary anti-Austrian movement then growing in his long-oppressed homeland and the enormous magnetic attraction of America, the land of the golden streets. To prevent him from going to America, his mother sent him to study in Ljubljana—a misguided move, for that city was a hotbed of political ferment. There Adamic joined the Yugoslav nationalist movement and spent some days in jail. After his release from prison, he was drawn to America, perhaps partly because he had talked with so many returned immigrants and had read such works as *Uncle Tom's Cabin* and *The Last of the Mohicans.*

When Ljubljana became too dangerous a city for him, he emigrated. He arrived in America in 1913 with twenty-five dollars in his pocket and celebrated New Year's Eve on his first night here. He had just turned fourteen. While working for a Slav newspaper in New York, he attended evening English classes. The paper folded in 1916, and Adamic found himself on the streets. In 1917 he entered the U. S. Army, spent three years in the service, and rose to the rank of sergeant. Following his discharge, he began a crucial period of his life. Aimless, rootless, he wandered across America, intoxicated by the exhilarating 1920s. He came in contact with "shadow America," to use Carey McWilliams' phrase.[22] Associating with hoboes, political malcontents, bootleggers, free thinkers, factory workers, and the unemployed, he saw the frightful underbelly of the America he had come to love. The immigrant was but one inhabitant of this subworld. Adamic thus became the "apostle of the excluded" (p. 12). In San Pedro, California, where a colony of South Slavs thrived, he worked as a clerk on the dock, a job that gave him free time to write.

After much trial and error, after exploring and then mastering English and the art of prose, Adamic wrote an important article, "The Yugoslav Speech in America." The article was accepted by the *American Mercury,* edited by H. L. Mencken, one of Adamic's literary heroes. Suddenly his work was in demand. In 1931 he published his controversial *Dynamite,* the story of labor-management strife in America. And in 1932 his *Laughing in the Jungle* appeared, the story of his early life in Slovenia and America. This work—a polished, introspective, occasionally profound work, the product of a professional writer deeply committed to exploring the complexities of American life—is rife with deep social consciousness, unlike Sanjek's autobiography. He found his metaphor: America as jungle, a concept he acquired from reading in the old country Upton Sinclair's *The Jungle.* His approach to America was to "laugh in the jungle." All he expected from America was "excitement and adventure."[23] He evolved from a halfhearted radical who believed that immigrants were American "dung" into a 1920s Menckenite afoot in a chaotic America. He became increasingly interested in proletarian movements. He immersed hinself in a frightening America, one lying beneath the national hysteria of 1920s prosperity; his was the non-WASP response to a world he found strangely intoxicating and often terrible. In 1928 he summed up his concept of America: "An endless comedy of futility and chaos" in which all kinds of people are trying to establish their own law and order and in which "Success is a religion, a fanaticism" (p. 216). And in Los Angeles he applied the metaphor for his Menckenite America: "L.A. is America. A Jungle" (p. 219). In that city all the bizarre elements congregate to create their ideal societies. Adamic became increasingly aware of social injustice and concluded that "one cannot afford to plunge too far into the economics and social issues of American life." One could be destroyed. A Menckenite in spirit, he laughed at America as a way of keeping sane. Adamic's narrative becomes a complex web of introspective analysis of the people he met who had fallen into this insane America. As he said, "hap-hazardness, chaos, violence, and accident had ruled their lives," these men and women, the "dung" who fertilized America (p. 239). And yet he believed that America offered promise of spiritual awakening. He was satisfied: he had come to America to experience it—to explore the great jungle, no more, no less. He had found what he wanted.

Early in his career, he became involved with controversial issues both in America and in his homeland. His 1934 bestseller, *The Native's Return,* told of life in Yugoslavia under the dictatorship of Alexander. Banned in Yugoslavia, the work found immediate popularity in America, where readers, mired in the depression, found curious comfort in the story of one immigrant's rise to fame and his emotional return to Slovenia. Later, with a grant from the Rockefeller Foundation, he began a nationwide study of immigrants of every ethnic persuasion. Three volumes resulted: *From Many Lands* (1940), *What's Your Name?* (1942), and *A Nation of Nations* (1945). His *My America* (1938) is a collection of assorted pieces including the poignant short story "Girl on the Road," the story of Hazel Culick, a poor, aimless, rootless American ethnic during the depression. The book also includes his passionate credo of ethnic purpose:

> Each of us living in the United States has his own America. That America is the aggregate, the sum-total of people, places, things, traditions, ideas, ideals, institutions, conditions, and diverse other forces and factors in the country which, in one way or another, for this reason or that, have touched or influenced one's life and contributed to one's education—or confusion—as an American and as a person.[24]

Adamic published two novels. *Cradle of Life* (1936) is loosely based on the life of a Croatian-American painter and friend of Adamic, Maksimilijan Vanka, who devoted his career to depicting the Croatian peasant. A sentimental, melodramatic work, it does not deal with ethnic experience in America. Of more ethnic interest is his *Grandsons* (1935), a novel whose potential is never realized. Working with a rich cultural theme— the influence of 1920s and 1930s America on three male descendants of a Slovenian immigrant killed in the Haymarket Riot of 1886—Adamic was unable to fuse his deeply felt social consciousness with his sense of the tragicomic America he had discovered. What results is a skeletal novel, often moving, often rich in its description of the 1920s, often eloquent in its depiction of the 1920s and 1930s as a period of spiritual vacuum, but Adamic never fleshes out the fascinating characters he establishes. Peter Gale, one of the three men, is a shadow person, with no reality. Now you see him; now you do not. Peter wants to write a book about the Haymarket Riot, but he cannot pull his life together. His brother is Andy (George Andrews), the biggest racketeer in Los Angeles. The third man, Jack Gale, is a Wobbly who goes to jail. These three men, the grandsons, carry the story of America at a crossroads. They are colorless men who lead empty lives and have no sense of belonging. Life is futile. Jack is killed while working as a migrant laborer; Andy is shot down by rival racketeers; chronically ill, Peter starts to die. The last line of the novel is symbolically apt for the generations of ethnic Americans removed from the American present: "I carried death in me all the time."[25] Death, violence, and despair all plague the new America. The ethnic sons find nothing to sustain them; no spiritual or intellectual core provides viable definition. And so they flounder; they lose; they die.

Adamic gradually moved away from fiction and became increasingly interested in polemic, social commentary, and immigrant sociology. His nonfiction works—often weakly structured, rambling, and chaotic—are pastiches of magazine articles. Some, like *Dinner at the White House,* are shrill, embarrassing diatribes. The years during and after World War II were difficult and tragic for Adamic. He became involved in internal movements to free Yugoslavia from Nazi occupation. Adamic's influence was considerable. While America supported the chetniks who opposed the communist Tito's partisans, Adamic made it clear that Tito was responsible for defending the nation from the Germans. Adamic's media blitz changed U.S.—British policy, which had supported the chetniks. When the war was over, Adamic supported Tito's Yugoslavia, despite the growing cold war and the fears of his fellow Americans. He had just completed a study of Tito, *The Eagle and the Roots* (1952), when he was found shot through the head on 4 September 1951. The circumstances were mysterious. Was it suicide? Assassination by someone from the right wing? By Soviets? The question has never been answered.

Adamic remains the most famous South Slavic-American writer. A man of tremendous talent and skill, he anticipated the new ethnic awareness that flourished in the 1960s and 1970s. Very early, he saw the immigrant and ethnic as crucial to any definition of America, and he understood that ethnicity is the fiber of our society: we are all immigrants here. At the same time, however, Adamic never fulfilled his promise. He published too quickly, revised too little, and toward the end of his life, became too involved with politics—that is, he allowed his writing to become propaganda. Had the depression and World War II not occurred, perhaps Adamic might have become a different writer—more the novelist, less the polemicist. Such speculation is purely idle, of course, suggested only by the potential for belles lettres we see in his early work. Nevertheless, Adamic made a contribution of no mean importance. This "intelligent peasant" (McWilliams, p. 11) gave a culturally disenfranchised ethnic America an identity, dignity, and pride.

Ironically, Adamic's potential as a novelist was realized by Frank Mlakar, Adamic's secretary, who was encouraged to write by the more famous Slovenian. Mlakar, born of Slovenian immigrant parents in Cleveland, Ohio, moved to New York during the depression to become a writer. He was assistant editor of *Common Ground.* A deeply intelligent writer and a conscious stylist, he wrote poetry, drama, short stories, and one superb achievement, *He, the Father* (1950), a novel that rivals the best of any ethnic American fiction. Mlakar moved to Australia in 1953 and died at age fifty-four, just after finishing *Francie*, a play. *He, the Father* made him a nationally known writer. *Time* called it a "powerful, Dostoevskian story,"[26] and the novel is, indeed, classically tragic. Osip Princevich, driven by guilt over his childhood obsession to kill his father, is tortured by the past. Mlakar draws a shattering portrait of the primitive Slovenian village of Gobelye, a town haunted by fear and tribal superstition. The father-son theme permeates the novel, which concerns Osip and his father, Osip and his son, and humanity's relation with God. Religious symbolism and a powerful admixture of Roman Catholicism and paganism dominate the work. Osip beats his father, steals his money, and goes to Cleveland with Lenka, whom he marries. There he is successful in Cuyahoga City's Chicken Village, the main colony of Slovenians in America. But Osip cannot escape the past. Tortured, he seeks the underbelly of America, symbolically digging in his dirt cellar, until he is at last ready to atone for his grievous sin. He returns to Slovenia, and on route his legs become paralyzed. A child again having come full circle, he is carried to the village in a basket. There, in Saint Jozef's Church, the home of God the Father, he is stoned to death by the frightened peasants who use him as a scapegoat for all their poverty, confusion, and despair. As Rose Marie Prosen stated in her perceptive discussion of the novel: "the passion and death of Christ function as the motif of *He, the*

Father. What is remarkable is the fusion of elemental forces and poetic symbols into a credible psychological novel that is subtle yet simple and never boring. . . . It is a horror story that does not preach the gospel of Christ. Instead, it renews the symbols of Christian mythology, rooted as they are in pagan ritual."[27] Although the dust jacket remarked that it is "a powerful and haunting novel that will not soon be forgotten, " *He, the Father* has fallen into undeserved obscurity. It certainly is a minor American classic.

If Mlakar transformed Slovenian-American experience into fiction, Rose Mary Prosen has converted her own ethnic sensibility into remarkable poetry. Born of Slovenian-American parents in Cleveland, Ohio, she very early became fascinated by her ethnic heritage. Her reminiscence, "Looking Back," winner of the first prize in Michael Novak's "Growing Up Slavic" contest, is a poet's awesome reflection on her rich past. Her final paragraph suggests the power of her language and vision:

> On Easter, 1976, I will remember the blessing of the basket; the ritual meal of colored eggs, baked ham, home-made bread, fresh horseradish, sausage and home-made wine; the sparkling windows of our house, the clean curtains, floors, walls and woodwork; all of us singing for the Great Feast Day; the sidewalks and porches hosed down; the yards raked, ready for seeding; the great basso voice of Mr. Snyder in the church choir, shaking the statues, the parishioners, the very earth, stirring roots, arousing the spirits of our ancestors in that Slovenian-American village in Newburgh. In my memory, his voice stirred the winds of the Asian steppes, raised questions: who are these, my people, my soul? The great Slavonic heart of a people dispersed and made singular through war and time and the elements; one tribe to settle in Cleveland, Ohio, to become again new men and women. I, too, am new.[28]

Such sentiment enriches her poetry; ethnicity provides the poetic tension that underlies her artistry. Published in many magazines *(Free Lance, Epos, New Review, Little Review)*, she has collected her work into two volumes: *Poems* (1971) and *O the Ravages* (1977). Her poetry is a tapestry of images garnered from years in a tight-bound Slovenian-American community, where the presence of factory, God, and kindred neighbors provides a stay against the chaos of the "outside" American present:

My mother makes my dresses. She lines our bureau
Drawers with sachet. She cooks dinner. My father
Gets first choice of the soup meat. My mother
Eats last, always. My sister and I feel proud,
Though she resents my shadow. I am older,
I will be the oldest of six children.

. . . .

There is a Depression. My parents argue about
Money. Beggars come to our door. I do not
Understand their eyes. On the first floor
Of our two-family house, a child dies. There are
Seven brothers and sisters in those four rooms.
The family buys a small white coffin. I do not
Cry. I am alert.[29]

Increasingly interested in the ethnic dimension of her life ("Our
children / pick up the seeds"),[30] Prosen is now converting
childhood memory into poetic expression. She is the first
Slovenian-American whose poetry approaches mainstream.

Other Slovenian-American writers flourished in the post–
World War II period, building on the early tradition established
by Adamic, dean of Slovenian-American letters. Stanley Zupan,
one-time English editor of *Glasilo KSKJ* and *Skyline,* has written
short stories and essays. Ludvik Puš wrote his memoirs, *Klasje v
viharju (Harvest in the Tempest,* 1970). Fred Orehek, an editor
of the Chicago *Tribune,* has written short stories. Talented
novelist and poet Ivan Jontez writes in both Slovenian and
English; his novels include *Senca preko pota (A Shadow Across
My Path,* 1940), *Jutro brez sonca (Morning without Sun,* 1949),
and *Trouble on East Green Street* (1956). Other short story
writers are Janko Rogelj, Robert Debevec, and Andrew Kobal.
Katka Zupančić wrote over three hundred poems, various plays,
and more than a hundred short stories and essays. Anna Krasna,
former editor of *Glas Naroda,* published short stories and poetry
(Za lepše dni, For a Better Future, poems, 1950). One of the
most radical writers, Joseph Kalar—at one time an editor of *New
Masses, Left Front,* and *Anvil*—wrote highly political short
stories, infused with descriptions of the exploitation of America's
working classes. His story "Collar" is included in Jack Conroy's
Writer in Revolt: The Anvil Anthology (1973). He was one of
three Slovenian-American writers (along with Adamic and

Mlakar) who made Edmund O'Brien's Best Stories series. Marie Prisland, one of the better-known writers in Slovenian-American communities, epitomized the immigrant as writer. After coming to America in 1906, she worked for six cents an hour and attended evening classes. Dedicated to the woman immigrant, she founded in 1926 the Slovenian Women's Union of America. In 1929 she created *Zarja (Dawn)*, a magazine. Her memoir, *From Slovenia to America* (1968), is a wise chronicle of one ethnic woman's journey from the Old World to the promised land, which was not quite what she had hoped it would be. Her memoir remains one of the most compelling, if familiar, stories of the immigrant achieving success in this strange land.

Like the Croatians, the Slovenians have a strong post–World War II émigré literature. Frank Bukvich spent most of the war in a concentration camp in Hungary. Educated at Graz University in Austria, he is now a naturalized American. His novels unclude *Brezdomci (The Homeless,* 1948) and *Ljudje iz Olšnice (People from Olšnice,* 1973), both of which revolve around the tragedy of war in Europe. Zdravko Novak, who emigrated in 1949, published over 200 short stories and articles and an influential book, *Utrinki (Fragments,* 1959). The most distinguished émigré, however, was Karel Mauser who arrived in America in 1950. A former seminarian, Mauser wrote from a Catholic perspective. A laborer with the Cleveland Twist Drill Company, he wrote only in his free time—and managed to produce over twenty successful novels, most of them concerning life in Slovenia but others focusing on the Slovenian-American experience. His trilogy, *Ljudje pod bičem (People under the Whip,* 1963–66), is considered his masterpiece, an account of Slovenia under Nazi and communist rule. In his short story "John Kovack," he draws a poignant picture of an old, enfeebled factory worker who can no longer do his job because his hands shake on the drill. A man shorn of purpose, he dies at his machine. The story is typical of Mauser's concern with the psychologically displaced person, whether in Slovenia or in America, the person who no longer belongs, the man or woman who blindly struggles to hold on to dignity in a world that no longer deems it important. Mauser was the consummate émigré writer who fused his Slovenian past with his American present. Unlike other émigré writers, he did not choose to dwell exclusively on the Slovenian past. His obscurity in this country, however, is lamentable. An accomplished novelist whose works have been translated into

German and Spanish, he remains unknown to his fellow Americans because he chose to write in Slovenian. Future translations of his most important works should introduce a significant Slovenian-American writer to a larger American readership.

Serbian-American Literature

Serbians were the least numerous of the groups that emigrated from South Slavic lands. Most of them came from the provinces of the Austro-Hungarian Empire, not from independent Serbia. They fled to America in pursuit of political and economic freedom. Immigration from Serbia proper was limited because of Serbia's independent status, as was immigration from Montenegro, an independent nation composed largely of Montenegrin Serbs. During the period up to 1920, George Prpić estimates, only fifteen percent of the incoming South Slavs were Serbs *(South Slavic Immigration,* p. 174). As colonies were formed in America, largely in the midwestern mine and factory cities, the number grew, until today there exists a sizable and influential Serbian-American culture. Although not so numerous as Croatians and Slovenians, the Serbs have a long cultural tradition that is distinct from that of the other two groups, mainly because of the Serbs' Eastern Orthodox religion, but similar in its rich folkloric heritage. That tradition has allowed them to make emphatic contributions to Serbian-American literature. The Serbians have also contributed two scientists, Michael Pupin and Nikola Tesla, whose discoveries have transformed the face of the globe.

Early Serbian-American literature followed the same patterns as did the literature of the Croatians and Slovenians. The early settlers, particularly during the great migration, established journals and newspapers to publish not only factual reporting but also poetry and fiction written by members of the peasant working class. Montenegrin Serbs from the Adriatic coast were here as early as the 1850s and established colonies on the West Coast. In 1857, for example, a Slavonian-Russian-Greek Orthodox Church and Benevolent Society was formed in San Francisco; it eventually became the first Serbian Orthodox Church in America. Sabastian Dabovich, son of a Montenegrin immigrant, was the first Orthodox missionary among the Serbians in America. Ordained in 1887, Dabovich became an influential leader who inspired his people not only religiously but culturally as well, for he believed in perpetuating the rich traditions of his people. He wrote many articles on the history and culture of the Serbians and edited a journal, *Orthodoxy.*

During the great migration, a number of Serbian and Montenegrin fraternal societies were organized, and their news-letters and journals register the first attempts at a Serbian-American literature. As others arrived from the homeland, they started newspapers. The *Amerikanski Srbobran (American Serb Sentinel),* the Pittsburgh organ of the Serbian National Federa-tion, began in 1905. The Yugoslav League of Independent Socialists started in San Francisco in 1909, publishing *Volja (The Will).* As late as 1939 seven Serbian papers were still published; the oldest was the weekly *Radnička Borba (Workers' Struggle)* in Cleveland, the South Slavic organ of the Socialist Labor party. John R. Palandech, distinguished Serbian publisher and writer, came in 1887 at age thirteen and began a long career as a journalist. Veljko Radojevich, the "sage and dean of Serbian journalism in the United States," edited the newspaper *Liberty* (1901–02) and the weekly *Serb Independence* (1902–08). Highly literate, committed to a "deep-rooted national philosophy" and "true national character," Radojevich is symbolically the father of the new Serbian-American literature that began to emerge at the turn of the century in the pages of the scattered publications appearing in the Serbian colonies.[31]

One of the early popular poets appeared at this time (1903–11), writing out of San Francisco and Oakland. Proka Jovkić, who took the name Nestor Zucni, was influenced by his literary mentor Maxim Gorky, whose idea of the futility of life Jovkić easily appropriated. Jovkić-Zucni worked as an editor for *Serb Independence,* but his primary contributions were patriotic lyrics lamenting his exile and praising life in the homeland. In his "Poem to a Beggar," he states that he cannot be content to stay at home, reducing his "universe to onion plants." "I prefer life where suffering, bitterness / Anxiety and revolt reign."[32] Con-scious of the continuing struggles in the homeland, he wrote poems that articulated the growing anger, frustration, and confusion that Serbians in America felt when they considered the disturbing happenings in the old country. Like most of the early poets, Jovkić-Zucni wrote in Serbian and turned his eyes to the land he had left behind.

Michael Pupin did not avoid the American experience, however, when he wrote one of the masterworks of Serbian-American literature: *From Immigrant to Inventor* (1922), which won the Pulitzer Prize for biography. Pupin, of course, was a brilliant scientist, but his one attempt at biography revealed him as a man of remarkable poetic sensibility as well. Born in the village of Idvor in Serbia in 1858, he was early influenced by Benjamin Franklin's experimentation with electricity. Like Adamic, however, he found himself embroiled in revolutionary politics, attempting to free the South Slavic lands from oppressive Austro-Hungarian rule. When he studied in Prague, his old interest in science reappeared, along with a fascination with America. When his father died, Pupin wanted to help the family financially, and so he came to America in 1874, attracted by a steamship poster offering the journey for a little over eleven dollars. At the immigration station at Ellis Island, he was told that he could not enter the country because he had only five cents in his pocket and no relative in the United States. The impetuous young Pupin, intoxicated with the idea of America, recalled the wide reading he had done. He informed the official that he did indeed know many Americans: Franklin, Abraham Lincoln, and Harriet Beecher Stowe. He was allowed in. With his five cents he bought a piece of prune pie, only to discover that it was filled with pits. Then, still wearing his red Turkish fez, he wandered aimlessly along the New York streets. He fought off a gang of rowdy, mocking teenagers, but his unpleasant experience had a happy outcome, for an onlooker offered him a job as a mule driver on a Delaware farm.

Soon his intellectual interests were rekindled. Eager to go to college, he studied Greek, Latin, and other subjects with a German scientist named Bilharz. He entered Columbia University in 1879. Pupin flourished there: he was president of the junior class, as well as a boxer and a wrestler. He graduated in 1883 and in that same year became a naturalized citizen. He returned to Europe for further education, returning to teach at Columbia as a professor of electromagnetics. In 1896 he discovered X-ray radiation and invented short exposure X-ray photography. In 1899 he developed high-inductive wave conductors, which were important in the creation of long-distance telephone service. But our concern here is with Pupin the man of literature. Vitally concerned with the welfare of his people and conscious of the interplay of science and humanity, Pupin worked on peace committees, served as adviser to the American government on the political situation in Eastern Europe, and helped form Yugoslavia in 1918. His personal testament, *From Immigrant to Inventor,* the story of his struggle to succeed in the new land, is an important book: a collection of rich observations, descriptions of folk traditions, examples of Serbian pride, and ethnic portraits. It is a moving statement by a "poet scientist" who has fallen in love with a new country. His book is a fusion of science and poetry. For example: "The joys and beauties of our seasons will tell you the story of this wonderful transformation of primordial energy from the chaos of the young stars, white hot with joy of life, to the cosmos of the old, cold, and moribund earth."[33]

What makes Pupin's work especially intriguing is its persistent motif of Serbian epic and folk tradition. The force of the oral tradition — the epic narratives of battle and heroism, especially the battle at Kosovo — is always present. Pupin often refers to the old ballads and songs that were passed down through the generations and that provided not only recreation during the long, cruel winters but also wisdom and models of behavior for youth to emulate. In the village of Idvor, he says, "the cultivation of the old traditions was the principal element in the spiritual life of the village people" (p. 4). The Serbian ballads and legends, the tales of Kosovo and Marko Kraljevic, were sung or told in the *kavanas* on winter nights. "Writing and reading did not flourish in Idvor in those days, but poetry did." (p. 5). The old men ("self appointed guardians of all the wisdom") recounted, often to the accompaniment of the *gusle,* the story of Karageorge and the Turks. The old *guslar* (minstrel), said Pupin, "was my first and best teacher in history" (p. 7). The power of such tradition had its effect on him: later in America he compared people he met with figures out of the oral tradition. He even rejected Protestantism because it seemed incompatible with the religion integral to the ballads he knew by heart. Also, interestingly, when he took his entrance exams at Columbia, his professors were amazed at his quotations from Greek and Latin writings; memorization was no problem, he said, for one who grew up with an oral tradition in which long narratives were committed to memory. Pupin also saw a direct correlation between the old ballads and his passion for American democracy: "The impressions which I carried away from [hearing the epic narratives recited] were a spiritual food which nourished in my young mind the sentiment that the noblest thing in the world is the struggle for right, justice, and freedom" (p. 8). Pupin's desire for political freedom and belief in the concept of a "strong man in defense of the weak and the oppressed" were consonant with the American sympathy for the underdog, the oppressed, and the importance of individual freedom.

Pupin's work reflects his preoccupation with American ideals. If Adamic saw Americans as shadowy, marginal people, Pupin rejected that reality and housed himself in the confined quarters of the academic hall. *From Immigrant to Inventor* was written "to describe the rise of idealism in American science" (Preface), but it is also a look at the other side of Adamic's coin: Pupin was an immigrant who bought the whole complex of American idealism that Adamic rejected. Pupin became an example of the Anglo conformity that many immigrants embraced, possibly because he arrived in 1874, just before the big influx of his people. His sense of isolation might therefore have been more pronounced than that of the later arrivals. As he followed the path that was to lead to a professorship at Columbia and world renown, he maintained his allegiance to his Serbian past but meshed that past with a tacit acceptance of the Anglo-Saxon culture that prevailed in his day, a culture that by definition opposed his being here. Studying the theatrical modulations of Edwin Booth was one thing, part of his effort to end his "apprenticeship," but his adulation of his native-born peers at Columbia is decidedly another. His playing the rustic Serbian peasant to their old-stock Anglo-Saxon American aristocrat serves as an alarming contrast to the experience of Ludwig Lewisohn, whose *Upstream* (published in 1922, the same year as Pupin's work) recounts his coming to grips with his own Jewishness when Columbia University turned anti-Semitic eyes on him. Ironically, Lewisohn, too, had been an Anglo conformist, but he underwent a rude awakening at Columbia. Pupin, however, admired the "spirit of aristocracy" (p. 120). He saw little snobbery at Columbia, he said, for it was a bastion of American gentlemen. Columbia taught him the rightness of the Anglo-Saxon culture: "There in the clean sunshine of their learning I saw the whole image of what I believed to be American civilization: a beautiful daughter of a beautiful mother, which is the Anglo-Saxon civilization" (p. 132). Here is a reflection of the old country worship of woman as ideal. He compared the Anglo-Saxon society to the Greek civilization, calling them "the two greatest" in history. He aspired to this society, and he obtained acceptance into it. If Adamic chose to stay in the immigrant milieu, Pupin left it behind; he was more comfortable with middle-class Anglo conformity, and he enjoyed living in an old Connecticut village. If Adamic's hero was the iconoclastic Mencken, Pupin's was the aristocratic Anglo-Saxon gentleman in the university. They represent, then, the extremes of reality and ideality confronting the immigrant.

Two Serbian-American novels that appeared in the 1940s reflect the same unabashed optimism and joy found in Pupin's work. Emilian Glocar's *A Man from the Balkans* (1942) is the story of Alexey, a Serbian immigrant celebrating his seventieth birthday. It is wartime, and Alexey has to register as an alien. Angered by the requirement because he has given so many years of hard work to America, he storms out of his house, and what follows is a nostalgic recapitulation of his past: his early life in Serbia, the poverty, his marriage and children. Scenes of the old village are vivid. One Christmas he comes home with a roasted lamb, closely pursued by a pack of wolves. As he reaches his house, he discovers his wife with her former boyfriend. The wolves rush in and kill her and the boyfriend. After setting fire to the house, Alexey flees to America. His life in America is anticlimactic; he marries and becomes productive and happy — until he has to register with the government. But the novel ends with Alexey surrounded by his family, happy and confident in his American future. A pedestrian, mechanical novel, *A Man from the Balkans* never realizes its dramatic and psychological potential: Glocar is content to convert his rich materials into static encomia to American greatness.

A better work is Milla Zenovich Logan's *Bring Along Laughter* (1947), a fictionalized story of a Serbian family in San Francisco. A humorous, spirited account of the misadventures of a rollicking family, the book delights with its broad humor, its zany characterizations, and its insistence that life is one big *festa*. Logan grew up in a rich Serbian atmosphere as the great-granddaughter of a Serbian who settled in San Francisco in 1851. After attending the University of California, she worked as a journalist in Sacramento and later became a publicist for labor unions, getting heavily involved in the many labor strikes of the 1930s. Her book — the title alone suggests its purpose — begins with a foreword: " 'What kind contents your book should be, and who is big fool who would read it?' a Serbian patriarch wrote me sternly from San Diego." The author tells us: "The people in this book are all on the same side; none are villains; all stand for one way of life."[34] Written "out of a deep nostalgia for a world that was warm, abundant and spicy" (p. viii), the book is more nonfiction than fiction, to be sure, despite its novelistic structure. Its often preposterous vignettes take us through disasters that would do other people in. During the great San Francisco earthquake, misfortune is converted into zany antics: "When a strong jog hurtled their bed across the room, my mother and father realized that this was the hour for the family to be together" (p. 3). The loss of material goods is trivial. When members of the huge, extended family assemble on the street (including Djede Luka with his parrot and pug dog), they embrace, shout "fala Bogu" ("thank God"), and go to the coffee house to celebrate. Thus begins the frolicsome account of Serbians in America, who refuse to let anything take away laughter. The work is filled with religious customs, family feuds, riotous feasting, sentimental weeping. When anyone questions their antics, the madcap grandmother, who holds the family together, will declare: "Is our nature" or "We don't ever change our nature"(p. 247). Laughter keeps them going; you have to work hard for a laugh in America. At the end the force of "Amerika" intrudes, as the old die and the young change. Filip becomes a Boy Scout and changes the spelling of his name to Philip, and Yovo plays baseball in the park. What does not change is their nature.

Logan's work is post–World War II literature, but it has little connection with the somber émigré poetry and fiction written by those who sought political asylum in America during and after the war. Jovan Dučić, long recognized as an important poet in his native country, has not dealt with the Serbian-American experience. His sonnets, *Love Poems and Adriatic Sonnets,* garnered attention outside his native land. In 1941 he came to America and settled in Gary, Indiana, where he remained until his death in 1943. His work is imbued with the power of life in the new land: "I felt the poetry of American life. . . . The first morning in New York, I became aware of the fact that if I didn't see America, my existence would never be complete."[35] But his poetry does not confront the Serbian life here; he uses ethnic material only to expand his poetic vision, and he speaks in universal and philosophical terms. Milan Petrović lived in America from 1949 to 1963, coming here after incarceration in Germany. His book of lyrics, *The Petrified Tears,* published in

Italy in 1962, consists largely of romantic evocations of his Serbian childhood—once again a turning away from the American present. Bozidar Purić emigrated from London to America in 1957; he was president of the Yugoslav government in exile during World War II. A poet in his native land, he chose to write literary criticism in America. Other poets include Mateja Matejić and Dragoslav Dragutinović. Jovan Kontić lived in the United States from 1946 to 1965, mainly in the Midwest, where he edited different newspapers and journals. He wrote two collections of short stories that deal with war in the old country. And in an unusual return to the source Ljubica Grković-Boljanić, born in Gary, Indiana, chose to write her poetry in Serbian. Deeply affected by her visits to Yugoslavia and her immersion in the life of her people, she became active in the Serbian-American community. Her poetry reflects her involvement with Serbian folklore, the life on the soil, the nostalgia for the old country, the influence of Serbian tradition on her and on all Serbs, no matter where they are dispersed.

Charles Simic, born in Belgrade in 1938, has evolved into a mainstream American poet whose work appears in anthologies of American poetry. When he was ten he went to Paris with his mother, and one year later he joined his father in America. He has degrees from the University of Chicago and New York University. He has translated widely from Russian, French, and Serbo-Croatian. He has been called one of the important younger American poets since the publication of his first volume, *What the Grass Says* (1967). Simic's lyrical verse is deeply introspective, concerned more with charting his psychological geography than with the ethnic experience he carries within him. He has not used his American-Serbian present extensively in his poetry, although he admits that an ethnic coloration and a Serbian sensibility pervade any number of them.[36] And the Serbian past informs the imagery of some of his best poetry:

> When I eat pork, it's solemn business.
> I am eating my ancestors.
> I am eating the land they worked on.
>
> Turnip-headed drunks, horse-thieves,
> Cutthroats, convicts, filthy laborers,
> I relive you within my blood.

If I add garlic to my pork
It is for one who became a minister,
Who left the land, city-bound,
Changed his name, never to be heard of again.[37]

Simic was in Belgrade during the war, and the specter of war haunts his poetry. The effect is often understated but nevertheless horrible:

> The trembling finger of a woman
> Goes down the list of casualties.
> The list is long. (p. 393)

An immigrant like Simic, Steve Tesich is just beginning to be recognized as an important American writer. Born in Yugoslavia in 1942, he came to the United States when he was fourteen. He studied at Indiana University and Columbia University, where he earned an M.A. in Russian literature. The author of short stories and a novel, he is making his mark primarily in the American theater. His play *The Predicators* was done in a workshop production at the American Academy of Dramatic Arts in New York City. The American Place Theatre produced *The Carpenters*. His third play, *Baba Goya*, was produced in 1973. His outlook on life is often absurdist, distilling from the decadence and confusion of contemporary American life a portrait of alienation, ennui, and futility. *Newsweek* said: "Tesich remains one of the most promising young American playwrights." Tesich's past obviously influences his work: "Like other expatriated East Europeans, writers such as Jerzy Kosinski, Tesich's vision of American madness seems colored and accented by his experience of European madness."[38] Recently Tesich has begun to write screenplays. His *Breaking Away*, released as a film in the summer of 1979, focuses on four teenagers during their first year out of high school. The film deals with the conflict between these four boys ("townies") and the college "frat" boys.

One recent novel attempts to define the Serbian-American experience. William Jovanovich's *Madmen Must* (1978) is the story of a young Serbian-American's search for self in the early 1940s, after America enters the war. The novel follows Big John Sirovich—cocky, brash, self-assured—as he seeks his special place in life. A brilliant student, he leaves behind his Serbian immigrant father who was a coal miner. John, the first American child, holds the promise of America in his hands. During the year after his departure from the Serbian-American community, he encounters all kinds of experiences that touch and influence him: California madness, an affair with a married woman, his attempt to save one of America's lost young men, long and feverish card games. The novel ends in 1942, when he stands proudly in a naval officer's uniform, saying good-bye to his father. The novel is, of course, a thinly veiled autobiography. Jovanovich is chairman of Harcourt Brace Jovanovich, which he has headed since he was thirty-four. Born in Colorado, he had a Montenegrin father and a Polish mother. He spent the war years in the U.S. Navy. His earlier collection of essays, *Now, Barabbas* (1964), contained many references to his Serbian heritage, especially in his discussion of the dissident Yugoslav writer Milovan Djilas. *Madmen Must* is his first attempt at fiction, and it fails to evolve a real Serbian sensibility. The novel tends to be a mechanical, often lethargic account of one young man's growing up, and Jovanovich fails to flesh out John's character so that his movement out of the parochial home and into the cosmopolitan, frenetic world is not convincingly motivated. What is most unfortunate is his failure to delve into the Serbian-American past. Jovanovich provides brief, fleeting glimpses of the small ethnic community and passages about his father (Tata), who was president of the Serbian People's Lodge. Serbia looms behind every action these hometown characters take. Early in the novel, when his father buries old Savo Lubradovich, we have an opportunity to see the many dimensions of the community:

> Once the priest had drawn the Orthodox crucifix in the air over the grave, one vertical line and two crossing, my father spoke in Serbian. He said that Savo's father had fought the Turks in the war of 1876, that Savo came to America in 1905 to work in the copper mines in Butte; he had gone back to fight in the First Balkan War, returned and worked some more and died, a long-time member of the Serbian People's Lodge. My father paused, looked at me standing at the foot of the grave, lowered his great head, his eyes showing nothing. . . . When he resumed, I was sure he would conclude by scolding the survivors. As president of the lodge, my father conducted the burials of those members who were bachelors, as many Serb coal miners in America are. He ended the eulogy by noting that each year the lodge lost members.[39]

Like the son, the reader also wants something more substantial, a striking of some responsive ethnic chord. Even the concluding dialogue between father and son is laced with Serbian consciousness. Tata says, "I killed Mexican scabs during the Ludlow Massacre strike on the hogback west of Walsenburg. I dug and loaded coal in four-foot-high rooms underground near Carbondale and Gebo and Raton. I took orders from Welshmen and others who never heard of Kosovo or Karageorge." The son replies, "Today in Yugoslavia, had you stayed, you'd be in the mountains dying" (p. 228). But the moment is trivialized by the novel's failure to grapple with that very Serbian psyche. When the novel appeared, the *New York Times* reviewer lamented this failure:

> Only when we glimpse and occasionally hear the immigrant generation does the book promise a fullness of life—promise to populate those barren stretches of the interior American landscape; but they are smothered before they can find the range and pitch of their voices and burst out of their anonymity. That is the book we had reason to expect, and should have.[40]

The reviewer's call for such fiction ("And that immigrant generation: Dalmatians, Croats, Serbs, Montenegrins, all unknown and still-unknown") points up a literary failing that I have suggested throughout this essay: the world of the Serbian, Slovenian, and Croatian in America is still unknown territory. America does not know about the lives and contributions of so many millions of its South Slavic fellow citizens. Largely virgin territory, it awaits writers who are confident of both their South Slavic heritage and their American present. Only they can effect an artistic creation that will capture the spirit and interrelationships of both. This is the challenge that directly faces the young South Slavic-American writer.

Notes

[1] Quoted and trans. in George J. Prpić, *South Slavic Immigration in America* (Boston: Twayne, 1978), p. 185, from Ljobomir Kosier, *Srbi, Hrvati i Slovenci u Americi: Ekonomosko-socijalni problemi emigracije* (Belgrade: Bankarstro, 1927), pp. 34–35.

[2] An immigrant from Croatia-Slavonia, quoted in Emily Balch, *Our Slavic Fellow Citizens* (New York: Charities, 1910), pp. 51–52.

[3] Paul Tymkevich, a Ruthenian Greek-Catholic priest, quoted in Balch, p. 419.

[4] *A Nation of Nations* (New York: Harper, 1945), p. 234.

[5] John D. Shea, *History of the Catholic Mission among the Indian Tribes of the United States* (New York: Shea, 1857), p. 401.

[6] Carl Wittke, *We Who Built America* (Englewood Cliffs, N.J.: Prentice-Hall, 1939), p. 430.

[7] Ivan Mladineo, *Narodni Adresar* (New York: privately printed, 1937), p. ix.

[8] Maurice R. Davie, *World Migration* (New York: Macmillan, 1949), p. 133.

[9] George Prpić, *The Croatian Immigrants in America* (New York: Philosophical Library, 1971, p. 209.

[10] *Od Atlantika do Pacifika* (Zagreb: Dionička Tiskara, 1905).

[11] A. Milćinović, "Hvatska pripovijetka i roman," *Kolo Matice hrvatske* (Zagreb: Dionička Tiskara, 1912), pp. 487-88.

[12] *Trailing Geronimo* (Los Angeles: Gem, 1926), p. 201.

[13] *In Silence* (New York: Fortuny, 1938), p. 12.

[14] *Scribner's Magazine*, Dec. 1937, p. 42.

[15] *Threatening Shadows* (Boston: Stratford, 1931), p. 29.

[16] Branimir Anzulović, "Croatian-American Literature," in *Ethnic Literature since 1776: The Many Voices of America*, ed. Wolodymyr T. Zyla and Wendell M. Aycock (Lubbock: Texas Tech Press, 1978), p. 152.

[17] "The Saga of Joe Magarac: Steelman," *Scribner's Magazine*, Nov. 1931, p. 505.

[18] Quoted on dust jacket of *Son of the Moon* (New York: Harper, 1948).

[19] *The Dave Kopay Story* (New York: Arbor, 1977), p. 26.

[20] Giles Edward Gobetz and Adele Donchenko, eds., *Anthology of Slovenian American Literature* (Willoughby Hills, Ohio: Slovenski Ameriški Inštitut, 1977). This volume includes short stories like Zakrajšek's "A Father's Love" and Frank Kerže's "Podboy's Return tò Slovenia." It is rich in fiction and essays originally written in or translated into English. Uneven in quality, the pieces range from the artistry of Mlakar Prosen and Rose Marie Prosen to sentimental throwaway pieces like Jim Deberec's "The Holiest Thing Alive" and Lavoslava Turk's "My Little Angels." The anthology, however, cannot be dismissed, and Gobetz's editorial observations are important and comprehensive.

[21] Quoted in Robert van Gelder, *Writers and Writing* (New York: Scribner's, 1946), p. 152. As van Gelder said, "He is engaged in a crusade to make immigrants feel they 'belong' " (p. 152).

[22] Carey McWilliams, *Louis Adamic and Shadow America* (Los Angeles: Whipple, 1935), p. 10.

[23] *Laughing in the Jungle* (New York: Harper, 1932), p. 40.

[24] *My America* (New York: Harper, 1938), p. xi.

[25] *Grandsons* (New York: Harper, 1935), p. 290.

[26] "Books," *Time*, 7 Aug. 1950, p. 72.

[27] Rose Marie Prosen, "Slovenian-American Literature: Louis Adamic's *Grandsons* and Frank Mlakar's *He, the Father*," *MELUS*, 5 (Winter 1978), 61.

[28] "Looking Back," in *Growing Up Slavic in America*, ed. Michael Novack (New York: Empac!, 1976), p. 8.

[29] "Chronicle: 1931-1945," in *The Ethnic American Woman*, ed. Edith Blicksilver (Atlanta: Kendall-Hunt, 1978), p. 95.

[30] "A Poem for Olga," in Blicksilver, p. 98.

[31] See Joseph S. Roucek, *Slavonic Encyclopedia* (New York: Philosophical Library, 1949), p. 1069.

[32] Quoted and trans. in Peter D. Bubesko, "American-Serbian Literature," in Zyla and Aycock, p. 525.

[33] *From Immigrant to Inventor* (New York: Scribner's, 1922), p. 385.

[34] *Bring Along Laughter* (New York: Random, 1947), p. vii.

[35] Quoted and trans. in Bubresko, from a manuscript in the possession of Leposava Dučić, in Zyla and Aycock, p. 543.

[36] Conversation with Simic, Farmington, Conn., Apr. 1978.

[37] "To All Hog-Raisers, My Ancestors," in *The Young American Poets*, ed. Paul Carroll (Chicago: Follett, 1968), p. 389.

[38] Jack Kroll, "All in the Family," *Newsweek*, 4 June 1973, p. 94.

[39] *Madmen Must* (New York: Harper, 1978), pp. 2–3.

[40] Saul Maloff, "Big John Grows Up," *New York Times Book Review*, 23 April 1978, p. 10.

Index

DATE DUE
